T0125230

COMPETITION, ECONOMIC PLANNING, AND THE KNOWLEDGE PROBLEM

THE COLLECTED WORKS OF ISRAEL M. KIRZNER

Austrian Subjectivism and the Emergence of

Entrepreneurship Theory

Competition, Economic Planning, and the

Knowledge Problem

Competition and Entrepreneurship

Discovery, Capitalism, and Distributive Justice

The Economic Point of View

Essays on Capital and Interest

The Essence of Entrepreneurship and the Nature and

Significance of Market Process

Ludwig von Mises: The Man and His Economics

Market Theory and the Price System

Reflections on Ethics, Freedom, Welfare Economics, Policy,

and the Legacy of Austrian Economics

ISRAEL M. KIRZNER

Competition, Economic Planning,

and the Knowledge Problem

Edited and with an Introduction by

PETER J. BOETTKE and FRÉDÉRIC SAUTET

LIBERTY FUND

Introduction and index © 2018 by Liberty Fund, Inc.

22 21 20 19 18 C 5 4 3 2 1

22 21 20 19 18 P 5 4 3 2 1

Library of Congress Cataloging-in-Publication Data

Names: Kirzner, Israel M., author. | Boettke, Peter J., editor. | Sautet, Frederic E., editor.

Title: Competition, economic planning, and the knowledge problem / Israel M. Kirzner ; edited and with an introduction by Peter J. Boettke and Frederic Sautet.

Description: Carmel, Ind. : Liberty Fund, Inc., [2017] | Series: The collected works of Israel M. Kirzner | Includes index.

Identifiers: LCCN 2017044924 | ISBN 9780865978621 (hardcover : alk. paper) | ISBN 9780865978638 (pbk.)

Subjects: LCSH: Competition. | Prices. | Economic policy. | Economics—Philosophy.

Classification: LCC HB238 .K56 2017 | DDC 338.6/048—dc23

LC record available at https://lccn.loc.gov/2017044924

LIBERTY FUND, INC.

11301 North Meridian Street

Carmel, Indiana 46032-4564

B'EZRAS HASHEM

CONTENTS

INTRODUCTION TO
THE LIBERTY FUND EDITION

The present volume of Israel Kirzner's Collected Works contains papers exploring the propositions that can be derived from the consistent application of the entrepreneurial process approach to economics. The articles specifically address competition and the related ideas of plan coordination, economic planning, and the knowledge problem.

Economists are often criticized for offering an abstract and overly simplified view of markets. While the notion of markets is central to the field of economics, it has remained a mysterious concept. The traditional view of "perfect" competition emerged in the 1930s. According to this model, markets are composed of a multitude of agents who have no influence on the prices of goods they buy and sell. Competition is a state of affairs whereby prices and quantities of goods and services are set independent of the actors' decisions, because atomistic individuals allegedly have no influence over market outcomes. The development of competition theory, including oligopolistic competition, during the years preceding World War II, reflected the growing tendency among economists to rely on blackboard theorizing instead of looking to the real world to direct their scholarship. The mathematical properties of economic systems rather than their explanatory potential drove economists' theoretical research.[1] This trend in research shifted the economic paradigm from one of markets as a space for exchange, as developed in the nineteenth century, to one of markets as a metaphor, or a tool to indict reality. In this "modern" approach, markets are disincarnated, and man has become a machine.[2]

The Keynesian transformation finished off whatever was left of the classical idea of the market.[3] John M. Keynes and, later, Paul Samuelson saw the well functioning of markets as an exception rather than the rule. In order for the microeconomy to function, one first had to have the macro balance right. Economists became the new high priests and

1. On this subject, see, for instance, Machovec (1995).

2. See Boettke (1997), Boettke, Coyne, and Leeson (2003), and Sautet (2015).

3. For more on this subject and papers that influenced Kirzner's view, see Friedrich Hayek (1948b), Paul McNulty (1968), and Shorey Peterson (1957).

counselors of the political princes and were called to design institutions and policies aimed at keeping the economy in working order. Both the content and use of economic science changed. The classical era during which economists were humble observers of social realities had come to an end.[4]

It was in this academic and political environment that market process theory developed. Ludwig von Mises's work in the 1920s on economic calculation can be considered as one of the first important landmarks in the field. Subsequently Mises developed an entrepreneurial theory of the market in *Human Action*.[5] He insisted that the market is a process resulting from the interactions of individuals cooperating under the division of labor. Mises's theory was centered on a change agent, the entrepreneur, which explained the true dynamic properties of the market through the continuous adjustments of individual actions. Another important landmark lies in the work of Friedrich Hayek, who offered an epistemic critique of market socialism, equilibrium analysis, and perfect competition. Hayek articulated the central role of dispersed knowledge in markets and its place in economics. He studied the social institutions that help solve markets' epistemic problem.

In the late 1960s, Kirzner started bringing the Misesian and Hayekian analyses together to flesh out an entrepreneurial theory of the market process based on what he later called the Hayekian knowledge problem. That approach became the core of market theory for the new generation of Austrian economists. Market process theory provides an understanding of competition different from that of equilibrium analysis. In fact, seeing the market as a process brings economics back to its nineteenth-century roots, in which competition is about real flesh and blood individuals striving to do better than other market participants by seizing opportunities for profit. In the Kirznerian view, competition is not a state of affairs; it is the process generated through the rivalrous actions of entrepreneurs. This view builds on the work of Mises and Hayek, for whom the important issue was to understand the process that leads to equilibrium, not to assume equilibrium as a starting hypothesis. The way individuals learn is a key element in understanding the market process.

4. See Boettke, Coyne, and Leeson (2006).
5. See especially chapter 15.

As Hayek explained: "if we want to make the assertion that under certain conditions people will approach [equilibrium], we must explain by what process they will acquire the necessary knowledge." (Hayek 1948a, 46) In Hayek's view, studying the properties of equilibrium is a mathematical exercise rather than an economic problem. Instead, the economic problem starts with the assumption that knowledge is dispersed and not available to anyone in its entirety. Perfect knowledge cannot be an assumption within the process of equilibration. Acknowledging the true dispersion of knowledge forces economists to theorize about individuals' decision mechanisms within the limits of the knowledge they possess. In this process, the entrepreneurial function plays the main role.

Through his emphasis on the entrepreneurial dimension of the market process, Kirzner revisited the debates on the meaning of competition and economic planning. At its core, explains Kirzner, competition must be understood as an entrepreneurially driven discovery process. This returns the human element to economic analysis. It sheds a new light on the socialist calculation debate and the limits of government planning, and it opens another window on age-old debates such as the nature of monopoly.[6] One of Kirzner's most important lessons is his emphasis on the discovery process as opposed to the focus of equilibrium analysis on allocative efficiency. As he explains: "The pattern of resource allocation during a given period may, for certain purposes, be considered profoundly unimportant as compared with the speed and smoothness with which misallocations can be discovered and corrected."[7]

In the eyes of famed historian of economic thought Mark Blaug, Austrian economists, and particularly Kirzner, have put forward an analysis that should purely and simply stand at the center of market theory. As Blaug writes in *Economic Theory in Retrospect*:

> I contend that perfect competition is a grossly misleading concept whose only value is to generate an endless series of examination questions. Economics would be a better subject if we discarded it once and for all. Having expunged perfect competition, we ought to follow it

---

6. While this topic may have brought some disagreements among economists of the Austrian school, it is to Kirzner's credit that he remained open to the idea that monopoly pricing could emerge within the unhampered market. See Kirzner (2013).

7. See Kirzner (2013, 112).

by also discarding Walrasian existence proofs and the Invisible Hand Theorem of welfare economics. First of all, everyone admits that these beautiful theorems are mental exercises without the slightest possibility of ever being practically relevant: first-best optima are never actually observed and in a second-best world, it is not in general desirable to fulfill any of the first-best optimum conditions; in other words, piecemeal welfare policies may be based on good or bad qualitative judgments but they are not based on rigorous analytical theorems. But once first-best, end-state competition is discarded as irrelevant, as precisely and rigorously wrong, and replaced by process-competition as imprecisely and loosely right, what are we left with? We are left with the content of every chapter in every textbook on imperfect or monopolistic competition, on oligopoly, duopoly and monopoly, in short, on industrial organisation as a sub-discipline in economics. In those chapters, firms jostle for advantage by price and non-price competition, undercutting and out-bidding rivals in the market place by advertising outlays and promotional expenses, launching new differentiated products, new technical processes, new methods of marketing and new organisational forms, and even new reward structures for their employees, all for the sake of head-start profits that they know will soon be eroded. In these chapters, there is never any doubt that competition is an active process, of discovery, of knowledge formation, of "creative destruction." I call this "the Austrian view of competition" because it is most firmly enshrined in the writings of such Austrian economists as Hayek, Schumpeter and, more recently, Kirzner. (Blaug 1996, 594–5)

This volume consists of four sections. The first section contains papers in which Kirzner explores the nature of competition and the role of prices. In the second section the reader will find papers on coordination, the knowledge problem, government planning, and the socialist calculation debate. Note that the section also includes a paper on Hayek's theory of coordination of markets that was originally published in German.[8] This paper is important on two counts. First it partially deals

---

8. The title is "Hayek's Theory of the Coordination of Markets: A Commentary to Accompany the Facsimile Edition of Hayek's *Preise und Produktion*."

with Austrian business cycle theory, a subject Kirzner has almost never explored in writing; and second, it is published in its original English version for the first time. The section that follows comprises articles on the role of information, knowledge, and advertising. The volume concludes with a section presenting two long articles about market process theory.

ACKNOWLEDGMENTS

We would first like to thank wholeheartedly Israel Kirzner for his unparalleled contribution to economic science. Kirzner's research program has deeply enriched the discipline and has shed light on some of economics' most difficult puzzles. Economists owe him an immense intellectual debt.

The publication of the Collected Works of Israel M. Kirzner would not be a reality without the participation of Liberty Fund, Inc. We are extremely grateful to Liberty Fund, and especially Emilio Pacheco, for making this project possible. To republish Kirzner's unique oeuvre has been on our minds since our time spent at New York University in the 1990s—where one of us was a professor (Peter) and the other a post-doc student (Frédéric). We are thrilled at the idea that current and future generations of economists and other scholars will have easy access to Kirzner's works.

Finally, we wish to thank Emily Washington for her invaluable help in the publication of this volume, as well as Dr. Stefan Kolev and Dr. Diana Thomas for providing their expertise with German quotations.

Peter J. Boettke and Frédéric Sautet

REFERENCES

Blaug, Mark (1996). *Economic Theory in Retrospect*, 5th ed. Cambridge: Cambridge University Press.

Boettke, Peter (1997). "Where Did Economics Go Wrong? Modern Economics as a Flight from Reality." *Critical Review* 11 (1).

Boettke, Peter, Christopher J. Coyne, and Peter T. Leeson (2006). "High Priests and Lowly Philosophers: The Battle for the Soul of Economics." *Case Western Reserve Law Review* 56.

——— (2003). "Man as Machine: The Plight of 20th Century Economics." *Annals for the Society of the History of Economic Thought* 43 (June): 1–10.

Hayek, Friedrich (1948a). "Economics and Knowledge," in Friedrich Hayek, *Individualism and Economic Order*. London: Routledge, 33–56.

——— (1948b). "The Meaning of Competition," in Friedrich Hayek, *Individualism and Economic Order*. London: Routledge, 92–106.

Kirzner, Israel M. ([1973] 2013). *Competition and Entrepreneurship,* Chicago: University of Chicago Press; reprint, Indianapolis: Liberty Fund. Citation refers to the Liberty Fund edition.

Machovec, Frank (1995). *Perfect Competition and the Transformation of Economics.* London: Routledge.

McNulty, Paul (1968). "Economic Theory and the Meaning of Competition." *Quarterly Journal of Economics* 82 (4): 639–56.

Mises, Ludwig von (1966). *Human Action,* 4th ed. San Francisco: Fox and Wilkes.

Peterson, Shorey (1957). "Antitrust and the Classic Model." *American Economic Review* 47 (no. 1): 60–78.

Sautet, Frédéric (2015). "Market Theory and the Price System," in Peter Boettke and Christopher Coyne (eds.), *The Oxford Handbook of Austrian Economics,* Oxford: Oxford University Press, 65–93.

THE
NATURE
OF
COMPETITION

CAPITAL, COMPETITION, AND CAPITALISM

Nothing is more fundamental to capitalism than competition, its very lifeblood. It is the interaction of consumers, resource owners, and entrepreneur-producers in free competitive markets which achieves the allocative efficiency and the affluence we take for granted in capitalist societies. At the same time, nothing can be more integral to the definition of capitalism than private ownership of the tools of production. It is, therefore, with puzzled surprise that one finds that private ownership of capital resources has been judged either unnecessary to, or incompatible with, the competitive market's operation.

On one hand, Professor K. Lancaster has recently asserted that a competitive market system does not require private ownership of capital. All the virtues of the system, he claims, could be achieved equally well in a system in which the state was the sole source of capital, providing it at a market-clearing price to all comers.[1] On the other hand, it is more often asserted that private ownership of capital, especially capital necessary to modern industry, operates as a barrier against the entry of new competition. The result is incompatible with the allocative efficiency usually found in the competitive market economy. I shall critically examine the second assertion, but our discussion will reveal certain weaknesses in the first assertion as well. The analysis will reaffirm the vital role private ownership of capital plays in the competitive market process by elucidating the way it supports the efficiency, flexibility, and resourcefulness of the capitalist system.

COMPETITION AND EFFICIENCY

The theory of the competitive market process teaches that where resources within a society leave opportunities for improvement via exchange, production, or some combination of both, they will appear as opportunities

Presented as a lecture at Hillsdale College, Hillsdale, Michigan, February 1974. From *Perception, Opportunity, and Profit: Studies in the Theory of Entrepreneurship* (Chicago and London: University of Chicago Press, 1979), 91–106. Reprinted by permission of Hillsdale College Press; the original source is *Champions of Freedom*, Ludwig von Mises Lecture Series, with presentations by Henry Hazlitt and others (Hillsdale, Mich.: Hillsdale College Press, 1974), 69–91.

for entrepreneurial profit. The lure of profit will lead entrepreneurs to discover these opportunities and pursue them until, through the competitive entrepreneurial process, resources have been reallocated in an equilibrium that eliminates both the profit opportunities and the misallocation. Freedom of entry is crucial to this process. The process depends heavily on the likelihood that, whenever anyone perceives an opportunity for improvement, he will be motivated by the lure of profit to exploit that opportunity. For this actually to occur it is necessary that no one who has perceived such an opportunity be barred from exploiting it. Efficiency in resource allocation might fail to be achieved if the resource is monopolized. Where access to a resource is blocked by its monopolized ownership, the monopolist-owner may find it to be in his own interest to limit production, even where the opportunities for utilization of the resource are fully perceived by other would-be producers. Critics claim that the institution of private ownership of capital serves as an obstacle to competitive market entry, arguing that capitalism is incompatible with competition. Let us state these criticisms more fully.

CAPITALISM AND COMPETITION: THE CRITICISMS

Critics argue that lack of capital may prevent the entrepreneur who has the better idea from following it through. Resources will continue to be used for producing less urgently needed products; resources will continue to be combined less efficiently in production, not because superior modes of utilization cannot be perceived (at least by some potential entrepreneurs), but because these visionary pioneers lack the capital resources needed to implement their projects.[2] As a special example, when a poor youth shows unmistakable signs of exceptional native ability, if he cannot afford an education, he may never take advantage of his talents, and thus society may never enjoy the fruits of his ability. Absence of access to capital has left a valuable resource unexploited.[3] If entrepreneurs who lack capital are unable to compete, then the ideas that do become implemented in production are not necessarily those whose superiority in serving consumers has been proved in the crucible of competition.

It is argued that incumbent firms, by virtue of their ownership of capital—a resource not accessible to many potential competitors—are able to enjoy a monopolistic or oligopolistic position. Capital requirements, serving as a barrier to entry, operate to confer imperfectly competitive market structures upon industries. Inefficiency in resource allocation is seen as inevitable because, given the imperfectly competitive structure of an industry, firms will find it in their self-interest to produce less than the competitive ideal. As E. S. Mason objects, "The capital resources necessary to establish a new firm in an effective competitive position may be so large as to eliminate potential competition as a practical consideration."[4]

This line of criticism, especially when advanced by laymen, is often unhelpfully jumbled with other arguments based on the size of incumbent firms. Many argue that monopoly power is granted by the necessity for a firm to be large in order to take advantage of the economies of scale. With a market limited in total size by demand conditions, economies of scale tend to keep down the number of firms in the market, a circumstance which, in the common view, defines the industry as imperfectly competitive. But this version of the criticism is based on confusion. While the argument that capital requirements constitute a barrier to entry is strengthened by the existence of scale economies,[5] since these will increase the amount of capital needed to compete effectively, the argument does not depend on the superficial identification of large size with monopoly power (an identification derived from considerations of limited size of markets). It depends, in its clearest form, strictly on the contention that capital requirements serve to bar entry into industries. We shall appraise capital requirements in this form.

OWNERSHIP, ENTREPRENEURSHIP, AND PROFITS

Critical discussion of the thesis of capital as barrier against entry requires that we first clarify several widely misunderstood aspects of entrepreneurial profits. The common view sees profits as ordinarily accruing to the owner of an enterprise.[6] The entrepreneur is seen as capturing profits through his successful deployment of the resources of his firm. This identification of the owner as the recipient of entrepreneurial profit has been responsible for difficulties economists purport to have discovered in the modern corporation. The modern large corporation is owned by stockholders who exercise virtually no day-to-day control over the use of the corporate resources. Ownership apparently has come to be divorced from control over firm assets. In the Berle-Galbraith view of things, this circumstance shatters the traditional view of profit's role in shaping the pattern of production. In the traditional view, the lure of profits spurs producers to serve consumers; in the corporation the production decisions are not made by owners, to whom profits accrue, but by a new class of corporate managers who find little personal incentive in providing corporate profits for stockholders. It is not our purpose to expose the fallacies in this Berle-Galbraith doctrine on the corporation at this point. We merely note that it rests on an uncritical acceptance of the view that entrepreneurial profits go to the owners of business firms. It is only because profits are believed to accrue only to owners that the stockholders' lack of power appears to contradict the assumption that corporate production decisions are actuated by the profit motive. Later on, we will revert critically to this aspect of the Berle-Galbraith view of the modern corporation.

In contrast to this widespread position linking profit with the ownership of assets, there flows from the Misesian analysis of the market process an entirely different view of entrepreneurial profits. Entrepreneurial profits, in this view, are not captured by owners, in their capacity of owners, at all. They are captured, instead, by men who exercise pure entrepreneurship, for which ownership is *never* a condition.

The Misesian theory of entrepreneurial profit can be described as an "arbitrage" theory of profit.[7] "What makes profit emerge is the fact that the entrepreneur who judges the future prices of the products more correctly than other people do buys some or all of the factors of production at prices which, seen from the point of view of the future state of the market, are too low."[8] Profits arise, then, from the absence of adjustment between the prices on different markets. Entrepreneurship does not consist in exchanging (or physically converting) owned assets of low value into assets of higher value. It consists in exploiting the difference between two sets of prices for the same goods. It consists in buying at the low price and selling at the higher price. Where the opportunities to buy and to sell are, as in pure arbitrage, truly simultaneous, in principle no initial resources are needed at all. The higher price obtained from the sale is more than sufficient to pay the low price that must be paid simultaneously for the purchase. In the more general case of entrepreneurship exercised across time, purchase must precede sale; the capture of profit requires the investment of capital.

But it is still correct to insist that the entrepreneur qua entrepreneur requires no investment of any kind. If the surplus (representing the difference between selling price and buying price) is sufficient to enable the entrepreneur to offer an interest payment attractive enough to persuade someone to advance the necessary funds, it is still true that the entrepreneur has discovered a way of obtaining pure profit, without the need to invest anything at all.[9]

Recognition that entrepreneurship, in the pure sense, does not require any prior ownership should not prevent us from seeing how an entrepreneur *may*, at the same time, be an owner. Instead of employing a resource in a standard, routine use for which its productivity at the margin is widely known and is already precisely reflected in its own market price, an owner of a resource may deploy it in a new, imaginative fashion yielding a sales revenue far in excess of its own current market price. But clearly the same entrepreneurial success might have been obtained by a nonowner purchasing the same resource in the market at its low price and deploying it in the novel way. Where the resource owner himself acted entrepreneurially in production, we should see him as having "purchased" the resource from himself at the current market price. When an entrepreneur has purchased a good for subsequent resale, he has become the owner of the good. When he does subsequently sell the good at a profit-yielding price, it might appear that it is as an owner that he has captured that profit. But reflection will confirm that the successful decision to which the entrepreneur must attribute his profit was made at a time when he was not yet the owner of the good he has now sold. The entrepreneurial decision is that which inspired him to buy the good in the first place for the sake of its expected sale at a later date. Clearly, then, while we see profits captured by owners, we must perceive that ownership has nothing to do with these profits, and by the same token, essentially nothing to do with the exercise of entrepreneurship.

CAPITALISTS AND ENTREPRENEURS

From the foregoing discussion there emerges with clarity the very important distinction that separates the role of the entrepreneur from that of the capitalist. The capitalist's role in the production process derives wholly from his ownership of resources. The capitalist is the resource owner who, in return for the promise of interest payments, is willing to permit his resources to be used in economic processes extending over time. The entrepreneur is one who perceives in a way the capitalist himself does not how these resources can be deployed in a way that can justify contractual interest payments to prospective investors. It is the entrepreneur who acquires these resources from the capitalist at the "low" price including interest in order to yield an even higher sales revenue at a later date.

To fulfill the capitalist role in production, it is necessary to own resources that can be offered in the market to producers, and to be prepared to wait for payment until these resources generate revenue in relatively time-consuming processes of production. Without prior ownership of productive resources, or funds able to command resources, it is as impossible to be a capitalist as to be a laborer without possessing the capacity to work. But to fulfill the entrepreneurial role, as we have seen, no prior ownership of any resources is needed. It is necessary for the prospective entrepreneur merely to be alert to the possibility of securing the means of production from capitalists and other resource owners to produce a final sales revenue greater than the sum of the amounts he must offer them in return.

It is true that, in the complexity of the real world, we must not expect to discover pure analytical categories. Those exercising entrepreneurship in the real world are likely to be resource owners at the same time. A laborer may borrow capital and produce a product which, after full payment of the costs of capital, leaves a surplus higher than the market value of his labor. And we have already noticed that the exercise of entrepreneurship will render the entrepreneur an owner of that which he has purchased, for the period between its purchase and its later sale. So those who have exercised entrepreneurship appear as current owners of assets. But this does not in any way diminish the power of our conclusion that entrepreneurship as an analytical category does *not* call for the prior ownership of anything as a prerequisite.

Acceptance of this important conclusion may be hampered by the circumstance that we may be unlikely to discover a pure entrepreneur or a pure capitalist. As Mises has pointed out, "every action is embedded in the flux of time and therefore involves a speculation";[10] the decision to lend capital is itself partly an entrepreneurial one, because it involves the possibility that the borrower may be unable to carry out his side of the contract. "A capitalist is always also virtually an entrepreneur and speculator."[11]

But the fact that every capitalist must be an entrepreneur does not in any way logically entail that to become an entrepreneur one must be a capitalist. Even where an entrepreneur happens to be a resource owner, we have seen that the entrepreneurship he has exercised has not depended in any essential way upon the accident of his being an owner of resources.

I emphasize here the sharpness of the distinction between the capitalist and the entrepreneurial roles not only for the sake of the economic insight the distinction confers. (A fascinating chapter in the history of economic thought concerns the gradual emergence of this insight.) My emphasis also illuminates the question with which this chapter is directly concerned, namely, the possibility that the capital requirements of modern industry operate as a barrier to competition. Let us see how this is the case.

BARRIERS TO ENTRY

For competition to be eliminated from any branch of production, prospective competitors must somehow be prevented from entering that branch of production. In the absence of institutional barriers erected by governmental authority, one can imagine prospective competitors being unable to enter an otherwise profitable line of activity *only as a result of barred access to needed resources*. Only if the needed resources for a particular line of production are monopolistically owned and barred to newcomers can producers feel secure from new competition. Obstacles to competition in production must have their source in monopolized resource ownership. It is important to perceive the implications of this way of looking at things.

If the resources needed for production are not monopolized, no one can be said to be barred from competing by his lack of resources. If oranges are widely available for purchase, no prospective producer of orange juice is barred from entering the industry if it promises profits merely because he lacks oranges. Nor does any one owner of oranges, in such circumstances, possess any kind of entrepreneurial advantage over nonowners: "If the supply of an important factor is not controlled monopolistically, ownership conveys no economic power."[12] No prior ownership of oranges is needed in order to capture, by the exercise of entrepreneurial imagination, the profits waiting to be won through the production of orange juice. Entrepreneurial entry into the orange juice industry can be barred only through monopolistically barred access to oranges.

The case is not one whit different for one said to be barred from competing by his lack of capital. Unless access to capital is monopolistically restricted, lack of capital can in no way be seen as barring competition; nor can ownership of nonmonopolized capital resources be seen as conferring any special economic power. Capital resources, where they are not monopolized, are available to entrepreneurs who perceive how they can be turned to a profit. It is because the entrepreneurial role requires no prior ownership, being sharply distinguished from that of the capitalist, that entrepreneurial competition can never be said to be barred by lack of capital. However, further qualifying observations are in order.

CAPITAL AND ENTRY

Despite our theoretical conclusion that the lack of capital resources cannot, unless they are monopolized, form a barrier to entrepreneurial competition, it will be objected that casual business experience supports the contrary position. In everyday business experience, it will be argued, it is commonplace to find potential entrepreneurs unable to assemble the capital needed to finance promising projects. Apparently capital requirements do hamper competition.

We shall see, however, that the facts presented by casual empiricism can be reconciled with our theoretical conclusion in a number of ways. In fact, such reconciliation will be useful in further clarifying the insights embodied in that conclusion, as well as in guarding us against applying it in inappropriate contexts.

1. What may deter a would-be entrepreneur from implementing what he believes to be a good idea may not be the inaccessibility of capital, but merely its high cost. Clearly, where an idea that seems profitable with capital available at zero cost turns out to be unprofitable under actual capital market conditions, the idea is not in fact a very competitive idea. "The necessity of having to raise large amounts of capital, . . . cannot be said to prevent entry, since if sufficient profits were anticipated the capital would be forthcoming."[13]

2. Of greater relevance are those circumstances in which an entrepreneur is fully prepared to offer market rates of interest for capital and yet finds it impossible to finance his project. The late F. H. Knight observed years ago that "demonstrated ability can always get funds for business operations."[14] But what if funds are available only at above market rates of interest that render proposed operations no longer profitable? And

what if the prospective competitor is an entrepreneur who happens not to have had the opportunity to demonstrate his ability?

Economists have fallen into the habit of recognizing these kinds of possibilities as "capital market imperfections." Put in this way, these possibilities seem to support the charge which we are here rebutting. Even without monopoly in the ownership of capital, it is implied, distortions in resource allocation may be generated by the absence of perfect markets in capital. Moreover, in specific cases imperfection in the capital market may be ascribed to monopoly. In a valuable but neglected paper, G. J. Stigler has carefully collected examples of statements by economists alleging imperfections in the capital market and has demonstrated that all too frequently such allegations reflect nothing but careless thinking.[15] I will briefly report Stigler's criticism and will subsequently point out an aspect of capital markets to which Stigler has not drawn attention.

Stigler explains that market perfection—permitting "all exchange which the traders prefer to non-exchange"—requires a single price throughout the market for a given good. The existence of more than one price implies that "one seller is receiving less than some other buyer is paying, and both would prefer to trade with one another than with whomever they are trading." Thus economists who discover cases where capital can be obtained only at rates higher than those obtainable elsewhere, describe these as cases of market imperfection. But, Stigler points out, "this is surely not sufficient evidence to allow us to conclude that capital is being allocated inefficiently—any more than the fact that some people walk is proof of an imperfection in the automobile market."[16] The existence of trading costs such as costs of transportation, of acquiring information on products and other traders, inspecting quality, collecting funds, may make the absence of a single price fully consistent with market perfection. "There is no 'imperfection' in a market possessing incomplete knowledge if it would not be remunerative to acquire (produce) complete knowledge."[17]

In other words, if capital can be obtained for a project only at rates higher than those available elsewhere, this is not necessarily evidence of market imperfection, nor does it follow that capital requirements somehow operate to hamper competition. Thus, to use one of Stigler's examples, if an investment in college education is likely to yield a 12 percent return, no necessary "imperfection" in the capital market is demonstrated by the fact that a would-be student cannot borrow funds at "the" interest rate of 6 percent. After all, it is possible that the likely default rate—clearly a very significant transaction cost—on student loans may make even a 12 percent interest rate unprofitable to lenders. So the difficulty would-be students find in competing in the market for those with college degrees, under such conditions, could not be attributed to lack of access to capital. Instead, it should be clear, capital fails to flow into investment in education simply because when costs of transactions are appropriately taken into account, such investment turns out not to be the most profitable use of funds.

To pursue the point a little further, suppose an unknown, penniless would-be entrepreneur has a genuinely good idea but cannot put it into operation because capitalists do not wish to risk their capital on a venture in which they must rely on both his unproved judgment and his undemonstrated integrity. We have here a good idea which, if the entrepreneur had been independently wealthy, he would have plunged into with enthusiasm; it will now fail to be implemented solely because he is penniless. We have seen that it would be wrong to describe this as the result of an obstacle in the competitive process. What we may be seeing in such a situation may merely be the efficient translation of very real transactions costs (namely, the cost of securing recognition for one's entrepreneurial judgment and personal integrity) into the appropriate allocation of resources.[18] These costs of securing recognition of one's competence and trustworthiness are truly social costs. They would exist under any system of economic organization; thus under socialism, too, planners would face the problem of determining the competence and integrity of those to whom to entrust social capital. It is true, of course, that were the penniless entrepreneur a wealthy man, these costs would be absent. So it may be argued that, given the existing pattern of resource ownership, capital requirements operate to restrict entrepreneurial entry. But such an objection would be quite without force. It would be similar to an objection charging inefficiency on the grounds that, on the West Coast, there are unexploited opportunities for the utilization of skilled laborers who reside on the East Coast, whose transportation costs are not justified by the opportunities. Were the initial pattern of the geographical distribution of labor supply different, these transportation costs would indeed not have been needed. Given the existing state of the world, they *are* needed; to ignore them is to fall into miscalculation. Quite similarly, given the asset ownership pattern at any date, a true social cost must be incurred in order to entrust scarce valuable capital to penniless, unknown entrepreneurs. This hardly qualifies as an obstacle to entrepreneurial entry.

3. The preceding paragraphs, based substantially on the work of Stigler, go far to demonstrate why it is wrong to negate our theoretical conclusion because of the difficulties found in practice in assembling capital for a given project. But still further considerations must be adduced, not mentioned in Stigler's treatment, which lend additional support to my position.

Let us suppose, again, that a bright, unknown, penniless entrepreneur finds it difficult to finance his good idea. Let us suppose that his idea is so good that it justifies incurring all the transaction costs previously mentioned, and that it is profitable even after making ample allowance for the costs of proving the entrepreneur's competence and integrity to potential investors. But, despite all this, he still finds it impossible to raise the necessary capital. Our treatment so far merely suggests, with Stigler, that such cases have yet to be proved to exist. But, as we shall see, we need not be satisfied with this stance. What can be shown is that, even if such cases do exist, the case arguing the existence of a barrier to competition is not one whit the stronger. The clue to the matter lies in the circumstance that, as cited earlier from Mises, a "capitalist is always also virtually an entrepreneur and speculator."

If a new idea holds forth promise, even after all trading costs have been taken into account, of a yield to capitalists higher than they can obtain elsewhere, their failure to exploit it constitutes an entrepreneurial error on their part. To describe such a situation, as Stigler, by implication, seems forced to do, as the manifestation of imperfection in the capital market is to assume, quite erroneously, that absence of entry barriers assures instantaneous attainment of equilibrium; or at any rate, the term "imperfection" is used in a way misleading to laymen. In fact, whenever there exist—without entry barriers—two prices for the same good, this represents, rather than some sinister market "imperfection," nothing but a disequilibrium situation created by entrepreneurial errors, which the competitive entrepreneurial process tends to correct. Two prices for the same good, for which transaction costs are unable to account, are the result of imperfect information on the part of market participants. It is the essence of the entrepreneurial process that a two-price situation provides the incentives for entrepreneurial arbitrage, tending to eliminate the discrepancy. Such processes are the essence of markets, and they can be relied upon wherever entrepreneurial entry is not blocked. Errors by capitalists constitute no exception to these general market laws.

If capitalists have, every one of them, failed to assess correctly the profitability of an idea advanced by a penniless entrepreneur, because they have underestimated the competence or the integrity of its promoter, this creates, for capitalist-entrepreneurs, an opportunity for profit. Unless capital is monopolistically owned, capitalists will tend to compete among themselves with respect to the true measure of the competence and integrity of penniless, unknown would-be entrepreneurs. We have no reason to doubt that capitalists do frequently misjudge the ability of entrepreneurs vying for their capital. We have no reason to doubt, either, that entrepreneurial competition among capitalists always operates to generate a tendency toward equilibrium—that is, for present purposes, toward a state of affairs where the competence and integrity of prospective men of ideas are correctly assessed.

CORPORATIONS, ENTREPRENEURS, AND THE BERLE-GALBRAITH THESIS

Our discussion permits us to return to the problem of fitting the modern corporation into our theoretical framework. We have seen that the Berle-Galbraith thesis perceives the modern corporation as destroying the traditional paramountcy of the profit motive in allocating resources. With the ownership of the corporate capital separated from its control, the argument runs, the profit motives of the owners can hardly control the way corporate resources are allocated. In fact, in Galbraith's view, the modern corporation marks a highly significant shift of economic power away from the owners of capital, who dominated in earlier periods, to the "organized intelligence" that constitutes Galbraith's "technostructure" in the economy of today.[19]

The perspective developed here enables us to see things with greater clarity. For our present purposes, we do not need to engage the Berle-Galbraith thesis on its principal premise, namely, the validity of a separation between corporate ownership and control. Shorey Peterson and others[20] have shown how fuzzy such an alleged separation must be. For present purposes, it is sufficient to differ drastically with Galbraith on what the significance of any such separation must be.

My position is, briefly, that where the corporate form of business organization permits a measure of independence and discretion to corporate managers, this is an ingenious, unplanned device that eases the access of entrepreneurial talent to sources of large-scale financing. Instead of the entrepreneur having to borrow capital—with all the transactions costs we have seen this to involve—the corporate form of organization permits would-be entrepreneurs to hire themselves out to owners of capital as corporate executives. The capitalists retain formal ownership, permitting them, if they choose, to divest themselves easily of their shares in badly managed firms or, in the last resort, to oust incompetent management. Yet the executives, to the limited extent that they do possess discretionary freedom of action, are able to act as entrepreneurs and implement their ideas without themselves becoming owners at all.

Space does not permit an elaboration of this way of seeing the modern corporation. But this brief glimpse of it should reveal the remarkable institutional flexibility of capitalism. With no entry into markets blocked by institutional intervention, the market is incredibly ingenious in successfully encouraging new forms of entrepreneurial competition in the deployment of social capital resources to their most valuable uses. So, far from the modern corporation reflecting any weakening of entrepreneurial profit's role, it exemplifies the subtle ways the lure of profits permeates markets in the highly capitalized industrial forms of our time.[21]

CAPITALISTS AND COMPETITION

My main purpose has been achieved. We have seen how the capitalist role in modern market economies cannot in any way be described as incompatible with the competitive process. But our discussion also permits us to dissent vigorously from a related critical assertion. At the outset I cited the argument that, to enjoy the well-recognized advantages of a competitive market economy, private ownership of capital is not at all necessary. This view argues that all the virtues of a competitive market can be achieved equally well in a system in which the state is the sole source of capital, providing it at a market clearing price to all comers. There are a number of difficulties with this line of argument, as there are with all similar proposals for "market" systems under socialism; we will deal here only with one of them.

We have seen how important a role, in the market for capital, is played by the special trading costs associated with the entrusting of capital into entrepreneurial hands. In the assessment of these costs, we saw a new scope for the exercise of entrepreneurship. The Misesian insight that every capitalist must at the same time be an entrepreneur permitted us to see how entrepreneurial competition among capitalists plays a vital role in the selection of which would-be entrepreneurs shall be entrusted with society's scarce and valuable capital resources. Were the state to be the sole source of capital, this level of entrepreneurial competition would be eliminated. We need not stress the potential abuses lurking in such a state monopoly of capital ownership. We may assume for the sake of argument that such a monopoly would not create those very barriers to entrepreneurial entry that critics of capitalism erroneously claim are erected by capital needs of modern industry. But certainly state control of capital resources would mean that private capitalists would no longer compete with one another in entrepreneurship to identify would-be entrepreneurs of the competence and integrity needed to put massive quantities of capital to work implementing their ideas. Without the profit motive to guide those who select the men of action, initiative, and leadership—even if the profit motive is retained for the level at which men of action, initiative, and leadership themselves operate—we will have abandoned one crucial segment of the market process that tends to allocate capital to the entrepreneurs most likely to succeed.[22]

We conclude, then, not only that private ownership of capital is not inconsistent with the competitive market process, but that it is in fact essential to the efficiency of the competitive market process.

NOTES

1. K. Lancaster, "The Dynamic Inefficiency of Capitalism," *Journal of Political Economy* 81 (September/October 1973): 1092.

2. "Absolute capital requirements may be so large that relatively few individuals or groups could secure the needed capital, or that entrants could secure it only at interest rates and other terms which placed them at a net cost disadvantage to established sellers" (J. S. Bain, *Barriers to New Competition* [Cambridge: Harvard University Press, 1956], p. 55).

3. For references to the literature on this see G. J. Stigler, "Imperfections in the Capital Market," *Journal of Political Economy* 75 (June 1967): 287–88.

4. E. S. Mason, *Economic Concentration and the Monopoly Problem* (Cambridge: Harvard University Press, 1967), p. 348.

5. See Bain, *Barriers to New Competition*, chap. 3.

6. See, e.g., A. A. Alchian, "Corporate Management and Property Rights," in *Economic Policy and the Regulation of Corporate Securities*, ed. H. G. Manne (Washington, D.C.: American Enterprise Institute, 1969), pp. 342–43.

7. On this see my *Competition and Entrepreneurship* (Chicago: University of Chicago Press, 1973), pp. 85ff.

8. L. Mises, "Profit and Loss," in *Planning for Freedom*, 2d ed. (South Holland, Ill.: Libertarian Press, 1962), p. 109.

9. I. M. Kirzner, *Competition and Entrepreneurship*, p. 49.

10. L. Mises, *Human Action* (New Haven: Yale University Press, 1949), p. 254.

11. Ibid.

12. H. Demsetz, "The Technostructure, Forty-Six Years Later," *Yale Law Journal* 77 (1968): 805.

13. S. R. Shenoy, "The Sources of Monopoly," *New Individualist Review* 4 (Spring 1966): 42.

14. F. H. Knight, *Risk, Uncertainty and Profit* (New York: Houghton Mifflin, 1921), p. 274, note 1; see also D. M. Lamberton, *The Theory of Profit* (New York: A. M. Kelley, 1965), p. 50.

15. G. J. Stigler, "Imperfections in the Capital Market," *Journal of Political Economy* 75 (June 1967): 287–92.

16. Ibid., p. 288.

17. Ibid., p. 291.

18. See Stigler's remarks on Keynes's distinction between borrower's and lender's risk (ibid., p. 291).

19. J. K. Galbraith, *The New Industrial State* (New York: Houghton Mifflin, 1967), chaps. 5 and 6.

20. Shorey Peterson, "Corporate Control and Capitalism," *Quarterly Journal of Economics* 79 (February 1965): 1–24; A. A. Alchian, "Corporate Management."

21. See H. G. Manne, *Insider Trading and the Stock Market* (New York: Free Press, 1966), for a discussion of how corporate executives may be in a position to win pure entrepreneurial profits for themselves.

22. For critical discussion of earlier proposals concerning the allocation of capital in noncapitalist "competitive" systems, see F. A. Hayek, *Individualism and Economic Order* (London: Routledge and Kegan Paul, 1949), pp. 172–76, 200ff.

PRICES, THE COMMUNICATION OF KNOWLEDGE, AND THE DISCOVERY PROCESS

Among the fundamental contributions that Professor Hayek has made to economic science, certainly one of the most significant and far-reaching must be judged to be his path-breaking articulation of the nature of the "economic problem which society faces" (Hayek 1949b: 77). It was in this context that Hayek decisively drew the attention of the economics profession to the unique problems that arise from the *dispersal of knowledge*.

> The economic problem of society is . . . not merely a problem of how to allocate "given" resources—if "given" is taken to mean given to a single mind which deliberately solves the problem set by these "data." It is rather a problem, of how to secure the best use of resources known to any of the members of society, for ends whose relative importance only these individuals know. Or, to put it briefly, it is a problem of the utilization of knowledge which is not given to anyone in its totality.
>
> (Hayek 1949b: 77–8)

Hayek's insight represented a breakthrough, of course, in the modern history of welfare economics, as well as providing a brilliant new way of stating the crucial arguments making up the "Austrian" side of the socialist economic calculation debate (see particularly Lavoie 1985). In addition, however, Hayek's emphasis on the role of knowledge constituted an important step forward in our understanding of the way in which markets work, and of how the price system in fact tends to solve the economic problem which society faces. Indeed it seems to be this aspect of Hayek's contribution that has attracted the most attention in the economics profession. While accounts of modern developments in welfare economics rarely refer to Hayek's dismissal of the allocative-efficiency

The author gratefully acknowledges the stimulation of and the ideas contained in a paper presented at the Austrian Economics Colloquium at New York University by S. Ikeda: "An essay on equilibrium prices, disequilibrium prices, and information." Reprinted from *The Meaning of Market Process: Essays in the Development of Modern Austrian Economics* (New York and London: Routledge, 1992), 139–51. First published in *The Political Economy of Freedom: Essays in Honor of F. A. Hayek*, ed. K. R. Leube and A. H. Zlabinger (Philosophia Verlag, 1984).

criterion (in favour of the co-ordination perspective), and while accounts of the socialist economic calculation debate have, notoriously, thoroughly and unforgivably muddled it up (Lavoie 1985), Hayek's insights into the role of prices in solving the knowledge dispersal problem have been widely cited, and often by the most orthodox of neoclassical economists. I shall argue in this chapter that, in spite of its citation of Hayek's work in this regard, the economic literature has regrettably failed to do justice to the full significance of that work. As a result professional concern with problems of knowledge dispersal has tended to remain, unfortunately, at a rather superficial level. In demonstrating the validity of this assertion it will be necessary to distinguish sharply between two quite different "communications" challenges arising out of knowledge dispersal, and (consequently) two quite different functions that markets may possibly fulfil in the context of the "economic problem which society faces." It may perhaps be helpful to start with an analogy drawn from a rather different context, that of automobile traffic through a busy urban street intersection.

AUTOMOBILES AND THE PROBLEM OF DISPERSED KNOWLEDGE

Consider cars approaching the intersection of two urban streets, the one north–south and the other east–west. The driver of a car approaching from (say) the north must decide whether or not to stop before proceeding south across the east–west street. The driver's decision will depend on his knowledge or expectations concerning the decisions that the drivers of other cars (that may possibly be driving towards the intersection from the other directions) will make when *they* reach the cross-roads. In order for traffic to move smoothly and safely through the intersection it is clearly necessary that these various decisions be somehow co-ordinated. Absence of co-ordination may, rather obviously, result in regrettable, costly (because perhaps quite unnecessary) delays at the intersection before proceeding through it, or in even more regrettable and costly automobile collisions. It is easy to see that such regrettable events are to be attributed at least in part to the dispersal of knowledge: the driver of one car knows, at the moment when he makes his decision, what he has decided to do, but the drivers of other cars do not know what the first driver has decided (or perhaps even that there *is* this first driver). *Their* decisions are then likely to fail to be co-ordinated as well as is possible with that of the first driver, and so on. Were an omniscient single mind to make the decisions for *all* the drivers, that mind might arrange the drivers' actions in smooth and safe fashion. In the absence of such a central omniscient mind, a well-designed (and fully enforced) system of traffic signals can achieve co-ordination by providing each driver of a vehicle with confident assurance as to what the other driver will decide to do. The green light beckoning a southward-bound driver is in fact assuring him that cars proceeding in the east–west street will not cross the intersection in the immediate minute or minutes ahead. A red light directs him to stop, while at the same time it provides conviction (in a well-designed system) that the waiting is not wasted (since it implies that cars are being permitted to proceed east and west). By timing the light changes appropriately, smoothly co-ordinated traffic conditions can be achieved. Let us analyse what we mean when we say that a signal system "achieves co-ordination." It will be convenient to focus on the manner in which the system eliminates *unnecessary delays*. (Rather similar considerations apply to the system's elimination of avoidable collisions.)

A successful traffic signalling system will not only succeed in avoiding collisions, it will avoid requiring cars to wait needlessly (such as at times when traffic along the other direction is extremely light). Superior co-ordination would permit the timing of light changes to reflect the relative intensities of traffic along the two intersecting streets. "To achieve co-ordination" is thus a phrase which, in the context of the automobile example, can have two quite distinct meanings.

First, a traffic signal system may be said to be achieving co-ordination when its timing, from the very installation of the system, is such as in fact to control the flow of traffic in some optimal manner. No undesired collisions, no unjustified waiting, result from unanimous obedience of the traffic signals. This successful achievement of co-ordination has clearly involved the efficient communication of correct information. The information fed to the drivers of cars has been such as (a) correctly to inform each of them of the consequences of the decisions of other drivers, leading them, in turn (b) to make those decisions that permit this above property (a) to hold, with the resulting set of drivers' decisions being such as (c) to result in no unnecessary waiting. This is certainly a valid sense of the phrase "to achieve co-ordination." But a second possible meaning may be intended by use of this phrase.

For this second meaning consider a traffic signal system that, when installed, is timed suboptimally. Southbound drivers find themselves waiting at red lights, let us say at 3.00 in the afternoon, for several minutes during which no traffic flows at all in the east–west directions. Clearly this waiting is unnecessary; it means that north–south drivers are compelled to act in a fashion that is not co-ordinated with the decisions of east–west drivers (since the latter have decided not to pass through the intersection at this time, yet the former have been prevented from taking advantage of those east–west decisions). But imagine now that the signal system is programmed in a manner that, at the beginning of each day, alters the system's timing to reflect yesterday's actual time-profile of traffic experience (registering not only the dearth of traffic in the east–west direction at 3.00 in the afternoon, but also the heavy volume of traffic in the north–south direction). Then the very experience that results today from the as-yet-imperfectly co-ordinated system plays its part in bringing about a revision in the system's timing, in a way that substitutes a better co-ordinated system in place of the less co-ordinated one. This kind of signal system (including its property of improving itself by "learning" from the unfortunate results of its earlier imperfections) may also be described as one that "achieves co-ordination." However, here the phrase refers to the property of the system that permits it to identify and begin to correct its earlier weaknesses. The system begins its co-ordinating task at the very time when its signals promote *un*coordinated activity on the part of drivers— since it is that very uncoordinated activity that provides the information necessary for improved timing. The system's ability to achieve co-ordination, in this sense, certainly does *not* mean that, at the outset, it achieved the sets of results (a), (b) and (c) described in the preceding paragraph. Drivers proceeding south who have been directed to wait needlessly at the red light have, in effect, been informed *incorrectly* concerning the rate of traffic flow in the east–west direction. Yet, as we have seen, the system, from the very outset, has possessed the property of "achieving co-ordination" in the sense of incorporating a feedback mechanism that deploys the results of its own inadequacies towards their systematic elimination. Here too the co-ordinating property of the system arises from the way that it provides information—but in a sense quite different from that relevant to the system that is *already* perfectly timed. In this second, initially faulty, system, the co-ordinating properties arise from its ability *to communicate information concerning its own faulty information communication properties.*

Let us return to the role of the price system in coping with the problems arising from dispersed knowledge—the "economic problem which society faces." We shall find (a) that prices tend to "achieve co-ordination" in *both* the senses we have noticed in the traffic signal example, while (b) the literature has in fact recognized (and cited Hayek in regard to) only one of these two senses.

EQUILIBRIUM PRICES AND MARKET CO-ORDINATION

Economists often speak, nowadays, of the competitive equilibrium price system as an effective way in which the individual decisions of many market participants can be co-ordinated. Prices are, indeed, often compared with signals. Without knowing the details concerning the preferences of other market participants or concerning the conditions surrounding production processes, decision makers, through the guidance of these price signals, are led—economists explain—to that pattern of attempted activities that permits all of them to be carried out without disappointment and without regret.

In the Marshallian market for a single commodity, for example, the equilibrium market price for that commodity inspires the pattern of market clearing bids and offers. The price is such as to motivate potential buyers to ask for exactly that aggregate quantity of the commodity that potential suppliers have been motivated—by that same price—to produce. No buyer has been misled by the lowness of the price to seek to buy *more* than is in fact offered for sale. (And no buyer is discouraged from bidding for what is in fact available to him at a price he is prepared to pay.) No supplier has been misled by the height of this price to seek to produce more than is in fact being sought to be bought. (Nor is any supplier discouraged from offering that for which a price acceptable to him can be obtained.) No buyer need in fact know anything at all about the conditions of supply, the availabilities or the costs of inputs, and the like. Nor need the seller know anything about the preferences of consumers, the availability to them of substitute commodities, and the like. All that market participants need to know, for the Marshallian market to co-ordinate buying and selling conditions perfectly, is the prevailing equilibrium price of the commodity. By offering to buy all they wish to buy at this price, buyers find that their offers smoothly dovetail with the offers of sellers to sell (with the latter merely offering to sell all they wish to sell at this same prevailing equilibrium price). The equilibrium price co-ordinates. All this is of course well understood, and is part of the basic equipment common to all economists.

Hayek's emphasis on knowledge is frequently cited in the context of this understanding of what equilibrium prices can achieve. Equilibrium prices are explained to be communicating to potential buyers and sellers, in highly economical fashion, the information necessary for co-ordinated decisions to emerge. It is because the detailed information concerning the preferences of individual potential buyers, and concerning the peculiar productive capabilities of individual sources of potential supply, is so scattered and dispersed that the co-ordinative ability of the equilibrium price system is so valuable and impressive.

This kind of co-ordinative ability recognized as being possessed by equilibrium prices is clearly analogous to the ability of an optimally timed traffic signal system smoothly and safely to co-ordinate traffic.[1] Equilibrium prices, like optimally timed signal changes, correctly communicate the information that (by virtue of the very notion of "correctness" in this context) motivates and enables individual decision makers to generate a smoothly dovetailing set of decisions; a set that will entail neither disappointment nor regret. We must now show that, in addition to this possible sense in which prices may be said to achieve co-ordination (i.e. when the prices are already equilibrium prices—analogous to the already optimally timed signal system), there is also a much more important other possible sense in which prices may be said to achieve co-ordination. This sense refers to the possible ability of *dis*equilibrium prices to generate systematic changes in market decisions about price offers and bids, in a way that, by responding to the regrettable results of initially *un*coordinated sets of decisions, tends to replace them by less uncoordinated sets. (Here, of course, the analogy is to the non-optimally timed traffic signal system that contains a feedback mechanism through which the regrettable results of initial poor timing generate a tendency towards improved timing.)[2]

DISEQUILIBRIUM PRICES AND MARKET CO-ORDINATION

Consider the market for a single commodity (say, a given quality of tea) that has *not* attained equilibrium. Imagine, for example, that in different parts of this market there have occurred during the past "day" sales of tea at widely differing prices. Imagine, moreover, that by the end of the day the total quantity of tea that has changed hands is far less than that which the

realities of supply and demand conditions in fact warrant, so that potential suppliers remain holding inventories of tea which could, in truth, have
been reduced by sale to eager buyers at prices that these suppliers would
have found attractive. These market conditions express the co-ordination
failures that have occurred: prices have failed to clear the market. The signals offered by bids and offers have failed to generate completely dovetailing
sets of decisions; market participants, because of inadequate information
concerning each other's attitudes, preferences and capabilities, have failed
to take advantage of existing opportunities for mutually gainful exchange.

These unfortunate market conditions can be expected to result, sooner
or later, in both disappointment and regret. Disappointment and regret
may occur because sooner or later buyers will, perhaps, realize that, had
they offered higher prices, they could have obtained more tea (and that
they would have been happy to do so, even at the higher price, rather
than go without tea because they foolishly believed it would be forthcoming at lower prices). Or sellers may realize that they might, had they only
offered to sell at lower prices, have sold more tea (and that they would
have preferred to do so rather than refusing to sell because of a mistaken
belief that higher prices were available). In these cases disappointments
arise as buyers (sellers) discover that their hopes to buy (sell) at low
(high) prices were unrealistic. Regrets arise at not having realized that
they would have been better advised to have offered to buy (sell) at higher
(lower) prices. In addition, of course, since tea was sold at many different
prices during the same day, many of those who sold (bought) at the low
(high) prices will regret not having done so at the higher (lower) prices at
which in fact tea exchanged elsewhere in the very same market.

These disappointments and regrets may generate sharp changes in
the decisions made by potential buyers and sellers (even in the absence
of change in the sets of "real" determinants of their preferences and
productive capabilities). Buyers who paid the high prices and sellers
who accepted the low prices may revise their market attitudes, so that
a tendency towards a uniform price may occur. Buyers (or sellers) who
had overestimated the willingness of potential suppliers (or buyers) to
sell (or buy) will realize their earlier errors and adjust their offers to the
realities. In fact it is precisely because all these adjustments are likely
to cause the initial sets of prices to give way to a different set (a set perhaps less divergent, and perhaps less likely to generate disappointments
and regrets) that the initial market must be described as having been in

disequilibrium. Without any outside forces whatever (such as changes in preferences or in supply conditions), the initial sets of buying and selling offers are likely to give way to different sets. Where the changes generated in this way are systematically in the direction of better co-ordinated sets of decisions (than in the initial period), we may surely describe the market (even in its early, grossly discoordinated state) as possessing, to some degree, an ability to achieve co-ordination. The very disappointments and regrets that result from initial co-ordination failures systematically bring about improved sets of market decisions. Here the appropriate analogy, surely, is to the initially faulty traffic signal system.[3]

It should be noticed that here too the "co-ordinative properties" of the (disequilibrium) market derive from the ability of prices to communicate information, *but in a sense quite different from that in which equilibrium prices may be said to co-ordinate through the accurate communication of information.* Equilibrium prices co-ordinate because they are *already* so adjusted ("pre-reconciled") that decisions that take these prices into account turn out to be mutually reinforcing. Disequilibrium prices can, if at all, be described as "co-ordinating" only in the sense that they reveal, to alert market participants, how *altered* decisions on their part (from those that contributed to the emergence of these disequilibrium prices) may be wiser for the future. Thus disequilibrium prices that are "too low" (and which therefore generated excess demand) suggest to some disappointed buyers that they should offer to pay higher prices. Or again, to the extent that disequilibrium has manifested itself in the emergence of many prices in the same market for tea, this very spread between high and low prices suggests to some alert entrepreneurs that arbitrage profits may be won through offering to buy at somewhat higher (than the lowest) prices and simultaneously offering to sell elsewhere at somewhat lower (than the highest) prices. The information that inspires these "co-ordinating" changes is indeed information that is supplied by the initial structure of prices, but so supplied only through alert *realization of the failures* of those initial prices to achieve the kind of co-ordination that we found in the case of equilibrium prices.

DISPERSED KNOWLEDGE, THE PRICE SYSTEM
AND ECONOMIC LITERATURE

We have thus seen that the Hayekian insights into the nature of the economic problem facing society permit us to recognize the co-ordinative role of prices in a sense far more important than that played by equilibrium prices. The circumstance that information is dispersed offers society a "communication" challenge not only because even the most fully co-ordinated set of decentralized decisions must *presuppose* and *contain* an effective signalling system. The circumstance that information is dispersed offers society a far more important "communications" challenge—that of generating flows of information or of signals that might somehow stimulate the *revision* of initially *un*co-ordinated decisions in the direction of greater mutual co-ordinatedness.

So long as economists saw the economic problem to be one of achieving an efficient allocation of social resources (in the same way as the individual economizer faces the problem of private resource allocation), there could, of course, hardly be appreciation for the "co-ordinative" contributions to social well-being that a price system can offer in helping overcome the problem of dispersed knowledge. As is by now fairly widely understood, as a consequence of what we have learned from Hayek, to talk of the problem of efficiently allocating society's resources is completely *to assume away and thus to overlook* the dispersed knowledge problem.

What is disappointing, in the way in which the profession has absorbed the Hayekian lesson, is that the literature appears to have failed to grasp the way in which the price system meets the "communications" challenge, offered by the circumstance of dispersed knowledge, that we have described as being by far the more important one. Instead it appears to have focused entirely on the more superficial sense in which a price system may be said to communicate information, namely on the signalling role fulfilled by equilibrium prices.

Now, for textbook purposes this limited exploitation of the Hayekian insights is arguably understandable and defensible. Thus a number of contemporary textbooks[4] cite Hayek's well-known example of the tin market.

> Assume that somewhere in the world a new opportunity for the use of . . . tin, has arisen, or that one of the sources of supply of tin has been eliminated. It does not matter for our purpose—and it is significant that it does not matter—which of these two causes has made tin more scarce. All that the users of tin need to know is that . . . they must economize tin. There is no need for the great majority of them even to know . . . in favor of what other needs they ought to husband

the supply. . . . The mere fact that there is one price for any commodity . . . brings about the solution which . . . might have been arrived at by one single mind possessing all the information which is in fact dispersed among all the people involved in the process.

(Hayek 1949b: 85f.)

It is certainly true that this particular example of Hayek's is concerned only with the communication-of-information function fulfilled by equilibrium prices. (This is quite clear, for example, from the concluding sentences referring to the single price and to the coincidence between the results of there being a single price for tin throughout the market, and the solution that might be arrived at by a single omniscient mind.) This example does not focus on the communication problem that confronts a price system in which, as yet, the bewildering arrays of market prices reflect only highly *un*coordinated decisions on the parts of potential buyers and sellers. Yet there is no need to criticize the textbooks for not going beyond the simplest communication function of prices. There can be no doubt that an understanding of this simpler Hayekian lesson at the beginning of one's study of economics can be profoundly beneficial.

What is more puzzling is that the deeper implications of the Hayekian lesson have somehow failed to be noticed, not only in the textbooks, but also in the more advanced literature that has referred to Hayek's contribution. Thus, a considerable mathematical literature has emerged exploring the extent to which market prices convey information in the face of stochastic supply and/or demand conditions (see, for example, Grossman 1976; Grossman and Stiglitz 1976, 1980; Frydman 1982). The questions asked in this literature concern whether or not uninformed market participants can derive correct information from market prices themselves. Nowhere is there enquiry as to whether entrepreneurial alertness and motivation may perhaps be "switched on" by the configuration of market prices, to conjecture (and to try out!) hunches that may in fact be closer to the truth (than the information that the prices themselves reflect). Similarly, in what surely must be regarded as the most extensive and wide-ranging development of the implications of the Hayekian insights, Thomas Sowell's monumental *Knowledge and Decisions,* one looks in vain for any discussion of the way in which prices and price differences may stimulate a deployment of existing information that might be superior to that which these prices themselves express.

To emphasize, as Sowell does throughout his work, that prices *summarize* economic knowledge (see especially Sowell 1980: 38) is of unquestioned value. But this insight into the relationship between prices and knowledge ignores the far more important truth that it is the very *inadequacies* that cloud the manner in which these price-summaries express existing knowledge that create the market incentives for their modification. The profit opportunities embedded in existing prices are thus extraordinarily effective communicators of knowledge (in a sense quite different from that in which prices summarize knowledge). Thus governmentally imposed obstacles to price flexibility not only (as Sowell so well, and in such rich detail, explains) prevent prices from telling the truth—they smother the emergence of those disequilibrium-price-generated incentives upon which the system depends for its very ability to discover and announce the truth.

HAYEK AND THE MARKET DISCOVERY PROCESS

Hayek himself (especially in the earlier work in which he developed his seminal insights concerning the social significance of the circumstance of dispersed knowledge) was not as explicit as one might have wished on the role of prices in the discovery process of the market. A reader mistakenly believing that the only sense in which prices may be said to carry information is that in which equilibrium prices correctly reflect ("summarize") the true supply and demand conditions might be excused for coming away from a reading of Hayek's papers on knowledge of 1937 and of 1945 (1949c, 1949b) without sensing any challenge to that belief. Although a number of passages in these earlier papers of Hayek criticized the standard view among welfare economists and others (i.e. the view that saw the economic problem as that of securing an efficient allocation by society of its given scarce resources) as reflecting undue emphasis on the equilibrium state (see for example Hayek 1949a: 93, fn. 2; 188), these papers did not explicitly show how disequilibrium prices play their role in solving Hayek's problems of dispersed knowledge. Yet, as we have seen, there can be no doubt, once one has understood the co-ordination problems implied by dispersed knowledge, about the role of disequilibrium prices in this regard. That Hayek did in fact intend his formulation of the knowledge problem to include also the role of prices in providing the incentives for their own modification appears clear from his discussions of competition as a process, and particularly from his later work on competition as a discovery procedure (Hayek 1949d, 1978b).

In Hayek's 1946 lecture "The meaning of competition" he brilliantly distinguished the *state* of perfect competition from the dynamic competitive *process*. One of the conditions required for the former is perfect knowledge; the central achievement of the latter that is "it is only through the process of competition that the facts will be discovered." When Hayek in this paper talks of "spreading information" (1949d: 96, 106), he is not referring to the instantaneous transmission, through equilibrium price signals, of already known information. He is referring, instead, to the "process of the formation of opinion" (p. 106). This process of opinion formation is one built out of a series of entrepreneurial steps, made possible by competitive freedom of entrepreneurial entry, and exemplified by the entry of one "who possesses the exclusive knowledge . . . to reduce the cost of production of a commodity by 50 percent" and thus "reduces its price by . . . 25 percent" (p. 101).

These insights were deepened and made even more explicit in Hayek's later "Competition as a discovery procedure." In this paper what is emphasized is not that prices act as signals transmitting existing information—but rather that it is the competitive process which *digs out* what is in fact discovered. The competitive process relies upon market data at any particular time only in the sense that "provisional results from the market process at each stage . . . tell individuals what to look for" (1978b: 181). The "high-degree of coincidence of expectations" that the market achieves "is brought about by the systematic disappointment of some kind of expectations" (p. 185). The "generally beneficial effects of competition must include disappointing or defeating some particular expectations or intentions" (p. 180). In fact, "competition is valuable *only* because, and so far as, its results are unpredictable and on the whole different from those which anyone has, or could have, deliberately aimed at."

What emerges from these Hayekian insights into the *discovery* properties inherent in the competitive process is the recognition, surely, that the incentives offered by market prices *during* this competitive process are the key elements in motivating competitive-entrepreneurial entry and discovery. In this sense prices play a role in "spreading information" quite different from their role as signals communicating *already discovered* information under equilibrium conditions.

COMMUNICATION AND DISCOVERY

Equilibrium prices permit market participants to "read" the relevant information needed for their activities to be mutually adjusted in co-ordinated fashion. Disequilibrium prices are far less helpful in this regard; in fact a good deal of the "information" that trusting market participants "learn" from disequilibrium prices is quite incorrect and may be responsible for waste and frustration. As communicators, as signals, disequilibrium prices are relatively poor performers (when compared, of course, with the questionably-relevant standard set in this regard by equilibrium prices). Indeed, markets and the market system have often been criticized for the co-ordination failures that disequilibrium prices both express and help generate. What Hayek's "Austrian" insights permit us to see is that the social function served by market prices is captured far more significantly by the concept of *discovery* than by that of communication.

In regard to discovery, market prices (especially disequilibrium prices) should be seen not so much as known signals to be deliberately consulted *in order to find out* the right thing to do, but rather as spontaneously generated flashing red lights *alerting* hitherto unwitting market participants to the possibility of pure entrepreneurial profit or the danger of loss. These discoveries, surely, constitute the crucial steps through which markets tend to achieve co-ordination, gradually replacing earlier states of widespread mutual ignorance by successively better co-ordinated states of society.

No doubt the economics profession has much to learn about the subtle manner in which this market discovery procedure works. Surely the future historian of economic thought will trace back future development in this branch of social understanding to those seminal and path-breaking papers in which Hayek taught us the crucial importance of dispersed knowledge in creating *the* economic problem which society faces.

NOTES

1. An important limitation in this analogy is that, for a traffic signal system to be effective, it must depend on some *extraneous* circumstance (e.g. compulsion or custom) to provide assurance that signals will in fact be obeyed by all drivers. No such extraneous circumstance is required in the case of the equilibrium price system. The very *meaning* of such a system is that the set of prices is such as spontaneously to motivate directly a completely co-ordinated set of activities.

2. Here, too, the analogy is incomplete. As will be seen in the next section of the chapter, the errors expressed in disequilibrium prices generate disappointments and regrets that may motivate those responsible for the errors *themselves* to revise, for subsequent periods, their bids and offers. For the traffic signal system we had to assume that someone in control (or some robot) responds to the consequences of imperfect timing; the signals which changed at the "wrong" time do not improve their timing as a result of their own determination to "learn" from past "errors" and "regrets"; their timing is changed by someone, or some machine, from the "outside."

3. For a more detailed account of such a co-ordination process see Kirzner (1963: Ch. 7).

4. See, for example, Kohler (1982: 28f.), Dolan (1983: 62), Gwartney and Stroup (1982: Ch. 3, especially pp. 56f.). (On pp. 57f. Gwartney and Stroup's book goes beyond the communication role of prices in equilibrium to draw attention to the co-ordination properties of entrepreneurial activity in the dynamic market process.)

REFERENCES

Dolan, E. (1983) *Basic Economics,* 3rd edn, London: Dryden Press.

Frydman, R. (1982) "Towards an understanding of market processes: individual expectations, learning and convergence to rational expectations equilibrium," *American Economic Review* 72: 652–68.

Grossman, S. (1976) "On the efficiency of competitive stock markets where traders have diverse information," *Journal of Finance* 31: 573–85.

Grossman, S. and Stiglitz, J. E. (1976) "Information and competitive price systems," *American Economic Review, Proceedings* 66: 246–53.

Grossman, S. and Stiglitz, J. E. (1980) "On the impossibility of informationally efficient markets," *American Economic Review* 70: 393–402.

Gwartney, J. D. and Stroup, R. (1982) *Economics, Private and Public Choice,* 3rd edn, New York: Academic Press, Chapter 3.

Hayek, F. A. (1949a) *Individualism and Economic Order,* London: Routledge & Kegan Paul.

Hayek, F. A. (1949b) "The use of knowledge in society," in *Individualism and Economic Order,* London: Routledge & Kegan Paul (originally published in *American Economic Review* 35, no. 4 (1945): 519–30).

Hayek, F. A. (1949c) "Economics and knowledge," in *Individualism and Economic Order,* London: Routledge & Kegan Paul (originally published in *Economica* 4, February 1937).

Hayek, F. A. (1949d) "The meaning of competition," in *Individualism and Economic Order,* London: Routledge & Kegan Paul.

Hayek, F. A. (1978b) "Competition as a discovery procedure," in *New Studies in Philosophy, Politics, Economics and the History of Ideas,* Chicago, Ill.: University of Chicago Press (first presented as a lecture, 1968).

Kirzner, I. M. (1963) *Market Theory and the Price System*, Princeton, N.J.: Van Nostrand.

Kohler, H. (1982) *Intermediate Microeconomics, Theory and Applications*, Glenview, Ill.: Scott, Foresman.

Lavoie, D. (1985a) *Rivalry and Central Planning: The Socialist Calculation Debate Reconsidered*, Cambridge: Cambridge University Press.

Sowell, T. (1980) *Knowledge and Decisions*, New York: Basic Books.

COMPETITION AND THE MARKET PROCESS: SOME DOCTRINAL MILESTONES

As the twentieth century nears its conclusion, economic policymakers (if not the economic theory textbooks) have to a considerable extent come to recognize that the advantages of competition are to be found in the dynamics of the process of competition, rather than in the imagined state of affairs identified in the textbook model of competition. For most of the century, however, the general professional opinion was quite different. Any optimality properties a market system may possess, it was held, are those generated by its approximating the conditions of the perfectly competitive model. And the support for free markets which, it was generally understood, neoclassical economics (in its pre-1930 vintage) provided, rested (so ran the conventional wisdom during the central decades of this century) upon the dominant role played in neoclassical economics by the model of perfect competition. This chapter offers a brief survey of some significant milestones along the road which have led professional opinion away from these latter positions (emphasizing the role of perfect competition in achieving societal economic efficiency) towards the contemporary recognition of the greater relevance of the dynamic process of competition for an understanding of the achievements of free markets.

The story to be told is complicated by (and indeed includes) the following circumstance. We wish to provide insight into the gradual dislodgment of the perfectly competitive model from the center-stage of professional concern; but the story accounting for that earlier centrality of the perfectly competitive (henceforth "PC") model, is itself a complicated, confusing, and controversial one. In fact, we shall argue, an important early step along the road away from the dominance of the PC model, consisted in a drastic revision of what had become the orthodox account

Originally published as "Concurrence et processus de marché: quelques repères doctrinaux," in J. Krafft, dir., Le processus de concurrence (Paris: Editions Economica, 1999), 16–32. The English translation, "Competition and the Market Process: Some Doctrinal Milestones," appeared in The Driving Force of the Market: Essays in Austrian Economics (New York and London: Routledge, 2000), 205–21. Reprinted by permission of Taylor & Francis Books UK.

of the earlier rise of that model. Indeed, as we shall see, the story of the late twentieth century (partial) decline of the PC model can be construed as being largely the story of continual critical reconsideration of the manner in which that model had, by the 1930s, captured the central attention of the profession. Our story of the decline of the PC model must then begin with an outline of the place of that model in the neoclassical world before 1930.

NEOCLASSICAL ECONOMICS AND THE PC MODEL

There is no doubt that the economics profession at mid-century believed that the PC model basically captured the way in which neoclassical economics had understood how markets work (before Edward Chamberlin and Joan Robinson). "The 'perfection' of the concept of competition, that is, the emergence of the idea of competition as itself a market structure, was a distinguishing contribution of neoclassical economics" (McNulty, 1968, p. 644). Indeed, in 1939 Hicks (deeply engaged in refining and polishing neoclassical economics) made an oft-quoted statement to the effect that "sacrificing the assumption of perfect competition" must threaten "wreckage of the greater part of general equilibrium theory" (Hicks, 1939, pp. 83–4).

It was, in this general view, the work of Chamberlin and Robinson—and nothing else—which challenged this dominance of the PC model (arguing that its lack of realism rendered it incapable of explaining real world market prices). (It was the Chicago School, in its mid-century incarnation, which held on methodological grounds that this lack of realism was unimportant and provided no grounds for questioning the practical usefulness of the PC model.)[1]

Yet this orthodox view (that the mainstream of neoclassical microeconomics before Chamberlin and Robinson focused primarily on the theory of PC price determination) has been riddled with challenges during the past several decades. Brian Loasby (1989, p. 62) cites Sraffa's famous 1926 paper as challenging the consistency of Marshall's theory of value because his insistence on increasing returns is incompatible with perfect competition. (Clearly Sraffa, like Hicks, understood neoclassical economics, and in particular Marshallian economics, to stand or fall with the PC model.) But, Loasby asserts, Sraffa was "quite wrong to assume that perfect competition was the basis of Marshall's theory of value" (ibid., p. 62). Indeed, Loasby has gone so far as to claim that "Marshallian competition is a Hayekian discovery process" (ibid., p. 55). In a recent work Frank Machovec has brilliantly reconstructed the place of competition in the history of economic thought (Machovec, 1995).

The main thrust of Machovec's *dogmengeschichtliche* revisionism concerns his denial of the view (propagated particularly by Stigler (1957)) that the classical economists were, in effect, thinking in terms of a (crude) PC model. But in developing his refutation of this widespread Stiglerian error, Machovec also challenged an equally widespread view concerning the neoclassical mainstream that dominated the profession from the 1880s. Machovec challenged the view that the major neoclassical economists (such as Marshall) grounded their theory in the PC model (or, more precisely, that the development of the neoclassical mainstream from the 1880s onward, consisted largely in a steady, gradual analytical refinement of the meaning and implications of perfect competition). In Machovec's view, nothing of the sort characterized the neoclassical mainstream before 1920. On the contrary, Machovec maintains, among the neoclassical economists around the turn of the century, Walras was virtually alone in resting his analytical system upon the PC conditions (a step to which he was inexorably pushed by the logic of his general equilibrium system) (Machovec, 1995, p. 241). It was only during the 1920s (in particular as an outcome of Knight's 1921 *Risk, Uncertainty and Profit*) that there occurred a "Kuhnian revolution—that is, a distinct change in concept and analytical apparatus . . . as the model of perfect competition became the keystone of analysis" (ibid., p. 159). Where conventional wisdom had seen the history of economics since Adam Smith as gradual refinement until the 1920s, of a single conception of competition (that of competition as a completed state of affairs), Machovec maintained that the classical economists and also at least the earlier neoclassical writers saw competition as a dynamic process: "The process view of the classicists and the early neoclassical writers was purged during the 1920s as the profession adopted an exclusively equilibrium framework for its microeconomic theorizing" (ibid., p. 236).

The present writer would, at least in one respect, in fact push Machovec's revisionism even further. The dominance of the PC model in the economics profession of the 1930s, 1940s, and 1950s, was to a significant extent an outcome of the monopolistic competition revolution of the early 1930s. In contrasting their own (static) models of monopolistically competitive equilibrium with (what they certainly believed to be)

the dominant earlier models, Chamberlin and Robinson were incidentally formalizing and emphasizing an analytical model of (perfect) competition which had, for most of the profession, hitherto remained less
than precisely articulated. Paradoxically, therefore, it was the very effort to
dislodge the PC model (in favor of the equally static, but less unrealistic
model of monopolistic competition) which thrust that PC model into the
analytical limelight. Certainly Chamberlin and Robinson shared the now-
conventional view (disputed by Machovec) that the state of perfect competition was central to the earlier neoclassical theory of value. The efforts
to challenge this centrality had the effect, we believe, of focusing more
sophisticated analytic attention on the PC model. Their efforts to dislodge the PC model thus had the paradoxical effect of rendering truthful
for the 1940s and 1950s, that dominance in economics (of the PC model)
which they had not quite correctly attributed to pre-1920 economics.

FURTHER THOUGHTS ON THE EARLIER
NEOCLASSICAL VIEW OF COMPETITION

As we have seen, Machovec has argued that the earlier neoclassicals had
shared (with the classical economists) a process view of competition. It was,
he maintained, only Walras's emphasis on the determinateness of general
equilibrium which pushed the PC model to the center of his own system
(until, under the influence of Knight, the Walrasian centrality for PC came,
according to Machovec's reading, to be adopted by the profession in the
twenties in rather revolutionary fashion). But this view (that the earlier neo-
classical economists thought of competition primarily, if not exclusively, in
its dynamic, process, sense) may be reading a little too much into their
work. The circumstance that a writer describes competition in a manner at
variance with the fully articulated Knightian version of the PC model, does
not at all imply that that writer is necessarily thinking in process terms.
This point is of some importance and requires some elaboration.

The most significant insight concerning the story of the PC model in
the twentieth century is surely the following: until Hayek's 1946 paper
"The Meaning of Competition,"[2] no one in the profession, it appears, had
seen (or at least made explicit) the crucial difference between competition
as a state of affairs and competition as a driving, dynamic process.[3] There
is little doubt that Machovec (following McNulty [1967] and others) is correct in reading the classical economists as seeing competition (not, as
Stigler had believed, as a perfectly competitive state of affairs which they

were not quite able to articulate correctly and precisely, but) as a rivalrous process. But, astounding as it must in retrospect appear, none of the host of writers before Hayek, during the first half of this century (and including those of the 1930s and later) who dwelt on the meaning and implications of the PC model, quite saw with clarity that this model was a strictly equilibrium model, from which all vestiges of process had been completely filtered out.[4]

To see this failure perhaps most clearly one can cite the 1952 work (published *after* Hayek's paper!) of Fritz Machlup, *The Economics of Sellers' Competition* (Machlup, 1952). This mid-century volume is surely the most careful and complete analysis of the many possible meanings of the term "competition," of the entire century. There are few aspects of the competitive process and of competitive equilibrium, as they had been treated in a vast literature, which are not carefully and sensitively dissected and labeled (often with newly-coined labels), in this volume.[5] Yet it becomes clear that Machlup (who incidentally and surprisingly makes no reference whatever to Hayek's 1946 paper) was, quite amazingly, unaware that the PC model does indeed logically confine one to the equilibrium state. This is apparent in his lengthy discussion of the meanings attached to the term "perfect market" (Machlup, 1952, pp. 117–24). It also emerges almost dramatically in his following statement:

> The disparagers of perfect competition are badly mistaken if they regard perfect competition as inimical to progress. Of course, if they define it as instantaneous entry of newcomers, it is obvious that "perfect competition is not only impossible but inferior"—as we read in Joseph A. Schumpeter, *Capitalism, Socialism and Democracy* (New York: Harper, 1943), p. 106. But such a model of perfect competition serves no purpose except to confuse the issue. Instantaneous entry of newcomers, instantaneous appearance of imitators, is not only impossible but nonsensical.
>
> (Machlup, 1952, pp. 555–6, fn)

One is tempted to surmise that Machlup's "Austrian" training had such a profound influence on his thinking, that, despite the range of nuances which he was able to distinguish in the enormous literature on competition, it somehow became impossible for him to accept that a theorist could seriously think of perfect competition in the way which Schumpeter (surely correctly) ascribed to mainstream theorists!

Machovec is insightfully correct in attributing Walras's emphasis on perfect competition to his equilibrium perspective. And, as Machovec argues, the dominance within economics which the PC model attained, was attained concomitantly with the profession's adoption of the mathematical economist's primary concern with equilibrium conditions. But, at least until Hayek's paper, economists seemed (in retrospect, almost incredibly) entirely unaware of the sharp distinction between the two possible uses of the adjective "competitive," namely, either as describing a process or as describing the equilibrium outcome (of some undefined process) seen as an already attained and settled state of affairs. Although this failure seems, from today's perspective, to be difficult to comprehend, we will not, I suggest, adequately understand earlier neoclassical writing on competition without recognizing the *fact* of this failure.

In particular we should, therefore, avoid the possible error of interpreting references in earlier neoclassical writing, to acts of competitive entry, as firm evidence of a process view of competition. As a result of the failure (to recognize the distinction we have emphasized), such references to acts of competitive entry may have been understood as aspects of a competitive *structure* (rather than as implying any understanding that such competitive acts of entry are strictly and inherently inconsistent with any equilibrium state).

This writer would therefore tend to see the development of neoclassical ideas on competition between the 1880s and 1930s as a more gradual analytical change than Machovec is prepared to accept. In brief, it would appear that, under the influence of increasing analytic formalization (manifested partly but not exclusively in increased use of geometrical—and eventually more general mathematical—tools) neoclassical economics came to focus more and more on the *outcomes* of economic processes and less and less on these processes themselves. As part of this change, references to competition came gradually to refer less and less to competitive processes and more and more to the results of such processes. Because the distinction between a competitive process and a "competitive" state of affairs was as yet entirely unclear, the neoclassical economists (such as Knight) engaged in explicit articulation of a precise characterization of competition (and who were, perhaps unselfconsciously, thinking in equilibrium terms) were able to nudge their fellow economists towards thinking within a structural, rather than a process framework. It is, then, not so much that an earlier dominant purely

"process" view of competition succumbed to a revolution in favor of the
"state-of-affairs" view of competition—as that an earlier somewhat non-
descript view of competition (in which elements of process and of outcomes were rather confusedly jumbled together) came gradually to be
purged of its process elements. While, from a late twentieth century perspective this change may appear negative in its extrusion of elements of
process understanding, we can at least recognize that the achieved internal consistency (attained through exclusively structural understanding of
perfect competition) may have had much to do with the new dominance
of the PC model, and the length of its period of such dominance.

HAYEK AND THE MEANING OF COMPETITION

Hayek's 1946 paper was undoubtedly a by-product of his concern in the
late 1930s and early 1940s with the role of markets in disseminating
mutual knowledge among markets participants. The remarkable series
of papers which emerged from this concern were published in Hayek's
1949 *Individualism and Economic Order*. His paper "The Meaning of
Competition" is described in that book as reproducing the substance of
a lecture delivered at Princeton in May 1946. Hayek begins his paper
recognizing that "some valiant attempts" had been made to bring discussion of the meaning of the term competition "back to earth."[6] But he
quickly points out that the general view is still that "the so-called theory
of 'perfect competition' provides the appropriate model for judging the
effectiveness of competition in real life, and that, to the extent that real
competition differs from that model, it is undesirable and even harmful"
(Hayek, 1949, p. 92).

Hayek vigorously disputed this view. He pointed out in particular that
this general view "throughout assumes that state of affairs already to exist
which, according to the truer view of the older theory, the process of competition tends to bring about . . . and that, if the state of affairs assumed by
theory of perfect competition ever existed, it would not only deprive of their
scope all the activities which the verb 'to compete' describes but would
make them virtually impossible" (ibid.). Hayek proceeded to articulate with
utmost clarity that the "modern theory of competition deals almost exclusively with a state of what is called 'competitive equilibrium' in which it
is assumed that the data for the different individuals are fully adjusted to
each other, while the problem which requires explanation is the nature of
the process by which the data are thus adjusted" (ibid., p. 94).

Hayek's paper reads like a breath of fresh air. Cutting through a veritable forest of confusion in the literature, he was putting his finger on the root difficulty with the profession's preoccupation with the PC model: its being an equilibrium model inherently incapable of offering help in understanding how equilibrium might possibly be approached. (It should be noted that his approving references to J. M. Clark and to Fritz Machlup[7] do not at all suggest that Hayek's fundamental insight had been anticipated by these writers. Rather they were being cited as lone writers who at least recognized that real world competition may have merit that does not depend on its being a close approximation to the PC model.)

THE SCENE AFTER HAYEK'S 1946 PAPER

Hayek's paper appears to have been virtually ignored in the subsequent literature (perhaps, in part, because it was not published in a journal). Mises (in his 1949 *Human Action* (p. 278, fn)) approvingly cited Hayek's paper as refuting the doctrines of monopolistic or imperfect competition. (Although Hayek did not in fact directly criticize these theories themselves in his paper, Mises obviously recognized the profound implications of Hayek's insights for the way in which Chamberlin's and Robinson's work had been interpreted by the profession.) Mises, whose own understanding of competition was, emphatically, steeped in the process mode,[8] instantly appreciated Hayek's contribution. But this writer has not found other references to Hayek's paper in the literature immediately after 1946.[9]

It was not that the profession failed to see the (obvious) difference between the term "competition" as used by businessmen and that term as used by economists.[10] But very few writers recognized that this difference reflected completely different perspectives on the market, *each* of which might be able to make a (separate) crucial contribution to economic understanding. Rather, the businessman's perception of active, rivalrous competition was dismissed as a crude expression of the way in which imperfect reality falls short of the sophisticated analytical ideal which the PC model expresses. In other words, the businessman's usage was seen as an uncouth use of language which fails to recognize that the market which he describes as competitive is, in fact, riddled with monopolistic elements—or, more pointedly, that precisely those elements which he sees as competitive, are, in fact, more properly to be labeled as monopolistic.

It is true that when this writer wrote his *Competition and Entrepreneurship*,[11] he was able in 1973 to trace a handful of references in the literature of the 1950s and 1960s to the need to supplement the theory of competitive equilibrium by a process theory, and to recognition that the PC model provides only the former.[12] Yet what were perceived as the most authoritative mainstream voices in those decades continued to articulate the conventional PC doctrine with renewed emphasis. George Stigler's well-known 1957 paper was, indeed, so emphatic in this regard that it may have, precisely as a result of that emphasis, provoked something of a reaction to the orthodoxy which he offered.[13]

Stigler offered a history of the PC model from the time of the classical economists until his own time. He treated Adam Smith's references to rivalrous competition as the early and somewhat crude articulation of a notion of competition which was to receive its refinement and precise formulation only in later generations, specifically in the pioneering mathematical work of Cournot (1838) and, finally, in the careful pronouncements of J. B. Clark and (in particular) of Frank Knight. It was this understanding of the classical economists' notion of competition which was to be challenged in the important (and above-cited) work of McNulty and, most recently, of Frank Machovec.

One important (and fairly prominent) contribution, published, as it happens, in the same year as Stigler's paper, challenged key aspects of the mainstream perception of the place of the PC model in early twentieth century neoclassical economics. This was the paper by Shorey Peterson, "Antitrust and the Classic Model."[14] In his paper Peterson maintained that it was not the case (as seemed to be argued by the later theories of monopolistic and imperfect competition) that the mainstream economic theory of the 1920s and earlier was one dominated by the PC model. The idea of such a "classic" model's having dominated "pre-Chamberlinian thought" seems "mildly shocking" to Peterson (who described himself as one of the "economists trained in the 1920s and before" (Peterson, 1957, pp. 60–3).

Instead, Peterson insisted, the economics which was learned from the treatises of J. B. Clark and Alfred Marshall understood that the rough and ready competition of the real world, particularly when buttressed by the threat of potential competition, sufficed to protect the consumers from the most serious of the distortions with which monopoly elements in the market might menace them. We should notice that in dwelling on this theme, Peterson does not seem to be disagreeing with the terminology in which all departures from the PC conditions are termed "monopolistic." Rather he appears to claim (on behalf of the mainstream economics of the 1920s and earlier) that the vigorous "imperfect" competition of the real world, riddled though it may be with such "monopolistic" elements, may suffice to impose efficiency and "order" upon market phenomena. It is this which supports Peterson's contention that John Maurice Clark's work on "workable competition" was not trying to "close a gap caused by failure of the older theory" (Peterson, 1957, p. 78), but was rather seeking to stem policy misunderstandings likely to be generated by "recent refinements of the competitive model" (ibid.). And it was this which led Peterson to express surprise that Schumpeter[15] should have read neoclassical doctrine as inconsistent with his own emphasis on the competition of new and better products and on the force of potential competition. Schumpeter's emphasis in these respects was rather to be seen as "essentially an unfolding of earlier thought" (ibid., p. 74).

An intriguing paper of the 1950s by John Maurice Clark (which served as the basis for his subsequent book (Clark, 1961)), was entitled "Competition: Static Models and Dynamic Aspects" (Clark, 1955), and was presented at the 1954 American Economic Association meetings. Despite the surprisingly ill-tempered remarks with which Machlup commented on this paper (Machlup, 1955), Clark was clearly groping towards a sound critique of the place which the PC model was playing in mainstream economics at mid-century. It is perhaps relevant to note that, while Clark was certainly thoroughly aware of (indeed insistent upon) the distinction between competition as a "static" state of affairs and competition as a "dynamic process," his distinction is not quite the same as that which distinguishes between the PC state and the competitive process which might hypothetically produce that PC state. For Clark, dynamic competition was not primarily important as a possibly equilibrating force, but rather as a more general force relevant, in particular, for economic progress and growth (as well as for the protection of the consumers against monopolistic exploitation). (It should perhaps be emphasized that our observation here is not intended to be in any way critical of Clark.) This crusade by Clark (which, as Machovec points out [Machovec, 1995, p. 293], was in reality a "struggle [that] was hopeless" in the face of the cold reception it received in the profession) sought to dislodge the dominance of the static PC model. It made no attempt to point out that that model, and the very idea of determinacy in market outcomes—surely the heart of neoclassical theory—acquires relevance only by being supplemented by a theory of competitive process.[16]

REFLECTIONS ON MAINSTREAM
ECONOMICS IN THE 1940S AND 1950S

Our brief sampling of the literature of the central decades of this century has revealed a certain confusion in regard to the perceived role of the PC model. As has become increasingly apparent since the 1950s, the central body of (contemporary) neoclassical theory saw (and still sees) the PC model as its primary tool, and as the main pillar upon which to build a normative case for a free market economy. For a George Stigler, or a Milton Friedman,[17] for example, questions of realism were relatively unimportant. They believed the pragmatic usefulness of the PC model justified its dominant role in economic theory. On the other hand, we have seen that there existed (quite apart from Hayek's completely developed, but virtually ignored, contribution) a definite if rather disorganized set of dissident views, associated with such names as Schumpeter, J. M. Clark, and Shorey Peterson. These writers were challenging (not so much the meaningfulness of an economic theory virtually confined, for its central understanding of the workings of a market economy, upon the PC models, as) the attitude which saw all observed departures from the PC conditions as representing harmfully monopolistic features of reality. Their critiques certainly set their work decisively apart from the extensive literature in the area of industrial organization which explored industries described as oligopolistic, seeing them as variants of monopoly situations (see, for example, Peterson, 1957, p. 76). We do not perhaps adequately appreciate how much the very perception of an analytical box labeled "oligopoly," sprang from the dominance of that orthodoxy in which the word "competitive" means nothing but one particular market structure, the PC model. Once one refuses to grant use of the adjective "competitive" to describe any act of entrepreneurial entry aimed at winning pure profit (on the grounds that such acts are, as a matter of definition, "monopolistic"), one has firmly closed one's eyes to the obvious (and surely genuinely competitive) feature which is common to all situations characterized by freedom of entry. What remains is only the task of classifying different combinations and/or degrees of quasi-monopoly—a task to which so much of oligopoly theory has in fact been devoted.

What distinguishes these dissident views (from those that would emerge in the subsequent decades) is perhaps their linkages to earlier pre-Chamberlinian conceptions of competition (which had not yet been pressed into what would turn out to be the PC mold). They were not Young Turks rebelling at an existing orthodoxy which they found in place; rather they were expressing dismay at the fashion in which this orthodoxy had displaced a less formal, but more meaningful and useful, earlier orthodoxy. Their work no doubt played a role in keeping alive the notion of active competition in the profession. But a retrospective survey of late twentieth-century economics shows that these voices were drowned out by a textbook literature in which the PC model continued to occupy a more and more central position in economic explanations of market economies.

THE LATE TWENTIETH-CENTURY TURN

During the latter several decades of the century, however, new voices have emerged to question the dominance of the PC model. These new voices have not in any sense constituted a unified "school"; often these voices clashed with each other. Yet the overall outcome achieved by the work expressed in these voices has been to dislodge the PC model (if not from its dominance of the textbooks, yet) from its long-established position of almost unchallenged dominance in professional understanding of how the market economy in fact works. In the space available here we certainly cannot adequately describe the way in which these new challenges to the PC model emerged and broadly reinforced each other. What we can attempt to do is to list briefly and identify some of these new voices, so that we can gain appreciation for the way in which, discordant though they may have been, they have nonetheless drilled a certain scepticism into professional consciousness in regard to the relevance of the PC model—a scepticism along an entirely different dimension from that introduced a half-century earlier by Chamberlin and Robinson.

Voices emphasizing the process character of market effectiveness include work from the early 1960s onwards by such writers as G. B. Richardson (1960), who was a pioneer in understanding the role of the interactive flow of information in the competitive market process; Murray N. Rothbard (1962), who (although barely mentioning Hayek's work) pursued Austrian ideas on competition with admirable consistency to some of their radical implications; and Paul J. McNulty (1967, 1968), who in the late

1960s articulated the Hayekian insights with great skill and effectiveness and deployed them to offer (as we have already seen) a powerful history-of-thought critique of George Stigler's views on the history of the PC model.[18]

Voices emphasizing the powerful effectiveness of freedom of potential entry include Sylos-Labini, who early in the 1960s had published a much discussed work on oligopoly (Sylos-Labini, 1962),[19] in which the role on entry was extensively explored. Although much of the subsequently-inspired work on the role of entry was conducted within the conventional "structural" framework, this work did focus attention on an aspect of real world competition which the PC model tended to suppress or at least ignore.[20] A powerful 1969 paper by Yale Brozen (Brozen, 1969) sharply criticized the way in which the term "barriers to entry" had been used, in the conventional literature, to include such dynamically competitive activities (or arenas) as advertising, economies of scale, and product differentiation.

Closely related to the foregoing were voices questioning that orthodoxy which defined degrees of monopoly and competition in terms of numbers. Harold Demsetz, in a pioneering paper on the regulation of public utilities (Demsetz, 1968) (one which had far-reaching implications for monopoly theory in general), sharply challenged the standard doctrine on "natural monopoly." There is, Demsetz pointed out, "no clear or necessary reason for *production* scale economies to decrease the number of *bidders*. Let prospective buyers call for bids to service their demands. Scale economies in servicing their demands in no way imply that there will be one bidder only. There can be many bidders and the bid that wins will be the lowest" (ibid., p. 57). It was this insight, so strange to conventional wisdom at the time it was introduced, that would subsequently generate the theory of "contestable" markets (see Baumol, Panzar, and Willig, 1982). While that theory was largely developed within the mainstream framework on market structures, it did much to widen economists' horizons on the nature and role of competition.

Much in the spirit of the foregoing was the new work of the early 1970s which challenged the then existing so-called "structural approach" to the evaluation of oligopoly situations. Some of that work was summarized in a prominent paper by J. Fred Weston (Weston, 1972). Weston, who himself contributed to this research, was particularly concerned to demonstrate empirically the competitive processes which take place in concentrated markets. Clearly this line of work, conducted primarily in the "applied" area of industrial organization (and eventually to be dubbed "the new learning"[21]), had important implications for the theory of competition. This line of work has indeed had continual influential impact on industrial organization theory and on antitrust economics during the latter decades of the century.

A RETROSPECTIVE REFLECTION

Although it may seem that the contrast emphasized in this chapter (between competition as a process or competition as a state of affairs) is purely semantic, this is not at all the case. It would be a mistake to understand the shift in recent professional thinking about competition, as one primarily concerned with the meaning of the word—or even about the economic policy implications of the use of that word. Rather, the shift we have briefly surveyed constitutes a gradual deepening of professional understanding of how a market economy works. As long as the PC model dominated microeconomic theory, appreciation for the economic success of the market economy saw that economy as more-or-less closely approximating the state of perfect competitive equilibrium, with its prices and quantities emerging spontaneously as if from a magic computer. As professional understanding of the dynamic character of the competitive process has deepened, the contributions of the market have come to be glimpsed more profoundly and more accurately. It is the rivalrous competition described by Adam Smith, the entrepreneurial process described by Ludwig von Mises, and the knowledge-discovery procedure described by Friedrich Hayek, which has been "rediscovered" by a significant proportion of the economics profession, as this century reaches its conclusion. This encouraging development should serve as a firm foundation for future research into the competitive process, during the decades ahead.

NOTES

1. On this issue see Knight (1946), Stigler (1949), and Chamberlin (1957).

2. This paper was read as a lecture in 1946 and published in Hayek (1949). It is of interest that Hayek had incautiously described as competition the situation in which "the individual producer has to adapt to price changes and cannot control them" (1944, p. 49). Galbraith read this as requiring that demand curves facing individual sellers "be completely elastic at the ruling price" (1948, p. 111, fn 29). Certainly this would not be in the spirit of Hayek's 1946 paper. For a looser reading of Hayek than Galbraith's, see Shorey Peterson (1957, p. 75).

3. The following statement of George Stigler (written 11 years after Hayek's paper—which he does not cite) is of interest in this regard. Stigler is referring to Adam Smith's use of the term "competition" in the rivalrous sense. Stigler comments: "Competition is a process of responding to a new force and a method of reaching a new equilibrium" (1957, p. 235). The fact that, as noted in the text, Stigler saw Adam Smith as something of a crude forerunner of Knight's (equilibrium) PC model, suggests that Stigler was himself perhaps not fully alive to the significance that might be read into his sentence.

4. A careful reading of Schumpeter (1942, pp. 77–80, 103–6) may arguably, but not conclusively, suggest an exception to the statement in the text.

5. On the use of new labels to distinguish between subtly different aspects of competition, see Machlup (1952, p. 105, fn 17).

6. In this regard Hayek cites Clark (1940) and Machlup (1942).

7. See above, note 6.

8. See especially Mises (1949, pp. 273–9).

9. Among the earliest references to Hayek's 1946 paper are perhaps the papers by McNulty (1967, 1968).

10. For some references on this point see Kirzner (1973, p. 89, fn).

11. Kirzner (1973). This work cited Hayek's paper as "penetrating and pioneering" (p. 91) in regard to the distinction with which the present chapter is concerned.

12. See Kirzner (1973, esp. p. 93, fn 13, and p. 89, fn 1).

13. The reference is to Stigler (1957); it was this paper to which McNulty (1967) was primarily responding.

14. The reference is Peterson (1957). This paper was included in the influential AEA-sponsored volume of readings in industrial organization (Heflebower and Stocking, 1958).

15. Peterson was referring to Schumpeter (1942, chs 7 and 8).

16. It would be a mistake to conclude this section without any reference to a valuable (but almost entirely neglected) work of the 1950s, which was thoroughly out of step with the static ("state-of-affairs") notion of competition. This was Lawrence Abbott's *Quality and Competition* (New York: Columbia University Press, 1955). Abbott's emphasis on the dynamics of quality competition differs in spirit (although not perhaps in policy implications) from the work on "quality-as-a-variable" of E. H. Chamberlin (see Chamberlin, 1957, ch. 6). For an appreciative awareness of Abbott's work, see Rothbard, 1962, vol. 2, p. 906, n. 28).

17. See Friedman (1953).

18. One of this writer's own books (Kirzner, 1973) was deeply influenced by Hayek and McNulty in this regard.

19. The standard work on barriers to entry had been Bain (1956).

20. For an example of such work see Needham (1969, ch. 7), reprinted in Breit and Hochman (1971).

21. Important samples of this and related literature were creatively assembled and edited by Yale Brozen (Brozen, 1975).

REFERENCES

Bain, J. S. (1956) *Barriers to New Competition*, Cambridge, Mass.: Harvard University Press.

Baumol, W. J., Panzar, J. C., and Willig, R. D. (1982) *Contestable Markets and the Theory of Industry Structure*, New York: Harcourt Brace Jovanovich.

Breit, William, and Hochman, Harold M. (1971) *Readings in Microeconomics*, 2nd edn, New York: Holt, Rinehart and Winston.

Brozen, Yale (1969) "Competition, Efficiency, and Antitrust," *Journal of World Trade Law*; reprinted in Brozen (1975).

—— (ed.) (1975) *The Competitive Economy, Selected Readings*, Morristown, N.J.: General Learning Press.

Chamberlin, Edward H. (1957) "The Chicago School," and "The Product as an Economic Variable," in E. H. Chamberlin, *Towards a More General Theory of Value*, New York: Oxford.

Clark, John Maurice (1940) "Toward a Concept of Workable Competition," *American Economic Review* 30 (June).

—— (1955) "Competition: Static Models and Dynamic Aspects," *American Economic Review* 45 (May).

—— (1961) *Competition as a Dynamic Process*, New York: Brookings.

Demsetz, Harold (1968) "Why Regulate Utilities?" *Journal of Law and Economics* 11 (April).

Ellis, Howard S. (ed.) (1948) *A Survey of Contemporary Economics* (published for the American Economic Association), Homewood, Ill.: Irwin.

Friedman, Milton (1953) "The Methodology of Positive Economics," in *Essays in Positive Economics*, Chicago: University of Chicago Press.

Galbraith, John Kenneth (1948) "Monopoly and the Concentration of Economic Power," in Ellis (1948).

Hayek, Friedrich A. (1944) *The Road to Serfdom*, Chicago: University of Chicago Press.

—— (1949) *Individualism and Economic Order*, London: Routledge and Kegan Paul.

Heflebower, Richard B., and Stocking, George W. (eds) (1958) *Readings in Industrial Organization and Public Policy* (published for the American Economic Association), Homewood, Ill.: Irwin.

Hicks, J. R. (1946) *Value and Capital* (1st edn, 1939), 2nd edn, Oxford: Clarendon Press.

Kirzner, Israel M. (1973) *Competition and Entrepreneurship*, Chicago: University of Chicago Press.

Knight, Frank H. (1946) "Immutable Law in Economics: Its Reality and Limitations," *American Economic Review* (May).

Loasby, Brian J. (1989) *The Mind and Method of the Economist*, Aldershot: Edward Elgar.

Machlup, Fritz (1942) "Competition, Pliopoly, and Profit," *Economica* 9 (new ser.: February and May).

——— (1952) *The Economics of Sellers' Competition, Model Analysis of Sellers' Conduct,* Baltimore, Md.: The Johns Hopkins University Press.

——— (1955) "Discussion," *American Economic Review* XLV (May), pp. 480–3.

Machovec, Frank M. (1995) *Perfect Competition and the Transformation of Economics,* London and New York: Routledge.

McNulty, Paul J. (1967) "A Note on the History of Perfect Competition," *Journal of Political Economy* 75 (August).

——— (1968) "Economic Theory and the Meaning of Competition," *Quarterly Journal of Economics* 82 (November).

Mises, Ludwig von (1949) *Human Action,* New Haven, Conn.: Yale University Press.

Needham, Douglas (1969) *Economic Analysis and Industrial Structure,* New York: Holt, Rinehart and Winston, ch. 7; reprinted in Breit and Hochman (1971).

Peterson, Shorey (1957) "Antitrust and the Classic Model," *American Economic Review* 47 (March).

Richardson, G. B. (1960) *Information and Investment,* Oxford: Oxford University Press.

Rothbard, Murray N. (1962) *Man, Economy, and State: A Treatise on Economic Principles,* Princeton, N.J.: Van Nostrand.

Schumpeter, Joseph A. (1950) *Capitalism, Socialism and Democracy* (1st edn, 1942), 3rd edn, New York: Harper.

Stigler, George J. (1949) *Five Lectures on Economic Problems,* London: Macmillan.

——— (1957) "Perfect Competition, Historically Contemplated," *Journal of Political Economy* 65 (February); page references to Stigler (1965).

——— (1965) *Essays in the History of Economics,* Chicago and London: University of Chicago Press.

Sylos-Labini, P. (1962) *Oligopoly and Technical Progress,* Cambridge, Mass.: Harvard University Press.

Weston, J. Fred (1922) "Implications of Recent Research for the Structural Approach to Oligopoly," *Antitrust Law Journal* 41.

THE DRIVING FORCE OF THE MARKET:
THE IDEA OF "COMPETITION" IN CONTEMPORARY
ECONOMIC THEORY AND IN THE AUSTRIAN THEORY
OF THE MARKET PROCESS

The crucial role played by the notion of dynamic competition in Austrian economics is by now well known. It is widely appreciated that perhaps the critical respect in which the modern Austrian paradigm differs from the mainstream approach consists in the Austrian rejection of the centrality in the latter of the perfectly competitive model, and its replacement by the idea of the entrepreneurial-competitive market process. In this process the essential element is the steadily expanding field of mutual awareness on the part of potential market participants. Whereas the perfectly competitive model expresses the equilibrium pattern of decisions expressing already attained, complete mutual knowledge, the competitive market process expresses the course of mutual discovery through which an equilibrium may possibly be approached.[1]

Although this fundamental difference has been articulated by the Austrians now for several decades,[2] there has been disappointingly little impact upon mainstream contemporary theory. Precisely during a period in which mainstream theorists have come to recognize the limitations of their models in explaining the equilibrating process,[3] and have come to appreciate the importance of changing knowledge in determining market outcomes,[4] the textbook paramountcy of the perfectly competitive model appears to be as solidly ensconced as ever. Despite the "uprising" of contestable market theory,[5] the perfectly competitive model appears not to have been dislodged. More to the point, perhaps, there is little in this uprising itself which reflects the insights of the theory of the dynamic competitive process.

I shall not attempt yet another Austrian assault on mainstream perfect competition orthodoxy. Instead I shall briefly review the principal insights

From *The Driving Force of the Market: Essays in Austrian Economics* (New York and London: Routledge, 2000), 222–38. Reprinted by permission of Hillsdale College Press; the original source is *Austrian Economics: Perspectives on the Past and Prospects for the Future*, ed. R. Ebeling (Hillsdale, Mich.: Hillsdale College Press, 1997).

embodied in the Austrian approach to understanding competition, in order to place emphasis upon certain insufficiently noticed features of this approach. Beyond these points of emphasis (and an attempt to illustrate the significance of this emphasis by reference to certain recent disagreements among Austrians), there will be very little new here.

The point upon which I wish to place emphasis can be stated simply: economists contrast monopolistic markets with competitive markets. But while this contrast is appropriate within the equilibrium understanding of the meaning of competition, this is not the case for a theory concentrating on the competitive market process. In the context of the theory of market process, competition should be recognized as universal—even for the market process which operates to bring about monopoly prices. To speak of the competitive market process is in fact to engage in periphrasis. There *is* no market process other than the competitive one. Competitive activity is the activity which constitutes the market process. So it is misleading to inquire, for example, into the conditions required to render the market process competitive. To understand the dynamic motion of competition is at the same time to grasp the nature of the market process—with or without monopoly. Although this insight is certainly not new,[6] it appears not to have been sufficiently emphasized. I will suggest in this chapter that this insight offers a useful vantage point from which to appraise certain issues debated in modern Austrian literature.

THE MODEL OF PERFECT COMPETITION

The equilibrium character of the perfectly competitive market model is now widely understood. The model presumes satisfaction of a series of conditions which together assure a pattern of decisions by market participants insulated from the possibility of disappointment or regret. No decision to buy or to sell can fail to be accepted in this model. Nor can hindsight ever reveal to any buyer or seller that a more attractive market opportunity has been missed. Each potential buyer (seller) correctly anticipates the lowest (highest) price available in the market, and, moreover, correctly expects to be able to buy (sell) as much as he wishes to buy (sell) at this price. The price which all market participants correctly anticipate is that price which, when indeed anticipated by all, inspires the decisions to buy and sell which dovetail completely. It is not merely that the buying and selling decisions so made do indeed mesh perfectly; it is, in addition to such "pre-reconciliation of plans,"[7] that the sets of expectations underlying and inspiring each of these plans have somehow come to correctly and mutually anticipate what each of the other plans will in fact bring about. In fact, the perfection of knowledge underlying the model is, ultimately, more than simply the correct anticipation by each participant of the actions of others; it involves, in the final analysis, the correct and self-fulfilling anticipation by each of the (correct and self-fulfilling) anticipations by each of the others, of the (correct and self-fulfilling) anticipations, *et cetera, et cetera, ad infinitum*.

To put the matter concisely, the perfectly competitive model portrays (as does each and every equilibrium model of a market) a pattern of mutual anticipations and executed decisions which, if somehow attained, would lead no participant to wish that he had acted differently. It was this equilibrium character of the model to which Hayek was referring when, over forty years ago, he criticized it as blandly assuming that "situation to exist which a true explanation ought to account for as the effect of the competitive process."[8] *If* such a perfectly competitive situation in fact exists, Hayek was exclaiming, the scientific challenge is surely to account for the chain of events which has led to the quite remarkable fulfillment of the extraordinarily demanding set of relevant conditions. Of course no such account can be expected from the model itself.

Unless one adopts a methodology in which the truthfulness of the assumptions of models is of no concern, all this must render the model of perfect competition far less useful than the standard microeconomics textbooks appear to believe. The model cannot be used to "explain" market prices; the model presumes that everyone has, somehow, correctly and self-fulfillingly guessed what the market price is going to be. The circumstance that (quite apart from the assumed correctness of the anticipated price) the model treats each market participant as a price-taker further underscores the uselessness of the model as an explanation for the manner in which prices are adjusted. No one in the model ever does change his price bids or offers.

These limitations of the model have not altogether escaped mainstream acknowledgment. One recent writer on the perfectly competitive model pointed out that "the competitive model is inherently unable to contemplate economic activity out of equilibrium."[9] An entire issue of the *Journal of Economic Theory* was devoted, several years ago, to exploring the rationale for the perfectly competitive model.[10] Yet the centrality of the model in mainstream microeconomics seems to continue virtually unchallenged. Even more disturbing, perhaps, is the circumstance that, where attention is paid to the need for a theory of the equilibrating process, and even where it is recognized that such a theory must involve systematic processes of knowledge and expectations modification, it is somehow not perceived that the notion of dynamic competition is precisely the analytical device needed for the required theoretical task.

COMPETITION AS AN ENTREPRENEURIAL/ DISCOVERY PROCEDURE

The emphasis by Austrians in recent decades upon dynamic competition has been part of their comprehensive attack on the dominance, in modern economics, of equilibrium analysis. Following Ludwig von Mises in his conception of the market as a dynamic entrepreneurial *process,* rather than as an array of mutually sustaining optimal exchange decisions, Austrians have drawn the attention of economists back to an earlier classical notion of competition as a rivalrous process.[11] This notion, so congenial to the experience of the businessman, underscores competition not in the sense of individual powerlessness in the face of the presence of competitors, but in the sense of a procedure inspired by the incentive of outstripping one's competitors in order to achieve market success. As Austrians came to appreciate, the essence of this rivalrous process lies in the pressure it applies, and the incentives it offers, to competing market participants to recognize the opportunities created by earlier decisions (which failed to offer the best possible conditions to other market participants), and the disappointments to be avoided in repeating earlier decisions (which erroneously insisted on unattainable exchange terms). To put it concisely, Austrians came to understand competition as a process of discovery. Both over-optimism and undue pessimism, as expressed in earlier rejected bids and offers and in earlier regrets (at attained, but less than optimal, exchange transactions) may come to be replaced in this process by more realistic assessments of market opportunities.

In other words, the changing patterns of bids and offers made in the course of the market process reflect, in the perspective of this Austrian approach, the lessons learned, rightly or wrongly, during that process. If the course of this competitive market process turns out to be equilibrating, this is seen, from this dynamic perspective, as the result of the systematic improvement in mutual knowledge (among market participants) generated by the competitive pressures. The possibility of systematic equilibrating tendencies is underscored by recognition of the entrepreneurial character of the competitive process.

Initial errors by market participants generate a disequilibrium pattern of market bids and offers. Some bids and offers are rejected as hopelessly unattractive. Prospective buyers may have been prepared to offer better terms, but had erroneously overestimated the eagerness of the potential sellers. And so on. Market experience may teach more realistic estimates in this regard. Again, bids and offers may be accepted, but may generate regret as market experience demonstrates that even more advantageous market opportunities might have been grasped. The changes in bids and offers stimulated by these market experiences represent entrepreneurial discovery of the true dimensions of market opportunities. Without deliberate search (by prospective buyers and sellers) for the best terms consistent with the attitudes of other market participants, decision makers come to learn how to avoid disappointment and elude regret. Their alertness to earlier disappointments and to regrettably overlooked opportunities teaches them, during an equilibrating process, to adopt more accurate attitudes in anticipating the reactions of others.

The net result is that, to the extent that entrepreneurial alertness indeed induces steadily more realistic estimates of the attitudes of others, the course of market transactions becomes steadily closer to a pattern avoiding both disappointments and regrets. The competitive-entrepreneurial process then becomes an equilibrating process leading, possibly, close to that very state of affairs assumed from the very beginning by the modelists of perfect competition. To the extent that economic history ever does display market conditions roughly consistent with the perfectly competitive model, this can then be accounted for by reference to the achievements of the dynamic process of competition. To the extent that economic history (as it invariably does) displays features which are thoroughly inconsistent with the perfectly competitive model, this may be accounted for by understanding how the dynamic process of competition has, as yet, not fully run its equilibrating course. Features of real world markets will typically reflect the errors which it is the function of the competitive process to identify and correct.

What drives this competitive process is the alertness of market participants to the profit possibilities created by past errors, and, to the unfortunate frustrations that would be the result of repeating past errors. This entrepreneurial process is competitive in the sense that it relies upon the freedom of alert entrepreneurs to enter markets and exploit these possibilities. It is the possibility of such entry which not only provides an incentive for alert potential entrants, but also, through acting as a threat, inspires parallel alertness on the part of incumbent market participants, spurring them to anticipate potential entrants through their own entrepreneurial decisions. Constantly looking over their shoulders, market participants are inspired alertly to notice and implement opportunities for offering superior options to the market. The competitive process is driven by the entrepreneurial element in each human being, by the propensity to notice the implications of earlier errors (which propensity is the essence of entrepreneurship). The competitive process itself consists of the systematic series of revised decisions on the part of market participants, generated by their entrepreneurial discoveries. I am now in a position to spell out more fully the point in this approach to competition which I wish to emphasize in this chapter.

COMPETITION AND MONOPOLY

It is ordinarily assumed that competition and monopoly are at opposite poles of a single continuum. Along this spectrum, being "more monopolistic" means being correspondingly "less competitive." At the one extreme one has the perfectly competitive market, at the other a market characterized by pure monopoly. (Theories of imperfect or monopolistic competition were designed to avoid confining economic theory strictly to these polar cases.) Each type of market is, in this perspective, characterized by a series of defining criteria. The criteria defining the polar cases are mutually exclusive; those governing intermediate cases partly overlap with those defining one or both of the polar models.

My claim here is that this way of looking at competition and monopoly might be appropriate for the classification of alternative static equilibrium models. To the extent, for example, that the demand curve confronting a firm is less than perfectly elastic, this may be interpreted as reflecting a degree of "market power" possessed by the firm. With perfect competition defined in terms of total absence of such power, a degree of power expressed in a downward-sloping demand curve may plausibly come to be labelled a degree of monopoly. This was indeed the approach expressed in Abba Lerner's classic attempt to conceive of a measure of monopoly power.[12]

But, I wish to point out, for an approach which puts the emphasis on competition as a dynamic process, the idea of competition and monopoly being at opposite poles of a single spectrum is confused and almost incoherent. For this approach, competition is the essential defining characteristic of the market process itself. No matter what the institutional contours of the market may be, no matter what the economic power possessed by market participants may be, the market process (if such a process does exist and occur) is itself necessarily competitive. It is a process during which entrepreneurial, competitive-minded market participants, whether incumbent participants or merely potential participants, discover the true shape of market possibilities and constraints. The only situation in which competition can be said to be absent is one in which markets do not operate. Such a situation presumes, as in the centrally planned economy, the existence of institutional prohibitions on market exchanges. In any *market* situation, however, no matter what the degree of monopoly may be (and regardless of how monopoly is to be defined), the market process itself must be a competitive one. There simply is no market process other than that consisting of competitively inspired discoveries of opportunities for gain through exchange.

If, for example, a firm is the monopolist in an industry (whether as the result of unique control over some essential input or as the result of governmental grant of exclusive privilege), the manner in which the monopolist's price and quantity of sales is determined in the market is one that emerges from the competitive interplay of the decisions of potential buyers (of the monopolized commodity) as well as of those of participants in related markets. There is no other procedure governing the sequence of prices and quantities as determined in a world of open-ended uncertainty. Textbooks present, of course, the monopolized market as one in which the monopolist is confronted by a given and known demand curve, from which he at once selects his profit-maximizing price–quantity combination. But in fact no monopolist knows his demand curve in advance. It is the market process that reveals what the contours of the market possibilities really are, so that for the monopolized market it is the competitive process that tends to ensure that the monopoly equilibrium is in fact approached.

It is reasonable to try to formulate the conditions defining a monopolized market, but it is almost incoherent to ask for the conditions that must be satisfied in order for a market process to be described as being competitive. A market process is competitive by the very nature of being a market process. Sometimes I try to characterize the competitive nature of the market process by drawing attention to "freedom of entry" (or its correlate, "absence of privilege"), but it would be confusing to state that a market process is competitive according to the extent to which it permits free entry. A market process consists of the decisions of those who enter or who might enter. At most one can say that the extent to which a social process can be described as a market process depends on the extent to which freedom of entry to buy and sell are permitted. Freedom of entry is indeed a defining characteristic of competition, but only because the market process is, by definition, a competitive one.

Admittedly all this does create a certain difficulty for economic terminology. A market may be monopolized or it may not be monopolized. How am I to describe a market in which exclusive monopolistic privilege is absent? Surely the adjective "competitive" has a reasonable claim, in economic history and in the history of economic theory, to be the label describing the absence of exclusive privilege? The terminological difficulty is a real one, and is, probably, responsible in part for the extraordinary confusion which has surrounded the concepts of monopoly and competition during the twentieth century. It is, therefore, useful to examine one recent example of the problem, an example taken from an internal disagreement within Austrian economics.

THE MISESIAN THEORY OF MONOPOLY

Standard theory defines competition in terms of the degree of elasticity of demand facing the firm. In the case of perfect competition this elasticity is infinite; there are so many firms in the industry, and knowledge is so perfect, that no one of them can sell anything above the going market price. The polar opposite case is then that of a single firm selling in a well-defined market. With outside entry somehow absent, this monopolist then confronts the market demand curve, and chooses his profit-maximizing position accordingly. Clearly, if this monopoly position does indeed yield pure profit, the question arises as to why outside entry is indeed absent. Why don't others enter in an attempt to grasp some of this profit? It was this insight which inspired Mises to recognize that, within the market system itself, the only possible source for monopoly was sole ownership of some scarce essential input. (Of course Mises made it clear that government intervention in a market system can—and has historically very frequently indeed—generated monopolized markets.) If government forbids others to compete with a licensed producer, this certainly places him in a monopoly position, able to earn a supernormal return (which competition will be unable to "compete away").

Without government blocking of competitive entry, the number of firms in an industry, no matter how small, does not insulate them from the cold winds of potential competition; they are subject to the threat of the process of competitive entry. With the possibility, however, of a single owner of a scarce essential resource, Mises argued, we must recognize the possibility that this owner may be able to obtain greater revenue out of his resource by withholding part of it from the market. Whether he uses the resource in production himself or whether he sells it to other producers, his revenues may turn out to be greater as a result of his refusing to sell all that he, in his capacity as resource owner, might be prepared to sell were he to be only one of a number of such resource owners. Mises did not consider this possibility to be of much practical importance. Certainly he was convinced that most situations usually described as monopolistic are either not monopolistic at all or are likely to be the result of government obstacles against entry, rather than being the result of unique resource ownership. Yet, from the theoretical perspective, the possibility of a true monopoly occurring within a market is an interesting one and Mises pursued it for the sake of theoretical completeness.

With exclusive resource ownership, the extra monopoly revenue (that results from withholding some of the available supply from the market) is clearly not in the nature of any pure entrepreneurial profit. Rather it is an extra rent obtainable from the scarce resource as a result of the economic power created out of the peculiar pattern of ownership coupled with the absence of close substitute resources:

> Entrepreneurial profit has nothing to do with monopoly. If an entrepreneur is in a position to sell at monopoly prices, he owes this advantage to his monopoly with regard to a monopolized factor m. He earns the specific monopoly gain from his ownership of m, not from his specific entrepreneurial activities.[13]

There is, therefore, no problem of explaining why entrepreneurial entry does not compete away this surplus revenue; this surplus revenue is not an entrepreneurial profit, it can be obtained only by virtue of ownership of the resource.

Just as in the case of other markets, price in the monopolized market emerges through the rough and tumble of competing entrants. Of course, with exclusive resource ownership the entrants are (apart from the competing potential buyers) the owners of (possibly distant) substitute resources, or producers of competing products. It is the process of such competition that guides the monopoly resource owner to his best obtainable position. Mises points out that the "monopolist does not know the shape of the curve of demand" for his resource.[14] Clearly Mises is relying on the competitive market process to guide the monopolist to the profit-maximizing position obtainable by withholding some of the resource.

MISES: A NEOCLASSICAL?

I shall not deal comprehensively with the various criticisms from within Austrian economics which the Misesian theory has drawn.[15] I shall concern myself here only with one line of criticism which I believe can be traced to the terminological ambiguities cited earlier.

Several years ago, Gerald O'Driscoll argued that the theory of monopoly presented by Mises is "a variant of the neoclassical theory."[16] By the neoclassical theory of monopoly, O'Driscoll means the approach which (a) ignores the case of monopolies created by the state, and (b) ignores, in effect, the problem of why monopoly profits do not attract competitive entry (or, at any rate, provide untenable solutions to this problem). "[Neoclassical] theory lacks any defensible, coherent answer to the entry question. Monopoly is postulated without being explained."[17] O'Driscoll contrasts the neoclassical theory of monopoly with the "property-rights" approach. In the property-rights approach, entry will indeed occur:

> A profitable open-market monopoly is not a stable situation and hence is not one to concern either the economist or the policymaker. The property-rights tradition is to concentrate on the many varied ways in which governments create, foster, and maintain monopoly.[18]

Although O'Driscoll exonerates Mises from the charge of ignoring the cases of state-created monopoly,[19] he charges him with having a neoclassical monopoly theory in two senses. First, resource monopoly is one source of neoclassical monopoly. Second, Mises's theory "is no more successful at answering the entry question than is neoclassical theory."[20] In what follows I shall not deal directly with the unimportant issue of the neoclassical label which O'Driscoll has polemically pinned on to the Misesian theory. Instead I will attempt to address the substance of O'Driscoll's quite astonishing charge that Mises has ignored the problem of competitive entry.[21]

O'Driscoll's charge is astonishing primarily because in any reading of Mises's vehement disagreements with the standard theories of perfect competition, pure monopoly, and monopolistic competition, the absolutely central role must surely be assigned to his insistence on the driving force of competitive entry (actual and potential) into profitable markets. It was precisely this Misesian insistence on the power of dynamic competitive entry that has inspired the revival of interest, within contemporary Austrian economics, in the market as a process, rather than as an equilibrium configuration. It was undoubtedly precisely because of this concern with competitive entry that Mises offered his drastic idea (as it must be judged by the standards of neoclassical equilibrium theory) of restricting the notion of monopoly (and its "welfare" consequences) to the level of resource ownership.

And this brings us to a second sense in which O'Driscoll's charge against Mises (that he ignored the problem of competitive entry) appears astonishing. Mises avoided the entry problem entirely by deliberately restricting the notion of monopoly, in its primary sense, to the resource owner. The entrepreneur-producer is never a monopolist *qua* entrepreneur. If he is a monopolist it is only due to the circumstance that earlier (possibly entrepreneurial) transactions may have made him, at a given point in time, the sole owner of a scarce essential resource. (In this case he is a monopolist *qua* resource owner, *not qua* entrepreneur.) To ask why competitive entry does not compete away a monopoly resource owner's monopoly gain, is, one suspects, to misunderstand that gain as a subspecies of pure entrepreneurial profit.

O'Driscoll states the central theoretical issue to be solved by a monopoly theory as being that of explaining why, if "monopoly yields a net revenue or surplus . . . does entry of new firms not occur? The profitability of monopoly should ensure its own demise."[22] The answer which Mises's theory of resource monopoly offers to the question of why competition does not wipe out the monopolist's special gain (attributable to his monopoly position) is that this special gain is, "admittedly" (if that is the appropriate adverb) by hypothesis, a result of his exclusive ownership of this (apparently essential) resource.[23] One presumes that O'Driscoll would argue that, if we accepted this interpretation of Mises, this will mean that (as O'Driscoll remarks on Ricardo) Mises has then "trivialized the central question" which O'Driscoll believes must be dealt with by any monopoly theory. Our point here is that for Mises (perhaps even more than for the writers whom O'Driscoll labels the "property-rights theorists"), the entry problem in fact erases the monopoly case completely from the agenda of the theorist insofar as concerns the entrepreneur. "A profitable open-market monopoly," at the entrepreneurial level, "is not a stable situation and hence is not one to concern either the economist or the policymaker."[24] Even more to the point, for our purposes, a "profitable open-market monopoly" at the entrepreneurial level is simply, for Mises, an unfortunate misnomer. When a single entrepreneur in an open market engages in a profitable venture he has, in Misesian terminology, engaged in it competitively, not monopolistically. Others could have entered into this line of activity. Their not having done so, so far from rendering the profit-making entrepreneur a monopolist, simply means that they have been out-competed by him. His activity is part of the entrepreneurial competitive process.

The only sense in which the idea of a monopoly retains any meaning for Mises is in the context of resource ownership. As explained in the preceding section, the monopoly gain that may, under appropriate conditions, be made by the monopoly resource owner, has nothing to do with entrepreneurial gain. It is a gain, obtainable by virtue of ownership of his resource, which would not have been forthcoming were the resource supply to be owned by more than one independent owner. There simply is no ignored "entry problem" that needs to be addressed by the Misesian theory of monopoly.

THE SOURCE OF THE MISUNDERSTANDING

That so perceptive and so Austrian an economist as O'Driscoll came to misunderstand Mises in this regard seems to illustrate the terminological difficulties and confusions referred to earlier. It seems evident that O'Driscoll, recognizing the Austrian emphasis on the competitive process, has thought of monopoly as a case to be contrasted with that process. It is in this context that O'Driscoll raises the entry problem. "No one would seek a monopoly position . . . unless he expected to earn returns in excess of revenues forgone. Why then do others not follow suit or imitate the first rent seeker, thus breaking down the monopoly and competing away that monopoly rent?"[25] Clearly O'Driscoll is thinking of an entrepreneur who has successfully sought a monopoly position. But this was not Mises's approach at all. He thought of a monopoly position somehow already existing (as a result of historical patterns of resource ownership, or whatever).[26]

In regard to the competitive-entrepreneurial process itself, it is utterly vain to search for any monopoly case. There can be none, such as we have seen, not merely because any monopoly gains, so won in an open market must tend to be competed away, but also because in an open market *every* action is taken competitively (i.e., with full awareness of the need to anticipate the actions of others, actual or potential competitors). And here we have a source of misunderstanding. Mises contrasted the special case of "monopoly price" with the more general case of "competitive price."[27] This use of terminology is readily understandable but may, I fear, easily lead to a degree of confusion. It might be understood that, by using the contrasting terms, "competitive price" and "monopoly price," Mises was implying that monopoly is the opposite of competition in the sense of the competitive-entrepreneurial process. Perhaps, as we have seen, O'Driscoll was led so to assume. But we have seen how this would be incorrect. The Austrian process of entrepreneurial competition has no contrast within the market. So long as there is a market at all, or to any degree to which a market is able to proceed, it proceeds through the sequence of transactions generated by dynamic competition.

Monopoly, for Mises, has been reduced to a particular, not-very-important case, of a resource-owner who, by virtue of history and market conditions, happens to be the sole owner of a scarce essential ingredient in the production of a good. Market outcomes in this context are, as always, determined through the course of the competitive market process. Monopoly resource ownership does not compromise the competitive character of the market process; it merely diverts it from the particular pattern which that process might have taken in the absence of monopoly resource ownership. Had this resource not been exclusively owned, the driving forces of competition among entrepreneurs seeking to buy the resource from competing sellers of the resource, would have tended to make it desirable for resource owners to sell all of their resource supplies (beyond what they might retain for their own consumer purposes or for speculation). With all supplies of the scarce essential resource concentrated in the hands of one owner, the forces of market competition may not tend to induce him to sell all of his supply; they may teach him how to enhance his sales revenue from the resource by throwing some of it into the sea. Such a possibility, Mises argued, would, if ever realized, pit the interests of the consuming public against those of the exclusive resource owner. It was this theoretical possibility that Mises recognized (without considering it to be of much practical significance).

COMPETITION AS THE FUNDAMENTAL
PRINCIPLE IN MARKET THEORY

In his doctoral dissertation, Frank Machovec documented the thesis that the dynamic notion of competition pervaded the bulk of economics in the neoclassical period up until the 1920s.[28] It was only during the twenties and thirties that equilibrium thinking, and thus the static model of perfect competition, assumed its current dominance in mainstream economic thought. It was presumably this prevalence of the dynamic notion of competition which led Mises into believing, as late as 1932, that the various schools of twentieth-century economic thought shared a common basic understanding of the workings of the market economy.[29]

Whatever the degree of shared understanding may have been, and whatever the diverse directions toward which these schools were respectively pointing,[30] the prevalence of the dynamic notion of competition at this time may lend support to a thesis I recently suggested. Our emphasis here has been upon the universality in market processes in all contexts, of the dynamically competitive element. Recently I suggested that it is the character of the discoveries which make up this dynamically competitive process to which the central economist's assumption of universal self-interest in fact pertains.[31] The self-interest assumption in economics, this suggestion argues, does not so much identify a particular pattern of choices among given available options, as it illuminates the discovery process through which market participants identify the options available to them. The self-interest assumption sees market participants as purposeful human beings alert to changing conditions and to the new opportunities these may create. The alertness which inspires the discoveries made by market participants in the course of the market process is an alertness fueled, not necessarily by selfish or materialistic goals, but by concern to further one's goals, whatever these may be. What is being suggested, then, is that the critical place filled by the self-interest assumption is not in the theory of the consumer decision, or the theory of the producer's

decision, but in the entrepreneurial decision. Because all market participants are, to some degree, entrepreneurial, the self-interest assumption
has universal relevance. From this perspective it turns out that the competitive character of market processes, and the self-interested character of
market behavior, are simply two sides of the same coin.

Something of this seems to have been present in the thinking on competition of major economists at the turn of the century. "Broadly defined,"
Herbert J. Davenport observed, "economic competition is a struggle for
maximum economic rewards (minimum sacrifice)."[32] The rivalrous character of dynamic competition and the self-interested purposefulness of
individual market behavior "fold into" each other. The ubiquity in markets of self-interest, and the universality in markets of dynamic competition turn out to be one and the same.

NOTES

1. Reekie (1984, pp. 37ff.); O'Driscoll and Rizzo (1985, ch. 6); Littlechild (1981);
Shand (1984, pp. 65–71).

2. See especially Mises (1966, chs 15, 16); Hayek (1948, 1978); Kirzner (1973).

3. See, for example, Fisher (1983).

4. See, for example, Frydman (1982).

5. See Baumol (1982).

6. See, for example, Kirzner (1973, pp. 19ff.).

7. See Shackle (1972, pp. 54, 124, 137ff.).

8. Hayek (1948, p. 94).

9. Silvestre (1986, p. 197). Earlier references include Arrow (1959); Richardson
(1960); Clark (1961).

10. 22 (2) (April 1980).

11. On this see McNulty (1967).

12. Lerner (1934).

13. Mises (1966, p. 360).

14. Ibid., p. 378.

15. See, for example, Armentano (1978).

16. O'Driscoll (1982, p. 190). O'Driscoll's sentence reads: "Some [modern Austri-
ans], such as Ludwig von Mises and Israel Kirzner, present a variant of the neoclassical theory." Certain of O'Driscoll's criticisms (pp. 205–6) do relate especially to this
writer's presentation of the Misesian theory (in *Competition and Entrepreneurship*).
However, the remarks in the text relate strictly to the sense in which O'Driscoll finds
Mises's own theory to be neoclassical. Accordingly no further references will be made
to O'Driscoll's specific criticisms of this writer's presentation.

17. Ibid., p. 199.

18. Ibid.

19. Ibid., p. 205.

20. Ibid.

21. O'Driscoll's charge is all the more surprising in that he uses, as the epigraph introducing his paper, a quotation from Mises explicitly emphasizing that in dealing with cases of monopoly price "one must first of all raise the question of what obstacles restrain people from challenging the monopolist" (ibid., p. 189).

22. Ibid.

23. It must certainly be recognized that, in the Misesian theory of resource monopoly, this monopoly is, to use O'Driscoll's language, "postulated without being explained" (ibid., p. 199). The theory deals with the implications of a particular possible situation. That is all.

24. Ibid.

25. Ibid.

26. For a discussion of the forces that might lead entrepreneurs to attempt to win the position of a Misesian resource monopolist, see Kirzner (1973, pp. 199ff.).

27. See, for example, Mises (1966, p. 357).

28. Machovec (1986).

29. Mises (1960, p. 214).

30. See Kirzner (1989, pp. 2ff.).

31. Kirzner (1990).

32. Davenport (1905, p. 201).

REFERENCES

Armentano, Dominick T. (1978) "A Critique of Neoclassical and Austrian Monopoly Theory," in Louis M. Spadaro (ed.) *New Directions in Austrian Economics*, Kansas City: Sheed, Andrews and McMeel.

Arrow, Kenneth (1959) "Toward a Theory of Price Adjustment," in Abramowitz *et al.* (eds) *The Allocation of Economic Resources*, Stanford, Calif.: Stanford University Press.

Baumol, William J. (1982) "Contestable Markets: An Uprising in the Theory of Industry Structure," *American Economic Review* March.

Clark, J. M. (1961) *Competition as a Dynamic Process*, Washington, D.C.: Brookings Institution.

Davenport, Herbert J. (1905) *Outlines of Economic Theory*, New York: Macmillan.

Fisher, Franklin M. (1983) *Disequilibrium Foundations of Equilibrium Economics*, Cambridge: Cambridge University Press.

Frydman, Roman (1982) "Towards an Understanding of Market Processes: Individual Expectations, Learning and Convergence to Rational Expectations Equilibrium," *American Economic Review* 72.

Hayek, Friedrich von (1948) "The Meaning of Competition," in *Individualism and Economic Order*, Chicago: University of Chicago Press.

—— (1978) "Competition as a Discovery Procedure," in *New Studies in Philosophy, Politics, Economics and the History of Ideas,* Chicago: University of Chicago Press.

Kirzner, Israel M. (1973) *Competition and Entrepreneurship,* Chicago: University of Chicago Press.

—— (1989) "The Economic Calculation Debate: Lessons for Austrians," *The Review of Austrian Economics* 2.

—— (1990) "Self-Interest and the New Bashing of Economics: A Fresh Opportunity in the Perennial Debate?" *Critical Review* 4(1–2).

Lerner, Abba P. (1934) "The Concept of Monopoly and the Measurement of Monopoly Power," *Review of Economic Studies,* June.

Littlechild, Stephen C. (1981) "Misleading Calculation of the Social Costs of Monopoly Power," *Economic Journal.*

Machovec, Frank (1986) "The Destruction of Competition Theory: The Perfectly Competitive Model and Beyond," unpublished doctoral dissertation, New York University.

McNulty, P. J. (1967) "A Note on the History of Perfect Competition," *Journal of Political Economy* 75.

Mises, Ludwig von (1960) *Epistemological Problems of Economics* (first published 1933, Princeton, N.J.: Van Nostrand.

—— (1966) *Human Action,* 3rd rev. edn, Chicago: Henry Regnery.

O'Driscoll, Gerald P., Jr. (1982) "Monopoly in Theory and Practice," in Israel M. Kirzner (ed.) *Method, Process, and Austrian Economics, Essays in Honor of Ludwig von Mises,* Lexington, Mass.: D. C. Heath.

O'Driscoll, Gerald P., Jr., and Rizzo, Mario J. (1985) *The Economics of Time and Ignorance,* Oxford: Basil Blackwell.

Reekie, W. Duncan (1984) *Markets, Entrepreneurs and Liberty: An Austrian View of Capitalism,* New York: St. Martin's Press.

Richardson, G. B. (1960) *Information and Investment,* London: Oxford University Press.

Shackle, George L. S. (1972) *Epistemics and Economics: A Critique of Economic Doctrines,* Cambridge: Cambridge University Press.

Shand, Alexander H. (1984) *The Capitalist Alternative: An Introduction to Neo-Austrian Economics,* New York: New York University Press.

Silvestre, Joachim (1986) "The Elements of Fixprice Microeconomics," in Larry Samuelson (ed.) *Microeconomic Theory,* Boston: Kluwer-Nijhoff.

The systematic character of the market process derives, in the Austrian view, from the interplay of the actions of entrepreneurial human beings. Entrepreneurs act imaginatively and creatively, seeking to identify and to grasp market profit opportunities (generated by earlier entrepreneurial limitations of vision). As a result of the interplay of such entrepreneurial acts of vision, product prices and quantities of product offered for sale tend to be nudged systematically in the direction of the market-clearing price/quantity configuration.

In the present article we draw attention to the essentially *competitive* character of this entrepreneurial process and draw out some critical implications for any assessment of governmental antitrust policies. We must begin by pointing out certain crucial ambiguities that have long plagued economists' use of the adjective "competitive." The problem was identified over half a century ago by F. A. Hayek; despite the valiant efforts of Hayek and others, the problem continues to confuse both economists and the public.

THE MEANING OF COMPETITION

For the mainstream of economic theory the notion of competition has come to be associated with the *absence of market power* (to effect change in price or product quality). A competitive market is one in which no firm possesses market power. There is a certain reasonableness to this use of the term. Competition is seen as the antithesis of monopoly. Monopoly is identified with possession of the power to name one's price without having to worry whether this will encourage one's potential customers to seek more favorable terms elsewhere.

Competition is therefore reasonably understood to mean the situation in markets where such monopoly power is absent. "Perfect" competition therefore came to mean the situation in markets where each and every participant lacks *any* power whatever directly to influence product price or product quality. The conditions needed to define such a perfect situation are, as we would expect, completely unrealistic, including (as we

From *The Freeman* 50, 3 (March 2000): 11–14. Reprinted by permission.

saw in the first in this series of articles) universal perfect information concerning all current market events and potential events. But this is not necessarily a damning weakness; the notion of the state of perfect competition is, after all, seen in mainstream economics not as a description of reality, but as a model able to serve (a) as a theoretical framework helpful for understanding real-world markets, and (b) as a yardstick of perfection against which to assess the seriousness with which real-world situations (of less-than-"perfect" competition) fall short, in terms of the resulting pattern of resource allocation, as compared with the perfectly competitive efficiency ideal. It is this model of perfect competition which is, in mainstream economics, seen as the heart of the law of supply and demand, and which has, in the history of modern antitrust policy, driven governmental efforts to "maintain competition"—that is, to secure a structure of industry reasonably close to the perfectly competitive ideal.

For Austrians, however, the term competition has a *completely different meaning*, both for understanding how markets work and for formulating public policy in regard to the structure of industry. Austrians find the mainstream meaning of "competition" not only unhelpful, but in fact grossly misleading in terms of economic understanding. For Austrians it is clear that to seek to emulate an "ideal" state in which no single entrepreneur can have impact on market price or output quality is in effect to seek to paralyze the competitive market process.

Following a long tradition in economics going back at least to Adam Smith, Austrians define a competitive market not as a situation where no participant or potential participant has the power to make any difference, but as a *market where no potential participant faces nonmarket obstacles to entry*. (The adjective "nonmarket" refers, primarily, to government obstacles to entry; it is used to differentiate such obstacles from, for example, high production costs that might discourage entry. These latter do not constitute noncompetitive elements in a market; to be able to enter means to be able to enter a market if one judges such entry to be economically promising—it does not mean to be able to enter without having to bear the relevant costs of production.) That is, a situation is competitive if no incumbent participant possesses privileges that protect him against the possible entry of new competitors.

The achievements that free markets are able to attain depend, in the Austrian view, *on freedom of entry, that is, on the absence of privilege*. It is because the law of supply and demand (as understood by Austrians) depends crucially on freedom of entry that this meaning of the term "competition" is so important. As we shall see, it is because of this importance that so much twentieth-century antitrust policy can be seen as positively harmful, as seriously obstructing the competitive-entrepreneurial market process.

SEMANTICS AND SUBSTANCE

Certainly the dispute concerning the meaning of "competition" is a semantic one. But, together with, and underlying, the semantic squabble (which, admittedly, should not overly concern us as economists; after all, new terms can be coined that are not subject to misunderstanding), there is a profound substantive disagreement concerning the way in which markets work. The mainstream notion of competition sees it as a *state of affairs:* the notion of competition has nothing to do with the *process,* through which the market achieves its results. For Austrians, on the other hand, it is the market process that is important. And that market process cannot be imagined at all without *necessarily* departing from that state of complete powerlessness which mainstream economics sees as perfectly competitive. For Austrians the adjective "competitive" captures the essential feature of the market *process.*

In other words, entrepreneurial actions that are, in the Austrian sense of the term,* seen as essentially and emphatically *competitive,* as critical steps in the market process, are, in the mainstream view, seen as *anti*competitive, as monopolistic, as aberrations to be eliminated for the sake of the efficient-market ideal. As a result of this confusion of thought in twentieth-century economics, governments ostensibly intent on maintaining the competitiveness of markets have been seen as having the obligation to outlaw and zealously stamp out the very actions through which ordinary competitive strategies are effected. A brief glance at typical tools in the antitrust kit can help illustrate this Austrian critique.

SOME TOOLS OF ANTITRUST
Obstructing mergers
Antitrust policy has traditionally frowned upon (and often prohibited) mergers between hitherto competing firms. The rationale is, given the mainstream perspective, obvious and plausible. Replacing two competing

---

* This is also the sense universally adopted by business people, and the sense once universally followed by economists as well.

firms by one larger firm cannot but constitute a reduction in the degree of market competition (in the mainstream definition of the term). Two less powerful firms have been replaced by one more powerful firm.

But the Austrian view must be that such a merger, provided the potential entry of others has not been and is not being artificially blocked, is itself an entrepreneurial act, a *competitive* act; *the blockage obstructs the way in which market competition is able to discover the best size of firms and thus the lowest cost at which production can be maintained.* (Even if a single firm supplies an entire industry, the industry is still competitive, in Austrian terminology, so long as the firm is kept on its toes by the potential threat of new entrants into *this* industry, as well as by the threat and/or reality of competition from industries producing substitute commodities.)

Outlawing price collusion

A group of powerful firms may collude to keep prices high; their motives may be to cartelize the industry, to eliminate interfirm competition and thus to force the consumer to pay more. For this reason antitrust policy has of course been directed toward preventing such price collusion. But the Austrian perspective sees matters quite differently. Even where the *motive* is indeed to paralyze interfirm competition, such collusion is itself a competitive step—since, *in the absence of artificial blockage against entry,* such collusion can be taken only in the face of the threat of competition from new entrants (who may in fact be able to profit by offering to sell at lower prices). No one knows when a price is "too high"; only the competitive process of entry (or of the threat of potential entry) can reveal the lowest level of price that can be sustained. So long as entry is open, the colluding firms may, in seeking to maintain their higher prices, be unwittingly attracting new entrants to reveal the truth that lower prices are sustainable. Or they may, if no such new entry occurs, be demonstrating that the cost structure indeed dictates these higher prices, as being the lowest ones sustainable in a competitive world.

Preventing predatory price-cutting

What seems, from the mainstream perspective, a clear strategy of eliminating competition occurs where a large firm temporarily keeps prices very low, thus forcing smaller competing firms out of the industry, and is then able to raise prices drastically with impunity. Careful theoretical and historical analysis has cast serious doubt on even the possibility that such a strategy could be successful and on the validity of the classic claims that such strategies were indeed employed around the turn of the century in U.S. industry. But the Austrian objection to government attempts to limit so-called predatory price cuts does not rest on this analysis. Rather the Austrian objection is that, *so long as entry is not artificially blocked,* even where "monopoly" positions have indeed been acquired through "predatory" price-cutting, these positions have been acquired as part of the competitive process, and can only be maintained in the teeth of new potential competition.

No one can know when a price cut that eliminates a competitor is intended to establish a "monopoly"; more to the point, even an attempt to establish a "monopoly," *taken in the face of freedom of entry,* is itself a competitive step. No one denies that economic muscle may be used to confront consumers with higher prices. But if competition can indeed conceivably serve the consumers better, then these higher prices are themselves the way—the *competitive* way—through which it becomes profitable for new entrants to discover how better to serve consumers.

INEXORABLE MARKET COMPETITION

Our desperately brief glance at antitrust attitudes should perhaps suffice to confirm our central Austrian thesis: What is needed to stimulate that all-powerful entrepreneurial-competitive process upon which the free market depends is nothing more than freedom of entry to anyone with an idea of how to profit by serving consumers more faithfully than they are being currently served. It is important to remember that no claim is made that freedom of entry entails that competitors refrain from attempts to monopolize markets. They *may* attempt to do so; and certainly their efforts may possibly place the consumer in a worse position (than he might be under a system reflecting perfect knowledge). The Austrian claim is that since no such perfect knowledge can exist, we must rely on the competitive-entrepreneurial process to reveal how the consumer may be better served. To *obstruct* this process in the name of competition (!) is to undermine the only way through which the tendency toward social efficiency is possible. By obstructing or preventing entrepreneurial steps taken that do not fit the "perfectly competitive" model of universal utter powerlessness—even if such obstruction or prevention stems from the best of intentions on behalf of consumers—government is necessarily tending, to a greater or lesser extent, to paralyze what is truly the competitive process.

COORDINATION, ECONOMIC PLANNING, AND THE KNOWLEDGE PROBLEM

ECONOMIC PLANNING AND THE KNOWLEDGE PROBLEM

INTRODUCTION

It is now about forty years since Professor Hayek decisively identified the key misconception underlying mainstream welfare economics. This misconception, Hayek argued, was responsible for failure to appreciate the critique of the possibility of rational economic calculation under central planning—a critique stated most forcefully and clearly by Mises, and further developed by Hayek himself. As has been demonstrated by Professor Lavoie (1985), the true import and significance of the Hayekian lesson was simply not grasped by subsequent welfare economists writing on the socialist calculation debate, even though Hayek's work was widely cited.

In this chapter we attempt both to restate and to extend Hayek's insight concerning the "knowledge problem" and its implications for central economic planning, whether comprehensive in scope or otherwise. In the following paragraphs we cite Hayek's own formulation of his insight, and make certain observations concerning it. In subsequent sections of the chapter we start from a rather *different* point of departure, and in this way eventually arrive at our restatement and extension of the Hayekian position—spelling out some rather radical implications of our restatement.

According to Hayek (1949: 77–8):

> The peculiar character of the problem of a rational economic order is determined precisely by the fact that the knowledge of the circumstances of which we must make use never exists in concentrated or integrated form but solely as the dispersed bits of incomplete and frequently contradictory knowledge which all the separate individuals possess. The economic problem of society is thus not merely a problem of how to allocate "given" resources—if "given" is taken to mean given to a single mind which deliberately solves the problem set by these "data." It is rather a problem of how to secure the best use of

From *The Meaning of Market Process: Essays in the Development of Modern Austrian Economics* (New York and London: Routledge, 1992), 152–62. Reprinted by permission of Cato Institute; the original source is *Cato Journal*, Vol. 4, No. 2 (Fall 1984): 407–25. Cato Institute.

resources known to any of the members of society, for ends whose relative importance only these individuals know. Or, to put it briefly, it is a problem of the utilization of knowledge which is not given to anyone in its totality.

Let us call *this* knowledge problem "Hayek's knowledge problem." We note, at this initial stage in our discussion, that the position might be taken that Hayek's knowledge problem does *not,* at least at first glance, render immediately irrelevant the paramountcy of the social efficiency norm. It is true, as Hayek pointed out, that the dispersed character of knowledge means that the economic problem is not that of allocating "given" resources, where "given resources" means resources given and known to a single mind. But surely knowledge itself is a scarce resource. Thus the task of the central planner may be seen, in the light of Hayek's knowledge problem, as that of making the most effective use of the available dispersed knowledge existing in society at a given moment—with the attainment of such use constrained by the communication and search costs made necessary by the dispersed character of the available information.

It might seem, therefore, that there is nothing in Hayek's knowledge problem which places it outside the scope of economic planning. The knowledge problem, it might be argued, complicates the planning task: it introduces a newly recognized, subtle and complex resource (knowledge); it compels attention to the special characteristics of this resource (its dispersed character); and it calls for attention to a special class of costs (those required for search and communication). But Hayek's knowledge problem can still, it might seem, be subsumed under the overall economic problem, traditionally conceived in resource allocation terms. The central theme of this chapter is to deny this understanding of the implications of Hayek's knowledge problem.[1]

In this chapter I shall argue that this problem of securing the best use of dispersed knowledge, in fact, *cannot* be translated into a special case of the more general problem of securing an efficient allocation of society's resources. It will follow that societal planning, by its very character, is incapable of addressing Hayek's problem—such planning can only frustrate and hamper those spontaneous market forces that *are* capable of engaging this knowledge problem. In order to develop these arguments it will be useful to introduce a "knowledge problem" that at first glance seems very different from Hayek's.

THE INDIVIDUAL PLAN AND THE KNOWLEDGE PROBLEM

In the course of everyday life man continually *plans*. Economists have come to formulate the individual plan as the seeking of a maximum: the planner is intent on arriving at a constrained optimum position. This is the concept of the economizing decision articulated with special precision and force by Lionel Robbins in 1932 (Robbins 1935), and widely adopted since then as the basic building block of microeconomic theory. We wish to point out that there is an inescapable potential "knowledge problem" surrounding this concept of the individual plan.

The notion of the plan presupposes some deliberately aimed at entity—say, utility or profit—that is to be knowingly maximized. It further presupposes known resource constraints. In Robbins' terminology, both the ends and the means are presumed to be *given*. It is the presumed knowledge of these planning circumstances by the planner that permits the economist to perceive the plan as the solving of a constrained maximization problem. The validity of the plan itself, it should be noted, depends entirely on the validity of the assumption that the planner in fact accurately knows the circumstances surrounding his prospective decisions. If the planner does not know what it is that he is seeking to achieve, or does not know what resources are at his command, or what the efficacy of these resources is with respect to sought-after goals, then his plan—no matter how carefully formulated—is unlikely to result in the best possible outcome.

We can now identify the knowledge problem potentially relevant to each individual plan. *Because of inadequacies in the planner's knowledge of his true circumstances, his plan may fail to yield an attainable optimum.* Let us call *this* knowledge problem the "basic knowledge problem." This will distinguish it from what we have called "Hayek's knowledge problem." It will also indicate our intention to demonstrate that Hayek's knowledge problem can be considered a special case of what we call the "basic knowledge problem." To be sure, what we have called the "basic knowledge problem" seems, at first glance, to bear little resemblance to Hayek's. Hayek's knowledge problem consists in the dispersed character of available information; our basic knowledge problem consists in an individual's simple ignorance of the circumstances relevant to his situation. Further reflection on both Hayek's knowledge problem and our basic knowledge problem, however, will reveal the important sense in which Hayek's problem is indeed a basic one. Let us first clarify a possible misunderstanding concerning the basic knowledge problem.

THE BASIC KNOWLEDGE PROBLEM
AND THE ECONOMICS OF SEARCH

It might be argued that the basic knowledge problem surrounding every individual plan can be entirely escaped through the addition of new planning stages. After all, if a plan seems likely to fail because of inadequate availability of a necessary resource, this threatened failure need not be final; it may possibly be avoided by appropriate preliminary planning to obtain this resource. Instead of simply formulating a single plan directed at the immediate attainment of the final objective, it is necessary to introduce intermediate objectives to be pursued in the course of additional preliminary plans. Perhaps, then, the basic knowledge problem, too, merely calls for judicious preliminary planning.

From this perspective the basic knowledge problem would appear merely to represent an inadequacy in the available supply of an important resource, namely, knowledge. This inadequacy would then be seen to call for a *planned search* to acquire the necessary information. In principle, it might then be thought that the basic knowledge problem can be escaped, at least to the same extent that any other problem arising out of a resource shortage can be escaped. To the extent that it is worthwhile, a preliminary plan of search to overcome the shortage of necessary information may totally eliminate the basic knowledge problem. To the extent that such a costly search is held not to be worthwhile, the basic knowledge problem would seem merely to express the inescapable scarcity constraints inherent in the planner's situation. For the economist such an inescapable scarcity problem means that there is no problem at all, in the relevant sense.

To the extent that the knowledge problem is escapable, it can (and presumably will) be escaped; to the extent that it is not worthwhile escaping, there would appear to be no basic knowledge problem at all—since we defined the basic knowledge problem in terms of failure to realize an *attainable optimum*. If lack of knowledge renders a hypothetical optimum unattainable, it can generate no basic knowledge problem. And if the cost of acquiring the knowledge is prohibitive, then the "hypothetical optimum," while indeed "attainable," is in fact no optimum at all.

But this line of argument cannot be sustained. The basic knowledge problem potentially surrounding each individual plan is by its nature inescapable. Certainly a deficiency in knowledge may be able to be rectified by search, and the individual planner will no doubt consider, in his preliminary planning, whether such search should be undertaken or not. But the basic knowledge problem—involving possible failure to achieve an attainable optimum—remains. In fact the possibility of preliminary planning to acquire knowledge only *expands* the scope of the basic knowledge problem.

Let us consider an individual engaging in a plan seeking to achieve a valued objective. Let us call this Plan A. In formulating the specific steps that should be taken in pursuing Plan A, the individual realizes that he lacks needed pieces of information. He thereupon engages in a plan to attain these preliminary objectives, namely these missing pieces of information. Let us call this search plan Plan B. We can see Plan A as having been *expanded* (as a result of realized ignorance) to *include* the planned attainment of needed preliminary objectives, so that Plan B is "nested" within expanded Plan A. And we can identify the later steps to be taken in the course of expanded Plan A—those steps subsequent to the attainment of the information obtained in Plan B—as Plan A'. (Plan A' consists in the steps that would have made up the originally envisaged Plan A had the planner in fact *not* lacked the needed information.) We can easily see that the basic knowledge problem is a potential hazard both for Plan B and Plan A'. Plan A, which includes Plan B and Plan A', is of course subject to the vulnerabilities of both of them.

Even if Plan B is completely successful in attaining precisely the optimal amount of information capable of being searched for (and believed to be worth the costs of such search), Plan A is nonetheless still subject to the hazards of the basic knowledge problem. After all, although our decision maker, in originally seeking to formulate Plan A, realized he lacked specific items of information (and therefore undertook preliminary Plan B), he may have in fact *lacked far more information* than he realized. (Most important, such unrealized information may have taken the form of a firm, but totally mistaken, belief in the validity of information that is totally false.) Moreover he may be mistaken in his belief that the items of information he realizes he lacks are necessary for the implementation of Plan A. He also may be mistaken in his belief that he really lacks these items of information (in the relevant sense of lacking). The truth may be that these items are already within his grasp.

For example, he may believe that Plan A, in the course of which he must communicate with individual Z, requires information concerning Z's telephone number, information that he believes himself to lack, so that he undertakes Plan B to search for Z's telephone number. But the truth may be quite different. The truth may be that Z is in fact the wrong person to speak to altogether, or again the truth may be that Z is now in the very same room with our planner, so that no knowledge of Z's telephone number is in fact needed for Plan A. Or, it may be, our planner does not really "lack" Z's telephone number at all; he may in fact have that telephone number clearly written and identified in the list of telephone numbers that lies next to the telephone that he uses. Given these possibilities for sheer error that surround Plan A' and/or Plan B, possibilities in which the planner is entirely unaware of the extent of his ignorance, Plan A (because it includes Plan A' and Plan B) may be far from optimal even if Plan B is wholly successful in terms of its own objectives. In addition it may be the case that Plan B overlooks more efficient available ways of achieving its own objectives (e.g. there may be less costly methods of search of which the searcher is unaware).

To sum up, the possibility of planned search for information perceived to be lacking does not eliminate the knowledge problem. First, the planned search may itself be undertaken without awareness that more efficient search techniques are easily available. Second, the information sought may in fact not justify the costs of search because the truth (of which the planner is unaware) is that the information is *not* of significance for the attainment of the planner's ultimate objectives. Third, quite apart from the information that the planner realizes he lacks and for which he may attempt to search, he may lack other information that he does *not* realize he lacks and for which he does not think of undertaking any planned research.

CENTRAL PLANNING AND THE KNOWLEDGE PROBLEM

We are now in a position to appreciate Hayek's insight into the problem of dispersed knowledge as revealing *the central planning task to be one that is deeply and inextricably bound up in the basic knowledge problem.* Let us put ourselves in the position of the central planners, earnestly and single-mindedly seeking after the most efficient possible pattern of resource allocation.

Our task as central planners is to formulate a plan for society in a manner analogous to that in which an individual plans his own course of action. We formulate our social plan with respect to specific social objectives and in the light of specific perceived arrays of available social resources.[2] This framework for the central plan is relevant (in principle and with the necessary changes having been made) both for comprehensive social planning and for central planning designed merely to supplement or modify, rather than totally replace, decentralized economic activity. The analogy between the social plan and the individual plan compels us, of course, to acknowledge the relevance of the basic knowledge problem for the social plan, in exactly the same way as we have seen it to be an inevitable and inescapable hazard for the individual plan. *Hayek's contribution permits us to recognize that the central plan may be subject to hazards (arising out of the basic knowledge problem) that might have been escaped by decentralized planning.*

That the centralized plan is inescapably subject to the hazards of the basic knowledge problem follows almost trivially from the very notion of the basic knowledge problem. Because the individual planner may not be aware of his true circumstances and may be totally unaware of his ignorance, his best formulated plans may fail to yield an attainable optimum. The central planners, too, may be unaware of their own ignorance concerning the true circumstances relevant to the social plan. Our understanding of the implications of dispersed knowledge deepens our appreciation of the seriousness of the basic knowledge problem, and reveals how the hazards of this problem *might* have been entirely escaped in the absence of the centralized plan.

Recognition of the fact of dispersed knowledge—especially as regards "the knowledge of particular circumstances of time and place" (Hayek 1949: 80)—immediately illuminates our understanding of the basic knowledge problem that threatens central planners. For a planning individual, the basic knowledge problem derives from the possibility that what he thinks he knows about his circumstances may differ from what he *might* have known (without additional resource expenditure) had he been more alert or aware of the true environment.

The same possibility, of course, is fully relevant for a central planner, but it is heightened by the central planner's peculiar predicament. What the central planner thinks he knows about the relevant circumstances *must necessarily take the form of what he thinks he knows about the availability of dispersed bits of knowledge that can somehow, at some cost, be mobilized in formulating and implementing the social plan.* There is little chance that the central planner can ever know where to find, or how to search for, all the items of dispersed information known somewhere in the economic system. Moreover there seems little chance that the central planner can ever be fully aware of the nature or extent of the specific gaps in his own knowledge in this regard. He may realize, in a general way, that there is information the location of which he is ignorant, but this gives him no clue where to look. The end result is that the planner is unlikely to be able to exploit all the information that is within his command. Clearly the dispersal of information is responsible for a new dimension of application for the basic knowledge problem.

Earlier we raised the possibility that Hayek's knowledge problem—despite its novelty—might be subsumed under the general economic problem, traditionally conceived in terms of achieving an efficient allocation of given resources (with available information included as an important given resource). We can now see how inappropriate it is for us to consider central planners as being able to grapple with Hayek's knowledge problem in terms of conventional planning to achieve a constrained optimum pattern of resource allocation. The unknown ignorance that is the heart of the knowledge problem created by the dispersal of information defies its being able to be squeezed into the Procrustean bed of the allocation plan. Just as the individual planner is unable to grapple deliberately with the basic knowledge problem surrounding all decision making, so too is the central planner unable to invoke planning techniques to grapple deliberately with Hayek's knowledge problem.

What renders the Hayekian knowledge problem critique of central planning so devastating is the circumstance that in a market system, with decentralized decision making, *the insoluble knowledge problem confronted by central planners tends to dissolve through the entrepreneurial-competitive discovery procedure.*

THE ENTREPRENEURIAL-COMPETITIVE DISCOVERY PROCEDURE

The Hayekian case of decentralized decision making has frequently been misunderstood. All too frequently this case is presented as arguing only that the decentralized market economy escapes the problem of dispersed knowledge because prices accurately *and economically* convey necessary information to relevant decision makers (replacing any need for them to know *all* the detailed information that is dispersed throughout the system). It must be emphasized that while this line of reasoning is certainly present in Hayek's work, it fails to do justice to the full implications of that work.

To argue that market prices convey information, and thus directly overcome the problem of dispersed knowledge, is to make a case for markets that depends upon a dubious assumption: namely, that markets are always at or close to equilibrium. It is only in equilibrium that it can be claimed that a market participant guided by market prices is automatically steered toward those actions that will co-ordinate smoothly with the actions of all the other (similarly guided) market participants. Moreover, to make the assumption that markets are close to equilibrium is essentially (quite apart from our other reasons for feeling uncomfortable concerning the realism of this assumption) *to beg* (rather than to overcome) the Hayekian problem of dispersed knowledge. After all, just as the phenomenon of dispersed knowledge offers a formidable challenge to central planners, this phenomenon offers markets a wholly analogous challenge, namely that of *achieving*, in fact, those arrays of market prices that will clear markets.

One does not "solve" the problem of dispersed knowledge by *postulating* prices that will smoothly generate dovetailing decisions. Dispersed knowledge is precisely the reason for the very realistic possibility that market prices at a given date are *unable* to clear markets and to ensure the absence of wasted resources. The truth is that the market *does* possess weapons to combat (if not wholly to conquer) the problem of dispersed knowledge. These weapons are embodied in the workings of the price system, but *not* in the workings of a hypothetical system of equilibrium prices. The importance of prices for coping with the Hayekian knowledge problem does not lie in the accuracy of the information which equilibrium prices convey concerning the actions of others who are similarly informed. Rather, its importance lies in the ability of disequilibrium prices to offer pure profit opportunities that can attract the notice of alert, profit-seeking entrepreneurs. Where market participants have failed to co-ordinate their activites because of dispersed knowledge, this expresses itself in an array of prices that suggests to alert entrepreneurs where they may win pure profits.

We know very little about the precise way in which pure profit opportunities attract entrepreneurial attention. But there can be little doubt about the powerful magnetism which such opportunities exert. To say that pure profit opportunities attract attention is not at all to say that awareness of these opportunities is secured by deliberate, costly search on the part of entrepreneurs. Rather it is to recognize that the lure of pure profit is what permits an individual decision maker to transcend the limits of a given, perceived planning framework and to escape, to some extent, the basic knowledge problem that surrounds all individual decision making. Man's entrepreneurial alertness operates at all times to place his narrow planning activities within the broader framework of *human action*.[3] *At the very same time* as man is routinely calculating the optimal allocation of given resources with respect to given competing ends, he keeps an entrepreneurial ear cocked for anything that might suggest that the available resources are different from what had been assumed, or that perhaps a different array of goals might be worth striving for.

This entrepreneurial element in human action is what responds to the signals for pure profit that are generated by the errors that arise out of the dispersed knowledge available in society. It is this yeast that ferments the competitive-entrepreneurial discovery process, tending to reveal to market participants more and more of the relevant information scattered throughout the market. It is this entrepreneurial-competitive process that thus grapples with that basic knowledge problem we found inescapably to confront central planning authorities. To the extent that central planning displaces the entrepreneurial discovery process, whether on the society-wide scale of comprehensive planning or on the more modest scale of state piecemeal intervention in an otherwise free market, the planners are at the same time both smothering the market's ability to transcend the basic knowledge problem and subjecting themselves helplessly to that very problem. The problem's source is Hayek's dispersed knowledge: central planning has no tools with which to engage the problem of dispersed knowledge, and its very centralization means that the market's discovery process has been impeded, if not brought to a full halt.

MARKETS, FIRMS AND CENTRAL PLANNING

At least as far back as Coase's 1937 paper on the theory of the firm, it has been recognized that each firm in a market economy is an island of local "central planning" in a sea of spontaneously seething competitive market forces. Within the firm, activities are co-ordinated by central direction, not by market competition via a price mechanism. Our discussion in this chapter throws light, perhaps, on the forces governing the location of the boundaries separating the realm of freely adopted "central planning" from that of the competitive price system.

We have seen that the replacement of market discovery (working through entrepreneurial alertness to profit opportunities) by central planning generates a new scope of potency for the basic knowledge problem arising out of the dispersal of knowledge. In a free market, therefore, any advantages that may be derived from "central planning" (e.g. the avoidance of "wasteful" duplication often apparently present in situations of market rivalry) are purchased at the price of an enhanced knowledge problem. We may expect firms spontaneously to tend to expand to the point where additional advantages of "central" planning are just offset by the incremental knowledge difficulties that stem from dispersed information. On a small scale the latter difficulties may be insignificant enough to be worth absorbing in order to take advantage of explicitly co-ordinated organization. Knowledge dispersed over a small geographical organizational area may mean a Hayekian knowledge problem that, unlike that relevant to large, complex entities, is solvable through deliberate search. Beyond some point, however, the knowledge difficulties will tend to reduce the profitability of firms that are too large. Competition between firms of different sizes and scope will tend, therefore, to reveal the optimal extent of such "central planning."

On the other hand if central planning is *imposed* on an otherwise free market, whether in comprehensive terms or not, such planning will almost always involve the knowledge problem, and to an extent *not* likely to be justified by any advantages that centralization might otherwise afford. Governmentally enforced central planning sweeps away the market's delicate and spontaneous weapons for grappling with the knowledge problem. Such centralized planning is by its very nature, and the nature of the knowledge problem, unable to offer any substitute weapons of its own.

CONCLUSION

We should remember that the nature of the knowledge problem is such that its extent and seriousness cannot be known in advance. Part of the tragedy of proposals for industrial policy and economic planning is that their well-meaning advocates are totally unaware of the knowledge problem—the problem arising out of unawareness of one's ignorance.

NOTES

1. Hayek (1979: 190) has more recently deepened our understanding of the problem of dispersed knowledge as going far beyond that of "utilizing information about particular concrete facts which individuals already possess." He now emphasizes the problem of using the abilities that individuals possess *to discover* relevant concrete information. This leads Hayek to point out that, because a person "will discover what he knows or can find out only when faced with a problem where this will help," he may never be able to "pass on all the knowledge he commands. . . ." In recent unpublished work Professor Lavoie, building on insights contained in the work of Michael Polanyi, also has emphasized the relevance of "tacit knowledge" for the social problem of utilizing dispersed knowledge. The present chapter arrives at similar conclusions but from a somewhat different starting point.

2. We avoid here raising any of the well-known difficulties that surround (a) the notion of a hierarchy of social goals analogous to a ranking of individual objectives and (b) the related notions of social efficiency and social choice.

3. On this compare Mises (1966: 253–4).

REFERENCES

Coase, R. H. (1937) "The nature of the firm," *Economica (NS)* 4: 386–405.
Hayek, F. A. (1949) "The use of knowledge in society," in *Individualism and Economic Order*, London: Routledge & Kegan Paul (originally published in *American Economic Review* 35 no. 4 (1945): 519–30).
Hayek, F. A. (1979) *Law, Legislation and Liberty*, Vol. 3, *The Political Order of a Free People*, Chicago, Ill.: University of Chicago Press.
Lavoie, D. (1985) *Rivalry and Central Planning: The Socialist Calculation Debate Reconsidered*, Cambridge: Cambridge University Press.
Mises, L. von (1966) *Human Action, a Treatise on Economics*, 3rd edn, Chicago, Ill.: Henry Regnery (originally published as *Human Action*, New Haven, Conn.: Yale University Press, 1949).
Robbins, L. (1935) *An Essay on the Nature and Significance of Economic Science*, 2nd edn, London: Macmillan (1st edn 1932).

KNOWLEDGE PROBLEMS AND THEIR SOLUTIONS: SOME RELEVANT DISTINCTIONS

INTRODUCTION

A central role in Hayek's thought has been played by his insights into the problems posed by the phenomenon of dispersed knowledge. These insights first emerged as a result of Hayek's participation in the inter-war debate on the possibility of socialist economic calculation and were crystallized in his classic 1945 paper "The use of knowledge in society" (1949a). Although these insights were originally born out of Hayek's economics, for the past three decades they have nourished those profound contributions to other branches of social philosophy which have come to dominate Hayek's recent work.

The classic 1945 passage in which Hayek definitively articulated his original, economic insight, reads as follows:

> The peculiar character of the problem of a rational economic order is determined . . . by the fact that the knowledge of the circumstances of which we must make use never exists in concentrated or integrated form but solely as the dispersed bits of incomplete and frequently contradictory knowledge which all the separate individuals possess. The economic problem of society is thus not merely a problem of how to allocate "given" resources—if "given" is taken to mean given to a single mind which deliberately solves the problem set by these "data." It is rather a problem of how to secure the best use of resources known to any of the members of society, for ends whose relative importance only these individuals know. Or, to put it briefly, it is a problem of the utilization of knowledge which is not given to anyone in its totality.
>
> (Hayek 1949a: 77–8)

Some thirty years later, in introducing his three-volume *Law, Legislation and Liberty,* Hayek recognized the seminal part played by these insights for his more general discussions of later years.

From *The Meaning of Market Process: Essays in the Development of Modern Austrian Economics* (New York and London: Routledge, 1992), 163–79. The original source is *Cultural Dynamics* 3, 1 (1990): 32–48, copyright 1990 by Sage Publications. Reprinted by permission of SAGE.

The insight into the significance of our institutional ignorance in the economic sphere . . . was in fact the starting point for those ideas which in [*Law, Legislation and Liberty*] are systematically applied to a much wider field.

(Hayek 1973: 13)[1]

Indeed, already in 1960, in *The Constitution of Liberty*, Hayek was applying his 1945 economic insights into a far wider field. Hayek there points out that the "sum of the knowledge of all the individuals exists nowhere as an integrated whole. The great problem is how we can all profit from this knowledge, which exists only dispersed as the separate, partial, and sometimes conflicting beliefs of all men." He proceeds immediately to observe: "In other words, it is largely because civilization enables us constantly to profit from knowledge which individually we do not possess and because each individual's use of his particular knowledge may serve to assist others unknown to him in achieving their ends that men as members of civilized society can pursue their individual ends so much more successfully than they could alone." All this leads Hayek to refer to the "identification of the growth of civilization with the growth of knowledge" (1960: 25), pointing out that the "more civilized we become, the more relatively ignorant must each individual be of the facts on which the working of his civilization depends. The very division of knowledge increases the necessary ignorance of the individual of most of his knowledge" (p. 26). Our discussion in this chapter explores the meaning of the problem of dispersed knowledge by probing the legitimacy of Hayek's extension of his original, narrowly economic insight to apply to civilization in general, and to its various institutions in particular.

THE EXTENSION OF HAYEK'S KNOWLEDGE PROBLEM

In his recent work Hayek has indeed concentrated on the significance of the "knowledge problem" (as, following Lavoie (1985: Ch. 3), we shall now call it) as extending far beyond the capacity of market processes to co-ordinate the mutual expectations which market participants hold concerning one another. Hayek has emphasized the significance of the knowledge problem for the evolution of social and cultural norms and institutions. The intricate webs of mutually sustaining expectations required for the emergence of our most valuable social institutions, Hayek argues, could never conceivably have been deliberately simulated by any centralized organization. What has nurtured the spontaneous emergence of such benign cultural norms and institutions, Hayek maintains, is the circumstance that social processes of spontaneous coordination have been able to evolve. It is only in this way that a social fabric consisting of innumerable threads of mutual expectations—a fabric the totality of which displays a complexity transcending the capacity of any single mind—could possibly come to be woven.

Now, it is no doubt incorrect and unfair to attribute to Hayek the categorical assertion that whatever institutions evolve spontaneously are more likely to be socially benign than any deliberately constructed institutions could possibly be. Yet various writers have noted their discomfort at feeling how close Hayek appears sometimes to be to such a view. Although Hayek points out that he "has carefully avoided saying that evolution is identical with progress," he makes it clear that "it was the evolution of a tradition which made civilization possible," and asserts flatly "that spontaneous evolution is a necessary if not a sufficient condition of progress" (Hayek 1979: 168). Buchanan, in particular, has placed his finger on the theme that has become increasingly important in Hayek's recent writings:

> This theme involves the extension of the principle of spontaneous order, in its *normative* implications, to the emergence of institutional structure itself. . . . There is no room left for the political economist, or for anyone else who seeks to reform social structures to *change* laws and rules, with an aim of securing increased efficiency in the large. Any attempt to design, construct, and to change institutions must, within this logical setting strictly interpreted, introduce inefficiency. Any "constructively rational" interferences with the "natural" processes of history are therefore to be studiously avoided. The message seems clear: relax before the slow sweep of history.
>
> (Buchanan 1986: 75–6)[2]

Buchanan struggles to exonerate Hayek from the charge of actually supporting the full extreme position outlined in the preceding paragraph, and to resolve apparent contradictions between Hayek's more consistently anti-constructivist statements and his own attempts (such as his proposal for the denationalization of money, and his proposals for political constitutional reconstruction) at institutional reform.[3] Yet the strong impression one gains from Hayek remains that he has profound faith in the possibility, in general, of benign institutional evolution.

In the present chapter I shall join Hayek's critics in questioning the asserted parallelism (between the achievements of free markets within a given institutional setting and the spontaneous evolution of institutions themselves) which has formed the foundation for Hayek's work in recent decades. I shall proceed by first carefully dissecting the original Hayekian knowledge problem into two distinct component problems, both of which have their counterparts in the context of the emergence of social norms and institutions. It will then become apparent that only one of these two component problems permits solution, in the context of institutional development, in a manner parallel to that in which its counterpart problem is solved in markets. The remaining component of the knowledge problem turns out, in the institutional development context, not to be solvable by the spontaneous process through which its counterpart problem in markets is solved. The purpose of our critique, it should be emphasized, is not so much to challenge the analogies which Hayek draws between market and society, as to explore some subtleties in the knowledge problem which Hayek has taught us to appreciate. That Hayek has himself not always seemed sensitive to these subtleties makes this task, of course, only all the more important.

THE KNOWLEDGE PROBLEM IN MARKET CONTEXT

Consider a single commodity market in competitive equilibrium. A market clearing price prevails. No market participant need know more than the market price to be able to carry out his plans without disappointment or regret. Each seller finds himself able to sell what he wishes to sell at the market price. Each buyer finds himself able to buy what he wishes to buy at the market price. The amount of knowledge possessed by each market participant need not be more than miniscule. No one need know the shape or position of either the demand or the supply curve. Yet the market price stimulates a series of independent decisions which permits all possible mutually gainful trades between any pair of market participants to occur. Suppose now that some catastrophe strikes the industry producing our commodity, drastically shifting its supply curve to the left. Market price will rise and buyers of the commodity will find themselves constrained to economize more than previously on the use of this product—and will be guided by the higher market price to do so, without ever learning about the catastrophe, knowing only that the market price is now higher than it had been before. Many textbook presentations of Hayek's vision of how markets solve the knowledge problem see this achievement of the equilibrium market as the paradigmatic illustration of the knowledge problem and its market solution.

What the market solution has achieved, these expositions show, is that the market is able to mobilize dispersed knowledge as if all the information were concentrated in a single mind. Although knowledge is in fact dispersed, to a degree making it inconceivable that all of it might indeed be available to a single mind, the market successfully and spontaneously yields a social result which exploits every relevant bit of knowledge.

Careful consideration of this achievement of the market in equilibrium reveals, we wish to point out, two quite different achievements. Each of these achievements, we argue, corresponds to a distinct component of Hayek's knowledge problem. Let us see how this is the case.

The market clearing price can prevail only because no market participant makes any offer to sell or to buy which is not accepted. Each market participant correctly anticipates the responses which others will make to any offer or bid he proposes. No attempted decision has been based on undue optimism; no attempted decision has thus been disappointed. Of course we can easily imagine situations in which this happy state of affairs does not occur. Market participants may mistakenly believe that others will buy even at very high prices or that others will be prepared to sell even at very low prices. Such over-optimistic mistakes are very natural: they arise because market participants may not know what the other market participants know about themselves, namely that they are not prepared to buy at the high prices (or sell at the low prices). As a result of this dispersed knowledge (people knowing only their own attitudes, not those of others), markets may easily fail to clear (since over-optimistic sellers may have held out for prices that were too high *etc.*). We shall recognize this possible failure, due to over-optimism (resulting from the dispersion of knowledge), as the first of the two knowledge problems we wish to identify. We shall refer to it as Knowledge Problem A.

A little thought will convince us, however, that Knowledge Problem A is not the only knowledge problem successfully solved in the case of the market clearing price. Over-optimism is not the only reason why the market clearing price may not be achieved throughout the market. Imagine a situation—the stylized conditions of which are postulated only to illustrate a point relevant to far more realistic and typical problems—in which a wall, or an ocean, separates one half of the market from the other (but with this separation entailing no costs of transportation for the journey from one market sector to the other). It could easily happen, in such a situation, that this separation generates two separate markets, in each of which a (different) market clearing price prevails. It should be clear that here, too (just as in the *single* market clearing price case discussed earlier), Knowledge Problem A has been successfully solved. No market participant (in the two separate "markets") has made a buying/selling proposal, fully expecting it to be accepted, which turns out to be rejected. No one has been over-optimistic concerning the responses of others to offers made available to them.

But it should also be clear that, in this case of the two "markets," even though in each of them the local price clears the market, errors have none the less been made. The existence of two separate prices (in these two markets) for the identical commodity indicates that those paying the higher price erroneously overlooked the possibility of buying more cheaply in the other market; those selling for the lower price erroneously overlooked the possibility of selling at a higher price in the other market. Some participants in the high-price market refrain from buying (because of the high price) and remain without the commodity, even while that commodity is available in the other market. This is matched by the circumstance that some participants in the low-price market refrain from selling (at the low price) while potential buyers willing to pay higher prices could have been found in the high-price market. Market participants have failed to grasp opportunities that *might* have been grasped—if only they had more accurate knowledge concerning what others *might* have been prepared to do. Clearly these errors (while not constituting a problem identical with Knowledge Problem A, which arose because market participants were over-optimistic) constitute a knowledge problem: market participants are (over-pessimistically) unaware of what others *might* be willing to pay (or be willing to sell for). We shall call this second problem, the problem of undue pessimism arising from dispersed knowledge, Knowledge Problem B.

THE TWO KNOWLEDGE PROBLEMS

A little thought will convince us that Knowledge Problems A and B really are distinct problems.[4] Both arise from the circumstance of dispersed information, but consist in distinctly different kinds of error. My incomplete information concerning what others would like to do may lead me over-optimistically to expect to sell at very high prices. Here my incomplete information has led me to expect behaviour on the part of others which will in fact not occur. The errors thus constituting Knowledge Problem A tend to be *self-revealing*—since they stimulate proposals which are bound to be disappointed. Knowledge Problem A, in the market context, generates a process of equilibration which appears well-nigh inevitable. As Hayek himself put it, in apparently referring to this kind of equilibration process, the relevant knowledge which a market participant "must possess in order that equilibrium may prevail is the knowledge which he is bound to acquire in view of the position in which he originally is, and the plans which he then makes."[5]

My incomplete information concerning what others would like to do may, on the other hand, unduly pessimistically lead me to believe it impossible to sell at quite low prices (at which others would in fact be delighted to buy), compelling me to give up the idea of selling altogether. Here incomplete information has led market participants (between whom the possibility for mutually gainful exchange exists) to overlook this possibility, to their mutual (but never sensed) misfortune. Knowledge Problem B is here responsible for failure to make a move required for Pareto optimality. This Knowledge Problem B does not result in disappointed plans; it results in failure to achieve potential gains (because they remain unperceived). Because the misfortune caused by Knowledge Problem B has been unperceived, there is (unlike in the case of Knowledge Problem A) no inevitability that the problem will ever be revealed and corrected. What market participants fail to know about each other today, they may easily continue to fail to know tomorrow.

In market clearing equilibrium, of course, *both* Knowledge Problems have come to be solved (in regard to the market under consideration). It is not only the case, in market clearing equilibrium, that each attempt to buy or to sell is successfully able to be carried out. It is also the case that no possibly mutually gainful trade between a potential buyer and seller (both of whom are participants in this market) fails to be consummated. We can easily understand how it has come about, in this equilibrium, that no one has been led over-optimistically to ask any too-high price (or to offer any too-low price). We understand, that is, that any such over-optimistic errors have *corrected themselves:* disappointments have taught market participants not to expect unrealizable responses. We understand, that is, how Knowledge Problem A has been solved.

But we are not so immediately able to understand how, in market clearing equilibrium, Knowledge Problem B, as well, has come to be solved. It is not at all so obvious how the many overlooked possibilities for mutually gainful trade—possibilities which, given initial dispersed knowledge, could hardly have failed to have been overlooked—have somehow come to be revealed. What has caused market participants to know (about each other's potential attitudes) what they did not know yesterday?

Of course, economic theory explains how Knowledge Problem B has come to be solved in market equilibrium. It turns out that this solution is in fact quite different from that which has solved Knowledge Problem A. Whereas Knowledge Problem A was self-correcting, Knowledge Problem B created *an incentive for its solution by discovery in the activity of profit-alert entrepreneurs.* Where undue pessimism caused possible Pareto-optimal moves to fail to be made, the opportunity was thereby created for the possible grasping of pure entrepreneurial profit. Potential seller X, being pessimistically ignorant of potential buyer Y's willingness to pay as much as $10 for an item, failed to offer it for sale, even though he would himself have been very pleased to sell it for as low as $3. This overlooked opportunity for a mutually gainful trade between X and Y constitutes an inviting opportunity for the winning of pure entrepreneurial profit. Anyone, say entrepreneur Z, alert to this opportunity can, without any capital resources whatsoever, offer to buy from X at, say, a price of $4 (so that X, on our assumptions, will be delighted to accept), paying this price out of the gross revenue available to him through his offering to sell to Y at a price of $9 (which, again, on our assumption, Y will gladly accept). Wherever mutual ignorance, due to dispersed knowledge, causes Pareto-indicated moves not to be made, we have before us a situation inviting the alert entrepreneur to make pure profit.

Economic theory teaches us that, in this way, there is a powerful market tendency for all pure profit opportunities to be noticed and grasped. Knowledge Problem B comes to be solved through entrepreneurial discovery of hitherto overlooked opportunities.

Thus our understanding that in market clearing equilibrium *both* Knowledge Problems have been solved—ensuring that both over-optimistic and unduly pessimistic mutual errors (that might arise out of dispersed information) are *not* being made—rests on two distinct completed processes of market learning. The process whereby Knowledge Problem A is solved is a process which, without relying on entrepreneurial, profit-motivated alertness, arises from well-nigh inevitable learning of the unrealism of over-optimistic expectations. The process whereby Knowledge Problem B is solved, is a process which must rely entirely on the discovery by entrepreneurs of available opportunities of which nobody was hitherto aware.

THE TWO KNOWLEDGE PROBLEMS IN A WIDER SETTING

As Hayek came to emphasize, the Knowledge Problem is not only a problem in the context of the market. It is a problem crucially relevant to the emergence of social institutions as well. Such institutions as the law, language, the use of money, the respect for private property, require a concurrence of mutual knowledge and expectations completely analogous to the mutual knowledge required for market equilibrium. What we wish now to point out is that the problem which the phenomenon of dispersed knowledge creates for the emergence of benign social institutions is made up (exactly as the corresponding Knowledge Problem in the market context was) of two distinct problems. Let us consider the use in society of a common unit for the measure of distance. Obviously, the common use of a single scale of measurement is an important element in social intercourse. It would be most cumbersome and most obstructive to the emergence of standardized dimensions relevant to innumerable possible situations were several different measurement systems to be in use in the same society. For the emergence of a common system of measurement we require that members of the society correctly expect others to be employing that measurement system. A system using feet and inches can prevail only when, and because, each correctly expects others to use that system. More precisely it can prevail only when and because each correctly expects others to expect that system to be universally used. And so on.

Clearly such mutually sustaining expectations may be absent— resulting in and expressing the absence of a common system of measurement. What Hayek has emphasized is that the spontaneous emergence of such institutions has occurred throughout history. Members of society have learned, without central direction, to participate in social systems of language, measurement, monetary exchange—all of which have required mutually sustaining patterns of expectations. As Hayek has taught us, much of our civilization consists of such spontaneously developed systems of mutually reinforcing anticipations.

What must, for our present purpose, be stressed is that these institutions do not necessarily require that all conceivable opportunities for Pareto-superior social institutions be grasped and exploited. The common use of the system of feet and inches for measuring length does not in the slightest degree require that it be the end result achieved by grasping all conceivable opportunities for more efficient measurement. It could be that a superior system of measurement might have emerged. The fact that it did not does not deny usefulness to the system of feet and inches. That system is based on the concurrence of expectations on the part of millions of members of society. No one of them is disappointed in his expectations that others will employ this system. The usefulness of the system depends entirely and solely upon the successful solution of Knowledge Problem A (ensuring that expectations not be disappointed). It does not intrinsically depend on the solution of Knowledge Problem B. Even if some superior measurement system *could* be somehow devised and put into operation (by persuading the members of the society of its merits and its imminence), failure to do so in no way affects the viability of the measurement system that has in fact been adopted.

It is so with all of the institutions we usually cite. Use of a common language does not depend on the emergence of the simplest, clearest form of interpersonal communication. It depends only on members of society having learned to expect a single vocabulary and grammar.

Spontaneous order, in the sense of the spontaneous emergence of a set of rules, such as rules of language, behaviour or law, requires only that *some* given set of rules come to be universally expected. For the existence of none of these institutions is it inherently necessary that we go beyond the solution of Problem A, the avoidance of disappointment regarding the behaviour of others.

THE SPONTANEOUS EMERGENCE OF INSTITUTIONS

We understand, therefore, Hayek's convictions concerning the possibility of spontaneously emerging benign social institutions. Such institutions can emerge, it is clear, by the same solution of Knowledge Problem A which contributes to the spontaneous emergence of market equilibrating tendencies. People do tend to learn correctly to expect what other people will do, and the emergence of such mutually sustaining expectations may constitute the establishment of stable social institutions.

But it is equally clear that the solution of Knowledge Problem B, involving the discovery of hitherto unexamined attractive opportunities for mutual gain through interaction, is *not* needed for the emergence of any single institution. What we wish to point out in the following pages is that, except in the context of the market, we have in fact no generally operative tendency at all for Knowledge Problem B ever systematically to be solved.

If this contention of ours be accepted, we will surely have established grounds for challenging any assertion that spontaneous processes are able, in general, to generate not only stable institutions expressing mutually sustaining expectations, but also tendencies, parallel to those operating in markets to solve Knowledge Problem B, towards the replacement of socially inferior institutions by superior ones. There *may* be long-run survival-of-the-fittest type tendencies (or, for that matter, other kinds of tendencies) for societies to generate more rather than less "useful" social norms and institutions. It is our contention here that any such tendencies are entirely distinct from the tendency, within markets, for socially useful opportunities to be discovered and exploited through the solution of Knowledge Problem B.

Institutions, whether more useful to society, less useful to society, or even downright harmful to society, require only the solution to Knowledge Problem A. This solution, in the context of wider social interaction, can indeed be counted upon to be forthcoming in the same way as it is forthcoming in the market context. For this reason institutions may and do indeed emerge spontaneously, constituting classic examples of spontaneous co-ordination.

But the replacement of an inferior institution (say, a measurement system based on feet and inches) by a superior institution (say, the metric system) requires more than the solution of Knowledge Problem A: it requires also the solution of Knowledge Problem B. Our contention is that no solution of Knowledge Problem B, parallel to its solution in markets, can be counted upon, outside the market context itself. Thus a belief in the spontaneous development of better and better social institutions cannot rely on the analogy with, or uncritical extrapolation of, our insights into the processes whereby Knowledge Problem B is solved in the attainment of Pareto-optimal outcomes in market equilibrium. Our contention requires some further elaboration.

THE SOLUTION OF KNOWLEDGE PROBLEM B:
THE EXTERNALITY PROBLEM

As will be recalled, the market process includes a tendency for the solution of Knowledge Problem B resulting from the incentives provided by pure profit opportunities. Alert entrepreneurs are attracted to notice suboptimalities (constituting expressions of Knowledge Problem B) because they respond to the scent of pure profit which accompanies such suboptimalities. By grasping the profit accompanying such suboptimalities, the entrepreneur benefits the market as a whole (since he moves prices and costs closer to equality, eliminating hitherto unnoticed, unexploited opportunities for mutually gainful exchange between unalert market participants). But there was no externality. The stimulus needed to attract the entrepreneur to benefit society was provided by the prospect of pure profit for himself. Every possibility for social gain through the overcoming of Problem B implies the attraction of private gain for the alert entrepreneur who can notice the opportunity. We wish to point out that no such fortunate coincidence of private and social profit occurs in the context of the emergence of social norms and institutions.

Let us imagine a society employing a measurement system based on feet and inches. Let us postulate that use of the metric system would substantially lower transaction and other costs throughout the system. There appears no obvious way in which any private entrepreneur could be attracted to notice the superiority of the metric system—let alone any chance of it being within his power to effect its adoption. The externality of the relevant benefit to society arising from a change to the metric system appears to block the translation of this unexploited opportunity, jointly available to members of society, into concrete, privately attractive opportunities capable of alerting entrepreneurial discovery.

The metric system remains unadopted as a result of a special case of Knowledge Problem B. Individuals are not aware that use of the metric system would be an improvement. Moreover, even if some (or all) were to become so aware, they (correctly) believe others (even where they are so aware) not to be using the metric system (because *they* believe that nobody is using the system). The possibility of *all* members of society simultaneously becoming aware of the social preferability of a metric system (or, at any rate, of all members of society somehow coming correctly to expect others to expect universal use of the metric system . . .) is a possibility running head-on into conflict with the concrete-like obstacle of Knowledge Problem B. How is it possible to generate among a population who have happily been employing the common measurement system of feet and inches the realization of the imminent actual workability and superiority of the metric system, or, at least, the expectation that others will from now on use only the metric system?

Solution to Knowledge Problem B always calls for entrepreneurial imagination. The externality feature endemic to Knowledge Problem B outside the market context discourages us from having faith in any spontaneous discovery procedure that is patterned after the process of entrepreneurial discovery which drives the market process.

HAYEK, MENGER AND THE EMERGENCE OF MONEY

Hayek frequently cites Carl Menger's insight into the spontaneous emergence of socially useful institutions (Hayek 1967a: 94; 1967b: 100–1; 1955: 83; 1973: 22; 1978: 265n). It will be instructive to observe how the most famous Mengerian example of the spontaneous emergence of such a socially benign institution, namely the spontaneous emergence of a commonly accepted medium of exchange (making possible the transition from a barter economy to the far more efficient monetary economy), in fact occurs in Menger's exposition (Menger 1981: 257–62; 1985: 151–5). We shall discover that the spontaneous social process through which the evolution of a widely used money occurs is *not* one in which Knowledge Problem B is solved *analogously to its solution in market processes of equilibration*. To understand how Knowledge Problem B is overcome in the Mengerian process through which money emerges, it may be helpful to consider a similar spontaneous social process which does not involve any knowledge problem at all.

Consider the way in which a well-trodden path through the snow may be spontaneously achieved, without any deliberate, centralized plan to create it. At first, some hardy soul who has an urgent need to get to a destination makes the difficult crossing through the high snow. It is a costly journey (in terms of getting wet) but is apparently worthwhile. The precise route taken across the snow may be quite random, or it may be dictated by the pioneer's destination as viewed from the pioneer's starting point. What is important is that the first hike across the snow lowers the costs to others of crossing the snow subsequently. The snow is somewhat less intimidating where the first crossing was made. Others (who might otherwise perhaps not have crossed the snow at all, or who might have chosen some different route across the snow) now feel it worthwhile to cross exactly where the pioneer made the first crossing. Notice (a) that the reduced cost to subsequent snow crossers is an unintended consequence of the first crossing and (b) that subsequent crossings will obviously tend to follow the path taken by the pioneer. Those who do indeed cross the snow in the footsteps of the pioneer make their own unintended contributions to the spontaneous emergence of a clear path across the snow. Each crossing treads down the snow a little more, thus further reducing the costs to others of walking across the snow. In this way, the familiar, socially benign phenomenon of a new path is the unintended consequence of self-regarding behaviour.

Now the sequence of actions which led to the spontaneous creation of the path has nothing to do with the solution of any knowledge problem. It is simply the fortunate implication of the different degrees of urgency with which people need to cross the snow (and also, possibly, of the different times at which different people need to cross the snow). No creative, imaginative, entrepreneurial leap was needed—and none has occurred—for the path to be spontaneously created. The emergence of the path occurred without central planning for it to be created—not because entrepreneurs were independently inspired to produce it, but because each step in the snow unintentionally induced further steps to be taken.

We should remember, incidentally, that, just as processes may occur in which (as in the path-in-the-snow case) each step reduces costs in a way that promotes benign, spontaneously achieved results, we can easily envisage exactly opposite kinds of process. We can easily envisage, that is, processes each step of which unintentionally, *but perversely*, changes costs to others (of taking further steps). If urban concentration increases the chances of economic survival in the city compared with the surrounding villages (or at any rate if villagers believe this to be the case), then the city may spontaneously sink into congestion which becomes progressively more and more horrible and intolerable. Feuding tribes or nations may find it wise to arm themselves against possible attack; but each such step taken may enhance the danger to others, leading to a spiralling sequence of armament building, heightening the suspicions on all sides and increasing the likelihood of war. Such tragic processes are well known and well understood (if not easily controlled). Our point is that, whether benign or otherwise, these spontaneous processes proceed as they do because each step taken systematically renders it more rational for other similar steps to be taken by others. This results in the familiar snowballing effect. Menger's process of the spontaneous emergence of money proceeds in exactly this fashion.

What drives the dynamic Mengerian process through which money evolves is the gradually increasing liquidity of some particular commodity that has come to be used, not yet as money, but as a means for indirect exchange between resourceful, bartering market participants. Starting from a barter economy, alert market participants find they can improve their chances of trading what they initially possess for what they would prefer to possess if they trade the former for something which they themselves do *not* wish to acquire for final consumption use, but which they believe *is* likely to be sought after by those who possess the items which these alert market participants *do* wish to acquire. As this occurs, the "liquidity" of this item (which they acquire even though they have no wish to consume it themselves) increases. That is, the very circumstance that *these* alert market participants are buying this item increases now the chance that *other* market participants will find that initial acquisition of this item increases *their* chances of finally obtaining the items *they* wish finally to consume. The dynamics of this process of increasing liquidity becoming attached to certain items can lead to the emergence of a degree of liquidity so complete as, in effect, to render an item no longer an ordinary commodity but rather a generally accepted medium of exchange. Let us consider carefully the sense in which Menger's process (unlike our path-in-the-snow example) does involve the solution of a knowledge problem. We shall then more carefully appreciate how Menger's process, while it very certainly does solve Knowledge Problem B, does so in a way quite different from the market process solution to Knowledge Problem B.

In an initial barter society, the inconveniences attributable to the absence of a generally accepted medium of exchange can be seen as caused by Knowledge Problem B. (Knowledge Problem A, in which participants in society entertain false expectations about what others will do, is not a problem here. Everyone correctly expects others to engage only in barter transactions. No one mistakenly expects to be able to receive "money" in exchange for offered commodities.) What is preventing use of a monetary medium is the failure of market participants to know, not what in fact others *are* doing, but what others *might* be very willing to do (if they, in turn, knew that others would act similarly). Because the transition from a barter economy to a monetary economy involves grasping a new, universally gainful opportunity which has not yet been perceived, barter remains the prevailing mode. Even were I to understand the superior efficiency of moving to, say, a silver monetary standard, I will not try to sell anything for silver because silver is not now money (i.e. I do not expect others so to accept silver). Where in fact others, like me, do understand the advantages of moving from barter to a silver monetary standard, I am correct in my judgement that silver is not money only because each one of us (who does understand the virtues of silver money) fails to know what *might* be acceptable to others. Surely if I knew that others knew that I knew their appreciation of the virtues of silver money, et cetera *ad infinitum,* silver *would* now be accepted by all as money. Thus the knowledge problem obstructing the transition to widespread use of a silver money is Knowledge Problem B.

The transition from a barter society to a monetary economy, outlined in the Mengerian process, has thus certainly involved the spontaneous overcoming of Knowledge Problem B. After the transition, market participants have learned to behave in new ways which benefit them all. But these lessons have been learned in a manner that does not parallel the entrepreneurial processes which tend to overcome Knowledge Problem B in the market context. In the market context Knowledge Problem B manifests itself in market errors which reveal themselves as opportunities for entrepreneurial profit making. In the Mengerian context this was not the case. (The alertness which market participants display in the course of the Mengerian process regarding the steadily increasing liquidity of the commodity in question is never alertness to prospects of *further* increasing that liquidity; what is involved is strictly alertness to the personal efficiencies to be achieved by taking advantage of that commodity's *already increased* liquidity.) No entrepreneur could, by himself, discover opportunities for pure profit by attempting to move the barter society towards the use of money. None the less a spontaneous process which did move the society in that direction occurred in Menger's story. Our point is that it occurred in the same non-entrepreneurial fashion that marks the creation of paths in the snow.

CONCLUSION

What stimulates solutions to Knowledge Problem B in markets is the circumstance that in the market context this problem consists in unexploited opportunities for mutually gainful exchange. Such opportunities offer opportunities for private entrepreneurial gain to their discoverers. This sets in motion the familiar entrepreneurial process tending to bring separated markets into full contact with each other, eliminating price discrepancies (and opportunities for further profit).

But in the broader societal context the manner in which Knowledge Problem B stands in the way of the emergence of feasible, cost-efficient, social institutions is not such as to offer opportunities for private gain to its discoverers. There is thus no systematic discovery procedure upon which we can rely for the spontaneous emergence of superior institutional norms.

This circumstance does not prevent genuinely spontaneous processes of institutional development from occurring. Paths in the snow happen. But it does mean that we cannot use, as copybook example for such spontaneous processes, *the manner in which markets systematically tend to solve Knowledge Problem B.* To be sure, the spontaneous emergence of *any* institution indeed relies on the very same processes through which Knowledge Problem A is solved in markets. Hayek is on firm ground in seeing his insights into the market qua discovery procedure as providing the foundation for his own later work on the spontaneous emergence of cultural norms and institutions and its link with the phenomenon of division of knowledge.

On the other hand, however, it has been our aim to point out in this chapter that these earlier economic insights into the spontaneously co-ordinative properties of markets do not, in themselves, provide any reassurance concerning the benign quality of the long-run tendencies of institutional development. Such benign tendencies may well be powerful and important in some or many instances; but the spontaneous co-ordination which occurs in markets provides us with no basis for any extension of the welfare theorems relating to markets to the broader field of the theory of institutional evolution. The explanation for such benign tendencies, if indeed they exist, must be sought elsewhere.

NOTES

1. In a footnote to this passage (p. 148, fn.10) Hayek cites his 1945 paper in this regard.

2. See also Gray (1982).

3. Buchanan (1986). See also Buchanan (1977) and Kirzner (1987).

4. See Kirzner (1963: Ch. 7) for an extensive discussion of the differences between these two problems, and the character of the distinct market processes of equilibration which they respectively set in motion.

5. See Hayek (1949b: 53). I am indebted to Mario Rizzo for drawing my attention to the importance of this passage.

REFERENCES

Buchanan, J. M. (1977) "Law and the invisible hand," in *Freedom in Constitutional Contract*, College Station, Tex.: Texas A&M University Press.

Buchanan, J. M. (1986) "Cultural evolution and institutional reform," in *Liberty, Market and State*, New York: New York University Press.

Gray, J. (1982) "F. A. Hayek and the rebirth of classical liberalism," *Literature of Liberty* 5 (4): 56–9.

Hayek, F. A. (1949a) "The use of knowledge in society," in *Individualism and Economic Order*, London: Routledge & Kegan Paul (originally published in *American Economic Review* 35, no. 4 (1945): 519–30).

Hayek, F. A. (1949b) "Economics and knowledge," in *Individualism and Economic Order*, London: Routledge & Kegan Paul (originally published in *Economica* 4, February 1937).

Hayek, F. A. (1955) *The Counter-Revolution of Science. Studies on the Abuse of Reason*, Glencoe, Ill.: Free Press.

Hayek, F. A. (1960) *The Constitution of Liberty*, Chicago, Ill.: University of Chicago Press.

Hayek, F. A. (1967a) "Kinds of rationalism," in *Studies in Philosophy, Politics and Economics*, Chicago, Ill.: University of Chicago Press.

Hayek, F. A. (1967b) "The results of human action but not of human design," in *Studies in Philosophy, Politics and Economics*, Chicago, Ill.: University of Chicago Press.

Hayek, F. A. (1973) *Law, Legislation and Liberty*, Vol. 1, *Rules and Order*, Chicago, Ill.: University of Chicago Press.

Hayek, F. A. (1978) "Dr Bernard Mandeville," in *New Studies in Philosophy, Politics, Economics and the History of Ideas*, Chicago, Ill.: University of Chicago Press.

Hayek, F. A. (1979) *Law, Legislation and Liberty*, Vol. 3, *The Political Order of a Free People*, Chicago, Ill.: University of Chicago Press.

Kirzner, I. M. (1963) *Market Theory and the Price System*, Princeton, N.J.: Van Nostrand.

Kirzner, I. M. (1987) "Spontaneous order and the case for the free market," *Ideas on Liberty: Essays in Honor of Paul L. Poirot,* Irvington-on-Hudson, N.Y.: Foundation for Economic Education.

Lavoie, D. (1985) *National Planning: What is Left?* Cambridge, Mass.: Ballinger.

Menger, C. (1981) *Principles of Economics,* New York: New York University Press (originally published as *Grundsätze der Volkswirtschaftslehre,* Wien: Wilhelm Braumüller, 1871: translated and edited by J. Dingwall and B. F. Hoselitz, Glencoe, Ill.: Free Press, 1950).

Menger, C. (1985) *Investigations into the Method of the Social Sciences with Special Reference to Economics,* transl. F. J. Nock, New York: New York University Press (originally published as *Untersuchungen über der Methode der Socialwissenschaften und der Politischen Oekonomie insbesondere,* Leipzig: Duncker and Humblot, 1883; translation first published as *Problems of Economics and Sociology,* Urbana, Ill.: University of Illinois, 1963).

THE ECONOMIC CALCULATION DEBATE:
LESSONS FOR AUSTRIANS

The thesis of this chapter is that the celebrated debate over economic calculation under socialism that raged during the inter-war period was important for the history of economic thought in a sense not generally appreciated. Not only was the debate an important episode, of course, for its own sake. It was, in addition, I shall claim, important as a catalyst in the development and articulation of the modern Austrian view of the market as a competitive-entrepreneurial process of discovery. Professor Karen Vaughn has written of her conviction that "the most interesting results of the controversy . . . were the further developments of economic theory to which it gave rise" (1976: 107). It will be my contention here that the crystallization of the modern Austrian understanding of the market must be counted among the most significant of these "further developments of economic theory." I shall argue that it was through the give-and-take of this debate that the Austrians gradually refined their understanding of their own position; the Mises-Hayek position at the end of the 1940s was articulated in terms far different from those presented in the Misesian statements of the early 1920s. Moreover, this more advanced Mises-Hayek position pointed beyond itself towards (and decisively helped generate) the more explicit Austrian statements of the 1970s and 1980s.

Now it may at first glance appear that my thesis contradicts the view of the most eminent historian of the calculation debate. Don Lavoie (1985), in his definitive account of the debate, has exhaustively explored the debate as what we have referred to as "an important episode for its own sake." His position with regard to the debate emphasizes two related points. First, Lavoie emphatically denies that, as a result of the thrust and parry of the debate, the Austrian side found it necessary "to retreat" from or otherwise modify its originally stated case challenging the feasibility of economic calculation under socialism. For Lavoie, the later statements of

From *The Meaning of Market Process: Essays in the Development of Modern Austrian Economics* (New York and London: Routledge, 1992), 100–118. Reprinted by permission of Springer-Verlag; the original source is *Review of Austrian Economics* 2 (1988).

Mises and Hayek do no more than restate—in better, clearer, fashion— the originally presented arguments. Second, Lavoie has demonstrated with admirable clarity and thoroughness that the Mises-Hayek arguments, from the very beginning, reflected the Austrian understanding of the market as a competitive discovery process. (He furthermore has shown that it was failure by the socialist economists to recognize this that led to confusion during the debate itself, while it was failure by later historians of the debate to recognize this that led to the widespread misinterpretations of the debate by post–Second World War writers.) Thus it may appear that my contention that the debate was itself responsible for the distillation of that Austrian understanding runs sharply counter to both these elements in Lavoie's thesis. It will perhaps be helpful to explain briefly why, in my view, there is no contradiction here.[1] In fact, such a brief explanation permits me usefully to introduce further the central ideas to be offered in this chapter.

THE ARTICULATION OF THE DISCOVERY-PROCESS VIEW

Professor Lavoie is entirely correct, I believe, in interpreting the original 1920 argument by Mises as reflecting the characteristically Austrian understanding of the market as an entrepreneurial process.[2] And, as Lavoie shows, once this is recognized, there is no reason whatever to read the later statements by Mises and Hayek as "retreating" from the original argument. My position, however, is that neither Mises nor (in his earlier papers on the topic) Hayek was aware of how sharply their Austrian view of the market differed from that implicit in the views of other contemporary schools of thought. Accordingly, the earlier statements of the Austrian position failed to articulate sufficiently clearly the "process" perspective that Lavoie (correctly) perceives as underlying those statements.

The truth is that, among most economists (Austrian, Marshallian or Walrasian) in the early twentieth century, there was a superficial, shared understanding of markets that submerged important distinctions that would become apparent only much later. In this shared understanding, there coexisted elements of appreciation for dynamic market processes and elements of appreciation for the degree of balance—the degree of equilibrium—held to be achieved by markets. To be sure, the Mengerian background of the Austrian version of this common understanding pointed unquestionably to the predominance of the process view, while the Walrasian version of this common understanding pointed consistently towards a strictly equilibrium view, but these conflicting signposts were simply not seen at the time. Mises's earlier statements, while they indeed adumbrated the process elements central to the Austrian tradition, did not emphasize these elements (and, as Lavoie suggests, a case can be made that for his immediate purposes in 1920 it was not at all necessary for Mises to emphasize these elements) so that when economists such as Lange came to consider the Misesian challenge from their own equilibrium perspective, they failed to recognize how seriously they were misunderstanding that challenge.

What occurred as a result of the vigorous inter-war debate was that the Austrians were inspired, not to retreat, but to identify more carefully the aspects of their understanding of market processes that their critics had failed to recognize. This process of increasingly precise articulation was not merely one of improved communication; it was a process of improved self-understanding. It is upon this process of improved self-understanding that I wish to focus in this chapter. While my own principal concern here is with the gradually developing articulation of the modern Austrian position, we should recognize at the same time that the debate was contemporaneous with a parallel process of the development of a more consistently articulated Walrasian neoclassical position. While it would probably be an exaggeration to see the calculation debate as significantly responsible for the development of a more explicit neoclassical perspective, it seems quite plausible to see the Lange-Lerner position in the calculation debate as at least a significant episode in that development.

What occurred, then, in the quarter century following Mises's original paper on socialist calculation is that a single, blurred picture of the market, common to most economists, came to be resolved into its two separate, distinct and well-focused components. The one component came to be perceived as the completely static general equilibrium market model; the second component came to be perceived as the dynamic process of entrepreneurial discovery. It was in the course of the debate that it gradually became apparent to the Austrians—but not to their opponents in the debate—that their position represented a critique of socialism only because and to the extent that markets under capitalism indeed constitute such a dynamic process of entrepreneurial discovery. Lavoie has himself put the matter as follows: "I have concluded that the Austrian economists have learned much by 'living through' the calculation debate.

Because they have had to cope with criticisms in past debates, they now have much better, clearer ways of putting their arguments" (1985: 26f). My contention is that what the Austrians learned was more than a technique of exposition; they learned to appreciate more sensitively how their own tradition understood the market process.

We can distinguish several distinct (but, of course, related) lines of development that occurred during this gradually improved articulation of the Austrian position. First, there was development in the positive understanding of the market process. Second, there was development in understanding the "welfare" aspects of the market process (in particular, in understanding the social function of economic systems or the nature of the "economic problem" facing society). Third, there was development in understanding the role of prices in grappling with this now better understood "economic problem" facing society. I shall be discussing each of these lines of development in this chapter. (There were, of course, parallel developments in neoclassical economics with regard to the positive understanding of markets in equilibrium, with regard to appreciation for the welfare properties of general equilibrium and with regard to the role of equilibrium prices in promoting complete dovetailing of decentralized decisions.)

SIMULTANEOUS LEVELS OF ECONOMIC UNDERSTANDING

My story of the developing articulation of the modern Austrian perspective is complicated, especially with regard to the calculation debate, by the circumstance that from that perspective there appear to be *three* distinct levels of economic understanding with regard to the price system. It may be useful for me to spell these out at this point. They are, respectively, (1) the recognition of scarcity, (2) the recognition of the role of information and (3) the recognition of the role of discovery.

1. The foundation of economic understanding consists, of course, in the recognition of scarcity and of its implications. At the individual level, the recognition of scarcity informs individual allocative, economizing activity. In society, the phenomenon of scarcity implies the social benefits that arise from a price system that translates the relative scarcities of particular resources or products into a price structure that encourages correspondingly effective "economic" utilization of these scarce resources by potential users, whether producers or consumers.

2. A deeper appreciation for the social usefulness of a market price system stems from the insight that prices may be efficient means of communicating information from one part of the economy to another. Where prices do in fact fully reflect the bids and offers made by market participants throughout the market, such prices afford a highly effective system of signals that obviate the need for the transmission of detailed, factual information to decision makers. If the source of supply of an important raw material has suddenly been destroyed, the jump in its market price will effectively convey the impact of this disaster to potential users, with great rapidity. Those who have themselves learned of the disaster do not have to inform potential users that it has occurred, the price rise suffices.

3. Finally, and building upon these two previous levels of economic understanding, the modern Austrian perspective decisively draws attention to the manner in which the price system promotes alertness to and the discovery of as yet unknown information (both in regard to existing opportunities for potential gains from trade with existing techniques and in regard to possibilities for innovative processes of production).

The complications introduced by Austrian recognition of the simultaneous relevance of all these levels of economic understanding should be fairly obvious. From the vantage point of today's explicit modern Austrian position, it is clear that full appreciation of the social benefits provided by the price system involves all three of these levels of understanding. That is, while an understanding of the social *consequences* of scarcity need not involve an understanding of the subtleties of information and discovery, Austrian recognition of the way in which the market price system effectively *grapples* with the scarcity confronting society depends very much upon the recognition of the function that prices play in communicating existing information, and of the function that prices play in alerting market participants to hitherto unglimpsed opportunities. On the other hand, however, neoclassical economics, which certainly recognizes the role of the price system in contending with scarcity, is likely to refer to this role without any recognition of the discovery process of the market (and, until recently, without recognition of the role of the market in communicating information). Because the earlier Austrian statements in the calculation debate did not distinguish between the various levels of economic understanding, and did not emphasize the discovery process upon which their own understanding of the market depended, it was quite easy (for the Austrians themselves as well as for onlookers) to believe that the Austrian critique of socialist calculation indeed proceeded from an understanding of how markets work that was shared by their neoclassical opponents. This was particularly the case because Mises found himself, in the earlier stages of the debate, contending with proponents of socialism who seem not at all to have understood the social problems raised by the phenomenon of scarcity, at the most fundamental level.

It was only after more competent economists—who *did* understand the economic problem created by scarcity—came to argue that Mises's reasoning failed to establish his case that the Austrians were compelled to articulate more carefully the basis of their understanding of the market process (and, hence, their contention that the socialized economy is unable to provide any counterpart to that process). Thus, Mises refers specifically to H. D. Dickinson and Oskar Lange as two socialist writers on the calculation problem who did appreciate the economic problems involved (1966: 702n.).

It is against the background of these complications that I now turn to consider, in somewhat greater detail and in more systematic fashion, the developing self-awareness on the part of the Austrians that came to be induced by the various stages of the economic calculation debate. As I have suggested, I shall pay separate attention to developments (a) in the positive understanding of how markets work, (b) in understanding the welfare and normative aspects of the economic problem facing society and (c) in understanding the role of prices in helping to deal with that economic problem.

THE MARKET AS A PROCESS OF DISCOVERY

With the benefit of hindsight, we now understand that, in the Austrian view of the market, its most important feature is (and was) the dynamic entrepreneurial-competitive discovery process. We know now that, for Mises, the idea of a price that does not reflect and express entrepreneurial judgement and hunch is virtually a contradiction in terms. (It is for this reason that Mises rejected Lange's contention that socialist managers may be able to take their bearings from—and to calculate on the basis of—centrally promulgated non-market prices.) We know now that for Mises the description of states of market equilibrium is mere byplay (1966: 251)—the description of something that will never in fact occur and that provides us with little of direct relevance to real world conditions (conditions that at all times display the characteristics of markets in disequilibrium). We know now that for Mises competition is an entrepreneurial process, not a state of affairs (1966: 278f.). We know these matters because they have formed a central theme in Misesian economics since the publication of *Nationalökonomie* in 1940. And we have every reason to agree with Lavoie and others that these insights were, at least implicitly, an integral element in the Austrian heritage from before the First World War. (Surely it is for this reason that Schumpeter's views on competition are so similar to those of Mises and Hayek.)

But, despite all this, it must be acknowledged, after a careful study of Mises's 1920 paper, that a first reading of that paper might easily lead to a quite different conclusion. It might easily be concluded from a reading of that paper (and of the corresponding passages in Mises's 1922 original German edition of *Socialism*) that the central feature in Mises's appreciation for markets was their continual ability to generate prices that, to a reasonable extent, approximated their equilibrium values. In his discussion of how market values of commodities enter into economic calculation, it does not seem important to Mises to point out that such market values may be seriously misleading (1920: 97ff.). He does at several points emphasize that "monetary calculation has its limits," its "inconveniences and serious defects" (pp. 98, 109), but the weaknesses that Mises identifies seem to consist almost exclusively in the inability of money prices to capture the significance of non-pecuniary costs and benefits and in the measurement problems arising out of the fluctuations in the value of money. He does not draw attention to the possibility that disequilibrium money prices may inspire market participants to make responses that are mutually inconsistent (e.g. an above-equilibrium price may inspire producers to offer goods that buyers will not buy at that price) or that cause them to overlook opportunities for mutually gainful trade (e.g. where a commodity is being sold at different prices in different parts of the same market). It might easily appear to the superficial reader that Mises was satisfied that market prices are (subject to the limitations to which he refers) reasonably accurate expressions of relative social importance; and that it is this that constitutes the achievement of markets that could not be duplicated under socialism. Under "the economic system of private ownership of the means of production," Mises asserts, "all goods of a higher order receive a position in the scale of valuations in accordance with the immediate state of social conditions of production and of social needs" (1920: 107).

It is true that Mises already in his 1920 paper drew attention to the special problems generated by *changes* in the basic data, with respect to which economic calculation is called for. Thus, it might be argued that for Mises in 1920, a central achievement of the market is its ability to inspire entrepreneurial alertness to such changes, so that, perhaps, his appreciation for the market did, after all, recognize it as "discovery procedure." But it seems difficult to make this claim. Certainly, we can feel confident that Mises in 1920 would have accepted the insight that markets inspire entrepreneurial discovery; but he did not, in his 1920 paper, refer to the problems raised by changing data in a way that presented markets as being essentially on-going processes of discovery. His references to change were merely in order to point out that, although a newly socialized economy might well usefully take its bearings from the patterns of production that had characterized the previously prevailing market economy, changes in underlying conditions and goals would rapidly render those patterns obsolete and inefficient (1920: 109). These brief references by Mises would not prevent a reader from concluding that Mises believed that markets are continuously close to equilibrium, even in the face of changing data. This failure to draw attention to the market as a process of discovery seems to exist in all of Mises's writings published before *Nationalökonomie*.

But in his 1940 *Nationalökonomie* (later to be translated and revised to become *Human Action*), Mises emphasized the importance of seeing the market as an entrepreneurial process with unsurpassable clarity. By that year, Hayek, too, had drawn explicit attention to the problems of equilibration that are somehow, to some degree, apparently successfully overcome in the course of market processes (1949b). Moreover, by 1940, Hayek, like Mises, was pointing out that some of those who were arguing in the 1930s for the possibility of socialism based on centrally promulgated non-market prices were guilty of "excessive preoccupation with problems of the pure theory of stationary equilibrium" and failed to understand how real world markets are likely to have the advantage in regard to the rapidity of "adjustment to the daily changing conditions in different places and different industries" (1949c: 188).

There seems to be little doubt that what led Mises and Hayek to emphasize these dynamic aspects of markets at the close of the 1930s was the position taken up by their opponents such as Lange, Lerner and Dickinson in the calculation debate. Where Mises's original statements were directed at those who were completely innocent even of the most fundamental level of economic understanding (involving at least an appreciation for the implications of scarcity), his challenge had now been picked up by competent economists—but economists whose understanding of the market was limited by "preoccupation with equilibrium theory." It was in restating their case in the face of the arguments of these economists that the Austrians were led to make explicit some of the "process" elements in their understanding of markets which they had hitherto not been impelled to emphasize.

This developing process of greater self-awareness among the Austrians continued during the 1940s. Mises's contribution in this period consisted of his revision and translation of *Nationalökonomie* into *Human Action*. It was the latter statement of his vision of the market process that was to have the most far-reaching influence on the further development of the Austrian view. It was this magisterial work that presented a dynamic interpretation of the market process in a manner so emphatic and clear as to render it henceforth impossible to overlook the profound differences between the Austrian and the mainstream neoclassical perspectives.

But it was Hayek who, in two celebrated papers during the 1940s, articulated certain key elements in the Austrian view in an exceptionally lucid and seminal fashion. In the first of these papers, "The use of knowledge in society" (1949a), Hayek drew attention to the role of the market in communicating information. In doing so, he explicitly linked his discussion with the socialist calculation debate. (I shall return later to further consideration of the part this paper has played in the crystallization of the modern Austrian position.) In the second of these two papers, "The meaning of competition" (1949d), Hayek was able to enunciate with great clarity the Austrian understanding of what competition really means and how the contemporary mainstream developments in treating competition in terms of the perfectly competitive state of affairs must be deplored as obscuring understanding of how markets work.

To treat competition exclusively as the perfectly competitive state of affairs, Hayek pointed out, is to confine attention exclusively to states of complete adjustment, to states of equilibrium. But to do this is already *to assume* "the situation to exist which a true explanation ought to account for as the effect of the competitive process" (1949d: 94). In other words, Hayek was in this second paper *attributing to dynamic competition the central role in providing a true explanation of how markets generate tendencies towards mutual adjustment of decentralized decisions.*

There seems no doubt that Hayek was led to these insights concerning the severe limitations surrounding the usefulness of the notion of perfect competition by his experience with the proposals of the proponents of "competitive socialism" during the 1930s. It became very clear that the illusion of transplanting competition to the environment of the socialized economy could have made its appearance only as a result of the mistaken belief that the role of competition in markets is best portrayed by the model of perfectly competitive equilibrium. Indeed, there are rather clear signs that Hayek's insights concerning the competitive processes were developed as a result of the calculation debate. Thus, in his 1940 essay, "Socialist calculation III: the competitive 'solution,'" Hayek pointed out that preoccupation with equilibrium analysis had led the socialist economists to misunderstand the role of competition. Apparently, Hayek wrote, "the concept of perfect competition . . . has made them overlook a very important field to which their method appears to be simply inapplicable." This important field includes much "machinery, most buildings and ships, and many parts of other products [that] are hardly ever produced for a market, but only on a special contract. This does not mean that there may not be intense competition in the market for the products of these industries, although it may not be 'perfect competition' in the sense of pure theory" (1949c: 188f.). This passage is not as explicit in its understanding of the problems of the perfectly competitive model as Hayek's 1946 paper, but it is clearly pointing towards the latter paper—and it has clearly been motivated by the effort to dispel the misunderstandings of the proponents of "competitive socialism." And from the "Meaning of competition" (1949d) to "Competition as a discovery procedure" (1968) was but a small step for Hayek (1978: ch. 12). Thus, the linkage between the unfolding of the calculation debate and Hayek's most advanced statement concerning the market as a process of discovery seems not merely eminently plausible, but quite unmistakable.

THE UNFOLDING OF THE DISCOVERY VIEW

What seems to have been the case is something like the following. The earlier Austrians were simply not aware of their own implicit acceptance of a process view, rather than an equilibrium view, of markets. One is not always aware that one is speaking prose or, perhaps more to the point, one is not always aware that one is breathing. If Jaffé found it necessary to "dehomogenize" the economics of the Walrasian, Jevonsian and Austrian schools (Jaffé 1976), this was not merely because outside observers failed to recognize the important distinctions that separated their respective views, but also because leading protagonists of these schools failed to do so as well. Consider the following statement—one is tempted to describe it as an astonishing statement—made by Mises in 1932:

> Within modern subjectivist economics it has become customary to distinguish several schools. We usually speak of the Austrian and the Anglo-American Schools and the School of Lausanne. . . . [The fact is] that these three schools of thought differ only in their mode of expressing the same fundamental idea and that they are divided more by their terminology and by peculiarities of presentation than by the substance of their teachings.
>
> (Mises 1960: 214)

Clearly, the major opponents of Austrian economic theory, in 1932, were perceived by Mises not as being the followers of Walras or of Marshall but as being the historical and institutionalist writers (as well as a sprinkling of economic theorists) who rejected marginal utility theory. Mises lists these opponents as including Cassel, Conrad, Diehl, Dietzel, Gottl, Liefmann, Oppenheimer, Spann and Veblen (Mises 1960: 215). Against the views of these writers, Mises saw the three major schools of economics united in their support of the subjectivist theory of value, which for Mises was synonymous with "the theory of the market" (p. 207). Differences between an emphasis on process, as against an emphasis on equilibrium, were simply not seen.

Between 1932 and 1940, however, the eyes of Mises and Hayek were, at least partially, opened. The work of the socialist economists, particularly Durbin, Dickinson, Lange and Lerner, was based on an understanding of how the market system works, which revealed and expressed the perceived primacy of equilibrium in the workings of that system. In confronting the arguments of these writers, based on this understanding that a parallel non-market price system can be devised for the socialist economy, Mises and Hayek felt called upon to draw attention to the primacy of the entrepreneurial-competitive process that they themselves associated with the market system.

Certainly, the mathematicization of mainstream microeconomics that was occurring (as Walrasian ideas became merged with the Marshallian tradition) during this period helped crystallize the equilibrium emphasis that came to characterize mainstream theory. What helped crystallize the process emphasis of the Austrians was the dramatic use made by the socialist economists of mainstream price theory, to refute the Misesian challenge—a challenge that Mises had believed to be based solidly on that very mainstream theory of price. It was this confrontation, one now sees, that provided much of the impetus for Mises's repeated attacks, in later years, against the misuse of mathematics in economics, the misuse of equilibrium analysis and the misunderstandings embodied in mainstream treatments of competition and monopoly.

It would be a mistake to suppose that the crystallization of the Austrian process view was completed by the early 1940s. In the writings of neither Mises nor Hayek were the differences between their own approach and that of the neoclassical mainstream clearly stated. I can attest to the difficulties that the graduate student studying under Mises in the mid-1950s had in achieving a clear understanding of precisely what separated the two approaches. It was extremely tempting at that time to set down the Mises-Hayek approach as simply old-fashioned, imprecise and non-rigorous. In helping the student appreciate the foundations of the Austrian approach, Hayek's papers cited in the preceding section were especially helpful. But the gradually achieved clarification of the Austrian process approach—a clarification still not completed—can be traced back unerringly to those first reactions by Mises and Hayek to the contentions of the brilliant socialist writers of the 1930s.

THE DEVELOPMENT OF AUSTRIAN WELFARE ECONOMICS

With the benefit of hindsight, it is possible to recognize that for Austrians a normative evaluation of the achievements of the market (or of alternative economic systems) must apply criteria for judgement that differ substantially from those that are encountered in mainstream welfare economics.

Now, of course, it was during the course of the inter-war debate on social-ist economic calculation that modern mainstream economics developed those major features that have characterized it since the Second World War. And it is difficult to avoid the conclusion that the developments in mainstream welfare economics owe much to clarifications attained dur-ing the course of the debate. This was probably most especially the case with A. P. Lerner, but appears to be true of welfare economics in general (see also Hutchison 1953: ch. 18; Little 1957: ch. 14). What I wish to argue in the present section of this chapter is that in the case of the Austrian approach to normative economics, too, it was the debate on socialist calcu-lation that triggered the process of clarification and articulation.

From the vantage point of the 1980s, it is clear that for Austrians none of the several notions that economists over the past two centu-ries have had in mind in evaluating the economic "goodness" of poli-cies or of institutional arrangements can be accepted. Classical ideas that revolved around the concept of maximum aggregative (objective) wealth are clearly unacceptable from the subjectivist perspective. Neoclassical attempts (by Marshall and Pigou) to replace the criterion of aggregative wealth by that of aggregate utility came to grief, for Austrians, in the light of the problems of interpersonal utility comparisons. Modern concepts of social efficiency in resource allocation that seek to avoid interpersonal comparisons of utility, based on notions of Paretian social optimality, are now seen as not being very helpful after all. Not only does the concept of the allocation of social resources imply a notion of social choice that is uncongenial, to put it mildly, to Austrian methodological individualism,[3] it turns out that the concept offers a criterion appropriate almost exclu-sively to the evaluation of *situations* (rather than processes). Following on Hayek's path-breaking (and now generally celebrated) papers on the role of markets in mobilizing dispersed knowledge, modern Austrians have converged on the notion of *co-ordination* as the key to normative discus-sion (Kirzner 1973: ch. 6; O'Driscoll 1977). As we shall see, this notion fits naturally into the Austrian understanding of the market process. Let us see how this modern Austrian idea developed, in large measure, as a con-sequence of the economic calculation debate.

In Mises's 1920 statement (pp. 97f.) and its almost verbatim repeti-tion in his 1922 book (Mises 1936: 115), Mises was very brief in his assess-ment of the economic function of market prices. Economic calculation carried on in terms of market prices expressed in money, he stated, involves three advantages. First, "we are able to take as the basis of cal- culation the valuation of all individuals participating in trade." This per- mits comparisons across individuals where direct interpersonal utility comparisons are out of the question. Second, such calculations "enable those who desire to calculate the cost of complicated processes of pro- duction to see at once whether they are working as economically as oth- ers." Inability to produce at a profit proves that others are able to put the relevant inputs to better use. Third, the use of money prices enables values to be reduced to a common unit. The statement of these advan- tages refers, it is conceded, to economic calculation as such, rather than to the broader issue of the social advantages of the price system. None the less, they seem to express a view of social "economy" that does not differ from a perspective of social allocation of scarce resources. And the same seems to have been the case with Hayek at least as late as 1935. He defined "the economic problem" as being the "distribution of available resources between different uses" and pointed out that this is "no less a problem of society than for the individual" (1949e: 121). Here, we have a clear idea of the textbook extension of Robbins's famous criterion of economizing activity from the level of the individual to that of society as a whole. What is important for my purposes is that both Mises and Hayek were judging the usefulness of the price system in terms that treat society as if it were compelled to choose between alternative pat- terns of use for given scarce resources.

Yet as early as 1937 Hayek was already beginning to draw attention to the economic problem raised by dispersed knowledge. He asserted that the "central question of all social sciences [is]: How can the combina- tion of fragments of knowledge existing in different minds bring about results which, if they were to be brought about deliberately, would require a knowledge on the part of the directing mind which no single person can possess?" (1949b: 54). In 1940, Hayek applied this insight to criti- cize the socialist economists in the calculation debate. The "main merit of real competition [is] that through it use is made of knowledge divided between persons which, if it were to be used in a centrally directed econ- omy, would all have to enter the single plan" (1949c: 202). But it was in 1945 that Hayek emphatically denied what he had himself apparently pre- viously accepted—that the economic problem facing society was that of achieving the solution to an optimum problem, that of achieving the best use of society's available means:

The economic problem of society is thus not merely a problem of how to allocate "given" resources—if "given" is taken to mean given to a single mind which deliberately solves the problem set by these "data." It is rather a problem of how to secure the best use of resources known to any of the members of society, for ends whose relative importance only these individuals know. Or, to put it briefly, it is a problem of the utilization of knowledge which is not given to anyone in its totality.

(Hayek 1949a: 77f.)

Moreover, Hayek was explicit in linking the economic calculation debate with this rejection of the idea that the economic problem facing society was the simple optimization problem. A year later, Hayek again referred to his new normative criterion in the course of his criticism of perfect competition theory. Referring to the assumption, central to that theory, of complete knowledge of all relevant information on the part of all market participants, Hayek comments that "nothing is solved when we assume everybody to know everything and . . . the real problem is rather how it can be brought about that as much of the available knowledge as possible is used" (1949d: 95).

Here then we have the strong assertion to the effect that standard approaches to welfare analysis are assuming away the essential normative problem. There can be little question that this assertion has revolutionary potential for welfare analysis. Although these implications for welfare analysis have been all but ignored by the economics profession (despite a fair degree of understanding of Hayek's related interpretation of the price system as a network of information communication), the truth is that Hayek opened the door to an entirely new perspective on the "goodness" of economic policies and institutional arrangements. Instead of judging policies or institutional arrangements in terms of the resource allocation pattern they are expected to produce (in comparison with the hypothetically optimal allocation pattern), we can now understand the possibility of judging them in terms of their ability to promote discovery. This innovative insight, whose importance seems difficult to exaggerate, was very clearly a direct by-product of the calculation debate.

As we found in regard to the positive recognition of the market as constituting a discovery process, progress in regard to the normative aspects of discovery has not ceased since the mid-1940s. It has been pointed out that emphasis on fragmented knowledge is not quite enough to dislodge mainstream welfare concepts. "Co-ordination" (in the sense of a *state* of co-ordination), while it may refer to co-ordination of decentralized decisions made in the light of dispersed knowledge, still turns out to involve standard Paretian norms. It is only "co-ordination" in the sense of the process of co-ordinat*ing* hitherto *un*co-ordinated activity that draws attention to the discovery norm identified through Hayek's insights (see chapters 8 and 9). Hayek has himself deepened our understanding of the problem of dispersed knowledge as going far beyond that of "utilizing information about particular concrete facts which individuals already possess." He now emphasizes the problem of using the abilities that individuals possess *to discover* relevant concrete information. Because a person "will discover what he knows or can find out only when faced with a problem where this will help," he may never be able to "pass on all the knowledge he commands" (1979: 190). All this focuses attention on the more general normative criterion of encouraging the *elimination of true error* in the individual decentralized decisions impinging on the uses made of society's resources. Clearly, this criterion is preeminently relevant to appreciation for the character of market *processes* (in which entrepreneurship and competition spur continual discoveries). Once again, therefore, we see how the socialist calculation debate was responsible for a very fruitful line of development that relates to modern Austrian economics.

THE FUNCTION OF PRICES

As Don Lavoie's history of the debate demonstrates, modern Austrian economics is able to comprehend the various stages in the debate with a clarity not hitherto attained. From the vantage point of our present understanding of the nature of dynamic competition, of the role of entrepreneurship and of the social significance of error discovery, we can see what Mises and Hayek "really meant"—even better, perhaps, than they were themselves able to do at the time they wrote. We can see how the inability of the socialist economists to comprehend what Mises and Hayek really meant stemmed from the mainstream neoclassical paradigm within which the socialist economists were working. And we can see how all this led to confusion and misunderstanding. What is important for the approach in this chapter is that it was the calculation debate itself that generated those key developmental steps in modern Austrian economics that were ultimately responsible for our contemporary improved Austrian understanding of "what it was all about." We turn now to review briefly the development of greater clarity within the Austrian tradition in regard to the function of market prices.

We have noticed Mises's brief 1920 reference to the role that market prices play in permitting economic calculation in the competitive market economy. It would be easy for a superficial reader of the 1920 paper (and of the 1922 book) to conclude that market prices play their part in achieving social efficiency through confronting each market participant with social valuations that reflect the activities of all other market participants and which, again, impose relevant efficiency constraints on the decisions of each market participant these prices now confront. Clearly, such an understanding of the role of market prices would not be greatly different from that understood by Lange in his now notorious reference to "the parametric function of prices, i.e. on the fact that, although the prices are a resultant of the behavior of all individuals on the market, each individual separately regards the actual market price as given data to which he has to adjust himself" (1964: 70).

As Lavoie has extensively documented, the true role of price in the Austrian understanding of the market economy is quite different from that understood by Lange. For Austrians, prices emerge in an open-ended context in which entrepreneurs must grapple with true Knightian uncertainty. This context generates "precisely the kind of choice that stimulates the competitive discovery process" (Lavoie 1985: 137). In this context, the entrepreneur "does not treat prices as parameters out of his control but, on the contrary, represents the very causal force that moves prices in coordinating directions" (1985: 129).

Mises paints the picture of the entrepreneurially driven market and of the role that prices play within it as follows:

There is nothing automatic or mechanical in the operation of the market. The entrepreneurs, eager to earn profits, appear as bidders at an auction, as it were. . . . Their offers are limited on the one hand by their anticipation of future prices of the products and on the other hand by the necessity to snatch the factors of production away from the hands of other entrepreneurs competing with them. . . . The entrepreneur is the agency that prevents the persistence of a state of production unsuitable to fill the most urgent wants of the consumers in the cheapest way. . . . They are the first to understand that there is a discrepancy between what is done and what could be done. . . . In drafting their plans the entrepreneurs look first at the prices of the immediate past which are mistakenly called *present* prices. Of course, the entrepreneurs never make these prices enter into their calculations without paying regard to anticipated changes. The prices of the immediate past are for them only the starting point of deliberations leading to forecasts of future prices. . . . The essential fact is that it is the competition of profit-seeking entrepreneurs that does not tolerate the preservation of *false* prices of the factors of production.

(Mises 1966: 332–5, emphasis in original)

This 1949 statement (presumably based on a similar passage in *National-ökonomie*, 1940) appears to attribute a role to prices that differs sharply from that which the superficial reader might have gathered from Mises's 1920 or 1922 statements. The contrast is between the role of prices that are assumed *already* to express with reasonable accuracy all relevant information and the role of prices seen as stimulating entrepreneurial anticipations for the future. It is difficult to escape the conclusion that what led Mises to his more profound articulation of the role that prices play in the entrepreneurial process was his dismay at the Lange-Lerner misunderstandings concerning the "parametric function of prices." His earlier statements concerning market prices had not been made primarily in order to explain the operation of the market system; they had been made in order to illustrate the kind of economic calculation that market prices make possible. These statements were directed primarily at those who fail to recognize how market prices, precisely or crudely, do enforce the constraints implied by scarcity. The experience during the calculation debate not only sensitized Mises to the existence of more sophisticated proponents of socialism, it also sensitized him to the more subtle insights embodied in his own, Austrian, appreciation of the way in which markets work.

In regard to the function of market prices, too (as we found in regard to the appreciation for the discovery procedure of the market and for the emergence of the "co-ordination" criterion for normative evaluations), the development of the modern Austrian position was not completed in the 1940s. Hayek's seminal 1945 paper "The use of knowledge in society," which drew explicit attention to the role of prices in communicating information, did not succeed in distinguishing between two quite different communication functions. It is one thing to recognize the role of equilibrium prices as economic signals which permit instantaneous co-ordination of decentralized decisions, based on dispersed bodies of knowledge. It is quite another thing to recognize the role of *disequi-librium* prices in stimulating entrepreneurial discoveries concerning the availability of dispersed information (whose existence had hitherto escaped relevant attention). The statements of both Mises and Hayek during the 1940s, stimulated by the calculation debate, betray sure signs of appreciation for the latter role. But precisely because of Hayek's pioneering and carefully presented insights into the first role (that relating to the signalling function of equilibrium prices), it is doubtful whether he came to recognize the sharp distinction that today's Austrians would surely wish to draw between the two roles (see chapter 8).

Be this as it may, the modern Austrian recognition of prices as *stimulating discovery* must be seen as a further development in an unfolding series of advances that must surely be judged as having been set in motion, in significant degree, by the calculation debate.

THE CONTINUING DEBATE

It would be a mistake to believe that the calculation debate has ended. Lavoie has stated the main purpose of his work as being "to rekindle the fires of the calculation debate" (1985: 179). There are signs that a new round in the debate is indeed called for. From the perspective of the present chapter, these signs must be read as calling for restatement of the Austrian position with even greater clarity and sensivity. The appearance of an important paper by Richard R. Nelson exemplifies this need (Nelson 1981). Nelson's critique of the market and his implied (moderate) defence of central planning were written with a fairly extensive familiarity and understanding of the Austrian literature in the calculation debate. None the less, it is this writer's opinion that Nelson's paper betrays insufficient understanding of the Austrian position. We have seen that the Austrian position has required successive stages of clarification. Nelson's contention illustrates very well how the most recent clarifications—and more still need to be contributed—are vital in this continuing debate.

NOTES

1. No claim is being made here that Professor Lavoie will accept this explanation or, indeed, that he will accept my view that no contradiction is involved.

2. See Lavoie (1985: 26) where he maintains this despite acknowledging that there "is always, of course, the potential danger that I have illegitimately read modern Austrian notions into the earlier Austrian contributions."

3. For a critique of this concept (and of the way the literature has misused Lord Robbins's concept of *individual* allocation of resources), see J. M. Buchanan (1964).

REFERENCES

Buchanan, J. M. (1964) "What should economists do?" *Southern Economic Journal* 30, January: 213–22.

Hayek, F. A. (1949a) "The use of knowledge in society," in *Individualism and Economic Order*, London: Routledge & Kegan Paul (originally published in *American Economic Review* 35, no. 4 (1945): 519–30).

Hayek, F. A. (1949b) "Economics and knowledge," in *Individualism and Economic Order*, London: Routledge & Kegan Paul (originally published in *Economica* 4, February 1937).

Hayek, F. A. (1949c) "Socialist calculation III: the competitive 'solution,'" in *Individualism and Economic Order*, London: Routledge & Kegan Paul.

Hayek, F. A. (1949d) "The meaning of competition," in *Individualism and Economic Order*, London: Routledge & Kegan Paul.

Hayek, F. A. (1949e) "Socialist calculation I: the nature and history of the problem," in *Individualism and Economic Order*, London: Routledge & Kegan Paul.

Hayek, F. A. (1968) "Economic thought VI: the Austrian School," in D. L. Sills (ed.) *International Encyclopedia of the Social Sciences*, New York: Macmillan.

Hayek, F. A. (1978) *New Studies in Philosophy, Politics, Economics, and the History of Ideas*, Chicago, Ill.: University of Chicago Press.

Hayek, F. A. (1979) *Law, Legislation and Liberty*, Vol. 3, *The Political Order of a Free People*, Chicago, Ill.: University of Chicago Press.

Hutchison, T. W. (1953) *A Review of Economic Doctrines, 1870–1929*, Oxford: Clarendon Press.

Jaffé, W. (1976) "Menger, Jevons, and Walras de-homogenized," *Economic Inquiry* 14 (4): 511–24.

Kirzner, I. M. (1973) *Competition and Entrepreneurship*, Chicago, Ill.: University of Chicago Press.

Lange, O. (1964) "On the economic theory of socialism," in B. E. Lippincott (ed.) *On the Economic Theory of Socialism*, New York: McGraw-Hill.

Lavoie, D. (1985) *Rivalry and Central Planning: The Socialist Calculation Debate Reconsidered*, Cambridge: Cambridge University Press.

Little, I. M. D. (1957) *A Critique of Welfare Economics*, 2nd edn, Oxford: Clarendon Press.

Mises, L. von (1920) "Economic calculation in the socialist commonwealth," translated in F. A. Hayek (ed.) (1935) *Collectivist Economic Planning*, London: Routledge & Kegan Paul.

Mises, L. von (1936) *Socialism: An Economic and Sociological Analysis*, London: Jonathan Cape (translation from the German of *Die Gemeinwirtschaft*, 1st edn 1922, 2nd edn 1932).

Mises, L. von (1940) *Nationalökonomie, Theorie des Handelns und Wirtschaftens*, Geneva: Editions Union.

Mises, L. von (1960) *Epistemological Problems of Economics*, Princeton, N.J.: Van Nostrand (translation of *Grundprobleme der Nationalökonomie*, 1933).

Mises, L. von (1966) *Human Action, a Treatise on Economics*, 3rd edn, Chicago, Ill.: Henry Regnery (originally published as *Human Action*, New Haven, Conn.: Yale University Press, 1949).

Nelson, R. R. (1981) "Assessing private enterprise: an exegesis of tangled doctrine," *Bell Journal of Economics* 12 (1): 93–111.

O'Driscoll, G. P. Jr. (1977) *Economics as a Coordination Problem, The Contributions of Friedrich A. Hayek*, Kansas City, Kans.: Sheed, Andrews & McMeel.

Vaughn, K. I. (1976) "Critical discussion of the four papers," in L. S. Moss (ed.) *The Economics of Ludwig von Mises: Toward a Critical Reappraisal*, Kansas City, Kans.: Sheed and Ward.

HEDGEHOG OR FOX? HAYEK AND
THE IDEA OF PLAN-COORDINATION

George Shackle once wrote a paper entitled "The Hedgehog and the Fox, A Scheme of Economic Theory" (Shackle, 1966, ch. 12). He referred to a line from the poet Archilochus, made famous in contemporary discussion by Isaiah Berlin: "The fox knows many things, but the hedgehog knows one big thing" (ibid., p. 30 fn). Shackle explains that the

> hedgehog is the system-builder, the seeker after . . . a theory which explains everything by a unified conception of what the cosmos is . . . Such a theory might be itself compact, like the acorn, but able to unfold the whole glory of the heavens and the earth, like the oak which so massively arises . . . from the minute germ. The fox by contrast is the scientist who is content with . . . understanding one thing at a time by reference, in each case, to an ultimately arbitrary pattern.
>
> (Ibid., p. 30)

Shackle himself suggests "that the economic theoretician must be content to know many things and not seek to know one big thing" (ibid., p. 31). (This is in contrast to a Paretian general equilibrium perspective which Shackle perceives as "perhaps an attempt to see the whole economic scene as the manifestation of the free operation of self-interest within a frame of law and order (ibid.). Shackle believes such an attempt must tacitly assume, that while "resources are scarce, knowledge is not scarce, but on the contrary every participant possesses, or can obtain, all knowledge relevant for his own choices" (ibid.).)

This chapter seeks an answer to the question whether Hayek is best understood as hedgehog or as fox. Certainly, in his extraordinarily long scholarly career, Hayek dealt with a remarkably extensive list of superficially disparate research areas, both inside and outside economics. Is it possible to see his work in all or most of these different areas—or at least

From *The Driving Force of the Market: Essays in Austrian Economics* (New York and London: Routledge, 2000), 180–202. Reprinted by permission of De Gruyter; the original source is *Journal des Economistes et des Etudes Humaines* 9, 2/3 (June/September 1999): 217–37.

his work in economics—as somehow flowing out of a single seminal insight ("one big thing")? Could one take, say, the idea of the dispersed character of knowledge and its implications for (both the need for and the possibility of) the coordination of individual plans and expectations in society, as the central unifying theme of Hayek's rich and multifarious scholarly output in the social sciences (or at least in his economics)? (Notice, however, that such a unifying theme, resting on the dispersed character of knowledge, would of course be the polar opposite of that "hedgehog" mentality which Shackle ascribed to the general equilibrium theorist.)

In his highly original and insightful survey of Hayek's contributions to economics, a survey written at a time when few in the economics profession were prepared to pay much attention to Hayek, Gerald P. O'Driscoll indeed took "the coordination of economic activities" as the unifying theme of Hayek's work: "Hayek's work is seen as variations of this theme" (O'Driscoll, 1977, p. xx). "Throughout all [Hayek's] work he maintained his conception of the 'economic problem' as a coordination problem . . ." (ibid., p. 28). O'Driscoll's book set out "to connect [Hayek's] many and diverse contributions to economics, and to show that they evidence an overall conception of economics as the study of decentralized planning and market coordination" (ibid., p. xxi). It is of considerable interest that in his 1975 Foreword to O'Driscoll's book, Hayek appears to endorse O'Driscoll's thesis (while confessing that he had himself *not* realized this unity in his own work). He notes the

> curious fact that a student of complex phenomena may long himself remain unaware of how his views of different problems hang together and perhaps never fully succeed in clearly stating the guiding ideas which led him in the treatment of particulars. I must confess that I was occasionally myself surprised when I found in Professor O'Driscoll's account side by side statements I made at the interval of many years and on quite different problems, which still implied the same general approach.
>
> (Ibid., p. ix)

Notwithstanding the meticulous care and detail with which O'Driscoll's book examines Hayek's contributions to economics, however, it seems that the thesis which has inspired the book and its title (that the coordination theme unites all those contributions) has (despite the presence of a chapter entitled "The Coordination Problem") been left implicit in the book's expositions, rather than being explicitly *argued* anywhere in the book. It may therefore be of some value to assess this theme afresh in its own right, by direct reference to relevant statements to be found in Hayek's own writings over the central decades of his scholarly career.[1]

We shall find numerous references in Hayek's work to such concepts as "coordination," "economic order," "spontaneous order" and the like— but in a way which suggests a good deal less than a single "big" idea uniting these concepts, and creating a seamless unity among his many areas of research. What will emerge from this chapter is that Hayek was indeed largely driven, in most of his work, by a set of closely related ideas and concerns (relating to knowledge, its dispersed character, and to the phenomenon of the spontaneous coordination of the activities of numerous individuals with different, but equally incomplete, awareness of the circumstances surrounding their respective aims of making rational decisions). Rather than constituting a substantial unifying theme, however, it seems fairer to see these closely related ideas and concerns as constituting what Professor Butos (Butos, 1985, p. 110) has termed "a band of continuity" in "the expanse of Hayek's work." Continuity does not itself constitute unity. Neither hedgehog nor fox, Hayek turns out to be a social scientist whose work in numerous separate research areas has been repeatedly inspired and enriched by a series of related insights, questions and concerns involving dispersed knowledge, spontaneous order, the compatibility of plans and expectations, and the like. It may be suggested that our exploration into these matters can, by warning against a possible oversimplification in interpreting Hayek's economics, deepen our understanding of some of the complexities in Hayek's work.[2]

THE AUSTRIAN THEORY OF THE BUSINESS CYCLE AND THE IDEA OF COORDINATION

In an earlier essay (Kirzner, 1995) the writer drew attention to a certain penumbra of doubt which surrounds the question of whether Hayek's 1931 *Prices and Production* foreshadowed his later concern with the idea of coordination. On the one hand, the fact is that a reader of that work can find little or no explicit reference to the coordination notion. Yet a number of late twentieth-century references to the Austrian cycle theory which that work made famous, have interpreted it unambiguously as a theory of how "artificially" low rates of interest "discoordinate" the intertemporal market (in which investment decisions are made). Present decisions to undertake capital-intensive projects are misled (by the low rate of interest) overoptimistically to anticipate the future availability of capital resources. Present activity is thus generated, based on expectations concerning the future decisions of market participants which fail to dovetail with the future reality of those decisions. Thus Professor Garrison has more than once referred to "intertemporal coordination" (Garrison, 1985) and "intertemporal discoordination" (Garrison, 1989, p. 24) in regard to Austrian cycle theory. Stavros Ioannides has, in his critical exposition of Hayek's theory, referred to the boom phase of that theory as distorting the structure of production "because the plans of producers and consumers are no longer compatible with each other" (Ioannides, 1992, p. 123). In similar vein Gerald O'Driscoll (whom we have already seen to emphasize the role of the coordination concept in Hayek's work) states that for Hayek "the crucial question for business cycle theory was the mutual correspondence of the plans of savers and investors and those of consumers and producers" (O'Driscoll, 1977, p. 73). Yet, as we have pointed out, Hayek's 1931 exposition of his cycle theory does *not* in fact emphasize this plan-coordination or plan-discoordination issue (or even the signalling function of prices, including rates of interest). Instead, that exposition is couched in terms of "misdirections of production" (Hayek [1931] 1935, pp. 105, 117). Now the idea of "misdirected production" is entirely consistent with the perspective of a central planner (whose central plan might replace all other possible individual plans, rendering the idea of plan coordination utterly irrelevant). Production might thus be considered "misdirected" (from the central planner's perspective), for example, if it involves currently-initiated long-term capital-intensive projects for which subsequently needed complementary resources turn out not to be available (in later stages of these projects, thus entailing their abandonment).

Yet it is the case that Hayek, in his 1981 lecture commemorating the fiftieth year since his original 1931 lectures at the London School of Economics (the lectures which were published as *Prices and Production*), recalled that the 1931 lectures "made use of what became the leading theme of most of my later work, an analysis of the signal function of prices in guiding production, a conception which I first expounded systematically ... in ... 'Economics and Knowledge'" (Hayek, 1981, p. 2). Now certainly the latter paper (published in 1937 as the written version of a lecture given in 1936) did, as we shall discuss below, systematically expound the communication and coordinating role of prices. (And apparently by 1981 Hayek had become thoroughly persuaded, presumably by O'Driscoll's 1977 book, that the understanding of this coordinating role did indeed constitute the leading theme of most of his work subsequent to the 1931–7 period—despite his own earlier unawareness of any such unifying theme in his work!) And two European scholars have indeed fairly recently strongly and explicitly argued this very thesis, that Hayek's concern with the phenomenon of the business cycle early in his career, is to be seen as the opening phase of a lifelong research program on the theme of "coordination in economic process" (Schmidtchen and Utzig, 1989).

Certainly our broader question in this chapter concerning possible unity among Hayek's apparently disparate areas of research, must take note of these ambiguities concerning the role, if any, of the coordination concept in Hayek's 1931 book. It will, however, be at least equally helpful (in addressing the broader question) to examine carefully those parts of Hayek's work which deal most explicitly and directly with the notion of plan-coordination. To this we now turn.

THE TETRAD ON ECONOMIC COORDINATION[3]

There is no doubt that our interest in the place of the idea of plan-coordination in Hayek's economics has its source in four important papers (all republished in his *Individualism and Economic Order* (Hayek, 1949a, chs 2–5)). These papers were written within a 10-year span during perhaps the most important decade of Hayek's research career. These papers are: (i) "Economics and Knowledge" (Hayek, 1937); (ii) "The Facts of the Social Sciences" (Hayek, 1943); (iii) "The Use of Knowledge in Society" (Hayek, 1945); (iv) "The Meaning of Competition" (Hayek, 1949b). It was in these papers that Hayek articulated most clearly and originally his insights concerning the implications of incomplete and dispersed knowledge, concerning the signalling role of prices in such a world of dispersed information, and concerning the character of the competitive market process as one tending to coordinate the expectations, plans and activities of imperfectly informed market participants. Again and again Hayek would refer to the ideas developed in these papers (particularly the first of these four) as encapsulating what he considered his most important and potentially seminal ideas. For example, in a footnote to the 1939 republication of his 1933 Copenhagen lecture (Hayek, 1933), he referred to his 1937 paper as elaborating on and partly revising the discussion, in the 1933 lecture, of the relationship between equilibrium and foresight; in his 1941 *The Pure Theory of Capital* (Hayek, 1941a) he cited his 1937 paper as showing how the idea of general equilibrium refers to a relationship between the plans of different members of society; in his (1955) *The Counter-Revolution of Science: Studies on the Abuse of Reason* (Hayek, 1955) he referred to his 1937 paper in regard to the communication-of-knowledge function of market prices; and in a 1965 paper (Hayek, [1965] 1967) he referred to this (1937) paper as having been the starting point of his own development from being a "very pure and narrow economic theorist" into a scholar concerned with "all kinds of questions usually regarded as philosophical" (Hayek, [1965] 1967, p. 91).

Not only is it the case that, as we have noticed, Hayek believed that important parts of his subsequent work grew out of the ideas of this "coordination tetrad," it is also the case that Hayek believed these ideas to be relatively polished concepts which had themselves grown, in turn, out of earlier, less satisfactory formulations on his own part. We have noticed his linking his 1937 paper with ideas expressed initially in his 1933 Copenhagen lecture; in his above-cited 1941 *Pure Theory of Capital* reference to his 1937 paper, he also suggests that the ideas of that paper originated "in a rather unsatisfactory form" in his 1928 paper on intertemporal equilibrium (Hayek, [1928] 1994). So that these four "coordination" papers represent together for Hayek both a maturer development and articulation of earlier insights,[4] and a foundation, at the very least, for important aspects of Hayek's later scholarly contributions, both inside economics and beyond economics. It will therefore certainly be useful to analyze somewhat more carefully what Hayek understood by the ideas which illuminate the "coordination tetrad" (or which appear, perhaps less centrally, in several related Hayekian contributions).

COORDINATION AND OTHER RELATED IDEAS

The truth is that our references (following O'Driscoll) to the "coordination tetrad," need to be qualified in a number of respects. These four seminal, classic Hayekian papers (as well as the other related contributions to which we will be referring) present an array of ideas which certainly *include* the notion of plan-coordination, but which also suggest a number of related insights which should *not* themselves be confused with the idea of plan-coordination. Let us take up some of the more obvious of these insights.

A. Order I

The term "order" is used by Hayek not only to refer to a state of affairs in which the plans of different market participants are mutually supportive ("coordinated" in the sense to be distinguished below), but also to refer to any specified set of institutional arrangements. For example, in the third of the "coordination tetrad" papers, Hayek refers to "the problem of a rational economic order," to attempting "to construct a rational economic order" (Hayek, 1949a, p. 77); elsewhere he refers to "the task which faces the designer of a rational order of society" (Hayek, 1955, p. 98), to reproaches "of irrationality leveled against the existing economic order" (Hayek, 1949a, p. 81). He sometimes (e.g. Hayek, 1978, pp. 183ff.) refers to the "market order," sometimes to the "social order" (Hayek, 1949a, p. 1). In these references Hayek appears to be simply referring to the "economic system," the "market system," or to a "social system." He is not referring directly to the *orderliness* which may or may not be achieved within any of the identified (or unidentified) sets of institutional arrangements. Clearly this use of the word "order" has, then, nothing to do with our own focus of interest in this paper (that focus being the idea of plan-coordination). We mention this usage only to avoid possible confusion (and also to note a certain source of such possible confusion that may be generated, for example, by Hayek's title (to the important volume in which the "coordination tetrad" papers were published), *Individualism and Economic Order*).

B. Order II

The use by Hayek of the word "order," that *is* relevant to the focus of this chapter, is that which implies the *orderliness* of some discussed set of activities or social arrangements. (And it is of course this use of the word "order" which is implicit in the correlative word "coordination," with which this chapter is directly concerned.) In a well-known paper written during the same years in which the "coordination tetrad" emerged, Hayek contrasts the view "which accounts for most of the order which we find in human affairs as the unforeseen result of individual actions," with "the view which traces all discoverable order to deliberate design" (Hayek, 1949a, p. 8). In this usage Hayek clearly understands "order" to refer to an orderliness which does *not* necessarily consist in the compatibility existing among independently-made individual plans. So that when we find Hayek identifying the "order" achieved by market competition as the "mutual adjustment of individual plans," involving "the circumstance that the expectations of transactions to be effected with other members of society, on which the plans of all the several economic subjects are based, can be mostly realized" (Hayek [1968] 1978, p. 184)—this is simply *one* kind of order. We can, in Hayek's terminology, envisage, at least, the possibility of designed order. Presumably such order would consist in the hypothesized successfully achieved consistency among the various distinct elements of a central design or plan; it would *not* relate to the dovetailing of individually made decisions and plans.

In his 1960 book *The Constitution of Liberty* (Hayek, 1960), Hayek cites an unidentified source for the following observation: "That there is some kind of order, consistency and constancy, in social life is obvious. If there were not, none of us would be able to go about his affairs or satisfy his most elementary wants." Hayek similarly points out that the "orderliness of social activity shows itself in the fact that the individual can carry out a consistent plan of action that, at almost every stage, rests on the expectation of certain contributions from his fellows" (ibid., pp. 159–60). In this, Hayek is illustrating the fallacy of the "enemies of liberty [who] have always based their arguments on the contention that order in human affairs requires that some should give orders and others obey" (ibid., p. 159).

From all this it appears that for Hayek, order in social phenomena consists in the mutual consistency displayed among individual elements that can be identified in those phenomena. We shall discover that this breadth in the conception of order in society has certain implications for Hayek's idea of coordination. We can also now understand what Hayek has in mind with his term "spontaneous order."

C. Spontaneous order

Our discussion in the preceding subsection of Hayek's broad notion of "order" has already noticed Hayek's emphasis on the undesigned achievement, in a market economy, of order "as the unforeseen result of individual actions." This is Hayek's celebrated notion of "spontaneous order."[5] The order achieved spontaneously in the market has been demonstrated by economic theory. "One of the achievements of economic

theory has been to explain how such a mutual adjustment of the spontaneous activities of individuals is brought about by the market" (Hayek,
1960, p. 159). "The study of spontaneous orders has long been the peculiar task of economic theory (Hayek, 1973, pp. 36–7). And just as the
term "order" has its correlate in the term "coordination," so too does
the term "spontaneous order" have its correlate, as we shall see, in one
sense (out of other possible senses) of the term "coordination."

But just as we have seen that the notion of order in social phenomena is, for Hayek, not defined as the mutual adjustment of numerous
independently-made decisions, it is quite similarly the case that the
term "spontaneous order" is not defined, for Hayek, as the spontaneous achievement of such mutual adjustment. By the notion of spontaneous order Hayek wished to refer more broadly, for example, to the
circumstance that "the spontaneous collaboration of free men often creates things which are greater than their individual minds can ever fully
comprehend. This is the great theme of Josiah Tucker and Adam Smith,
of Adam Ferguson and Edmund Burke" (Hayek, 1949a, p. 7). Now the
achievement of an outcome which no one has deliberately created, an outcome which is "greater" than anything the individuals (whose "spontaneous collaboration" spontaneously achieves this "greater" social outcome)
could ever comprehend, does not require that that outcome be defined
in terms of mutual compatibility of individual plans. Presumably when
Hayek refers to the mutual compatibility of individually made plans that
is achieved by the spontaneous interplay of market competition, he sees
this as one example of something "greater" than what the individual market participants have been aiming at. Such compatibility is thus an example of spontaneous order rather than its defining characteristic.

It is worth emphasizing this aspect of the Hayekian spontaneous
order concept. It might perhaps plausibly be argued that if one were to
seek the "one big thing" that might qualify Hayek as "hedgehog," it might
well be found in his concern with spontaneous order. Certainly some of
Hayek's later work in the spontaneous evolution of benign social institutions focuses not so much upon the coordination of individual decisions,
as upon the creation of something greater than anything which any of the
innumerable individuals (out of whose actions these social institutions
spontaneously emerge) could possibly have had in mind. Our purpose
in drawing attention to this is not to support (or rebut) any such claim
(concerning the centrality of the spontaneous order concept in Hayek's

work). It is rather to point out that the "spontaneous" aspect of social outcomes must not be confined to outcomes that can be parsed as consisting of sets of mutually compatible individual decisions. Nor (given the breadth with which we have seen Hayek to have defined "order"), could we in good conscience even confine the concept of spontaneous order to the creation of benignly "greater" things (than the individuals could have had in mind). The same scientific fascination which surrounds the spontaneous emergence of benign social outcomes, should apply also to the spontaneous emergence of social outcomes which the individuals (out of whose activities these outcomes emerge) would abhor.[6] Any centrality in Hayekian thought of the spontaneous order concept must be distinguished from a possible focus upon plan-coordination.

D. Coordination I

Closely related to the foregoing discussion is the notion of the coordination of the activities of many individuals in order to achieve some desired overall patterned outcome. Here the starting point is either (or both) of two realistic premises: (a) that individuals may be motivated by self-regarding goals that do not include the achievement of the desired social outcome; (b) that individuals may (as a result of the Hayekian phenomenon of dispersed knowledge) be only incompletely informed concerning the circumstances of time and place needed for the achievement of the desired social outcome. Given these premises, the achievement of the desired social outcome calls, as the most elementary economics recognizes, for a way of achieving coordination of individual activities. Certainly, as we have seen, Hayek's work drew attention again and again to the counterintuitive possibility of spontaneous market coordination to achieve a desirable social outcome. (The subtleties which Hayek certainly recognized surrounding the question of what constitutes the pattern of outcomes which is "desirable"—or whether indeed "desirability" involves any "pattern" at all—need not detain us for present purposes.) It should be noticed, in regard to this coordination notion, that (just as we saw in regard to the notion of "order") such coordination is certainly not defined in terms of the mutual compatibility of independently-made plans or independently-held expectations—since such coordination includes (in principle) coordination sought to be achieved by central command, superseding individually made plans. The defining feature of this notion of coordination is the desired character of some social outcome.[7]

Although most of the passages in which Hayek uses the word "coordination" are *not* referring to the central coordination of activities (by command) in order to achieve some desired social outcome (but refer instead to what we shall below term "Coordination II"), nonetheless it seems fair to say that at least sometimes it *is* the goal of achieving some desired overall outcome which underlies his use of the term "coordination." (An example of such a use is Hayek's 1941 reference to what individual entrepreneurs in a market economy "have to do in order to bring about that coordination of their efforts which a central planner could never achieve" (Hayek, [1941] 1997, p. 146).)

A second example seems to be present in a sentence in which Hayek states that "in a system in which the knowledge of the relevant facts is dispersed among many people, prices can act to co-ordinate the separate actions of different people *in the same way as subjective values help the individual to co-ordinate the parts of his plan*" (Hayek, [1945] 1949a, p. 85; emphasis added).

The same idea is surely implied in a number of passages in which Hayek draws attention to the circumstance that "the spontaneous actions of individuals will . . . bring about a distribution of resources which can be understood *as if it were made according to a single plan*" (Hayek [1937] 1949a, p. 54; emphasis added). It is, Hayek stares, "the main merit of real competition that through it use is made of knowledge divided between many persons which, if it were to be used in a centrally directed economy, would all have to enter the single plan" (Hayek, 1949a, p. 202). Late in his career Hayek expressed unhappiness at the modern term "the economy," and made a plea that this term be reserved for describing "a complex of deliberately co-ordinated actions serving a single scale of ends" (Hayek, 1976, p. 108).

E. Coordination II

Here we come to the place in Hayek of that central idea which has motivated the present chapter (and which, I believe, led Gerald O'Driscoll, as we have seen, to see all of Hayek's work as variations of the coordination theme)—namely, coordination as the state (or the process leading towards the state) in which the individual plans of independently-acting persons display mutual compatibility. Such compatibility may be couched, as in the preceding sentence, in terms of plans, or it may be couched in terms of decisions, or of expectations. The earmark of "coordination II" is that it refers to the dovetailing of individual purposeful efforts without any necessary concern with or interest in (either on the part of any of the individuals involved in these efforts, or on the part of the observing or theorizing scientist, or on the part of anyone else) the desitability or undesirability of the overall "social" outcome of these purposeful efforts. Certainly most of the references to coordination to be found in Hayek's work (while, as we have seen, they may sometimes if not always be defined in terms consistent with some overall social outcome that is somehow deemed desirable) in fact refer to the (spontaneous) coordination (through the market process) of the independently-made plans of market participants. In a 1939 paper[8] Hayek wrote of a market system achieving "effective coordination of individual effort," through "the free combination of the knowledge of all participants, with prices conveying to each the information which helps him to bring his actions in relation to those of others" (Hayek, [1939] 1997, p. 194). In a 1941 paper (in a passage with a thrust typical of numerous others, in which the word "coordination" may however not be explicitly used) Hayek stated that "in order to achieve the extensive division of labour on which our civilization is based, the direction of production must . . . be decentralized to a high degree, and some method must be found for coordinating these separate plans which does not depend on conscious central control" (Hayek, [1941] 1997, pp. 143ff.). The fundamental idea in this coordination concept is that we (the economic or social scientists) are interested in the extent to which the decisions made by an individual correctly anticipate (and take advantage of) the decisions in fact being made by others.

Perhaps the single most important and original insight which Hayek contributed to economic understanding is contained in his 1937 detailed interpretation of the state of equilibrium as being simply that state in which "the different plans which the individuals . . . have made for action in time are mutually compatible" (Hayek, [1937] 1949a, p. 41). This interpretation was first suggested in germinal form by Hayek, it appears, in his 1933 Copenhagen lecture, where the compatibility of plans was explicitly linked to the compatibility of expectations. The concept of equilibrium assumes, Hayek stated in that lecture, that everybody possesses correct foresight concerning "the behaviour of all the other people with whom he expects to perform economic transactions" (Hayek, [1933] 1939b, p. 140). From this interpretation of the equilibrium state it is possible to achieve an understanding of the market process which is hardly available to more conventional ways of seeing equilibrium (for example as the solution to a system of simultaneous equations of supply and demand functions, or as representing, as if in mechanics, a balance of the forces of supply and demand). It was this interpretation of equilibrium as expressing a pattern of mutually sustaining expectations, which enabled Hayek to highlight the role of dispersed information in market processes, and to perceive the signalling role of market prices in communicating information. And it was surely this interpretation which led Hayek to appreciate the possibility of a spontaneous order in which, without central direction, market prices generate an array of decisions on the part of independently-acting, independently-motivated, and independently-informed individuals which do, to a remarkable degree, reflect mutually sustaining expectations.

Having in this section briefly examined the various ideas and concepts surrounding the notion of "coordination II" to be found in Hayek's writings (particularly those in, or influenced by his "tetrad on economic coordination"), we are in a position to summarize some of the separate (if overlapping) themes that we should identify in those writings. Although to do so is to do nothing new in regard to the substance of Hayek's contributions, it will enable us to raise doubts concerning possible claims that we can find any "one big thing" at the foundations of Hayek's work in so many different areas.

SOME SEPARATE (BUT OVERLAPPING) THEMES IN HAYEK

Several enduring themes pervade Hayek's work. These are well-known. Yet it may be helpful, for the purposes of this paper, to list some of them systematically here. The themes we select for this listing are those most salient in Hayek's "tetrad on coordination" (and thus most relevant to the possible identification of plan-coordination as the "one big thing" that might qualify Hayek for hedgehogdom).

A. Equilibrium

In his famous 1933 Copenhagen lecture, Hayek pronounced "the fundamental problem of all economic theory," to be "the question of the significance of the concept of equilibrium and its relevance to the explanation of a process which takes place in time" (Hayek, [1933] 1939b, p. 138). There can be no doubt that this "fundamental problem" was never far from Hayek's concern as an economic theorist (and of course this is true for most economic theorists, of most schools of thought). Even when

Hayek was to criticize "modern economists" for their "perhaps excessive preoccupation with the conditions of a hypothetical state of stationary equilibrium" (Hayek, [1935] 1949a, p. 167),[9] the relevance of the equilibrium concept and its centrality for economic understanding was not in question. Hayek is famous for having been a pioneer in the idea of intertemporal equilibrium (Hayek, [1928] 1994), and even after he expressed his impatience with the profession's preoccupation with the equilibrium concept, he considered intertemporal equilibrium to be a central building block for his own system of understanding.[10] In regard to the coordination problem, we note that Hayek did not object so much to the professional attention to what is called the state of "competitive equilibrium" (in which "the data for the different individuals are fully adjusted to each other"), as to its failure to explain "the nature of the process by which the data are thus adjusted" (Hayek, 1949a, p. 94). We have already noticed how important for Hayek's work on coordination was his path-breaking reinterpretation of equilibrium in terms of the mutual compatibility of plans. Our purpose in identifying "equilibrium" as an important theme in Hayek's work is not to throw doubt on the importance for Hayek of the plan-coordination idea; it is simply to take note of the separateness of these ideas. To *interpret* equilibrium as expressing plan compatibility is not quite the same thing as to *replace* the role of equilibrium itself in economic understanding, by that of plan-compatibility.

B. Spontaneous order

We have already taken note of the importance in Hayek's work of his celebrated notion of spontaneous order. For present purposes there is no need to elaborate further on what has already been said. Hayek's interest in spontaneous order clearly grows (as it does for most economists) out of his interest in the notion of equilibrium. It is Hayek's reinterpretation of equilibrium as expressing the mutual compatibility of independently-made plans which permitted him to see the price system as a signalling system, communicating information (concerning the actions of other market participants) to the entire market. Although we have seen that for Hayek the term "spontaneous order" is not defined in plan-compatibility terms, it remains a central feature of his spontaneous order that it refers, in a market system, to the spontaneous knowledge-communication process through which plan-compatibility can be approached.

C. The Knowledge Problem

Distinct from, but of course closely related to the above, is the role of (what has come to be known as) Hayek's "Knowledge Problem." This refers to the "problem of the utilization of knowledge which is not given to anyone in its totality" (Hayek, [1945] 1949a, p. 78). The circumstance of dispersed knowledge came to be identified by Hayek as what renders plan-compatibility a challenge, and what renders central planning a virtual impossibility. So that this knowledge problem, a theme referred to again and again since the "coordination tetrad," is related to the possibility of spontaneous order, to the attainment (or at least to the tendency towards the attainment) of equilibrium. But it is, of course, distinct from each of them. (In fact, precisely in Hayek's emphasis on the difficulties which the knowledge problem poses for central planning, there is implicit the insight that this problem is *not* uniquely linked to the criterion of the compatibility of independently-made plans.)

D. The micro-basis for "macroeconomics" and cycle theory

One theme which certainly runs through almost all Hayek's work is his recognition of what is now called the "microfoundations" of macroeconomics. This recognition was vigorously expressed already in Hayek's 1931 *Prices and Production:*

> it is on the assumption of a knowledge of the decisions of individuals that the main propositions of non-monetary economic theory are based. It is to this "individualistic" method that we owe whatever understanding of economic phenomena we possess . . . If, therefore, monetary theory still attempts to establish causal relations between aggregates or general averages, this means that monetary theory lags behind the development of economics in general. In fact, neither aggregates nor averages do act upon one another.
>
> (Hayek, [1931] 1935, p. 4)

Certainly this theme is of overriding importance for Hayek (and O'Driscoll rightly emphasizes this in his own emphasis on the centrality of plan-coordination in Hayek's work); but, of course, to insist on the micro-basis of the theory of the business cycle is, by itself, not the same as insisting on the centrality of plan-compatibility in such theory.

E. Plan-coordination

This theme (which we identified above as "coordination II") is the focus of our interest in this chapter. Its importance in what we have seen O'Driscoll perceptively to have labelled Hayek's "tetrad on economic coordination," cannot be questioned. Into this concept of plan-coordination Hayek poured his deep and subtle understanding of individual decision-making, and in the social processes generated by the interactions among individual actions in markets. This concept embraces the implications of the dispersed character of knowledge in society, of the possibilities for the attainment of spontaneous order, and of the meaning of equilibrium and of equilibrating processes. Our understanding of the competitive process can, after appreciating the lessons of the coordination tetrad, never be the same. And certainly one can appreciate the insight of those recent expositions of Hayek's cycle theory which have, as we noticed very early in this chapter, read it directly in (intertemporal) plan-coordination terms. One does not have to accept the doctrinal-historiography of such expositions to understand sympathetically "where they are coming from." Yet our brief dissection of the various themes which we have identified as important for Hayekian economics must surely convince us that, whatever the degree of overlap with, and whatever the extent of other linkages between, the plan-coordination insight and the other themes, they must, at any rate, be recognized as distinct themes.

HAYEK AND THE WORLD OF SOCIAL SCIENCE BEYOND ECONOMICS

A fascinating theme which, I believe, has thus far been only partly explored, is the extent of and the source of the continuity between Hayek's work outside economics and his earlier purely economic work.[11] For the purposes of this chapter we take brief note of this as yet insufficiently examined issue only insofar as it may possibly throw light on our own search for the "one big thing" that could permit us to see Hayek as "hedgehog." A most revealing passage in a 1965 paper of Hayek's can perhaps be helpful. The year 1965 was several years after Hayek had published his *Constitution of Liberty*. The paper seems not only to reflect certain key ideas of that book, but also to anticipate a good deal of what Hayek would be expounding several years later in the three volumes of *Law, Legislation and Liberty*.

In this 1965 paper Hayek ([1965] 1967) is making a plea against what he calls the "rational constructivism" of Bacon, Hobbes and Descartes, which contends "that all the useful human institutions were and ought to be the deliberate creation of conscious reason" (ibid., p. 85). This rationalism Hayek contrasts with the rationalism of the medieval thinkers who were "very much aware that many of the institutions of civilization were not the inventions of the reason but what, in explicit contrast to all that was invented, they called 'natural', i.e., spontaneously grown" (ibid., p. 84). Hayek, developing this latter (non-constructivist) rationalist perspective, suggests further "that in all our thinking we are guided (or even operated) by rules of which we are not aware, and that our conscious reason can therefore always take account only of some of the circumstances which determine our actions" (ibid., p. 87). This leads him to his now well-known conclusion that "the only manner in which we can in fact give our lives some order [in the face of ever new and unforeseeable circumstances] is to adopt certain abstract rules or principles for guidance, and then strictly adhere to the rules we have adopted in our dealing with the new situations as they arise" (ibid., p. 90). Hayek is then led to remark on what in his "personal development was the starting point of all these reflections," explaining how he "was led from technical economics into all kinds of questions usually regarded as philosophical" (ibid., p. 91). He sees it all to have begun with his 1937 "Economics and Knowledge" paper (the first of the "coordination tetrad"). That paper, he writes in 1965, showed how economics must explain "how an overall order of economic activity was achieved which utilized a large amount of knowledge which was not concentrated in any one mind."

Pursuing these insights further through "a re-examination of the age-old concept of freedom under the law, the basic conception of traditional liberalism, and of the problems of the philosophy of law which this raises," Hayek acquired, one gathers, "insight into the relations between the abstract rules which the individual follows in his actions, and the abstract overall order which is formed as a result of his responding, within the limits imposed upon him by those abstract rules, to the concrete particular circumstances which he encounters." These insights, it is made clear, have provided Hayek with "a tolerably clear picture of the nature of the spontaneous order of which liberal economists have so long been talking" (ibid., p. 92).

In other words, Hayek's insights into philosophy and political philosophy represent far-reaching extrapolation of ideas first outlined (within the narrow scope of purely technical economics) in the first of the coordination tetrad papers. We notice immediately that in this extrapolation the focus is no longer upon the simple coordination or dovetailing of individual decisions within a set of market institutions, but upon the achievement of an "abstract overall order," through rigorous adherence on the part of individuals to abstract rules, in broader social interaction, in the face of ever new and unforeseeable circumstances. The extension by Hayek of his economics insights of 1937 to his political philosophy insights of the 1960s is not so much a rigorous analytical development, as it is the pursuit of a fertile hunch based on an ingenious analogy. We notice also that Hayek saw this continuity in the development of his thinking outside narrow technical economics (as proceeding from his 1937 paper in the coordination tetrad), some 12 years before his 1977 statement (in his above-cited Foreword to O'Driscoll's book) in which he clearly appears to confess that, until he saw that book, he had been unaware of how the idea of plan-coordination had served as a guiding idea in most of his economic writings. It becomes thus very obvious that to recognize (as he did in 1965) that the coordination-of-dispersed-knowledge insights of his 1937 paper led him eventually to many of his later contributions to philosophy and political philosophy, is not at all inconsistent with unawareness at the very same time of the place of plan-coordination in his own post-1937 contributions to economics itself. All this confirms our scepticism concerning any "hedgehog"-understanding of Hayek's life-work in the social sciences, or even in economics proper. At the very time he was pursuing the fertile hunch (suggesting an analogy between the spheres of economics and of political philosophy—but in ways that did *not* involve individual plan-coordination) he was, in his work on the pure theory of capital, for example (as in other economic contributions of the 1940s), engaging in technical economic analysis without consciously or deliberately invoking those coordination insights which loomed so prominently in his intellectual-autobiographical memory. We are now in a position to draw together what we have found.

CONTINUITY RATHER THAN UNITY

We have already cited Professor Butos's reference to "a band of continuity" running through Hayek's work. What we have seen in this chapter is confirmation that such continuity must be distinguished from unity. There is no "one big thing" that might permit us to see Hayek as "hedgehog," as developing an array of theories in various branches of social science, or of economics, that might all be recognized as flowing directly out of one, big seminal insight. Instead we find an array of overlapping themes and insights in Hayek's "tetrad," which appear to have inspired him to develop useful prescientific hunches, based on analogy, which his subsequent work—work of extraordinary scholarly devotion and breadth—permitted him to transform into systematically developed scientific contributions. Plan-coordination is one—very plausibly the most important one—of these enduring themes which inspired much of Hayek's work and which establishes that continuity of which Professor Butos wrote.

The truth seems to be that up until the mid-1930s Hayek's economics focused on two quite distinct areas, both of them involving the elaboration of pioneering contributions by Hayek's mentor, Ludwig von Mises. These two areas were (a) what came to be known as the Austrian theory of the business cycle,[12] and (b) the Austrian position concerning the difficulties surrounding the possibility of socialist economic calculation.[13] Now Mises himself never did focus explicitly on plan-coordination in all of his work; he never did focus on the dispersed character of knowledge, and on the consequent coordination problem. (This does not mean that Mises' seminal insights in each of the above two areas cannot be faithfully articulated in plan-coordination terms; it merely means that Mises himself never explicitly recognized this possible articulation.) Certainly for Mises these two areas of economics, while each of them reflected their common basis in the standard economic theory of prices, were quite separate areas of research. There is no reason whatever to suppose that, up until the mid-thirties (by which time Hayek's major contributions to both areas were virtually complete) Hayek saw these areas as anything but separate and distinct sets of theoretical argumentation.

It is true that (e.g. in his 1931 *Prices and Production*, and in his 1933 Copenhagen lecture) Hayek's work in both of these areas in the early 1930s was leading him to fresh insights which were to develop into his "tetrad on economic coordination." And it is this writer's conviction that these fresh insights constitute Hayek's enduring original contribution to economic understanding. (They also led him, as we have seen, to extend these insights, by analogy, to areas beyond economics proper. And this writer has elsewhere expressed reservations concerning some of Hayek's resulting conclusions; see Kirzner ([1990] 1992).) But what we have seen in this chapter must warn us against any sweeping thesis suggesting that, consciously or unconsciously, Hayek's entire work in economics, work extending from the 1920s to the 1970s and beyond, is to be seen as the consistent development of his plan-coordination insights.

Neither hedgehog nor fox, Hayek emerges as an extraordinarily fertile and broad scholar, one whose work in so many different areas can, naturally enough, be seen to reflect his consistent fascination with a series of related and overlapping themes and insights, to which he arrived in perhaps the central decade of his career as economist. Hayek's contributions to Austrian economics revolve around these overlapping themes; his lasting influence will, without question, depend on the extent to which these themes and insights will continue to inspire current and future Austrian scholars. In this centenary year commemorating Hayek's birth, we can pay no greater tribute to his work than to reaffirm the continuity which these themes and insights confer upon Hayek's lifelong scientific odyssey.

NOTES

1. It is perhaps worthwhile to remind ourselves that of course many economists (besides Hayek or other "Austrian" economists) have emphasized the idea of "coordination" (sometimes of "spontaneous coordination") as central to the understanding of economics. Thus, for example, Milton Friedman writes that the "basic problem of social organization is how to co-ordinate the economic activities of large numbers of people" (Friedman, 1962, p. 12). Axel Leijonhufvud titled a published collection of his essays in *macro*economic theory, *Information and Coordination* (Leijonhufvud, 1981), explaining (at p. v) that "macroeconomics," for Leijonhufvud, "is the study of the coordination of activities in large, complex, economic systems."

2. It should be emphasized that it is entirely possible, and perhaps even plausible, that O'Driscoll's book (as well as Hayek's above-cited Foreword to it) are not at all necessarily inconsistent with our conclusions in this chapter.

3. This phrase was perceptively coined by O'Driscoll (1977, p. 67).

4. And we have already noticed the possibility, at least, of tracing these coordination ideas to Hayek's earlier formulation of his business cycle theory. On this see further Kirzner (1995, pp. 38–40).

5. On the development of Hayek's insights into spontaneous order, see Leube (1994).

6. For a criticism of what this writer believes to be Hayek's insufficient appreciation of this possibility, see Kirzner ([1990] 1992).

7. In a recent subtle, provocative paper, Daniel B. Klein (Klein, 1997, pp. 325ff.) has read Hayek as speaking of coordination *exclusively* in terms of what we have called "Coordination I." He has labelled this coordination idea "metacoordination" (in order to distinguish it from another type of coordination, which he labels "coordination" *simpliciter*, or "Schelling coordination"). As will become evident in the subsequent subsection in the text ("Coordination II"), this writer believes that, at least part of the time, Hayek was using the term "coordination" not in the sense of Klein's "metacoordination," but in the sense of the achievement of mutual compatibility among independently-made individual plans (without regard to any overall desirability of this outcome). It is this latter sense of the term "coordination" (involving simply the objective criterion of mutual plan compatibility) which is the focus of our attention in this chapter. This sense of "coordination" is, in fact, closer to (but not identical with) Klein's "Schelling coordination." For a detailed exposition of what this writer believes to constitute "coordination" (i.e. what we call here "Coordination II"), including aspects of it which do not dovetail at all neatly with Klein's taxonomy, see Kirzner (1998).

8. In regard to this passage (and to other similar observations in other of his works) Hayek refers the reader to his 1937 paper (Hayek, [1937] 1949a).

9. For a similar criticism of the profession's preoccupation with equilibrium, see Hayek (1949a, ch. IX, p. 188).

10. See for example Hayek (1941a, ch. II).

11. Our reference in this section is not to Hayek's early work in psychology (see Hayek, 1952), but to his work in political philosophy and other areas such as philosophy and the history of ideas.

12. For Hayek's reference to Mises's earlier work in this area see Hayek (1984).

13. See Hayek's acknowledgement of Mises's contribution in this area, in his introduction to the collection of essays on this problem which he edited in 1935 (Hayek, 1935a).

REFERENCES

Buros, William N. (1985) "Hayek and General Equilibrium Analysis," *Southern Economic Journal* 52 (October), pp. 332–43; page references are to the reprint in J. C. Wood and R. N. Woods (eds) (1991) *Friedrich A. Hayek, Critical Assessments*, Vol. IV, London and New York: Routledge.

Friedman, Milton (1962) *Capitalism and Freedom*, Chicago: University of Chicago Press.

Garrison, Roger W. (1985) "Intertemporal Coordination and the Invisible Hand: An Austrian Perspective on the Keynesian Vision," *History of Political Economy* 17 (Summer), pp. 309–21.

——— (1989) "The Austrian Theory of the Business Cycle in the Light of Modern Macroeconomics," *Review of Austrian Economics* 9.

Hayek, Friedrich A. (1928) "Das intertemporale Gleichgewichtssystem der Preise und die Bewegungen des Geldwertes," *Weltwirtschaftliches Archiv* 28; English translation in Israel M. Kirzner (ed.) (1994) *Classics in Austrian Economics, A Sampling in the History of a Tradition,* Vol. III, London: William Pickering, pp. 161–98.

———— (1931) *Prices and Production,* 1st edn; page references are to the 1935 second edition, London: Routledge.

———— (1933) "Price Expectations, Monetary Disturbances and Malinvestments," reprinted as ch. IV in Hayek (1939b).

———— (1935a) *Collectivist Economic Planning,* London: Routledge and Kegan Paul.

———— (1935b) "Socialist Calculation, The State of the Debate," in Hayek (1935a); page references are to the reprint in Hayek (1949a).

———— (1937) "Economics and Knowledge," *Economica* 4 (February); page references are to the reprint in Hayek (1949a).

———— (1939a) "Freedom and the Economic System," Public Policy Pamphlet No. 29, Chicago, University of Chicago Press; page references are to the reprint in Hayek (1997).

———— (1939b) *Profits, Interest and Investment,* London: George Routledge and Sons.

———— (1941a) *The Pure Theory of Capital,* Chicago: University of Chicago Press.

———— (1941b) "The Economics of Planning," *The Liberal Review* I, pp. 5–11; page references are to the reprint in Hayek (1997).

———— (1943) "The Facts of the Social Sciences," *Ethics* LIV (1); page references are to the reprint in Hayek (1949a).

———— (1945) "The Use of Knowledge in Society," *American Economic Review* XXXV (4), pp. 519–30; page references are to the reprint in Hayek (1949a).

———— (1949a) *Individualism and Economic Order,* London: Routledge and Kegan Paul.

———— (1949b) "The Meaning of Competition," in Hayek (1949a).

———— (1949c) "Individualism—True and False," in Hayek (1949a).

———— (1949d) "Socialist Calculation: The Competitive 'Solution,'" in Hayek (1949a).

———— (1952) *The Sensory Order,* London and Chicago: University of Chicago Press.

———— (1955) *The Counter-Revolution of Science: Studies on the Abuse of Reason,* Glencoe, Ill.: The Free Press.

———— (1960) *The Constitution of Liberty,* Chicago: University of Chicago Press.

———— (1965) "Kinds of Rationalism," *The Economic Studies Quarterly* XV (3); page references are to the reprint in Hayek (1967).

———— (1967) *Studies in Philosophy, Politics and Economics,* Chicago: University of Chicago Press.

———— (1968) "Competition as a Discovery Procedure"; page references to English version in Hayek (1978).

———— (1973) *Law, Legislation and Liberty,* Vol. 1, *Rules and Order,* Chicago: University of Chicago Press.

———— (1976) *Law, Legislation and Liberty,* Vol. 2, *The Mirage of Social Justice,* Chicago: University of Chicago Press.

—— (1978) *New Studies in Philosophy, Politics, Economics and the History of Ideas*, Chicago: University of Chicago Press.

—— (1979) *Law, Legislation and Liberty*, Vol. 3, *The Political Order of a Free People*, Chicago: University of Chicago Press.

—— (1981) Ms. of introductory remarks to "The Flow of Goods and Services," lecture at the London School of Economics, January 27.

—— (1984) *Money, Capital and Fluctuations: Early Essays*, ed. Roy McCloughry, Chicago: University of Chicago Press.

—— (1997) *Socialism and War, Essays, Documents, Reviews*, Vol. 10 of *The Collected Works of F. A. Hayek* (ed. Bruce Caldwell), Chicago: University of Chicago Press.

Ioannides, Stavros (1992) *The Market, Competition and Democracy; A Critique of Neo-Austrian Economics*, Aldershot: Edward Elgar.

Kirzner, Israel M. (1990) "Knowledge Problems and Their Solutions: Some Relevant Distinctions," *Cultural Dynamics*; page references are to the reprint in Kirzner (1992).

—— (1992) *The Meaning of Market Process; Essays in the Development of Modern Austrian Economics*, London and New York: Routledge.

—— (ed.) (1994) *Classics in Austrian Economics, A Sampling in the History of a Tradition*, 3 vols, London: William Pickering.

—— (1995) "Hayeks Theorie der Koordination von Märkten," in *Vademecum zu Einem Klassiker Der Marktkoordination* (to accompany the facsimile republication of Hayek's *Preise und Produktion*), Dusseldorf: Verlag Wirtschaft und Finanzen GMBH.

—— (1998) "Coordination as a Criterion for Economic 'Goodness,'" *Constitutional Political Economy* 9, pp. 289–301, reprinted as chapter 7 in the present volume.

Klein, Daniel B. (1997) "Conventions, Social Order, and the Two Coordinations," *Constitutional Political Economy* 8, pp. 319–35.

Leijonhufvud, Axel. (1981) *Information and Coordination. Essays in Macroeconomic Theory*, New York and Oxford: Oxford University Press.

Leube, Kurt R. (1994) "Law and Economics, Some Preliminary Remarks on Hayek's Early Student Years and his Development of the Theory of Spontaneous Order," in Christoph Frei and Robert Nef (eds) *Contending With Hayek: on Liberalism, Spontaneous Order and the Post-Communist Societies in Transition*, Bern: Peter Lang.

O'Driscoll, Gerald P. (1977) *Economics as a Coordination Problem, The Contributions of Friedrich A. Hayek*, Kansas City: Sheed, Andrews and McMeel.

Schmidtchen, Dieter and Utzig, S. (1989) "Die Konjunkturtheorie Hayeks: Episode in einem forscherleben oder Ausdruk eines lebenslangen Forschungsprogramms?" *Wirtschaftspolitische Blätter* 2 (in honor of Hayek's 90th birthday).

Shackle, George L. S. (1966) *The Nature of Economic Thought, Selected Papers, 1955–1964*, Cambridge: Cambridge University Press.

The first major contribution of Don Lavoie's remarkable career as a scholar was surely his superb doctoral dissertation, later published as *Rivalry and Central Planning: The Socialist Calculation Debate Reconsidered* (1985). In this contribution, Lavoie's reconsideration developed the penetrating insight that Mises' critique of the possibility of rational calculation under socialist central planning proceeded from that same Misesian theoretical vision which saw the competitive market process as a *fundamentally* entrepreneurial one.

The present chapter seeks to explore this insight further. This exploration will proceed, in part, by commenting on a footnote in Lavoie's book.[1] In that footnote, Lavoie cited an objection to certain aspects of Mises' thesis which had been raised by Professor Buchanan. Buchanan had contended that the Austrians, Mises and Hayek, had focused on a less fundamental difficulty for central planning (the difficulty of calculation), instead of on the more important difficulty, that of motivation.

> Even if the socialist state should somehow discover an oracle that would allow all calculation to be made perfectly . . . efficiency in allocation will emerge only if . . . men can be motivated . . . to make decisions in accordance with cost criteria that are different from *their own* . . . This amounts to saying that even if the problems of calculation are totally disregarded, the socialist system will generate efficiency in results only if men can be trained to make choices that do not embody the opportunity costs that they, individually and personally, confront.[2]

Buchanan was pointing out that we must expect central planners to be motivated to see the relevant alternatives *that face them as individuals,* rather than those that are relevant to the society which they are ostensibly serving.

Lavoie's footnote responded to this criticism by expressing his own conviction that the Misesian "problem of knowledge" is "more fundamental" than Buchanan's "problem of motivation." In Lavoie's words:

From *Humane Economics: Essays in Honor of Don Lavoie,* ed. Jack High (Cheltenham, UK: Edward Elgar, 2006), 29–46. Reprinted by permission.

One could reverse Buchanan's argument and say that even if socialist managers could somehow, as he puts it, be "converted into economic eunuchs . . . to make decisions in accordance with cost criteria that are different from their own," the central difficulty of obtaining the relevant information would still remain. Even fully motivated planners would not know how to plan rationally.[3]

In other words, the difference between Buchanan and Lavoie has been reduced to a difference concerning which of the two problems should be considered more "fundamental." Lavoie adduced no grounds for his own preference, in this regard, over Buchanan's.

The present chapter seeks to go somewhat beyond Lavoie's response. Our further exploration of the interface between the economics of socialist calculation and the economics of the process of entrepreneurial competition will permit us to argue, I believe, that there are analytical grounds for maintaining that the Misesian "problem of knowledge" is indeed anterior to Buchanan's problem of motivation. Unless one could imagine that Mises' calculation problem has somehow been solved, questions of motivation, we shall see, cannot even begin to be asked. In fact, it will turn out somewhat paradoxically, these "analytical grounds" can themselves be held to be rooted in certain other passages to be found in Buchanan's own rightly celebrated scholarly contributions. A superficial reading of this paper may suggest that this response to Buchanan's critique of the Austrians is its central purpose. I would like to emphasize that this is not the case. Our response to Buchanan's criticism is in fact merely an *illustration* of the central insight sought to be identified in the paper. This central insight, having to do with the very foundations of Austrian "welfare theory," emerges from a careful appreciation of the "welfare-economics" context of the socialist calculation debate.

THE SOCIALIST CALCULATION DEBATE
AND THE ECONOMICS OF WELFARE

This writer has elsewhere[4] pointed out that the inter-war socialist calculation debate is to be credited with advances both in the mainstream economics of welfare, and in the Austrian understanding of the social usefulness of the market economy in terms of the *coordinative* process which the market promotes. Abba Lerner's *The Economics of Control* (1944) is a classic example of the way in which mainstream twentieth century welfare economics grew out of the debate. Similarly Hayek's celebrated 1945 paper "The use of knowledge in society" (reprinted in his 1949 *Individualism and Economic Order*) represents a pivotal juncture in twentieth century Austrian thought; it was in that paper that Hayek's "knowledge problem" was brought explicitly to the fore. It was the explicit identification of this Hayekian knowledge problem which made it clear that Austrians could not be part of the dominant mid-century tendency in mainstream economics to treat society as an entity seeking "to allocate its resources" (in the same way in which Lionel Robbins had, in 1932, articulated the nature of individual economizing behavior as the allocation of scarce resources among competing ends). It was this Hayekian insight that crystallized the Austrian rejection of mainstream welfare economics, and which led to subsequent Austrian explorations into the normative meaning of the Misesian competitive-entrepreneurial market process. Certainly this 1945 paper of Hayek's is the obvious product of a decade of work in which Hayek had been grappling with a variety of attempted socialist refutations of Mises' demonstration of the inherent impossibility of central planning (due to the impossibility of economic calculation in the absence of the market).

For mainstream welfare economics the economic debate between the proponents of socialism and those of the market economy revolved around the question of which of these two systems can be expected to generate a more efficient allocation of society's given resources, in terms of that society's given arrays of consumer preferences. But Hayek's work, culminating in his 1945 paper, made explicit what had up until that time only been implicit in the work of Mises and other Austrians, viz., that (not only because of the generally well-recognized difficulties surrounding the interpersonal comparison of utilities, but more importantly) because of the problems arising out of the dispersed nature of knowledge in society, it is (except at the metaphorical level) simply *meaningless* to talk of a society "allocating its resources" as if to maximize its "total" welfare.

In fact, when one examines Mises' classic statements[5] concerning the impossibility of central planning, one discovers that he never did directly assert that *a society* is economically "better off" under a market system than under a centrally planned system. He simply pointed out that under a market system the decision makers (and, in particular, the entrepreneurs) *are* able to calculate by using market prices, while under a socialist system the central planners had no market prices (for resource services) with which to work, and were, therefore, simply *unable* to calculate. Mises seemed to take it for granted that the reader would then understand how the market system functions to coordinate, and thus to render, to some extent, mutually consistent, the calculative decisions of all market participants, while the impossibility of calculation by would-be central planners inevitably spelled the inherently chaotic nature of the socialist economy. But, at least in his statements dealing directly with the problems of socialist calculation, he did not make direct "welfare comparisons" between the two systems.

Indeed, reflection must render it evident—if perhaps in a way surprising—that such a direct "welfare" comparison cannot in fact be made. The would-be socialist central planner *is* (at least in theory) seeking efficiently to allocate society's resources—that is, to allocate them in a manner which "maximizes" the satisfaction of those goals which the planner deems relevant for "society" (and with the ranking of importance of these competing goals, which the planner has adopted). The standard notions of efficiency in allocative choice are certainly relevant to the task of the would-be central planner. His very undertaking takes it for granted that society is to be treated, in effect, as a decision-making entity—with the central planner assigned the technical function of determining the particular pattern of resource allocation to be decided upon. Success in this undertaking would mean that society has been efficient in "its" allocative function. Mises' argument was not only that such success is out of the question, but also that there is simply no way in which such success can even be systematically attempted. However, Mises did seem to be measuring the possibility or impossibility of successful planning under socialism by the measuring rod which, by the very definition of central planning, is the relevant one, viz., allocative efficiency as seen from the perspective of a single entity, the "society" in regard to which central planning is being undertaken. But such a measuring rod is, it should be clear, quite inappropriate for any assessment of the "economic success" (or failure) of a market economy. A market economy is by definition made up of a multitude of independently-made individual decisions. In such a context to talk of decisions made "by society" is, at best, to engage in metaphor. "Society" does not, as a simple matter of fact, choose; it does not plan; it does not engage in the "allocation of resources"; it does not have ends; it does not have means; to talk of society facing "its" allocative, economizing problem is, strictly speaking, to talk nonsense. And it was Professor Buchanan who was one of the first explicitly to point this out.

BUCHANAN AND THE ILLEGITIMACY OF THE IDEA OF SOCIAL "ALLOCATION"

In his remarkable 1963 Presidential Address to the Southern Economic Association,[6] "What should economists do?," Professor Buchanan sharply criticized economists for having illegitimately transferred the notion, emphasized by Lionel C. Robbins (*The Nature and Significance of Economic Science, 1932*), of the allocation of scarce resources among competing multiple ends, from the context of the individual (where the notion is valid and important) to that of society (where the notion has no validity at all).[7] Buchanan cited Milton Friedman, for example, as defining economics as "the study of how a particular society solves its economic problem." But this formulation (which was, already at the time of Buchanan's address, taking over virtually every principles textbook on the market) is an illegitimate transferral of what Robbins had articulated strictly at the individual level. The economists whom Buchanan was criticizing "are wholly concerned with the allocation of scarce resources among competing ends or uses," with respect to "social welfare functions." Buchanan insisted that "theirs is not legitimate activity for practitioners in economics"[8] as he defines the discipline. Buchanan talks of a "bridge between personal or individual units of decision and 'social' aggregates." This bridge, he points out, is "most difficult to cross"; his "whole plea" to economists is: "stay on the side of the bridge where you belong."[9] On *that* side of the bridge, Buchanan was arguing, one simply cannot talk of "the economic problem which faces society."

THE ECONOMICS OF SOCIALISM AND BUCHANAN'S BRIDGE

Our point here can be made briefly; it is an obvious, almost a trivial, one. Any discussion of the possibility of economic calculation under socialism must take it for granted that Buchanan's bridge *has* been crossed. What the central planner seeks to do is precisely to solve the allocation problem held to be faced by society. Buchanan wished to define the science of economics in "catallactic" terms,[10] that is as the science of interpersonal exchanges. Of course such a definition rules out the economics of pure socialism (under which, by definition, there are no private exchanges at the level of input services). Was Mises, in his exploration of the "economics of socialism" (by demonstrating the impossibility of socialist planning), then illegitimately extending the realm of economics beyond the boundaries which Buchanan wished to see in place? Would Mises really maintain that economists *can* cross Buchanan's bridge, and endorse the simple aggregation of individual objectives and constraints so as to be able to talk meaningfully of the allocation problem "facing society"? To anyone familiar with Mises' consistent insistence on the principle of methodological individualism, a positive answer to this latter question is simply unthinkable. Do we not then, in reading Mises, face a dilemma? I believe the solution to this apparent dilemma is a straightforward one: by demonstrating the impossibility of socialist economic calculation, Mises was doing more than proving the impossibility of rational central planning; he was in fact also proving that the very *objective* of socialist planning, that of efficiently allocating a "society's" resources among "its" multiple competing goals, is, strictly speaking, a *meaningless* objective. His demonstration, so far from violating Buchanan's guidelines for economists, constituted a case study illustrating the *validity* of Buchanan's insight (on the basis of which he promulgated those guidelines) that the bridge between "individual units of decision" and "social" aggregates *cannot* be crossed. Mises' foray into the economics of socialism was a thoroughly iconoclastic one; it showed that the only valid theorem possible in that field of inquiry was the theorem demonstrating the *non-existence* of the field! Buchanan (of the Southern Economic Association Presidential Address) could not have asked for more. Let us develop our argument somewhat more explicitly.

ON THE ECONOMIC PROBLEM

Many years ago I heard (or read) a semi-humorous remark about the discipline of economics which resonates, and which has somehow stuck in my memory. The remark was to the effect that economics is able to instruct decision makers on *how to avoid trying to run in two opposite directions at the same time.*

This remark surely sees the central idea in normative economics as revolving around the notion of *consistency* among decisions. Such consistency is, of course, fundamental to the very meaning of a *plan*. A plan consists of a series of steps which have been calculated to achieve aimed-at objectives; these steps must not be mutually frustrating. A plan which calls for simultaneously running in two directions is simply incoherent. Economic thinking, the above semi-humorous remark maintains, is peculiarly suited to pointing out to would-be decision makers that the various steps they are considering may in fact be mutually frustrating; they may be attempts to run in two directions at the same time. Achieving efficiency in the allocation of resources is simply the achievement of consistency among the components in one's pattern of resource expenditures. A shopper's decision to buy an additional quantity of beef is inefficient if that beef is purchased at the cost of a quantity of fish which the shopper values more highly than she does the beef. To genuinely value the fish more highly than the beef, and then to buy the beef rather than the fish, is to seek to run in two directions at the same time. All this is what we seek to instill into our freshmen students of economics, in the very first lecture.

But if the economic problem consists in avoiding the hazards of indeed trying to run in two directions at the same time, we must surely identify who is facing this economic problem; *who* is tempted to run in two directions at the same time? Certainly each individual potential decision maker, each individual formulating a plan for his activities over the next few minutes, or few days, or few years, must be aware of the need to achieve mutual consistency, coherence, among the various elements of his plan. Yet, mindful though we may be of the difficulty (or impossibility) of crossing "Buchanan's bridge," it is difficult to avoid the recognition, as one contemplates different areas in the beehive of economic activities in a society, that some of these activities are, surely, "inconsistent" with activities being engaged in elsewhere in the beehive. The automobile industry may be rapidly expanding at the very same time that the availability of gasoline to this society has been sharply reduced; medical schools may be training an increased number of specialists in fields of medicine for which the need is rapidly declining; and so on. We do think that such situations may be, from a social perspective, incoherent; and we do ask how the economic organization in a society might reduce or eliminate the likelihood of such incoherencies.

So that, having thoroughly accepted the Hayek-Buchanan rejection of the Milton Friedman formulation cited above, of economics being the study of how a society solves its economic problem, we do, nonetheless, think of a *society as if it were* somehow running in two directions at the same time. Have we, in so doing, contradicted ourselves? Are *we* running in two directions at the same time?! Several passages in Hayek show how we are not only *not* contradicting ourselves, but that the *apparent* contradiction illustrates a profoundly important truth—often completely overlooked in modern mainstream economics.

THE NOTION OF SOCIETAL EFFICIENCY— WITHOUT CROSSING BUCHANAN'S BRIDGE

In his celebrated (and, in fact, revolutionary) papers on the place of knowledge in a society's economy, Hayek made observations which open our eyes to a remarkable circumstance. When the market achieves a single price for a commodity, he wrote in 1945, it has brought about "the solution which (it is just conceptually possible) *might have been arrived at by one single mind* possessing all the information which is in fact dispersed among all the people involved in the process."[11] In other words, a properly functioning market system tends towards the achievement of that pattern of resource allocation which a would-be socialist central planner would have sought to achieve (and which Mises had shown to have been impossible for that central planner to have achieved). In his earlier (1937) paper on knowledge, Hayek had made a similar observation. There he wrote of how a market might, without central direction, spontaneously bring about "the combination of fragments of knowledge existing in different minds [thus achieving] results which, if they were to be brought about deliberately, would require a knowledge on the part of the directing mind which no single person can possess." In this way, Hayek was pointing out, "the spontaneous actions of individuals will, under conditions which we can define, bring about a distribution of resources which can be understood *as if it were made according to a single plan*, although nobody has planned it."[12]

Now to talk, even hypothetically, of the distribution of resources in a society being understood as if made according to a single plan, is, in effect to assert that that society *can* be treated as an entity confronted by "its" allocative economic problem. Yet certainly, by the date of his 1945 paper, Hayek was thoroughly convinced that the task of calculating the optimal allocation of a society's resources (of achieving that pattern of allocation such "that the marginal rates of substitution between any two commodities or factors must be the same in all their different uses") is "emphatically *not* the economic problem which society faces."[13] The dispersed character of relevant knowledge in a society means that the "economic problem of society" is not "how to allocate 'given' resources—if 'given' is taken to mean given to a single mind . . ." but rather the problem "of the utilization of knowledge which is not given to anyone in its totality."[14] Yet, as we have seen, this seminal insight did not prevent Hayek from speaking, in that very same paper, of the solution to the problem facing, in effect, a single planner for the entire society. What Hayek seemed to have realized was that if all the dispersed bits of knowledge *could* be concentrated in a single mind, then, for that mind we could talk meaningfully of the attainment of social efficiency, in the sense of avoiding running in many different directions at the same time. We would *not* need to cross Buchanan's bridge in order to be able to talk meaningfully in these terms. To be able to engage in the quest for Paretian optimality one needs, not to cross the bridge of "social aggregation," but to transcend the gulf created by dispersed knowledge. *Without* aggregating objectives, *without* aggregating available resources, we *would*—if Hayek's "knowledge problem" could be spirited away—talk meaningfully of a society as a single entity for which considerations of consistency ["efficiency"] are relevant. We can now appreciate, I believe, an aspect of Mises' demonstration of the impossibility of central planning which seems not to have been recognized. But let us first review briefly the notion of *coordination* in Austrian normative economics.

COORDINATION AND EFFICIENCY

One certainly does not have to be an Austrian economist in order to understand that markets fulfill the social function of tending to coordinate independently-made individual decisions.[15] But Austrian economics has been characteristically consistent in the development of the idea of coordination as the primary, if not the sole, criterion for normative discussion in economics.[16] It was not by chance that Dr. Gerald P. O'Driscoll entitled his pioneering (1977) study of Hayekian economics, *Economics as a Coordination Problem.* Much earlier Mises had written, "The coordination of the autonomous actions of all individuals is accomplished by the operation of the market."[17] The notion of coordination does not, of course, presume the possibility of treating society as a single entity. But it does enable us to recognize the possibility of spontaneous cooperation among independently-acting individual members of society. Surely all the "invisible hand" insights of economics since the eighteenth century, consist of the recognition that, in the market, actions of individuals interact in a way which achieves outcomes which these individuals, if isolated from one another, could never have achieved. It is this idea of coordination which enables us to speak of the "social" benefits effected by markets—without crossing any Buchanan bridge. If automobile industry executives are making plans to increase the production of cars at the same time that oil industry executives are planning to reduce their supply of gasoline, this may reflect a coordination failure. If the number of patients planning to seek medical help for obesity is declining at the same time that medical schools are expanding teaching and research in the obesity field, these decisions may not seem to be well coordinated. The idea of coordination and discoordination does enable us, despite all the methodological individualism in the world, to transcend the level of individual efficiency, and to talk of efficiency (or its absence) at the level of society. It is possible to talk of a society as if it were seeking to run in two directions at the same time. To do so does *not* require us to violate Buchanan's guidelines for the definition of economics; it does not require us to see society as an entity confronted by an allocation-of-scarce-resources problem. What we must now recognize, however, is that *our ability to treat society as an entity for which coordination-efficiency considerations are relevant, depends on the possibility of economic calculation in that society.* This is the central insight, mentioned (but not identified) in the opening section of this chapter, which it is the objective of this chapter to identify and to emphasize.

CALCULATION AND COORDINATION

Mises showed that, because the socialist economy does not generate market prices for resource services, would-be socialist planners cannot calculate. A socialist society must then consist of large numbers of individuals who are indeed controlled by a central authority whose commands they must obey—but whose individual objectives, individually-possessed scraps of local information, and individual abilities to contribute to potential social cooperation, must necessarily remain systematically uncoordinated. The central planner is simply and absolutely unable to ensure that the various commands (which issue from his attempted central plan) are not, in fact, ordering different segments of the economy to attempt to achieve mutually inconsistent and incoherent objectives. Although we can, from the perspective of assumed omniscience thus assert that the central planner's commands are necessarily incoherent, we must, *for that very reason,* also recognize that (once we recognize the abject ignorance

which must in fact envelop any would-be central planner) we can no longer talk of coordination (or discoordination) *at all* in regard to the socialist economy. We cannot sensibly talk of the socialist economy attempting
to run in two directions at the same time (or of its not so attempting)—
since such an economy *must* consist of discrete individuals between
whom no meaningful system of social cooperation can exist. A multitude
of economically discrete individuals may constitute a unified entity from
the perpective of tribal values, of military considerations, or from other
"sociological" perspectives, but from the perspective of economic science
they remain discrete individuals. There *is* in the socialist society no entity
in regard to which we can talk of its activities being coordinated or not.
Of course we can and do point out that any attempted central *plan* for
a socialist society must lack coherence and coordination among its elements. It is precisely this that is meant by the assertion that central planning is impossible. But what we have seen now is not merely that the
impossibility of economic calculation under socialism renders the idea
of a central plan impossible. We have now seen that the impossibility of
economic calculation under socialism prohibits us from thinking of the
socialist society as an economic entity—that is, as an entity for which it
is meaningful to say that it is or is not seeking to run in many directions
at the same time. Without the possibility of calculation, society is something for which the notion of coordination-efficiency is simply irrelevant.
We may say that the plan drawn up by a would-be central planner consists of mutually inconsistent elements, and therefore is not a plan at
all. But, precisely because it is thus not possible to plan for a society, that
society must, from the economic perspective, necessarily remain a multitude of discrete individuals—not an economic entity at all.

PARADOX AND PARADOX

We saw earlier that Hayek had pointed out that it is exclusively in the
non-centrally-planned (that is, in the market) society, that we can sensibly talk of the successful achievement of the resource-allocation pattern
that might (conceivably) have been the objective of a central plan. In the
socialist economy, for which such a central plan is presumably the objective, such a plan can, for reasons identified by Mises and Hayek, *not* be
attained. But precisely in the market economy, where individuals are free
to undertake their own separate (possibly mutually contradictory) projects, it *is* possible to see how the forces of entrepreneurial competition

can propel such individual plans into a mutually coherent pattern—one that would have been the objective of a central plan under socialism. This fascinating paradox is the heart of the Mises-Hayek position in the socialist calculation debate. We can now recognize that a closely similar paradox emerges in regard to the very possibility of treating a society as an efficiency-relevant entity.

In a market society, the price system enables us to recognize possible situations in which the activities of its individual members are not coordinated. The price system enables us to understand how powerful market forces are at work, in such a system, to identify and to eliminate such states of discoordination. In other words, although the individual members of a market society act independently and autonomously, we can meaningfully treat the totality of these individuals as an economic entity. If automobile executives are expanding the output of cars while oil company executives are reducing refinery capacity, we can meaningfully say that this economy is "attempting" to run in two directions at the same time.

But in the socialist society, we have seen, we are simply (and paradoxically) unable to talk in this fashion. Precisely in the society organized to marshall society's resources in a unified and centrally-planned fashion, it is, as we have seen, impossible to talk sensibly of that society's constituting a single economic (that is, efficiency-relevant) entity.

As a result of the central planner's inability to calculate, it is certainly possible for the socialist plan to call for a scale of automobile production that is inconsistent with refinery capacity set forth in the same plan. We may certainly, then, consider this an incoherent plan. But we will not, except at the metaphorical level, describe this plan as one in which society is attempting to run in two directions at the same time. We will not do so for the fundamental reason that, under socialism, the term "society" has no economic meaning, other than as constituted by a multitude of discrete individuals. It is the necessary incoherence of all conceivable socialist plans which inexorably implies the disintegration of any economic sense for the term, "society."

BUCHANAN'S OBJECTION AGAINST MISES— AN ANSWER FROM BUCHANAN

We noted at the outset of this chapter that Lavoie had cited Professor Buchanan's objection to the Austrian emphasis on calculation as the source of the problem undermining the possibility of socialist central planning. The more fundamental difficulty, Buchanan had argued, was that we cannot expect human central planners to be motivated to make decisions on the basis of cost considerations that are different from their own. Even if Mises-Hayek problems of calculation could be imagined away, central planning would not attain efficiency (as defined from the perspective of the *social* importance to be attached to alternative objectives). We saw that Lavoie pointed out that, while this is certainly the case, the reverse observation could also be made. Even if central planners *were*, somehow, trained to be motivated solely by socially-relevant considerations, the calculation difficulties pointed out by the Austrians would still remain. I believe we are now in a position to see how the Austrian problems of knowledge and calculation must, on analytical grounds, be recognized (in assessing the possibility of central economic planning) as anterior to Buchanan's motivational grounds (valid though these latter grounds certainly are). And what enables us to see this is Buchanan's own 1963 critique of mainstream definitions of the economics discipline.

As we have seen earlier in this chapter, Buchanan's presidential address to the Southern Economic Association sharply criticized the mainstream view that economics is the discipline which studies how society solves its (allocative) economic problem. He pointed out that such a perspective illegitimately assumes that there is meaningful content in economics for "social welfare."[18] It assumes that "society" is "the entity that confronts the economic problem about which we, as professional economists, should be concerned, the entity, presumably, whose ends are to count in the appropriate calculus of margins."[19] In other words, Buchanan was arguing that considerations of methodological individualism make it strictly impossible to treat "society" as such an economizing entity.

But if this is the case—and it certainly is—then what are we to make of the very *notion* of central planning? If we are not to see "society" as an entity to which the notion of an economic allocation problem is relevant, how can we even talk of attempting to formulate a central plan? Clearly, by showing how, in the absence of market prices for resources, a would-be central planner could not calculate, and thus could not plan, Mises was, from his own starting point, in effect simply re-affirming Buchanan's insight that we cannot treat society as an economizing entity. To put it in terms already proposed earlier in this chapter, Mises' theorem in the field of socialist economics was a theorem which proved the field to be non-existent. While, as we saw in the preceding section of this chapter, in a market society the price system permits us to treat the totality of the individuals in the society as an economic entity (to which coordination-efficiency considerations are relevant), the impossibility of socialist economic calculation requires us to see the socialist society as nothing more than a multitude of discrete individuals. It is this which requires us to recognize that the Austrian calculation problem (for the possibility of central planning) is anterior to Buchanan's "motivational" problem. The latter problem shows us how, if we already assume that socialist society faces "its" resource-allocation problem, motivational considerations must frustrate central planning attempts at successfully addressing the task of resource allocation. The Austrian economic calculation problem, on the other hand, shows us how, in a socialist society, the very objective of treating that society as an entity for which efficiency (that is, consistency) considerations are relevant, crumbles in our hands as soon as we seek to grasp it. Valid as are the questions which Buchanan's "motivational" problems raise for socialist planning, those questions cannot in fact begin to be asked at all—because of the Austrian calculation considerations.

A critic may perhaps object that we are arguing as if, because a heavy metal weight happens to be too heavy to be lifted, one is to conclude that there is therefore no weight "there" at all to challenge would-be weight-lifters. Surely, the objection may be raised, the circumstance that a socialist society is unable to tackle its economic allocation problem, does not justify our claiming that it faces no allocation problem at all. (And therefore, perhaps, one might argue, with Buchanan, that the more important reason for the failure of central planning is the "motivational" problem.) But the analogy of the weight too heavy to be lifted, entirely misses the point; the appropriate analogy is a quite different one. Think of an array of tiny gold-colored beads arranged (without any string running through them) in a perfect circle on a sidewalk. Because these beads are so small and so close to one another, a casual observer walking on the sidewalk may mistake them for a gold ring. The observer then, let us imagine, tells his small child, who is with him, to pick up the gold ring and give it to him. Now this request is futile, of course, not because the child may possibly not be motivated to obey it (which is certainly possible), but, more "fundamentally," *because there is no ring*; any attempt by the child to "pick up" the ring must fail; in fact, not only must it fail, it must fail *by demonstrating to us* that there is no ring here at all, only discrete gold-colored beads. To attempt to solve socialist society's allocation problem is to demonstrate that there is no such societal problem; there are only discrete individual members of this "society."

ENTREPRENEURIAL COMPETITION AND THE NOTION OF COORDINATION-EFFICIENCY IN THE MARKET SOCIETY

The paradox that it is precisely the freedom of independently-acting competing entrepreneurs which is responsible for those regularities in markets which economic science explains, has often been noted. The very possibility that, out of the actions of many individuals, anything resembling economic *law* might emerge, results, not from these individuals being constrained to obey central commands, but precisely from their freedom of any central directives. What we have emphasized in this chapter is the related and parallel paradox that it is precisely the freedom of independently-acting competing entrepreneurs which (by generating the system of market prices, only on the basis of which they are individually able to "calculate") permits us to talk of the possibility of coordination-efficiency as regards "society." It is only the price system in the market society which permits us to say that an increase in automobile production is inconsistent with a decline in oil refinery capacity. (It is after all *conceivable* that the previous refinery capacity was far greater than needed; only considerations of price can definitively stamp these two industry changes as mutually inconsistent.) It is the price system which permits individuals to calculate the prospects of pure profit in alternative projects. And it is, as we know from elementary economic theory, only the pure profitability of a prospective project which permits us to say that the pursuit of that project is coordinative, in the sense that it reveals the prior existence of market discoordination, which successful execution of that project will have corrected. Thus it is the very freedom of the individual participants in the market system to act, in regard to their property and persons, as they choose (which freedom, of course, is the basis for the price system) that is responsible for the possibility of treating society as an entity to which consistency-efficiency considerations are relevant. But while this result is certainly replete with the spice of paradox, it can for that very reason offer us deeper insight into the nature of entrepreneurial competition.

The entrepreneur, after all, is alert to pure profit possibilities. Such possibilities exist where incumbent producers have failed correctly to exploit available opportunities for serving consumers more adequately. To the outside observer the patterns followed up until now by existing producers are the "normal," settled, ways of doing things; to them the invading entrepreneur is the iconoclast who disrupts the settled pattern of events. To such outside observers, fresh entrepreneurial activity is the unpredictable wild card, following no regular pattern, which continually but spasmodically churns the market and prevents us from realizing stable, law-like regularities in market outcomes. It is for this reason that mainstream economics, in its search for the underlying regularities submerged beneath the roiling surface waves churned up by unpredictable entrepreneurial innovation, found it necessary to filter out all entrepreneurial activity from its (equilibrium) models of markets.[20]

But for Austrian economists matters appear quite differently. From their perspective what the entrepreneur does is not to be seen as the abrupt injection of *inherently* disruptive, unpredictable courses of action into an otherwise near-stable, orderly environment. Rather what the entrepreneur does is—with all the surprise and unpredictability of what he does—to *reveal* potential *contradictions* in the activities of incumbent producers in *apparently* stable industries. Industry A has for years been producing with resources whose alternative uses are in Industry B (and in which these resources have relatively high value). This circumstance will have helped determine the market price of the products of Industry A. A brash new entrepreneur innovates with new methods of production (or of delivery, or of retailing, or of organization, or whatever) such that the resources required for production and delivery in Industry A can be drawn from Industry C, where their value is, let us imagine, sharply lower (than the corresponding resources which, in the "settled" state of Industry A, had been diverted from possible use in Industry B). This brash new entrepreneur sets Industry A into turmoil. His apparently disruptive activity may indeed be gloriously creative and innovative; it may indeed be surprising in its novelty—and may have been, for these very reasons of creativity and novelty, totally unpredictable. But this activity has revealed the illusive quality of the earlier apparently tranquil and settled state of the industry. Production in Industry A has now been revealed to have been inefficiently costly. It has been the *apparently* disruptive activity of the innovative entrepreneur which has in fact uncovered the contradictions and the inconsistencies inherent in earlier patterns of production.

It is because *all* successful entrepreneurial activity can be seen as identifying and unmasking such pre-existing contradictions, that Austrian economics sees entrepreneurial competition as *fusing the disparate activities of individual market participants into a meaningful global, societal entity.* Only because the market offers freedom and scope for entrepreneurial creativity, originality and innovation, is it, in our disequilibrium world of dispersed information and constant exogenous change, meaningful to think of a market society as a whole in consistency-efficiency terms.

MISES, RIVALRY AND CENTRAL PLANNING

What Lavoie's reconsideration of the socialist calculation debate accomplished, was to teach the profession that Mises' critique of socialist planning can only be appreciated against the background of Mises' understanding of the competitive-entrepreneurial character of the market process. What we have sought to do in the present chapter is to make explicit what is in fact already implicit in Lavoie's work. That is, we have seen, how the very notion of what is "economically good for a society," can only consistently be parsed in the context of freedom for entrepreneurial competition.

Mises made no direct "welfare comparisons" between socialism and capitalism because, at one level, no such comparison can be made. The socialist planner *seeks* to address Milton Friedman's "economic problem facing society"; certainly no such allocative-efficiency problem can be formulated for capitalism, at all. On the other hand, however, we have noted the almost directly opposite conclusion. When one focuses, not on society's resource-allocation pattern, but upon the possibilities for coordinative efficiency, upon the extent to which society as a whole may be guilty of attempting "to run in opposite directions at the same time," then it is only under capitalism that the presence or absence of such guilt can be meaningfully talked of. Under socialism, we have seen, the notion of a society being a single entity subject to consistency-efficiency questions, evaporates as soon as such questions begin to be formulated.

NOTES

1. Don Lavoie, *Rivalry and Central Planning, The Socialist Calculation Debate Reconsidered* (1985), p. 102n.

2. James M. Buchanan, *Cost and Choice, an Inquiry in Economic Theory* (1969), pp. 96ff.

3. Don Lavoie, *Rivalry and Central Planning* (1985).

4. See Israel M. Kirzner, "The Economic Calculation Debate: Lessons for Austrians" (1988), see especially pp. 111–15.

5. For English-language versions of Mises' 1920 and 1922 statements, see respectively: (a) Ludwig von Mises, "Economic Calculation in the Socialist Commonwealth" (1935); (b) Ludwig von Mises, *Socialism: An Economic and Sociological Analysis* (1936), pp. 113–35.

6. Buchanan's address was subsequently published in the *Southern Economic Journal*, 30 (January 1964), pp. 213–22; it was also republished as the title essay in James M. Buchanan, *What Should Economists Do?* (1979) (to which all subsequent page references will relate).

7. As noted above, similar insights had been introduced earlier in F. A. Hayek, "The use of knowledge in society" (1945), pp. 519–30; reprinted in F. A. Hayek, *Individualism and Economic Order* (1949), pp. 77–91.

8. Buchanan, *What Should Economists Do?* (1979) p. 23.

9. Ibid.

10. Ibid. p. 23ff.

11. F. A. Hayek, "The Use of Knowledge in Society," in *Individualism and Economic Order* (1949), p. 86 (italics added).

12. F. A. Hayek, "Economics and knowledge," *Economica*, IV, 1937, pp. 33–54; reprinted in Hayek, *Individualism and Economic Order* (1949), p. 54 (italics added).

13. *Individualism and Economic Order* (1949), p. 77; italics in the original.

14. Ibid. pp. 77–8.

15. For examples illustrating this, see Milton Friedman, *Capitalism and Freedom* (1962), p. 12; Axel Leijonhufvud, *Information and Coordination, Essays in Macroeconomic Theory* (1981).

16. For further discussion of the coordination criterion in Austrian economics, see Israel M. Kirzner, *The Meaning of Market Process* (1992), chapter 11; Israel M. Kirzner, *The Driving Force of the Market, Essays in Austrian Economics* (2000), chapter 7. For the centrality of the coordination criterion in Lavoie's work, see *Rivalry and Central Planning* (1985), pp. 54n, 111, 172–3. For a comprehensive survey of Austrian thought in regard to welfare economics, see Roy E. Cordato, *Welfare Economics and Externalities in an Open Ended Universe, A Modern Austrian Perspective* (1992).

17. Ludwig von Mises, *Human Action, a Treatise on Economics*, 3rd edition (1966), p. 725; the first edition of *Human Action* was published in 1949.

18. Buchanan, *What Should Economists Do?* (1979), p. 22.

19. Ibid.

20. On this point see Israel M. Kirzner, *Discovery and the Capitalist Process* (1985), pp. 3–4.

REFERENCES

Buchanan, James M. (1969), *Cost and Choice, an Inquiry in Economic Theory*, Chicago: Markham Publishing Co.

Buchanan, James M. (1979), *What Should Economists Do?* Indianapolis: Liberty Fund.

Cordato, Roy F. (1992), *Welfare Economics and Externalities in an Open Ended Universe, a Modern Austrian Perspective,* Boston, Dordrecht, London: Kluwer Academic Publishers.

Friedman, Milton (1962), *Capitalism and Freedom,* Chicago: University of Chicago Press.

Hayek, F. A. (1945), "The use of knowledge in society," *American Economic Review,* XXXV (4), pp. 519–30.

Hayek, F. A. (1949), *Individualism and Economic Order,* London: Routledge and Kegan Paul.

Kirzner, Israel M. (1988), "The economic calculation debate: lessons for Austrians," *Review of Austrian Economics,* 2, reprinted in Israel M. Kirzner (1992), *The Meaning of Market Process, Essays in the Development of Modern Austrian Economics,* London: Routledge.

Kirzner, Israel M. (2000), *The Driving Force of the Market, Essays in Austrian Economics,* London: Routledge.

Lavoie, Don (1985), *Rivalry and Central Planning, the Socialist Calculation Debate Reconsidered,* Cambridge: Cambridge University Press.

Leijonhufvud, Axel (1981), *Information and Coordination, Essays in Macroeconomic Theory,* New York: Oxford University Press.

Lerner, Abba (1944), *The Economics of Control,* New York: Macmillan.

Mises, Ludwig von (1935), "Economic calculation in the socialist commonwealth," in F. A. Hayek (ed.) *Collectivist Economic Planning,* London: Routledge and Kegan Paul.

Mises, Ludwig von (1936), *Socialism: An Economic and Sociological Analysis,* London: Jonathan Cape.

Mises, Ludwig von ([1949] 1966), *Human Action, a Treatise on Economics,* 3rd edn, Chicago: Contemporary Books.

O'Driscoll, Gerald P. (1977), *Economics as a Coordination Problem,* Kansas City: Sheed Andrews and McMeel.

Robbins, Lionel C. (1932), *An Essay on the Nature and Significance of Economic Science,* London: Macmillan.

COMMENTS ON THE DEBATE BETWEEN PROFESSORS
LEONTIF AND STEIN ON NATIONAL ECONOMIC PLANNING

Some time ago, Paul Samuelson recalled a great debate that took place at Harvard many years earlier. The debate was between two formidable opponents, Joseph Schumpeter on the one hand, and the Marxist Paul Sweezy on the other; the topic was "The Future of Capitalism." In the chair was one of today's very distinguished lecturers, Professor Wassily Leontief. "Great debaters," Samuelson observed, "deserve great moderators," and that night Leontief was in fine form. At the end he fairly summarized the viewpoints expressed:

> The patient is capitalism. What is to be his fate? Our speakers are in fact agreed that the patient is inevitably dying. But the bases of their diagnoses could not be more different.
>
> On the one hand there is Sweezy, who utilizes the analysis of Marx and Lenin to deduce that the patient is dying of a malignant cancer. Absolutely no operation can help. The end is foreordained.
>
> On the other hand, there is Schumpeter. He, too, and rather cheerfully, admits that the patient is dying. . . . But to Schumpeter, the patient is dying of a psychosomatic ailment. Not cancer but neurosis is his complaint. Filled with self-hate, he has lost the will to live.[1]

We have again had the very same patient—*mirabile dictu* still alive—on the examining table (if not on the psychiatrist's couch). And, once again, two eminent doctors, this time Professor Leontief himself being one of them, have differed in their diagnoses. Both authorities are dissatisfied with the patient's overall condition. Their anxious attention has focussed on the patient's heart, the market. Dr. Stein has given us, on the whole, a reassuring report. The market, he finds, is a basically healthy organ. The patient's somewhat erratic performance in recent years must be attributed, not to cardiac-related problems, but to gaps in our economic knowledge, reinforced by unwise public opinions. Tampering with the patient's

Originally titled "Discussant: Israel M. Kirzner," in *Economic Policy and the Market Process: Austrian and Mainstream Economics*, ed. K. Groenvelt, J. A. H. Maks, and J. Muysken (Amsterdam: Elsevier, 1990), 76–84. Reprinted by permission.

heart through the introduction of planning, Dr. Stein warns, is highly dangerous. Alleviation of the patient's condition is to be looked for in an array of considerably milder prescriptions including a regimen of intensified economic research, expanded collection of statistics, and a wiser public.

Dr. Leontief, in contrast, finds the patient's condition far more serious and calling for much bolder and more imaginative treatment. The patient's heart, Dr. Leontief regretfully discovers, suffers from grave congenital defects which inevitably manifest themselves in resource misallocation, spasms of unemployment, and idle capacity. Drastic open-heart surgery is called for, Dr. Leontief believes, which will subordinate the fitful operation of the market to carefully designed and computerized planning procedures. This treatment, it is believed, while it will indeed drastically alter the aged inner works of the system, can get the patient back on his feet behaving in a manner which his old business friends will find reassuringly familiar. If these businessmen really love this patient, we infer, they will delay not one Congressional session longer, and will support immediate surgery regardless of the financial or ideological sacrifices called for.

From this clash of opinion among the experts there emerges clear agreement on one crucial point, namely, that the debate over national economic planning hinges on the ability of the market system, the profit system, the free enterprise system, to deliver the goods, and, in particular, on the degree to which a national economic planning system (with or without a coercive machinery for its implementation) can emulate or surpass the performance of the free market. This is, as Professor Stein has made clear, by no means a new question. But the lectures do provide scope for some critical observations.

Two small details in Professor Leontief's remarks are especially noteworthy. The first of these consists in his careful explanation that national economic planning will provide to citizens a series of alternative detailed *feasible* plans from among which they can then choose. Professor Leontief does not claim that any of these feasible plans, among all *conceivable* national patterns of production, is in any sense an *optimal* one. After all, a set of alternative plans, based as they must be on past input-output structural patterns, may simply fail to include equally feasible possibilities which, in the light of current tastes and technological knowledge, might easily be judged as in some sense better than those on the planners' menu of options.

The second detail to be noted arises out of yet another of Professor Leontief's delightfully apt metaphors. In discussing how planners can harness the force of the profit motive towards the implementation of their plan, Leontief likens their task to that of the hydraulic engineer charged with regulating a major water system. In his work the engineer must take full advantage of the force of gravity, but must plan dams, dikes, and locks in such a manner as to take advantage of gravity without permitting it to create floods or devastating droughts. For Leontif the profit motive, the driving force in the market system, is like gravity both in its potential for good if controlled; and its potential for disaster if left uncontrolled.

A similarly powerful metaphor has been used elsewhere by Professor Leontief which confirms this perception by him of the market process.[2] In that metaphor the economy is seen as a sailing ship propelled by a powerful wind, the profit motive. But to permit the vessel, we are warned, simply to go before the wind without use of the rudder, is to ensure that the ship will veer off its course and land on the rocks.

Both of these rich metaphors clearly present Professor Leontief's appreciation of the market as a force which carries with it no assurance whatever that the direction towards which, without guidance, it tends is a desirable one rather than a catastrophic one. Now this view surely calls for comment. To be sure any defense of the market must recognize and come to grips with a number of well-known possible problems in its operation. But to see the entrepreneurial profit motive as a force as likely to result in harm as in benefit, cannot but cause surprise.

The crux of the matter is that every opportunity for entrepreneurial profit arises from the existence of *two* market prices for essentially the same product or the same bundle of inputs. This price divergence, which offers the opportunity for profit is, therefore, at the same time, evidence of an earlier failure of coordination among members or sectors of the economy. The drive to capture profits is, then, a drive to locate pockets of inefficiency. The successful capture of pure entrepreneurial profits occurs only through action which tends to eliminate the price spread and the inefficiency which was its cause. The ceaseless agitation of the market is thus not propelled by an undirected force, but by an extraordinarily sensitive detector of gaps in coordination. This agitation consists, therefore, in a continuing tendency to coordinate economic activity in the face of ceaseless changes in consumer preferences, resource availabilities, and technological knowledge.

In thus sniffing out existing failures of coordination, therefore, the market achieves more than merely a tendency towards the attainment of a set of mutually feasible activities. It tends towards *optimality*. But optimality is something which, as Professor Stein has suggested, and as Professor Leontief has, if I understand him correctly, not denied, national economic planning is unable to claim.

The distinction between feasibility and optimality is so important, and so instructive for an understanding of the limitations of national planning, that I venture a small parable of my own as an illustration of that distinction.

Imagine someone wishing to buy exactly thirty dollars worth of groceries at the local supermarket, who happens to be rather weak in arithmetic, and is quite intimidated by the tens of thousands of variously priced items on the shelves. The shopper is well aware that there are many millions of ways in which to spend his thirty dollars. If an expert offers to provide a list of half a dozen arithmetically airtight ways of spending thirty dollars, based on records of how this same shopper and other shoppers spent their grocery budgets in the past, our shopper is surely entitled to be doubtful. Our shopper may well feel that, while each of these alternative buying proposals is *feasible* in the sense that it requires no more than thirty dollars and leaves no money unspent none of them is likely to be *optimal*. There is no assurance that any of these proposals has taken into account the shopper's own changes in tastes since last week, or the supermarket's changes in offerings, or even the likelihood that last week's purchases were themselves suboptimal. The shopper may well feel that a better market basket—even if one arithmetically less than perfect—might result from a keen, curious, and enterprising *personal* exploration of the supermarket corridors.

Both of our distinguished lecturers have referred to widespread dissatisfaction with the performance of contemporary capitalism. It is this dissatisfaction which underlies the call for national economic planning, to supplement or supplant sole reliance on a faltering market system. Our perception of what it is that the free market tends to achieve suggests, surely, an alternative and superior path along which to search for improvements.

Professor Stein has referred to the past forty years as decades during which we have formed the broad consensus that we should assign the principal economic role to the free market, and confine the role of the government to the task of maintaining a stable and competitive framework within which the market might operate. We need not necessarily dispute this reading of the dominant view of things during the past four decades. But it must surely be pointed out that, in its rather uninhibited interpretation of the assigned role of the state, the dominant view has, during this very same period, permitted and encouraged an unprecedented explosion in the volume of governmental activity, manifesting itself in an enormous growth in the size of government itself, in a volume of regulation and intervention which has seriously constricted and distorted the scope for the competitive market process, and, above all, in an inflation of the money supply which has introduced profound and potentially catastrophic distortions all of its own.

May it not just be possible that what our sluggish and fitful patient needs for recovery is not a heart-transplant, nor even a crash program of economic research and expanded gathering of statistics, but simply fresh air, sunshine, good food and exercise, free of the addictive drug of monetary inflation, of the crushing weight of a bloated public sector, and of the mass of regulations which hamper the flow of the spontaneous and invigorating juices of free competition?

NOTES

1. P. A. Samuelson, *The Samuelson Sampler* (Glen Ridge: T. Horton and Co., 1973), p. 261.

2. W. Leontief, "Sails and Rudders, Ship of State," in L. Silk (ed.), *Capitalism the Moving Target* (New York, Praeger, 1974).

HAYEK'S THEORY OF THE COORDINATION OF MARKETS: A COMMENTARY TO ACCOMPANY THE FACSIMILE EDITION OF HAYEK'S *PREISE UND PRODUKTION*

It is generally recognized that *Preise und Produktion* played a pivotal role in the development of Hayek's life's work in economics. It is thoroughly appropriate, therefore, that the publication of this facsimile edition of this classic work should inspire us, in the years immediately following the conclusion of Hayek's labors, to re-examine that pivotal role, from the perspective made possible by our present fuller appreciation of the totality of that contribution. *Preise und Produktion* was of course pivotal for several areas of Hayek's work, especially for his monetary theory, for his cycle theory, and for his theory of capital. This commentary will not, however, examine these important facets of Hayek's work. Instead we will seek to examine that aspect of *Preise und Produktion* which concerns the centrality in Hayek's economics of the *coordination achieved by the market,* among the individual plans made by diverse market participants.

There can be little doubt that in Hayek's own assessment of his work, as seen from the vantage point of the last decade of his life, one of the leading elements in his economic understanding was that encapsulated in the notion of *plan-coordination,* and of the function of market prices to serve as signals helping achieve such coordination. There can be little doubt, too, that in retrospect, at least, Hayek saw his *Preise und Produktion* as expressing this leading element of his life-long contribution. When, in 1981, exactly fifty years after he first delivered the London School of Economics (LSE) lectures for which this work was prepared, Hayek delivered a commemorative lecture at the same platform, he introduced it by remarking that in these 1931 lectures he had "made use of what became the leading theme of most of my later work, an analysis of the signal function of prices in guiding production, a conception which I first expounded systematically a few years later in my presidential address to the London Economics Club on 'Economics and Knowledge.'"[1]

Previously unpublished translation of "Hayeks Theorie der Koordination von Märkten," printed here by permission of Israel M. Kirzner. Originally published in German in Friedrich A. Hayek, *Preise und Produktion* (Düsseldorf: Verlag Wirtschaft und Finanzen, 1995).

It must be confessed that a reading of *Preise und Produktion* yields few *direct* clues to Hayek's awareness in 1931 of the idea of plan-coordination and of the signal function fulfilled by market prices in effecting such a coordination of plans. Nonetheless, as we shall see, there are strong grounds to support Hayek's retrospective 1981 judgment concerning his 1931 work. We will in fact be able to argue: (i) that germs of the coordination and price signal insights of Hayek's 1937 and 1945 papers[2] can be found already in Hayek's papers of the late 1920s; and (ii) that it was *Preise und Produktion* (which Hayek describes as having been—uncharacteristically—written out "in a few weeks, in the excitement about a new insight gained, and not from notes accumulated over years"[3]) which in fact crystallized these ideas *in the specific context of monetary and capital theory*; and (iii) that it was the more careful development (in the years after 1931) of the ideas rapidly sketched out in *Preise und Produktion* which enabled Hayek in his 1933 Copenhagen lecture,[4] and especially in his above-mentioned 1936 presidential address to the London Economics Club,[5] to articulate the coordination insights in more systematic and more general terms. We shall feel justified, therefore, in claiming that *Preise und Produktion* indeed played a pivotal role in the development of what we believe to be Hayek's most important contribution to economic understanding,—the idea that market-processes are to be understood as processes of plan coordination, with market prices playing the key role in communicating the information necessary for the achievement of such coordination.

THE CENTRAL THESIS OF *PREISE UND PRODUKTION*— WITH AND WITHOUT THE COORDINATION INSIGHT

The apparent paradox that a work in which no direct clues to the coordination insight are to be found can yet be claimed to have played a pivotal role in the development of that insight, requires that we remind ourselves of the central thesis of the book. Following on the work of Mises and earlier writers, Hayek showed in *Preise und Produktion* how an inflationary monetary environment can generate a boom fuelled by a powerful but undetected tendency towards the malinvestment of capital, and how the subsequent depression phase of the business cycle is to be understood as the market's way of revealing and exposing the economic disaster constituted by that malinvestment. The kernel of this "Austrian" theory of the business cycle is that the pattern of production generated during (and in fact constituting) the boom phase will eventually prove impossible to be sustained. The bust is the inevitable revelation of the unsustainability of the pattern of production which constituted the boom. There appear to be three parallel, but arguably distinct, ways to tell the story set forth in this theory. The first way, as we shall see, finds no need to make any reference whatever to plan coordination or discoordination, nor even to any errors or to error-correction. The second way, while making no reference to plan discoordination, does proceed by focussing on the *mistakes* made during the boom, and their *correction* during the subsequent downturn. It is the third way of expounding the Austrian theory of the trade cycle which explicitly refers to plan discoordination. We shall, in what follows, set forth our more careful articulation of these three ways of stating the Austrian cycle theory. It will be our thesis in this commentary that while the third way of expressing the theory has become the standard contemporary statement of that theory, Hayek himself in 1931 did *not* employ that mode of expression. Instead, like Mises before him, he mainly employed the first (of these three modes of exposition)—but with ample clues suggesting also the second mode of exposition. Nonetheless, we shall claim, Hayek's 1931 statement *pointed* rather clearly in the direction of the third mode of exposition, and can therefore be recognized as a stepping stone, at least, towards the coordination insights which loom so importantly in Hayek's later work. Let us review somewhat more carefully the three possible modes of expounding the Austrian theory of the business cycle.

(1) The Austrian theory can be expounded baldly in terms of capital availability. During the boom entrepreneurs are led (by artificially low nominal rates of interest) to behave as if the available capital resources are more plentiful than is actually the case. Sooner or later the truth will reassert itself: the capital needed to complete projects that have been initiated, will simply not be there when needed. Projects will inevitably fail for lack of capital; the boom has led to the unavoidable bust.

In 1928 Mises expressed this way of telling the story briefly as follows: "In a given economic situation, the opportunities for production, which may actually be carried out, are limited by the supply of capital goods available. Roundabout methods of production can be adopted only so far as the means for subsistence exist to maintain the workers during the entire period of the expanded process. All those projects, for the completion of which means are not available, must be left uncompleted. . . . However, such businesses, because of the lower loan rate offered by the banks, appear for the moment to be profitable and are, therefore, initiated. However, the existing resources are insufficient. Sooner or later this must become evident."[6]

In his maturest statements of the theory, Mises again apparently had such a mode of exposition in mind. "The whole entrepreneurial class is, as it were, in the position of a master-builder whose task it is to erect a building out of a limited supply of building materials. If this man over-estimates the quantity of the available supply, he drafts a plan for the execution of which the means at his disposal are not sufficient. He over-sizes the groundwork and the foundations and only discovers later in the progress of the construction that he lacks the material needed for the completion of the structure."[7] Notice that although Mises refers to "over-estimation" of available building materials, the notion of error and error-correction are not at all necessary for this mode of exposition.[8] What is crucial is simply that during the boom, production projects are initiated which will later not be able to be completed, because of lack of capital resources. At the same time, of course, it is easy to see how this exposi-tion *might* be cast in terms of error and error-correction. Only error could, after all, permit the initiation of unsustainable projects. This in fact is the second possible mode of exposition.

(2) In this mode of exposition what is emphasized is that the boom consists of *wrong, mistaken,* production decisions. Artificially low rates of interest (resulting from the inflationary monetary environment) mislead entrepreneurs to invest in processes of production which are "too long" (as judged from the perspective of the true, lesser willingness of consum-ers to postpone consumption). Sooner or later these mistakes will be revealed for what they are—as unsustainable mistakes. The true, higher time preferences of consumers will reassert themselves and manifest themselves in the market shortage of the capital needed to complete initi-ated production projects. At that time the errors embodied in the earlier plans will have been revealed through the failure of those projects. This painful process in which the earlier errors are exposed constitutes, in this way of telling the story, the *correction* of the earlier mistakes: production projects are once again forced correctly to dovetail with the actual avail-ability of capital, with the true higher time preferences of the consuming public. We have already noticed[9] that Mises's 1928 statement referred to such a perspective. He wrote, in regard to the downturn following the boom: "Then it will become apparent that production has gone astray,

that plans were drawn up in excess of the economic means available, that speculation, i.e., activity aimed at the provision of future goods, was misdirected."[10] In *Preise und Produktion,* too, there are several such references to "Fehlleitungen der Produktion,"[11] and one to "Kapitalfehlleitungen" (with the latter word in quotes in the original).[12]

The difference between the first and the second of these two ways of telling the Austrian story of the trade cycle is obvious. The first way does not invoke any concept of error. The boom consists of disequilibrating decisions which must, sooner or later, be overwhelmed by the forces of equilibration. That is all. As Lachmann explained, Hayek's theory of the cycle depended on Paretian general equilibrium insights. For Hayek "the task of trade cycle theory was to show how it came about that [the] major [equilibrating] forces were temporarily impeded . . . , and since the cycle was supposed to start with a boom and end with a depression, he saw in the depression the ultimate triumph of the equilibrating forces."[13] The second way of telling the same story simply translates the concepts of disequilibration and equilibration into the language of error and its correction. The boom, in which equilibrating forces are successfully held at bay, consists in "wrong" decisions (i.e., wrong from a perspective which recognizes the true arrays of data which must sooner or later exercise their force), while the downturn now consists of the painful but necessary "correction" of earlier errors, as the true arrays of data in fact succeed in making themselves inescapably felt. Sometimes expositions of the Austrian theory combined elements of both the first and the second modes of telling the story. As example of this was offered by Machlup in a classic 1935 paper in which he briefly presented the Austrian theory of the cycle. "Absolute or relative overlengthening of the investment period is the probable result of expansion of producers' credit. The length is excessive in the sense that without any 'outside' influences (without change in data) internal forces will lead to a reshortening of the investment period, sooner or later. The 'internal forces' consist in a divergence between the individual time preferences . . . and the time structure of production."[14] Certainly there is not much more than a nuance of difference between a story told in "positive" terms of disequilibration and equilibration, and one told in "normative" terms of entrepreneurial error and its subsequently painful correction by the forces of the market. Our emphasis on this nuance of difference has the purpose of focussing attention on the *third* mode of telling the Hayekian story.

(3) In this third way of telling the story, the focus is not on disequilibration and equilibration per se, nor on error and correction (in any narrow sense) but upon the discoordination of the plans of market participants (which occurs during the boom) and upon the subsequent achievement by the market (painful though this achievement may be for entrepreneurs) of greater coordination between the intertemporal plans of the producers, and the intertemporal plans of the consumers. Late twentieth century expositions of the Austrian theory of the trade cycle seem frequently to follow this mode. Thus in a 1989 paper Roger Garrison described the Austrian theory of the business cycle as amounting "to a theory of intertemporal discoordination."[15] In a 1992 book a critic of the Austrian theory describes the "deeper structure" of production generated in the boom (as explained in Austrian theory) as unstable "because the plans of producers and consumers are no longer compatible with each other."[16] In a book perceptively dedicated to the demonstration of the decisive centrality of the notion of coordination to Hayek's economics, Gerald O'Driscoll wrote: "For Hayek, the crucial question for business cycle theory was the mutual correspondence of the plans of savers and investors and those of consumers and producers."[17] As noted earlier, one would search *Preise und Produktion* in vain to discover explicit bases for such statements. Nonetheless, we wish to maintain, these interpretations of the 1931 Hayek are *not* flatly incorrect. Let us take note of the explicit emergence, in Hayek's subsequent work, of his understanding of the signalling function of prices, and of how this function serves to bring the decisions of market participants into mutual coordination.

PRICES AS SIGNALS: MARKET PROCESSES
AS COORDINATIVE PROCEDURES

In his book, devoted (as already noted) to the explication of Hayek's ideas on coordination, O'Driscoll refers to Hayek's "tetrad on economic coordination."[18] These four papers[19] (all republished in Hayek's 1949 *Individualism and Economic Order*) were first published and/or delivered as lectures in the decade beginning with 1936. In this ten-year period Hayek developed nothing less, in effect, than a completely fresh articulation of Austrian microeconomics. In this fresh articulation, the focus was placed squarely upon the *plans* of individual market participants, and upon the ability of competitive markets to achieve a tendency towards the mutual coordination of such individual plans. Hayek's new approach drew explicit attention to the role of knowledge, ignorance, and learning in the competitive market process. At any given moment we can expect mutual ignorance to be responsible for some degree of discoordination among the decisions being made by market participants. From the disappointment of plans, generated by such discoordination, there is, under typical conditions, a likelihood (but by no means any inevitability) that market participants will learn better to anticipate one another's decisions and attitudes. In this way, with market prices functioning as signals, as surrogates for explicit communication of market information, the competitive market process is likely to generate important tendencies towards greater mutual coordination. In the limit this can be imagined, as a useful (but also possibly misleading) exercise, to lead, ceteris paribus, to the state of equilibrium (in which all decisions made are fully mutually coordinated, with nobody's decisions leading to subsequent disappointment or regret). This, in a nutshell, was the heart of Hayek's monumental achievement—an achievement that was hardly noticed by the economics profession at the time, and which was developed in a decade in which Hayek was generally viewed as having been decisively defeated in the theoretical battlefield areas of the late thirties.

Certainly this Hayekian microeconomic understanding does not depend in any way upon the Austrian theory of the trade cycle. This new understanding, adumbrating major contributions to Austrian price theory, to the theory of competition, and to welfare economics, is completely distinct from Austrian monotary theory, capital theory, and trade cycle theory. It might therefore be argued that *Preise und Produktion* published five years before the decade in which Hayek developed these microeconomic insights (and itself containing no explicit references to any processes of coordination or discoordination) should not be seen as an anticipation of the coordination perspective. It might be argued, that is, that the later statements which we have noticed which presented Hayek's 1931 thesis in terms of coordination and discoordination, represent an unjustified revisionist reinterpretation of the 1931 work, through the hindsight made possible by Hayek's later contributions. We believe that such argument would be unfair. In fact, we shall claim, the subsequent reinterpretation of Hayek's 1931 thesis in coordination terms (a reinterpretation which we owe primarily to the pioneering, *dogmengeschichtliche* insight of Gerald O'Driscoll)[20] provides an illuminating perspective on the role of *Preise und Produktion* in Hayek's life's work. There is every reason to see Hayek's later contributions to Austrian microeconomics as, at least in part, the unintended outcome of a scientific discovery procedure in which *Preise und Produktion* played an important part.[21] Let us examine some of Hayek's contributions that pre-date the 1931 work.

HAYEK IN THE NINETEEN TWENTIES: THE BACKGROUND FOR *PREISE UND PRODUKTION*

The earliest published statement by Hayek of the Austrian cycle theory (the theory he was to elaborate in *Preise und Produktion*) was in a long footnote to a 1925 paper.[22] That paper was published in English translation in 1984 (in the collection of early Hayek papers edited by Roy McCloughry),[23] and Hayek (in his 1984 introduction to that collection) drew special attention to that footnote. The footnote was added, Hayek recalled, at the urging of Gottfried Haberler, who persuaded him in 1925 that a brief reference in the text of the paper to the theory of the cycle as expounded by Mises was simply inadequate. The brief statement in the text (together with a footnote reference to Mises's treatise on monetary theory) referred to the consequences of an artificially low rate of interest engineered by the banks. Such a rate "makes capital investments continue to appear to be profitable though in fact they exceed the economically permissible level and hence must sooner or later be partly lost."[24] In the long footnote which Hayek added as an elaboration of this brief statement, he referred to "a disproportionate development of the production of goods of higher order" and to "an excessive accumulation of capital." Certainly this statement, barely recognizing the error-element in the boom, makes no reference to any coordination failure among the intertemporal plans being made by market participants. Yet the long footnote clearly treats capital not as a homogeneous blob of productive capacity, but as a complex, multi-dimensional entity the components of which may be thrown out of order by the false stimulation of the artificially low rate of interest. It was this distinctive feature of Hayek's exposition which he was to pursue in subsequent writings and which, we wish to suggest, would eventually lead him to the "coordination" approach.

The next significant link in the development of Hayek's approach is probably to be found in his celebrated 1928 paper "Intertemporal Price Equilibrium and Movements in the Value of Money."[25] For our purposes the significant feature of this paper was its recognition of the system of intertemporal exchange ratios and the related sharply reduced emphasis upon the significance of the "general price level" at any particular moment in time, and especially the paper's sharp critique of the belief that sound economic policy requires stability over time in this general average level of prices. This attack upon excessive attention to the average of all prices became a central feature of Hayek's subsequent writings on the monetary (i.e., the "Austrian") theory of the cycle. This paper was undoubtedly, quite apart from its other contributions, an important link in the development of Hayek's deep suspicions of uncritical aggregative thinking in economics, of that type of thinking which recognizes significant relationships only between aggregates (of output, capital, labor) or averages (of prices). This paper set the stage for Hayek's own focus on the *time structure* of production, the structure of capital, and on possible aberrations in these structures which might remain totally invisible to economists concerned only with the sum total of output or the total value of the capital stock.

As we shall see, it was to be this insistence by Hayek upon the *internal structure* lying beneath the surface of economic aggregates and averages, whether output, capital stock, or price "level," which inspired his *Preise und Produktion* and which, it can be argued, was eventually to generate Hayek's insights into the coordinative function of the market process and into the signalling role played by market prices in inducing compatibility among the decisions of individuals.

PREISE UND PRODUKTION—
THE MICROFOUNDATIONS OF MACROECONOMICS

Preise und Produktion opens, in fact, with the observation explaining that this work "stellt teils eine Zusammenfassung und vor allem eine Fortführung von Gedankengängen dar, die ich im Laufe der letzten sechs Jahre in einer Reihe von Abhandlungen entwickelt habe"[26] (with a footnote referring, among other papers, to those we have here cited in the preceding section). There is little doubt that profound skepticism concerning simplistic aggregative thinking in economics played a crucial role in *Preise und Produktion*. Years later, in the essay prepared in connection with Hayek's receiving the 1974 Nobel prize in economics, Fritz Machlup cited Hayek's book as a pioneering recognition "that we have not completed our task before we have ascertained the micro-economic basis of all macro-economic theorizing."[27] Hayek argued that "if we try to establish *direct* causal connections between the *total* quantity of money, the *general level* of all prices and, perhaps, also the total amount of production," we are in effect cutting off monetary theory from general economic theory. "For none of these magnitudes *as such* ever exerts an influence on the decisions of individuals; yet it is on the assumption of a knowledge of the decisions of individuals that the main propositions of non-monetary economic theory are based. . . . In fact, neither aggregates nor averages do act upon one another. . . ."[28] Hayek in fact went on to assert that "from the very nature of economic theory, averages can never form a link in its reasoning,"[29] and described *Preise und Produktion* as "an attempt to show in a special field the differences between explanations which do and explanations which do not have recourse" to aggregates and averages.[30]

It is clear that it is this "individualistic" method (which Hayek saw as the basis for the advances made by the "modern 'subjective' theory" over the classical school)[31] which is responsible for the *"Preise"* in the title of this book. And it is in its third chapter (entitled "The Working of the Price Mechanism in the Course of the Credit Cycle") in which Hayek explores in detail how the various phases of the cycle are to be under-stood in terms of "the changes in relative prices which bring it about that goods are directed to new uses."[32] And, of course, it is the central thesis of the work that the cycle itself is to be seen as consisting in "die *realen Verschiebungen* im Aufbau der Produktion."[33] Years later Hayek himself traced his insights to his new interest in the 1920s in the "steering pro-cess in the market economy. I was then becoming increasingly aware that the guide function of the process determining the effectiveness of our efforts . . . could operate satisfactorily only if monetary demand cor-responded to real demand, not so much in the aggregate as in the relative proportions of the different goods which were demanded and supplied."[34] There can be little doubt that it was *Preise und Produktion* which crystal-lized these insights for Hayek.

What we wish to argue here is not only that *Preise und Produktion* crystallized these earlier Hayekian insights, but that this crystalliza-tion pointed towards those advances in Hayek's thinking which would later on be systematically developed in Hayek's "tetrad on economic coordination."

We have already noticed that although, in the main, Hayek's 1931 expo-sition is couched in the "positive" terms of equilibration and disequilibra-tion (via the mediation of market prices, whether or not these have been distorted by an inflationary environment), that exposition nonetheless occasionally slips into terminology which pronounces the production decisions made in the boom as having been *wrong*, involving "misdirection" or "malinvestment" of capital. One might perhaps have expected Hayek's subsequent writings to have expanded on these hints. However, when Hayek's 1931 lectures (in their original English version) encountered the notoriously savage criticisms of Sraffa[35] and of Keynes,[36] it was precisely this "structural" feature of Hayek's theory which they seemed completely to ignore. (In his response to Keynes's critique Hayek indeed complained on this score: "It seems never to have occurred to him that the artificial stimulus to investment, which makes it exceed current saving, may cause a dis-equilibrium in the real structure of production which, sooner or later, must lead to a reaction."[37] Because Sraffa and Keynes focussed their criticisms on the macro implications of Hayek's thesis (completely ignoring Hayek's interpretation of the boom as the manifestation of a disequilibrated distortion in the structure of production),[38] Hayek found himself forced to defend himself on ground not at all of his own choosing. So that the best known of Hayek's defenses of his 1931 work did not, in the main, emphasize that central aspect of his cycle theory which seems closest to his later insights in terms of the plan-coordination function of the market process. Nonetheless there is a very clear trail which can be followed, leading from *Preise und Produktion* directly to Hayek's "tetrad on economic coordination." This trail proceeds very clearly through Hayek's notable Copenhagen lecture of 1933. This circumstance has been valuably emphasized by Gerald O'Driscoll.[39]

FROM *PREISE UND PRODUKTION*
TO "ECONOMICS AND KNOWLEDGE"

Hayek's Copenhagen lecture[40] is known for its pioneering emphasis upon the role of expectations in economic dynamics. It deserves also to be remembered for its brief but novel interpretation of economic equilibrium in terms of the compatibility of the plans of market participants, and of their mutual sets of expectations.

> It is evident that the various expectations on which different individuals base their decisions at a particular moment either will or will not be mutually compatible; and that if these expectations are not compatible those of some people at least must be disappointed. It is probably clear also that expectations existing at a particular moment will to a

large extent be based on prices existing at that moment and that we can conceive of constellations of such prices which will create expectations inevitably doomed to disappointment, and of other constellations which do not bear the germ of such disappointments and which create expectations which—at least if there are no unforeseen changes in external circumstances—may be in harmony with the actual course of events.[41]

Here we have a remarkably clear anticipation of the insights which Hayek was to articulate in more detailed fashion in his later work on coordination. And, indeed, in the 1939 first publication of the English version of the Copenhagen lecture, Hayek noted (in a footnote to an earlier paragraph on the same page as the statement we have cited) that these ideas were subsequently further elaborated and revised in his 1937 paper—"Economics and Knowledge"—the first paper in the coordination tetrad (and expressing, in Hayek's later judgment, "the decisive point of the change in my outlook").[42]

It is worth emphasizing (as O'Driscoll has indeed already emphasized) that this early statement of the "compatibility of plans" approach was initially presented explicitly by Hayek in the narrow context of his work on industrial fluctuations. This permitted Hayek to see the boom as caused by entrepreneurs in general being "equally misled by following guides or symptoms which as a rule prove reliable." More concretely, "the prices existing when [entrepreneurs] made their decisions"—the decisions which drive the boom—"and on which they had to base their views about the future have created expectations which must necessarily be disappointed."[43] But this was to be followed by Hayek's perceiving that this new approach enabled economists to restate not only Austrian cycle theory but also the most fundamental elements of economic theory in general in an entirely new language—that of initial plan incompatibility, the discovery and communication of information, and the process of plan coordination. What began as an insight into a classic Austrian theory of the trade cycle had come, by 1936, to be perceived (or at least glimpsed) as the key to a crucially important new way of understanding the most basic theorems of economic science.

This writer has elsewhere[44] argued that it was the interwar debate on the possibility of rational economic calculation under socialism, which was largely responsible for the later refinements in the understanding of competitive market processes achieved by Mises and by Hayek. Our consideration of the background from which *Preise und Produktion* emerged, and of the Copenhagen lecture which followed that work within a couple of years, has taught us that this work appears to have played a similarly important role in those later refinements. When one takes note of the circumstance that Hayek's earliest attention to the socialist calculation debate appears to have been expressed in his two papers published in the book on the subject which he edited in 1935[45]—midway between his Copenhagen lecture and the publication of his first paper in the coordination tetrad—one is in fact tempted somewhat to revise one's reading of the relevant intellectual development. Certainly it was the calculation debate which served as the catalyst for the Mises-Hayek insights into the dynamic character of the market process. But, in the case of Hayek, it is a plausible conjecture that it was the insights emerging from *Preise und Produktion* (as pursued in the Copenhagen lecture) which in turn helped direct his attention to the calculation debate, and to the subtle nuances of the Austrian appreciation for the market process, which undergird that side of the debate. All this permits us to consider more broadly the role played by *Preise und Produktion* in the evolution of Hayek's later coordination insights, as perceived from the perspective made possible by the completion of his life's work.

PREISE UND PRODUKTION—
THE BASIS FOR A LIFELONG RESEARCH AGENDA

We have already noticed early in this commentary that Hayek, looking back from the perspective of 1981, saw *Preise und Produktion* as embracing the "signal function of prices in guiding production," an idea he linked to his 1937 paper, "Economics and Knowledge." And we have taken note of the circumstance that late twentieth century expositions of Hayek's cycle theory tend almost invariably to state that theory explicitly in terms of the discoordination of plans which occurs during the boom. This perspective, gained towards the conclusion of Hayek's life's work not only in economics but also in related fields in political science, history of ideas, philosophy, and social understanding in general, appears to have acquired fairly wide acceptance. In a paper published in honor of Hayek's ninetieth birthday, Dieter Schmidtchen and Siegfried Utzig expressed a similar attitude. They pointed out, in regard to Hayek's cycle theory, that the "Problem der fehlerhaften Koordination stand auch im Mittelpunkt von Hayeks Interesse, als er später der Frage nachging, wie das auf viele Köpfe der Gesellschaft verteilte Wissen, verwertet werden kann und welch Rolle die Preise dabei spielen . . . Betrachtet man Hayeks Arbeiten in der hier skizzierten Weise, so ergibt sich, dass seine Beschäftigung mit dem Phänomen Konjunktur am Anfang eines lebenslangen Forschungsprogramms zu dem Thema 'Koordination im Wirtschaftsprozess' stand."[46] We have seen that such a retrospective judgment seems to have been first articulated by O'Driscoll in his 1977 book.[47] In fact, it is distinctly possible that O'Driscoll's judgment may have influenced Hayek's own retrospective self-assessment. Indeed, in his foreword to O'Driscoll's book, Hayek seems to have recognized this very possibility. "It is a curious fact," he wrote, "that a student of complex phenomena may long himself remain unaware of how his views of different problems hang together. . . . I must confess that I was occasionally myself surprised when I found in Professor O'Driscoll's account side-by-side statements I made at the interval of many years and on quite different problems, which still implied the same general approach."[48] (Hayek proceeds then to refer specifically to "such different problems as those of industrial fluctuations and the running of a socialist economy.") It was presumably this "surprise" which Hayek was acknowledging in 1977 that moved him to qualify the retrospective self-assessment he offered in his 1984 introduction to the collection of his early essays published in English under the editorship of Roy McCloughry. In that introduction he saw the development of his ideas (at about the time that he was writing *Preise und Produktion*) in terms of the "steering process in the market economy." Hayek immediately qualified this by confessing that, looking back on the field more than half a century later, "I find it difficult to say how much of what I am now inclined to read into these early attempts I was clearly aware of at the time."[49] In the next, concluding section of this commentary the writer will suggest a sense in which, from the hindsight of the 1990s, we can indeed view *Preise und Produktion* as initiating a consistent development in Hayek's thinking—a development in which different perspectives upon coordination played important roles.

COORDINATION AND COORDINATION

It is generally acknowledged that *Preise und Produktion* was written with Hayek accepting the propositions of general equilibrium theory, at least as the background for the articulation of his theory of the trade cycle.

Despite the contrary view expressed by Roger Garrison,[50] few would disagree with Lachmann's judgment that Hayek's "early work was clearly under the influence of the general equilibrium model" and that at one time he "appeared to regard a strong tendency towards general equilibrium as a real phenomenon of the market economy."[51] (In fact *Preise und Produktion* has, in the work of some modern writers, been linked to the equilibrium-centered models of new-classical macroeconomics.)[52] We do not wish to dispute the characterization of the 1931 Hayek as subscribing to general equilibrium theory. Instead we wish to argue, in this section, that the "coordination" insights implicit in *Preise und Produktion* would initiate developments in Hayek's thinking which were to lead to a decisive *change* in his attitude towards equilibrium theory. It is because this decisive change was to prove so central to Hayek's "far-flung oeuvre,"[53] that we can support the thesis that *Preise und Produktion* indeed played an important role in his subsequent scientific work over six decades.

The point we wish to make is a simple one. There are, as we shall see, two distinct meanings that may be attached to the word "coordination." One of these meanings is fully consistent with exclusive emphasis upon the general equilibrium state; the second meaning is not. The coordination notion implicit in *Preise und Produktion* is, unsurprisingly, that which *is* consistent with general equilibrium. Yet Hayek's further development of this first notion of coordination eventually led him, in effect, to appreciate the importance of the *second* sense of the coordination notion. In this way Hayek was led, along a trail which certainly began with *Preise und Produktion,* towards a way of understanding the market process which was, in many ways, quite inconsistent with the equilibrium framework within which *Preise und Produktion* had been written. Let us develop this thesis somewhat more fully.

"Coordination" may, in the first sense, refer to the fully coordinated *state of affairs.* Each decision made correctly anticipates the other decisions being made. No plan is frustrated because others act differently from what had been expected. In this sense the word "coordination" is not merely consistent with the equilibrium state in market theory, it in fact expresses (a particular interpretation of) precisely that state.

On the other hand "coordination" may also refer to the *process* in the course of which initially uncoordinated decisions *may be brought into greater mutual compatibility.*[54] In this sense the word refers not at all to the attained state of equilibrium, but, instead, to the equilibrating process which a market may be held to generate. It refers to that process of mutual discovery through which a state of attained coordination may possibly be achieved.

In *Preise und Produktion* the inflationary monetary environment was shown to promote discoordination (in the sense that the resulting state of affairs—the situation during the boom phase of the cycle—expresses decisions which erroneously anticipate other decisions, which will in fact not be made). In his subsequent further development of what is implied by such a state of discoordination, Hayek was led (as we have seen earlier in this commentary) to recognize the crucial role of knowledge and of expectations in generating either more fully or less fully coordinated sets of decisions. It was this recognition that was to lead Hayek in his tetrad on coordination, decisively to reject the preoccupation with equilibrium theory which characterizes mainstream twentieth century economics, and to focus attention, eventually, on those processes of mutual discovery through which dynamic competition in the market nudges mutual expectations towards greater compatibility (and sustainability).[55] In this mature Hayekian vision, the significance of prices as signals rests not in their ability to sustain the state of coordination already present in the attained state of equilibrium. Rather it consists in the ability of disequilibrium prices to elicit those entrepreneurial profit-seeking moves upon which, possibly, a significant tendency towards equilibration may depend.

In finally arriving at this insight into the coordinative character of the market process (as against the coordinated state of equilibrium) Hayek was, it can be argued, converging towards the position occupied by his old mentor, Ludwig von Mises. Mises had, in his 1949 *Human Action*, emphatically rejected standard equilibrium theory in favor of an appreciation for the entrepreneurial process generated by disequilibrium conditions.[56] *Preise und Produktion* was written, one recalls, as a result of Hayek's wish to present Mises's brief statement of the Austrian theory of the trade cycle in a more carefully and more fully articulated form.[57] That work generated, we have argued, a dynamic intellectual development in Hayek's views. In the course of that development Hayek's perspective on the role of knowledge sharply *diverged* from the views of Mises.[58] Yet this same intellectual development, we have now seen, was finally to bring Hayek's mature understanding of the market process extremely close to Mises's own mature articulation of that process. It is a fascinating circumstance that Hayek's *Preise und Produktion* set him on a path which most

190 COORDINATION, PLANNING, AND THE KNOWLEDGE PROBLEM

intriguingly illustrates what he has called "my curious relation to Ludwig von Mises, from whom I have probably learnt more than from any other man. . . ."[59] For the purposes of the present commentary, what is important is that this path consists of what Hayek was later to see as his "most original contribution" to economic theory,[60] that is, of the interpretation of market processes as *processes of mutually coordinating discoveries*.

NOTES

1. F. A. Hayek, manuscript of introductory remarks to "The Flow of Goods and Services," lecture at London School of Economics, January 27, 1982, p. 2.

2. F. A. Hayek, "Economics and Knowledge," *Economica* 4 n.s., no. 13 (1937): 33–54 (Hayek's presidential address to London School Club, November 10, 1936); "The Use of Knowledge in Society," *American Economic Review* 35, no. 4 (September 1945): 519–30. Both papers are reprinted in F. A. Hayek, *Individualism and Economic Order* (London: Routledge and Kegan Paul, 1949).

3. F. A. Hayek, manuscript of introductory remarks to "The Flow of Goods and Services," p. 1.

4. F. A. Hayek, "Price Expectations, Monetary Disturbances and Malinvestments," translation of German-language article in *Nationalökonomisk Tidsskrift* 73, no. 3 (1935) (based on a lecture given in Copenhagen, December 7, 1933), published in English translation as chapter 4 in Hayek's *Profits, Interest and Investment and Other Essays on the Theory of Industrial Fluctuations* (London: George Routledge and Sons, 1939).

5. See above, note 2.

6. Ludwig von Mises, "Monetary Stabilization and Cyclical Policy" (translated by Bettina Bien Greaves from the German original *Geldwertstabilisierung und Konjunkturpolitik*, 1928), in Ludwig von Mises, *On the Manipulation of Money and Credit*, ed. Percy L. Greaves, Jr. (Dobbs Ferry, N.Y.: Free Market Books, 1978), pp. 125f.

7. Ludwig von Mises, *Human Action: A Treatise on Economics* (New Haven: Yale University Press, 1949), p. 557.

8. This holds also for Mises's 1928 statement (above) which is followed in the original text by a sentence referring to the plans which inspired the boom projects as having been "misdirected": see below in the text here.

9. See preceding note.

10. Mises, "Monetary Stabilization and Cyclical Policy," p. 126.

11. "Misdirections of production"; F. A. Hayek, *Preise und Produktion*, published as no. 3 in *Beiträge zur Konjunkturforschung* (herausgegeben von Österreichischen Institut für Konjunkturforschung (Wien: Julius Springer, 1931), pp. 99, 110.

12. "Misdirections of production"; ibid., p. 94.

13. Ludwig M. Lachmann, "Austrian Economics under Fire: The Hayek-Sraffa Duel in Retrospect," in *Austrian Economics, Historical and Philosophical Background*, ed. Wolfgang Grassl and Barry Smith (New York: New York University Press, 1986), p. 227.

14. Fritz Machlup, "Professor Knight and the 'Period of Production,'" *Journal of Political Economy* 43, no. 5 (1935), reprinted in *Classics in Austrian Economics: A Sampling in the History of a Tradition*, ed. Israel M. Kirzner (London: Pickering, 1994), vol. 2, pp. 304ff.

15. Roger W. Garrison, "The Austrian Theory of the Business Cycle in the Light of Modern Macroeconomics," *Review of Austrian Economics* 3 (1989): 24.

16. Stavros Ioannides, *The Market, Competition and Democracy: A Critique of Neo-Austrian Economics* (Aldershot: Edward Elgar, 1992), p. 123.

17. Gerald P. O'Driscoll, Jr., *Economics as a Coordination Problem: The Contributions of Friedrich A. Hayek* (Kansas City: Sheed Andrews and McMeel, 1977), p. 73.

18. O'Driscoll, *Economics as a Coordination Problem*, p. 67.

19. Hayek, "Economics and Knowledge"; "The Facts of the Social Sciences," *Ethics* 54, no. 1 (October 1943): 1–13; "Use of Knowledge"; "The Meaning of Competition," lecture delivered at Princeton University, May 20, 1946.

20. See O'Driscoll, *Economics as a Coordination Problem*.

21. See Israel M. Kirzner, *The Meaning of Market Process: Essays in the Development of Modern Austrian Economics* (London: Routledge, 1992), chap. 6, for the view that the socialist economic calculation debate was also an important catalyst in this process of discovery; see also further below in this paper on this point.

22. F. A. Hayek, "Die Währungspolitik der Vereinigten Staaten seit der Überwindung der Krise von 1920," *Zeitschrift für Volkswirtschaft und Sozialpolitik* n.s. 5 (1925), vols. 1–3, 25–63, and vols. 4–6, 254–317.

23. F. A. Hayek, "The Monetary Policy of the United States after the Recovery from the 1920 Crisis," in *Money, Capital and Fluctuations: Early Essays*, ed. by Roy McCloughry (Chicago: University of Chicago Press, 1984), chap. 1.

24. Hayek, *Money, Capital and Fluctuations*, p. 10. In the text the statement is accompanied by a footnote reference to Ludwig von Mises, *Theorie des Geldes und der Umlaufsmittel*, 2nd ed. (Munich: Duncker und Humblot, 1912), pp. 373ff.

25. Published as "Das intertemporale Gleichgewichtssystem der Preise und die Bewegungen des 'Geldwertes,'" in *Weltwirtschaftliches Archiv*, no. 2 (1928): 33–76; English translation, F. A. Hayek, *Money, Capital and Fluctuations*, chap. 4.

26. "[It] presents partly a synthesis and above all an extension of theories which I have developed in a series of articles during the course of the last six years." Hayek, *Preise und Produktion*, p. vi.

27. Fritz Machlup, "Friedrich von Hayek's Contribution to Economics," *Swedish Journal of Economics* 76 (December 1974), reprinted in *Friedrich A. Hayek: Critical Assessments*, ed. John Cunningham Wood and Ronald N. Woods (New York and London: Routledge, 1991), vol. 2, pp. 200ff.

28. F. A. Hayek, *Prices and Production*, 2nd revised and enlarged edition (London: Routledge, 1935), p. 4.

29. Ibid. p. 5.

30. Ibid.

31. Ibid. p. 4.

32. Ibid. p. 69.

33. "The real changes of the structure of production"; Hayek, *Preise und Produktion* (1931), p. vii.

34. Hayek, *Money, Capital and Fluctuations*, p. 1.

35. Piero Sraffa, "Dr. Hayek on Money and Capital," *Economic Journal* 42 (March 1932): 42–53, and "A Rejoinder," *Economic Journal* 42 (June 1932): 249–51.

36. J. M. Keynes, "The Pure Theory of Money: A Reply to Dr. Hayek," *Economica* 11, no. 34 (November 1931): 387–97.

37. F. A. Hayek, "Reflections on the Pure Theory of Money of Mr. J. M. Keynes (cont.) II," *Economica* 12, no. 35 (February 1932), reprinted in Wood and Woods, *Friedrich A Hayek*, vol. 1, p. 79.

38. It is plausible to argue that it was only this blindness to the maladjusted nature of the capital structure represented by the boom which can account for what Hayek described as the "surprisingly superficial" (*Critical Assessments*, vol. 1, p. 107) objections raised by Sraffa against the Austrian thesis that the subsequent downturn is expressed in capital losses as the maladjustments are revealed. See further on this point in Lachman, "Austrian Economics under Fire," pp. 233f.

39. O'Driscoll, *Economics as a Coordination Problem*, p. 102.

40. See above, note 4.

41. Hayek, *Profits, Interest and Investment*, p. 104.

42. F. A. Hayek, interview reported in *Hayek on Hayek: An Autobiographical Dialogue*, ed. S. Kresge and L. Wenar (London: Routledge, 1994), p. 80.

43. Hayek, *Profits, Interest and Investment*, p. 141.

44. See Kirzner, *Meaning of Market Process*, chap. 6.

45. F. A. Hayek, ed., *Collectivist Economic Planning* (London: George Routledge and Sons, 1935). These two papers were republished as chapters 7 and 8, respectively, in Hayek's *Individualism and Economic Order*.

46. "The problem of erroneous coordination was at the center of Hayek's interest when he later pursued the question of how the knowledge distributed across many people in society could be employed and which role prices could play in this process . . . when one views Hayek's works in the way sketched out here, one sees that his preoccupation with the phenomenon of the business cycle stood at the beginning of a life-long research program on the topic of 'coordination in the economic process.'" Dieter Schmidtchen and Siegfried Utzig, "Die Konjunkturtheorie Hayeks: Episode in einem Forscherleben oder Ausdruck eines lebenslangen Forschungsprogramms?" in *Wirtschaftspolitische Blätter*, no. 2 (1989; in honor of Hayek's ninetieth birthday), p. 233.

47. See also G. P. O'Driscoll, Jr., and S. R. Shenoy, "Inflation, Recession and Stagflation," in *The Foundation of Modern Austrian Economics*, ed. E. Dolan (Kansas City: Sheed and Ward, 1976), p. 205, where the Austrian cycle theory is presented as arguing that monetary expansion misinforms producers concerning the intertemporal plans of consumers.

48. O'Driscoll, *Economics as a Coordination Problem*, p. ix.

49. Hayek, *Money, Capital and Fluctuations*, p. 1.

50. Roger W. Garrison, review of *Money, Capital and Fluctuations: Early Essays*, by F. A. Hayek, *Market Process* 3, no. 2 (1984), reprinted in *Austrian Economics*, ed. S. C. Littlechild (Aldershot: Edward Elgar, 1990), vol. 2, p. 312.

51. Ludwig M. Lachmann, "From Mises to Shackle," *Journal of Economic Literature* 14 (1975): 60.

52. For a careful assessment of this thesis, see William W. Butos, "Hayek and General Equilibrium Analysis," *Southern Economic Journal* 52 (October 1985): 332–43. Some of the judgments expressed below parallel ideas argued by Butos.

53. Stephan Böhm, "Hayek on Knowledge, Equilibrium and Prices," *Wirtschaftspolitische Blätter*, no. 2 (1989): 201.

54. On this see Kirzner, *Meaning of Market Process*, pp. 141–46, 190–92.

55. The high point in Hayek's exposition of this insight was in his 1968 paper "Competition as a Discovery Procedure," first published in English some 47 years after *Preise und Produktion!* See F. A. Hayek, *New Studies in Philosophy, Politics, Economics and the History of Ideas* (Chicago: University of Chicago Press, 1978), chap. 12.

56. See Kirzner, *Meaning of Market Process*, chap. 7, for further elaboration on the complementarity between the views of Mises and Hayek after the mid-forties.

57. For the acknowledgement of Mises's influence of *Preise und Produktion*, see the preface to Hayek's second English edition of that work (1935).

58. See Kresge and Wenar, eds., *Hayek on Hayek*, p. 72, for the statement that Hayek's 1937 paper was an attempt to show Mises he was wrong regarding the nature of the equilibrating market process.

59. Ibid., p. 68.

60. Ibid., p. 79.

INFORMATION, KNOWLEDGE, AND ADVERTISING

THE OPEN-ENDEDNESS OF KNOWLEDGE:
ITS ROLE IN THE FEE FORMULA

As I think back to our meeting a year ago, I recall the sense of numbness which surrounded us then, so soon after Leonard Read's passing. We had not yet had sufficient time to ponder the uniqueness of the philosophy with which Leonard had imbued FEE.

This evening I intend to explore some aspects of that uniqueness, and to express my fervent hope and confidence that such uniqueness will continue to permeate every nook and cranny of FEE's activities in the years to come. I will begin by noting two related but separate paradoxes that have over the years repeatedly caught my attention.

TWO PARADOXES

First paradox: FEE's style is one of modesty, humility, tolerance, a steadfast refusal to browbeat those who do not agree with us. Now at least superficially, this attitude of tolerance and modesty appears to be inconsistent with what our fellow Trustee, the late Ben Rogge used to call "FEE's predictability." Let me quote from a talk Ben made here four and a half years ago:

> Quite frankly, I know of no other organization on our general side of the street whose position on any given issue is as predictable as FEE's. No ifs, ands or buts. No equivocation. Just right down the line, ramrod straight, for a society based on the principle of anything that's peaceful.

All of us remember how Leonard Read used to detest anything that resembled a "leak." Well now, surely this inability to compromise, this apparently intransigent attitude would seem difficult to reconcile with the characteristic courtesy, tolerance and genuine humility of FEE's style. That is my first apparent paradox.

"The Open-Endedness of Knowledge: Its Role in the FEE Formula," a talk that was given at the Annual Meeting of the Foundation for Economic Education, May 15, 1984, and reproduced in its entirety in a pamphlet published by the Foundation for Economic Education, Irvington-on-Hudson, N.Y. Reprinted by permission.

Let me turn to a second apparent paradox. FEE expresses, by its very being, a passionate belief in the sanctity of individual freedom, in the dignity and profound moral worth of a free society. Well, this profound belief surely seems difficult to reconcile with FEE's refusal to evangelize for what it believes in so passionately. Certainly, countless friends of FEE over the years have puzzled over FEE's refusal to reach out aggressively to win the hearts and minds of the public. If freedom is so sacred, then how can we sit back and refuse to sell it? That is my second paradox.

THE OPEN-ENDEDNESS OF KNOWLEDGE

I shall argue here that not only can these apparent paradoxes be satisfactorily resolved, as I believe they can, but that an understanding of this resolution is crucial for the very *raison d'être* of FEE. The resolution of these apparent paradoxes, I suggest, brings us close to the very core of FEE's mission and its identity. I believe the key to all this can be provided by what I shall call the *open-endedness of knowledge*.

What do I mean by the open-endedness of knowledge? I think the open-endedness of knowledge can be shown to involve two separate but complementary insights, the coupling of which may be held responsible for the uniqueness of FEE's message, its philosophy and its approach.

First of all, *knowledge is open-ended in the sense that no matter how much we know, this is as nothing compared with what we know that we do not know.* We all remember Sir Isaac Newton's remark about playing with pebbles of knowledge on the beach while the great ocean of scientific knowledge remains out there untouched before us—a magnificent and lofty thought.

Surely, one critically important premise of FEE's philosophy is this very lively awareness of the limits of our knowledge. In Leonard Read's own words, "Reflection reveals the fact that the more one knows, the more he knows he does not know." So, knowledge is open-ended in the sense of always being seen as incomplete. It is always only a fragment of that which is available to be known.

But I have said that the open-endedness of knowledge involves two ideas. There is a second idea included as an integral part in this notion of the open-endedness of knowledge. Knowledge is open-ended also in the sense that no matter where the limits and boundaries of one's present knowledge may lie, free human beings possess *an innate propensity to transcend spontaneously those barriers, those limits,* to continually escape those limits, through discovery of new horizons of knowledge the very existence of which was hitherto unsuspected. Life consists, in this sense, of a never-ending series of spontaneous leaps of discovery. The life of freedom is thus a continual expression of the dynamics of continual discovery. The free life, a life for which the open-endedness of knowledge is a central ideal, is one in which the sense of potential—unending potential, unending discovery—is at the heart of one's being. Open-endedness in this sense is the very opposite of the state of stagnancy.

THREE FACETS OF FEE'S PHILOSOPHY

Now I would like for the next few minutes to illustrate and explore the significance of this open-endedness of knowledge for each of *three* separate facets of FEE's philosophy and approach. The three will be as follows: *First,* the basic understanding of economic relationships. After all, FEE is a foundation for "economic education." This is number one. *Number two* will be the deep commitment mentioned earlier to the dignity and fertility of individual freedom. (The "fertility of freedom" is a phrase coined by the late Fritz Machlup; it expresses a profoundly important idea.) As to FEE's ideal of a free and peaceful society—what role does the open-endedness of knowledge play in that ideal? *Third,* what role does the open-endedness of knowledge play in FEE's soft-spoken, non-aggressive style of communicating its message and its philosophy to the world? I shall suggest that for each of these three facets of FEE's approach and philosophy, there is a close tie with our appreciation for what I call the open-endedness of knowledge.

OPEN-ENDEDNESS OF KNOWLEDGE
AND ECONOMIC UNDERSTANDING

Let us consider the first of these three facets of FEE's work—the open-endedness of knowledge as a source for economic understanding. Here I may be excused for referring to the essential differences that separate Austrian economics, the economics that we've learned from Mises and Hayek, from the standard mainstream view. To the standard mainstream view in economics, since about 1930, the view of the world has been one in which the future is essentially known, in which the participants in markets are in effect completely informed about the relative decisions made throughout the market by fellow participants. This is a world of equilibrium, a world in balance, a world in which quantitative economic predictions are entirely feasible. Now, as all of you know, Austrian economics has a quite different view of the world, and a quite different view of the way in which economic relationships can be grasped. I quote from Ludwig von Mises:

> The fundamental deficiency implied in every quantitative approach to economic problems consists in the neglect of the fact that there are no constant relations between what are called economic dimensions. There is neither constancy nor continuity in the valuations and in the formation of exchange ratios between various commodities. Every new datum brings about a reshuffling of the whole price system, the whole price structure. Understanding, by trying to grasp what is going on in the minds of the men concerned, can approach the problem of forecasting future conditions. We may call its method unsatisfactory and the positivists may arrogantly scorn it. But such arbitrary judgments must not and cannot obscure the fact that understanding is the only appropriate method of dealing with the uncertainty of future conditions.

It was Mises' disciple, Friedrich Hayek, who fully explained the importance for economic understanding of recognizing the limitations of knowledge. It was as a result of his attempt to explicate the Mises-Hayek side of the celebrated socialist economic calculation debate that Hayek first articulated the significance for market competition of dispersed information. Hayek taught us that the crucial element in market competition is the circumstance that knowledge is never concentrated in a single mind—always dispersed. We never know everything. None of us. No single mind can possibly know everything. No single mind can possibly grasp the entire economic problem that tends to be solved through spontaneous market processes. In more recent work, Hayek has emphasized the character of market competition as, in his terminology, a *discovery procedure*—and I quote:

> Competition is . . . first and foremost a discovery procedure. No theory can do justice to it which starts from the assumption that the facts to be discovered are already known. There is no predetermined range of known or "given" facts, which will ever all be taken into account. All we can hope to secure is a procedure that is on the whole likely to bring about a situation where more of the potentially useful objective facts will be taken into account than would be done in any other procedure

which we know. It is the circumstances which makes so irrelevant for the choice of a desirable policy all evaluation of the results of competition that starts from the assumption that all of the relevant facts are known to some single mind. The real issue is how we can best assist the optimum utilization of the knowledge, skills and opportunities to acquire knowledge, that are dispersed among hundreds of thousands of people, but given to nobody in their entirety. Competition must be seen as a process in which people acquire and communicate knowledge; to treat it as if all this knowledge were available to any one person at the outset is to make nonsense of it.

Hayek's broader philosophy has proceeded from these fundamental insights to appreciate their even more far-reaching implications. And Hayek in fact says that the very basis of civilization rests on these insights concerning ignorance: "Civilization rests on the fact that we all benefit from knowledge which we do not possess."

So far it might seem that these Austrian insights rest fundamentally on the awareness of human ignorance, on the limitations of human knowledge, but in fact they rest also on that second element in the open-endedness of knowledge that I have referred to. These insights rest, that is, also upon an appreciation for the propensity within human action to discover what was hitherto unknown—what I like to call the *entrepreneurial* propensity in human action. It is this propensity that is responsible for entrepreneurial alertness for pure profit opportunities, for entrepreneurial discovery, for bursting asunder the limits of existing knowledge. It is upon this alertness that we rely for the manner in which the market continually propels prices and decisions in the direction of greater mutual coordination. It is entrepreneurial alertness to existing errors that leads to their discovery and their eventual tendency to be corrected. So much for the open-endedness of knowledge, as an ingredient in economic education.

OPEN-ENDEDNESS OF KNOWLEDGE
AND THE COMMITMENT TO FREEDOM

Let me turn to the second of the three applications of the open-endedness of knowledge. This, you will recall, referred to the importance of the open-endedness of knowledge for our commitment to the dignity of freedom and its fertility in a free society. Here a great deal depends, I would suggest, on our instinctive recoil from the arrogance of benevolent dictatorship. Let me quote Leonard Read here:

> There are numerous virtues and vices that account for the rise and fall of societies. Near the top of the list, are the two opposites, humility and pride . . . Pride sprouts and grows from ignorance and self-blindness. Those with a haughty spirit foolishly believe they know the most, whereas they know the least. While they don't know how to make a pencil, or why grass is green, or who we are, they "know" how to run our lives. In their blind pride, the least taste of political power drives them to become power addicts. Until such persons seek help there is little we can do to curb their addiction. What we can and must do is to develop in ourselves the strength of character to resist the temptations of power.

In another place, Read refers to how a market works by bringing together all the trillion bits of expertise. He says these will work themselves out to the extent that individuals are free from the dictates of those who are unaware of how little they know, those who are unaware of the open-endedness of knowledge.

But I would suggest that our disgust for the arrogance of dictators is only part of the story. Surely, our commitment to a free society rests also on our appreciation for the immensely valuable spontaneous discoveries that the human spirit can generate when left free. It is our admiration for individual creativity that is responsible for our reverence for the free society. So here we have both of those elements in the open-endedness of knowledge—undergirding our regard for freedom in a free society: (1) our recoil, our disgust for the arrogance of those who believe they know how to run other people's lives, and (2) our awareness, our appreciation for the propensity in human beings to continually expand what they know, what they can create.

OPEN-ENDEDNESS OF KNOWLEDGE AND FEE'S STYLE

Let me turn to the third aspect of FEE's work and illustrate the significance of the open-endedness of knowledge for FEE's unique style and approach in communicating its message to the world. Here I think two points of contact ought to be noticed between the open-endedness of knowledge and FEE's characteristic style. We recall that this style involves first of all an innate courtesy, modesty and tolerance. (No name-calling,

Leonard Read taught us, no arrogance!) Second, the FEE "style" reflects a confidence, a faith, if you like, that those who can benefit from our message *will find us almost of their own accord.* They will discover us. Certainly this confidence is a remarkable feature of FEE's style.

I have one final quote from Ben Rogge, taken from a high school commencement address. He was talking to these youngsters about what they might expect of college. Ben said:

> Hopefully, you will . . . come to know how little you know, in fact how little is known about man and his world by even the most knowledgeable around you. This is to say that you may come to carry with you through life a deep sense of wonder and of awe, not of what you do understand, but of the deep and mysterious processes which neither you nor anyone else fully understands.

And Read once again:

> Humility is an awareness of how much there is to learn . . . No person can be a know-it-all at the same time that he seriously seeks knowledge. For anyone to be intolerant of others is to assess himself as the infallible I, *the authority* in rendering final judgments. Such authoritarianism is the very opposite of the freedom one avowedly stands for.

Open-endedness of knowledge is the root of FEE's modest, tolerant style. But then we said there was another aspect to that style—the confidence, the faith, that those who can benefit from our teachings, from what we have to offer will find us out, will seek us out. Listen to Leonard Read:

> Forget the "selling freedom" notion! Right method calls for concentration on the improvement of the most approachable person on earth— one's self. This is practical because accomplishment is possible. This tactic disposes of the numbers problem, the impossible—selling the masses. Do not seek followers! . . . What seek ye? The achievement of understanding and clarity of explanation so that those who wish to learn may come upon enlightenment. If you are successful, those with inquiring minds will find you out.

Here, surely, we have Leonard Read thinking of the spontaneous discovery potential that will bring our audience to our doors. If we hold up the standard, if we show them what a free society means, they will find us out.

PARADOXES RESOLVED

Let us return to the two apparent paradoxes that I mentioned earlier this evening. I believe that it should be easy for us now to see that these paradoxes dissolve immediately just as soon as we recall the significance of this open-endedness of knowledge. We asked how a passionate commitment to freedom could be reconciled with an attitude that refuses to go out and sell the freedom principles to others. We asked how FEE's refusal to compromise, refusal to recognize exceptions could be reconciled with its attitudes of modesty and tolerance. But these questions are easily answered. A passionate love of freedom as well as FEE's modest style and courtesy *both* grow out of our awareness of our own fallibility and of the arrogance of those who presume to know enough to control others.

But our awareness of how little we know does not and cannot prevent us from being absolutely certain of that one thing, namely how little we know. *That* we know! If we appear intransigent, if we appear uncompromising, this is because we are absolutely sure of this one thing that we do know with certainty; that is, that human knowledge is open-ended and inescapably limited.

Concerning this item of knowledge, we cultivate no false modesty. We know for sure how little we know. And we know for sure how this open-endedness of human knowledge is responsible for the spontaneously coordinated operation of free markets. And we know for sure how this vitiates so much fashionable economics.

It is this understanding that we have of the open-endedness of human knowledge—including our understanding of the potential for spontaneous discovery that rests in the human breast—it is this understanding that nourishes our conviction that what we need to do is to deepen our own understanding of the nature of a free society with full confidence that others will seek us out. We do not need to sell. We do not need to attack, to indulge in name-calling.

THE FORMULA FOR FEE'S FUTURE

In a word, FEE's unique style, its unique and quietly passionate commitment to a free society, its commitment to the basic principles of sound economic understanding—all of these fit cohesively into a single integrated whole. This I submit is an important element in FEE's formula. And I do believe that a renewed self-appreciation at this time by the friends, supporters and trustees of FEE for these basic principles can continue to provide stimulation and motivation for FEE's activities for many years to come.

Let us never lose our courtesy and our tolerance. Let us never forget our distaste for the arrogance which lies at the root of all threats to a free society. Let us never lose our confidence in the intellectual alertness of a free citizenry. Let us persevere in our search for understanding in our economic studies.

I believe that by mobilizing the dedicated and informed enthusiasm of our trustees and supporters, together with the loyal, competent expertise of FEE's staff, that we can proceed to translate these abstractions—and they are abstractions—we can translate these abstractions into the day-to-day activities of FEE.

We need never fear new ideas. We need never be unsure concerning new proposals, provided we appraise each one of them against our own standards and our own criteria involving leak-proof economic understanding, unified with unfailing courtesy to others in the way in which we reveal our own passionate love of freedom. Let the open-endedness of human knowledge be our inspiration and our guide as we navigate our way through a future of limitless possibilities for free human beings.

KNOWING ABOUT KNOWLEDGE: A SUBJECTIVIST
VIEW OF THE ROLE OF INFORMATION

In recent years a good deal of effort has been expended on exploring the role human knowledge plays in the economic process and the degree to which received economic theory takes cognizance of this role.[1] Here I shall argue that, valuable as these explorations have been, they appear in the main not to have exploited the insights that can be derived from an explicitly subjectivist approach to the role of knowledge and information in economic affairs. A consistent emphasis on subjectivism, in this as in other departments of economic theory, yields an understanding of the market process that seems to have escaped notice.

SUBJECTIVISM AND KNOWLEDGE: SOME PARADOXES

The profound importance of subjectivism in identifying human knowledge as central to economic science was perhaps most clearly recognized by Hayek. In his chapter "The Subjective Character of the Social Sciences," Hayek emphasized that "most of the objects of social or human action are not 'objective facts' in the special narrow sense in which this term is used by the Sciences and contrasted to 'opinions,' and they cannot at all be defined in physical terms. So far as human actions are concerned the things *are* what the acting people think they are."[2]

The theory of price, Hayek explains, "has nothing to say about the behavior of the price of iron or wool, of things of such and such physical properties, but only about things about which people have certain beliefs and which they want to use in a certain manner."[3] "Only in so far as we can find out what the knowledge and beliefs of the people concerned are in the relevant respects shall we be in a position to predict in what manner a change in the price of the product will affect the prices of the factors."[4] It is the advance of subjectivism in economic theory that has focused attention on "the problem of the compatibility of intentions and expectations of different people, of the division of knowledge between

Presented at a conference on Austrian Economics held at Irving, Texas, December 1976. From *Perception, Opportunity, and Profit: Studies in the Theory of Entrepreneurship* (Chicago and London: University of Chicago Press, 1979), 137–53. © 1979 by The University of Chicago. Reprinted by permission.

them, and the process by which the relevant knowledge is acquired and expectations formed."[5]

In developing my own thesis concerning the relevance of the subjectivist approach to the economic role of knowledge, I shall argue for what may seem a paradox. Because consideration of this apparent paradox will prove most enlightening, I state it at the outset. Subjectivism teaches us, we have learnt from Hayek, that it is not iron and wool themselves that enter into our economic explanations, but rather the knowledge and beliefs men hold about iron and wool. One might expect, therefore, that in considering economic explanations concerning *knowledge,* a subjectivist approach would emphasize not knowledge itself, but rather what people know about knowledge. What we shall discover, however, is that a subjectivist approach leads to recognition of precisely that kind of knowledge *about which men know nothing at all.* Or the paradox may be put in somewhat different terms. Subjectivism suggests that things about which men are completely ignorant are things that, in the sense relevant to economic theory, *simply do not exist.* Yet, in the case of knowledge itself, consistent pursuit of the subjectivist approach turns out to direct attention precisely to the existence of opportunities for the acquisition of knowledge about which *no* one knows. While in less consistently subjectivist approaches such opportunities are held *not* to exist, it is to the very important and very real existence of these opportunities that subjectivism points.

We shall come to this paradox by considering yet another paradox concerning knowledge, to which several writers have drawn attention. It is now a quarter of a century since Shackle pointed out that knowledge is "a very peculiar commodity." "All the goods," wrote Shackle, "that serve to educate or entertain us or enable us to communicate with one another, all the books, newspapers, films, theatrical performances, lectures, postal services and television sets, and all the apparatus of scientific research, could have no use or existence if the experiences they will give us could be known for certain beforehand in exact and complete detail. . . . To admit knowledge and information as . . . exchangeable goods is to expose a flank on which the theory of consumers' behaviour, as we find it in our literature, is defenceless; for knowledge would not be bought if it were already possessed; and when we buy knowledge we do not know what we are going to get."[6]

More recently, Boulding has noticed this peculiarity of knowledge and has to some extent pointed toward the implications we shall be drawing therefrom. "We have," Boulding observes, "the paradox . . . implicit in the very concept of knowledge, that we have to know what we want to know before we can start looking for it. There are things that we ought to know, and which we do not know that we ought to know, that remain largely unknown and unsought for."[7] I contend that the market performs a crucial function in discovering knowledge nobody knows exists; that an understanding of the true character of the market process depends, indeed, on recognizing this crucial function; and, finally, that contemporary economists' unawareness of these insights appears to be the result of otherwise wholly laudable attempts to treat knowledge objectively—that is, as consisting entirely of units of available information that are to be acquired only through calculated expenditure of resources.

KNOWLEDGE AND ACTION

Before turning to the detailed discussion of these contentions, let me clear up possible ambiguities concerning the sense in which I am interested in knowledge. We are, in the subjectivist spirit, concerned with knowledge only insofar as it informs action. We are not, that is, concerned with the extent to which people discover facts or theories that bear no relation to human action. Nor are we concerned with the truth or correctness of the knowledge people possess or of the knowledge they might (if they knew of its availability) wish to possess. We are interested only in the images (to employ Boulding's term) that might become ensconced in people's minds and might, in consequence, motivate and shape their concrete actions.

It follows, of course, that our discussions have nothing to do with the subtleties with which philosophers have invested the theory of knowledge. Knowledge for our purposes includes not only knowledge in the strict philosophical sense, but also beliefs, expectations, and even speculations and guesses, to the extent that people's actions can be recognized as the consistent expression of these beliefs, expectations, and speculation. A subjectivist view of economics sees the world as the outcome of the interplay of deliberate human actions. These actions are the systematic outcomes of the awareness that purposeful human beings have concerning themselves and their environment, in both the present and the future. When we discuss the ways people acquire knowledge, we refer to the ways they acquire the opinions and views, doubts and guesses, as well as certainties, that account for their actions.

ON PERFECT KNOWLEDGE IN ECONOMIC THEORY

All the contributions to the economics of knowledge and information focus uncomplimentary attention on the assumptions made in orthodox microeconomic theory concerning perfect knowledge. These assumptions played, of course, a pivotal role in much of the received theory, especially in the context of perfectly competitive market models. While it was Hayek who apparently first made explicit the place perfect knowledge occupies in the notion of market equilibrium,[8] a host of subsequent economists have worked on the consequences of relaxing this assumption. As we shall see, a good deal of their work has consisted in developing models of search behavior, models that recognize that people are more or less ignorant, and that they are prepared to shoulder the costs of search in order to partially remove their ignorance.

This transition from a world of assumed perfect knowledge to one of consciously accepted search costs has led to a certain revision in the perception of what the earlier perfect knowledge assumption is to mean. Whereas the earlier understanding of the perfect knowledge assumption appears to have been that we are to imagine a world in which people already know everything (without asking ourselves *how* such omniscience might have been arrived at),[9] the more recent perception is that the perfect knowledge assumption postulates the *costless acquisition* of knowledge. If search costs are zero, we are to understand, the perfect knowledge assumption follows as the logical result of the newer theories of search. "In the theory of the competitive market, there is . . . an . . . assumption about 'perfect knowledge.' What this means in effect is that the acquisition of knowledge of prices or exchange opportunities in a perfect market is costless, so that knowledge is, as it were, a free good."[10] And one recent attack on the received microeconomic theory of perfect competition rests, in part, on the irrationality of complete acquisition of information in a world in which information is not costless.[11] What is objected to in this critique is not, that is, the assumption of perfect knowledge itself but the implied assumption that market participants go to the pains of acquiring such costly complete information. But we shall see that the assumption of perfect information does not *have* to imply the *deliberate acquisition* of knowledge; nor, on the other hand, does the availability of costless information necessarily imply that people *will* in fact be perfectly informed. Let us consider how knowledge is acquired.

ACQUISITION OF KNOWLEDGE: THE TWO POSSIBLE WAYS

The literature on the economics of information has, at least since Stigler's pioneer article,[12] stressed the role of *deliberate search* for information. This deliberate search is understood to be conducted in exactly the same way as all economic activity. The prospective gross rewards from search are appraised, the relevant costs are carefully calculated, and the appropriate "rational," maximizing decision is taken concerning the extent of search activity to be engaged in. The wealth of literature patterned on this model has tended to suggest that the *only* way knowledge is acquired is through deliberate, cost-conscious search or learning activity. Any ignorance that remains, one is to understand, constitutes the deliberately planned optimal level of ignorance, decided upon in view of the costs of learning. In Stigler's words, "There is no 'imperfection' in a market possessing incomplete knowledge if it would not be remunerative to acquire (produce) complete knowledge: Information costs are the costs of transportation from ignorance to omniscience, and seldom can a trader afford to make the entire trip."[13]

But this view of things is clearly subject, at least to some degree, to the Shackle-Boulding paradox referred to earlier. The theory of search cannot, it is clear, avoid making the assumption that, before undertaking the search, one *already* knows enough about the territory to be able to calculate rewards and costs. So that, if we are to view the acquisition of knowledge as deliberately undertaken, one must postulate some prior knowledge *not* acquired through deliberate search or learning activity. One may, of course, imagine a long sequence of searches for knowledge, each set in motion by the information gathered deliberately from the preceding search. But this cannot free us from the conclusion that at the *start* of the necessarily finite sequence of searches, at least, some knowledge was possessed that was not itself the result of deliberate search. More generally, since economic decision making presupposes some perceived ends-means framework, every decision, including the very first decision to search for more information, must presuppose some given knowledge. The knowledge upon which the first decision to search for knowledge depended was itself *not* acquired deliberately.

The truth surely is that, of the mass of knowledge, beliefs, opinions, expectations, and guesses that one holds at a given moment and that inspire and shape action, only a fraction can be described as being the result of deliberate search or learning activity. Surely a very great volume of one's awareness of one's environment, and of one's expectations concerning the future, is the result of learning experiences that *occurred entirely without having been planned.* The knowledge one obtains from the advertising message thrust before one's eyes was, more likely than not, *not* deliberately searched for; the knowledge one obtains when one is addressed by one's neighbor, or importuned by a beggar, is simply acquired, not at all deliberately. Simply being alive as a human being subjects one to all sorts of sense impressions that continually alter one's awareness of the world. "So far as men are concerned," Shackle has pointed out, "*being* consists in continual and endless fresh *knowing.*"[14] To be sure, one is often highly dissatisfied with both the quantity and the quality of information so gained; it is this dissatisfaction, of course, that inspires the search for more and better knowledge. But it would surely be absurd to postulate the complete cessation of flows of knowledge spontaneously acquired. In fact, such spontaneous acquisition of knowledge and information is so pervasive that it is often far too easily taken for granted. It includes not only serendipity in the usual sense, but also spontaneous discovery of the most common and mundane items of daily knowledge. To describe the knowledge so acquired as having been costless or a free good is somewhat misleading. To be sure, the spontaneous learner has incurred no cost or sacrifice through his learning. But this is not so much because the knowledge was costlessly available as because the knowledge was simply not sought deliberately.

It seems reasonable *not* to attribute the prevalence of the assumption of perfect knowledge in so-called neoclassical theories of perfectly competitive equilibrium to an imagined zero-cost availability of knowledge to be acquired. Rather, the perfect knowledge assumption seems to have taken the notion of knowledge spontaneously and undeliberately acquired so much for granted that it imagines *everything* is already known in this way. Now, of course, we should and do protest this monstrous assumption. But we should note that this assumption is not quite the same as to assume that people have taken deliberate advantage of the opportunity to acquire knowledge without cost. So that it is not enough, as Hollis and Nell believe, in order to attack the neoclassical assumption of perfect knowledge, to show that the cost of deliberate acquisition of knowledge is greater than zero. After all, the circumstance that the deliberate acquisition of knowledge may be too costly for a particular individual does not by itself remove the possibility that the knowledge may, *without* any deliberate search decision, already have somehow been spontaneously communicated to him.

So it is necessary for us, it appears, to steer a careful course between errors that lurk on two sides. On the one hand, we must avoid the error of imagining that *all* action is inspired only by knowledge deliberately acquired. This view seems to be suggested by the literature on the economics of search. This view suffers, as we shall see, from its neglect of both the positive and the normative implications of information about which one does not at present know, or whose deliberate acquisition seems too costly. This view appears to have deflected attention from the pervasive processes of learning that do *not* depend on deliberate, costly search.

On the other hand, we must avoid the opposite error of imagining that action inspired exclusively by *spontaneously* acquired perceptions of one's environment can ever be seriously thought of as *completely* informed action. Such a view suggests that any facts in which one might have an interest somehow slip instantly, without effort of any kind, into one's consciousness. We must avoid this error, not because it underestimates the costs of deliberate search for knowledge, but because it blithely assumes such deliberate search, even at zero cost, not to have been necessary at all.

THE SOCIAL SIGNIFICANCE OF KNOWLEDGE ABOUT WHICH NOTHING IS KNOWN

The emphasis laid here on knowledge not deliberately acquired is by no means intended to minimize the importance of information purposefully sought. Deliberately learned knowledge must, of course, fill a critical role in social betterment. And the economic analysis of the way search is likely to be conducted, and the institutional framework likely to promote worthwhile search, must hold great importance for our understanding of economic development. Here I wish merely to draw attention to the extent to which social progress depends on a quite different source, in *addition* to deliberate search, for the information that propels and guides human actions. It may be helpful in this regard to contrast ignorance of knowledge that might be spontaneously, undeliberately absorbed, with ignorance of knowledge that might be deliberately sought out or learned.

Ignorance of knowledge or information that might be known through deliberate search or learning can be explained and accounted for. Such ignorance is in fact to be defended as justified by the high cost of search or learning. Such ignorance has, then, been deliberately accepted; in a sense it is *optimal*. To know more would mean to sacrifice something more important than the knowledge to be gained. And, again, such ignorance, if it cannot be defended on the grounds of cost-benefit calculations, *must* then clearly be attributed to ignorance concerning the search or learning possibilities that are in fact available. An item of information i_1 may fail to be sought out, that is, simply because knowledge of how to discover i_1 is lacking. The advantages to society that more complete, deliberately sought knowledge may confer may be missing, therefore, either because these advantages are not worthwhile to obtain or because of the lack of a necessary prerequisite, that is, knowledge about knowledge. Each of these possible explanations, while each possibly calling for further levels of explanation, fully responds to our initial surprise as to why available information remained unlearned.

Ignorance of knowledge that might be spontaneously, undeliberately absorbed can, on the other hand, *never be explained in terms of anything other than itself.* Such ignorance is simply there. It cannot be accounted for on the grounds of high search or learning costs, since no searching or learning is needed at all even, to repeat, at zero cost. Such ignorance cannot be accounted for by noting that knowledge concerning the specified knowledge is lacking, since it has been postulated that the specified knowledge can be absorbed quite undeliberately and spontaneously. Ignorance of knowledge that can be absorbed without decision is simply the expression and the evidence of a sheer failure to notice what is there to be seen. It can be given a name—lack of entrepreneurial alertness—but it cannot be explained in terms of the standard economics of microtheory, the theory of deliberate individual decisions.

By the same token, it follows that, whereas in the case of ignorance of knowledge available only through search one must assume that the ignorance must persist until some exogenous change occurs, this does *not* hold for ignorance of knowledge capable of being spontaneously absorbed. Since we can explain why information available through search was deliberately left unlearned, we cannot postulate learning to occur without introducing some change in the circumstances. If search was not worthwhile yesterday, it will not be worthwhile today unless a change has occurred in the value of the expected information or in the costs of search. If worthwhile search was not undertaken yesterday because the opportunity to search was not noticed, it will not be undertaken today unless it has been noticed.

On the other hand, ignorance concerning knowledge that might become spontaneously, undeliberately absorbed *can* be expected to gradually fade. This is so because an item of information that was staring one in the face yesterday, but in some unexplained way remained unnoticed, need *not* necessarily remain unnoticed today. In fact if, as we shall argue, one can assume a tendency to become aware of opportunities that do stare one in the face, then it follows that, as time flows on, men are subject to a spontaneously increasing awareness of information hitherto veiled in ignorance. Of course, this steadily receding tide of ignorance is at all times in opposition to and often overwhelmed by a precisely contrary trend—a continual and spontaneous *widening* of the universe of current facts concerning which knowledge is conceivable but absent. What Shackle calls the kaleidic world[15] is one of continual renewal of ignorance. Constant change constantly turns omniscience into ignorance; but, as we have seen, this continually renewed ignorance is subject to its own relentless erosion through spontaneous discovery.

There is one further important characteristic of ignorance as it relates to knowledge that might be undeliberately discovered, a characteristic that arises from the unexplainable nature of this ignorance. This characteristic is that such ignorance must, in a specific sense, be considered *regrettable*. Since there is no explanation or defense of this ignorance, such ignorance can only be described as a pity, possibly a tragedy. An opportunity stares one in the face; it is inexplicably ignored. Once one has gained the relevant knowledge, one looks back on one's ignorance without having anything to excuse it. One realizes one's earlier error and that is all. Of course, where one's later knowledge shows that the earlier ignorance was unavoidable, as where certain knowledge of the information gained was simply unavailable at the earlier date, one is unable to *condemn* one's earlier ignorance. But nonetheless when, let us say, one discovers that another had guessed the future correctly and had as a result won enormous profits, one must necessarily concede that one made what has turned out to be an error, an understandable error, but an error nonetheless.

Ignorance that *might* have been dispelled by diligent search, but for which the cost of search was too high, cannot be regretted in this way. If the cost calculations were valid, the ignorance was optimal; no error occurred. To regret this ignorance is to regret that the world is not different than it in fact is. But where ignorance was *not* the result of deliberate refusal to learn and has later been shown to have been entirely unnecessary, then one looks back at one's ignorance as upon a deplorable and embarrassing error. From a broader point of view, therefore, it must appear highly desirable to choose among alternative social institutional arrangements those modes of organization that minimize this kind of ignorance—that is, those modes of organization that generate the greatest volume of spontaneous, undeliberate learning. Whether such a choice among institutional arrangements is possible is an issue to which we shall return very shortly. We turn first to remind ourselves briefly that ignorance of spontaneously discoverable information has a special relevance in the decentralized market economy.

IGNORANCE OF OTHER PEOPLE: THE TWO KINDS

It was Hayek who most clearly spelled out the role of knowledge and its absence in the understanding of the market process, and of the wholly fictional state of equilibrium to which that process appears to point. For equilibrium, Hayek taught us, we require a special kind of knowledge, the knowledge of other people's plans. Disequilibrium, it followed, consists of ignorance of other people's plans.[16]

Now, as long as one confines attention to ignorance that is able to disappear only through deliberate, cost-calculating search, it follows that a process of equilibrium necessarily consists of a series of deliberate search efforts on the part of market participants. And it is along this line of analysis that the literature on the economics of information has sought to explicate the market process. A key feature of the market processes so explained, one should notice, is that the speed of the equilibrium process is optimal in the sense that for no participant in the process would it have been desirable, in view of the relevant costs, to have gained knowledge more rapidly.

But we have argued that deliberate search is *not* the only way ignorance is dispelled. And this leads us to recognize that the ignorance

that characterizes the market disequilibrium may well include ignorance concerning the plans of other people that is, in principle, entirely
unnecessary—ignorance that will tend to disappear spontaneously
without deliberate search. I will argue for a view that sees the competitive market process as wholly separate and distinct from any systematic,
deliberate search adjustment processes that will certainly occur. The market process I will identify will consist, therefore, of a process of *spontane-*
ous discovery of the plans of other market participants. Let us see how this
view can be sustained. To do this, we return to the question of whether
the pattern of institutional arrangements can have any systematic consequences for the rapidity with which ignorance can be dispelled through
spontaneous, undeliberate learning.

ON ENCOURAGING ALERTNESS

I have argued that at least some kinds of ignorance tend to disappear
through spontaneous discovery. It would be a mistake to imagine, however, that spontaneous discovery is a wholly unexplainable process, or
that it is a process that confers its benefits on all men equally.

The truth is that the ability to learn without deliberate search is a
gift individuals enjoy in quite different degrees. It is this gift, surely,
that we have in mind when we talk of *entrepreneurial alertness.* Entrepreneurial alertness consists, after all, in the ability to notice without
search opportunities that have been hitherto overlooked. To be sure,
entrepreneurial alertness may also include the ability to notice opportunities for profitable deliberate search. But this opportunity has been
discovered by the alert entrepreneur *without* search. Since individuals obviously differ in their entrepreneurial alertness, it is clear that
opportunities for social improvement will tend to be exploited most
fruitfully if institutional arrangements can be patterned so as to translate such opportunities into opportunities that will be encountered by
those whose entrepreneurial alertness is the most acute, the most sensitive, and the most accurate.

Moreover, the process of spontaneous discovery is—admittedly to an
as yet very limited degree—a process whose determinants we can at least
tentatively discern. It is true that economists and psychologists have a
great deal of work to do to explain the forces that influence the pattern of
spontaneous learning for different individuals. But surely we are already
in a position to identify the more powerful among these forces.

If the advertiser projects his message to the potential consumer in color, or with comic illustration, or accompanied by a certain piece of music, surely this is because the advertiser knows not merely how to lower the cost to the consumer of learning his message, but how to encourage spontaneous learning by the consumer with no deliberate search at all.

And, again, if we know anything at all about the process of spontaneous discovery of information, it is that this process is somehow altogether more rapid when the relevant information will be of benefit to the potential discoverer. Entrepreneurial alertness, that is, is sensitive not so much to information per se as to information that can be deployed to one's advantage.

It follows, then, that for opportunities for social improvement to be more rapidly discovered and exploited, these opportunities must be translated into opportunities that are not merely *encountered* by those whose entrepreneurial alertness is best developed, but into opportunities that are to the advantage of these potential entrepreneurs, and that most effectively excite their interest and alertness. Let us now consider the market process.

THE ROLE OF THE MARKET

Our discussion suggests a view of the market process, both at the level of positive analysis and at that of normative appraisal, that appears not yet to have been clearly enunciated in the economic literature.

We know of various perceptions of the role of the competitive market. The orthodox neoclassical view expressed in the literature of welfare economics sees the market as allocating social resources efficiently. This view suffers both from its concentration on the state of equilibrium and of complete information and from its acceptance of norms of social welfare that rest on illegitimate aggregation of individual preferences. The "catallactic" view espoused by Buchanan sees the market as the set of institutions that facilitate the exploitation of the opportunities for mutually profitable exchange between individuals.[17] Hayek has emphasized the role of the market as a discovery process mobilizing and exploiting the available but scattered scraps of knowledge strewn through the society.[18] Our discussion permits us, I believe, to interpret both the Buchanan and the Hayek positions in a rather novel fashion.

What the market process does is to systematically translate unnoticed opportunities for mutually profitable exchange among individuals into forms that tend to excite the interest and alertness of those most likely to notice what can be spontaneously learned. In this way the opportunities for social improvement via mutually profitable exchanges tend to be most rapidly discovered and exploited.

Where coordination—the mutual recognition of an exchange opportunity by its potential participants—has not occurred, the market translates this into an opportunity for pure entrepreneurial profit available to those with the keenest scent for profit. The ease of calculation provided by money is thus not merely a device lowering transaction costs relevant to deliberate search. It represents a social arrangement with the ability to present existing overlooked opportunities in a form most easily recognized and noticed by spontaneous learners. I have argued at length elsewhere that the competitive-equilibrating process should be understood as an entrepreneurial process, involving continued alertness to shifting opportunities for pure entrepreneurial profit.[19] We now see this process much more deeply, I believe, as a process whereby the general tendency for continued spontaneous discovery of available information is powerfully nudged into its most effective and expeditious channels. This process does *not* consist of deliberate search, it consists of a systematic but wholly unplanned process of undeliberate discovery. The market process disseminates knowledge whose very existence has not been known to its spontaneous learners. The process essentially consists not in a series of deliberate searches for information (although, to be sure, such searches may very well be entailed as by-products of the process). It consists in the spontaneous translation of as yet unexploited exchange opportunities into opportunities for pure profit able to attract the attention of the most alert entrepreneurs. These latter opportunities, noticed and acted upon by entrepreneurs, effectively communicate the knowledge needed to ensure consummation of exploitable exchange opportunities.

SUBJECTIVISM AND KNOWLEDGE

Our discussion—billed as a "subjectivist view on the role of information"— has, as promised at the outset, emphasized the role of knowledge about which nothing is known. But the subjectivist approach to social phenomena in general emphasizes that what is important about the objects that surround us is not the objects themselves, but only the knowledge and beliefs about them that inform and shape human actions. It might seem paradoxical, therefore, that I claim that my own emphasis on knowledge about which nothing at all is known is a subjectivist emphasis. But the paradox is easily explained, and the explanation may be of some value in elucidating the meaning of subjectivism.

The foundation of subjectivism in the analysis of social phenomena consists, of course, in the insight that these phenomena are generated by deliberate, purposeful human action. Since action grows out of perceived configurations of ends and means, subjectivism focuses attention on the way these ends and means have been perceived—on knowledge and beliefs concerning them. Now, it might seem that subjectivism then requires us to see action as made possible not only by the availability of the means alone, but by the availability of a more complex package that also includes bundles of information concerning the means and ends. The knowledge and beliefs thus possessed then appear, along with the more narrowly conceived means themselves, as the ingredients of action. The subjectivist view on iron and wool, then, would see not iron alone and wool alone, but iron packaged with information concerning iron, and wool similarly packaged.

A more penetrating understanding of subjectivism surely suggests that the knowledge presupposed by the action postulate is *not* of a character that permits it to be seen as packaged along with the objects or ideas that constitute the means and the ends for action. Instead, subjectivism sees action as inextricably *embedded* in the complex of perceptions and images that make up the consciousness of the human agent at each moment. The means employed in human action can be discussed quite separately from the human agent, but to discuss the knowledge and beliefs that actuate action separately from the human agent would be to imagine away the very notion of a human agent. Consciousness must be treated as primordial to action, so that the knowledge, beliefs, and images that constitute consciousness must for a science of human action be treated as ultimate givens. One must at some point desist from searching for what the agent knows and believes about his knowledge and beliefs. He simply *has* this knowledge and these beliefs.

To be sure, over time the complex of perceptions and images making up consciousness presents a shifting, flexible, and kaleidic scene, and these shifts constitute learning in the broader sense. There is no doubt that a large volume of these shifts are deliberately engineered by the individual, as when he reads a book, listens to a lecture or a harangue, watches a movie, or tours a foreign country. But subjectivism requires us to recognize that, just as man's consciousness itself is an ultimate datum for a science of human action, so also must room be found for spontaneous changes in man's consciousness—changes that are *not* to be viewed as deliberately engineered.

Shackle, as we have seen, pointed out that the knowledge that actuates the deliberate search for knowledge cannot coincide with the knowledge sought. I have argued that the knowledge that propels action of any kind must inevitably embody unsought learning. Our discussion has led us to understand the role of the market process in stimulating undeliberate learning in a socially significant way. I believe this new insight into the market process grows out of applying a consistent subjectivist perspective to the role that knowledge and information play in human action.

NOTES

1. See, e.g., F. A. Hayek, "Economics and Knowledge," and idem, "The Use of Knowledge in Society," *American Economic Review* 35 (September 1945): 519–30, both reprinted in *Individualism and Economic Order* (London: Routledge and Kegan Paul, 1949); D. M. Lamberton, ed., *Economics of Information and Knowledge* (New York: Penguin Books, 1971); J. Hirshleifer, "Where Are We in the Theory of Information?" *American Economic Review* 63 (May 1973): 31–39.

2. F. A. Hayek, *The Counter-revolution of Science* (Glencoe, Ill.: Free Press, 1955), pp. 26–27.

3. Ibid., p. 33.

4. Ibid.

5. Ibid.

6. G. L. S. Shackle, "On the Meaning and Measure of Uncertainty: I," *Metroeconomica* 4 (1952): 87–104, as reprinted in *Uncertainty in Economics and Other Reflections* (Cambridge: Cambridge University Press, 1955), pp. 17–18.

7. K. E. Boulding, "Knowledge as a Commodity," in *Beyond Economics: Essays on Society, Religion and Ethics* (Ann Arbor: University of Michigan Press, 1968), p. 146.

8. Hayek, "Economics and Knowledge."

9. Shackle has suggested that this assumption came from "adopting codes appropriate to the science of *inanimate* events, where the question does not arise how massive bodies come to be aware of their duty to attract each other with a force proportionate to the inverse square of their distance" (G. L. S. Shackle, *Epistemics and Economics* [Cambridge: Cambridge University Press, 1972], p. 53).

10. K. E. Boulding, "The Economics of Knowledge and the Knowledge of Economics," *American Economic Review* 56 (May 1966): 3.

11. M. Hollis and E. J. Nell, *Rational Economic Man* (Cambridge: Cambridge University Press, 1975), p. 228.

12. G. J. Stigler, "The Economics of Information," *Journal of Political Economy* 69 (June 1961): 213–25.

13. G. J. Stigler, "Imperfections in the Capital Market," *Journal of Political Economy* 75 (June 1967): 291; see also G. J. Stigler, "The Xistence of X-Efficiency," *American Economic Review* 66 (March 1976): 213–16.

14. Shackle, *Epistemics and Economics*, p. 156.

15. Ibid., p. 76.

16. See note 8.

17. J. M. Buchanan, "What Should Economists Do?" *Southern Economic Journal* 30 (January 1964): 213–22.

18. See Hayek, "Use of Knowledge in Society."

19. I. M. Kirzner, *Competition and Entrepreneurship* (Chicago: University of Chicago Press, 1973).

INFORMATION-KNOWLEDGE AND ACTION-KNOWLEDGE

The distinction between information and knowledge, as these words are commonly used, is fairly clear and quite important. We wish to point out, however, that the importance of this distinction becomes very substantially greater when we understand it as pointing to a different distinction—that between two levels of knowledge itself. The purpose of this note is to develop this insight and remark on whether modern economics accommodates these matters.

INFORMATION AND KNOWLEDGE

Imagine a professor employed at an urban university visiting a university in the suburbs to participate in a seminar. He travels by train, the trip taking about an hour. From the suburban train station it is a short walk to the host university campus. After the conclusion of the seminar, our visiting professor tarries to converse with old acquaintances at the host university until he realizes that, unless he leaves immediately for the train station, he is likely to miss the 3:30 train, the next train being 30 minutes hence. The prospect of missing the train spurs him to take leave of his old colleagues and to head for the station. In his pocket he has a detailed set of instructions telling how to get to the train station from the host campus. However, our professor does not consult these instructions, feeling sure that he knows the way to the station—after all, it is only a few hours since he walked successfully *from* the station to campus. Unfortunately this conviction of his is not quite valid, and he takes a wrong turn, walking for several minutes in a wrong direction. By the time he discovers his mistake, and finds his way to the station, he has missed the 3:30 train. Frustrated, he has no choice but to take out his reading materials and recline the best he can on the benches at the train station until the next train to town. He realizes that this cost is due to his not having known the way to the station; his possession of the information (in the form of the set of instructions in his pocket) was not sufficient to avoid this cost.

Our professor may or may not regret his failure to consult his instructions. He *may* be regretful, in the sense that he may, in retrospect, value

From *Econ Journal Watch* 2, 1 (April 2005): 75–81. Reprinted by permission.

making the 3:30 train as being worth the disutility and inconvenience of having to stop, open his coat, extract and read the instructions. Or, he may *not* be regretful: in the light of what he thought he knew, he may judge his decision to have been efficient. In fact, if the value he places on the inconvenience of extracting and reading the instructions is more than the inconvenience of missing the 3:30 train, he may be even more convinced of the wisdom and efficiency of his decision; he may tell himself that it was not worth his while to have consulted his instructions even if he *knew* that he would, by not consulting them, miss his train.

Most of us (and this writer) would say that our scholar suffered the dreariness of waiting because, although he possessed the *information* on how to get to the station in the shortest possible time, he did not possess the *knowledge* of that information. His possession of the needed information means that he had it within his power—by consulting his set of instructions—to gain knowledge of the most direct way from the campus to the train station. Information is an input that may be used in a process of "production" (= of learning) that results in the possession of knowledge. This difference between information and knowledge is straightforward, and conforms to everyday use of language.

What we wish to point out in this paper, however, is that the *distinction* between information and knowledge goes much further than this, and can be seen to be much more important (in a *different* context) than the difference between input and (intermediate) output.

INFORMATION-KNOWLEDGE AND ACTION-KNOWLEDGE

Imagine now a mother at home with a teething child. The child is suffering from pain, and loudly and aggressively proclaims his unhappiness. The mother has tried just about everything, but nothing in her toy chest or refrigerator seems able to soothe, pacify, or distract the child. At that very moment, an itinerant vendor knocks at her door, hawking a colorful toy priced at five dollars. At her wits' end, the mother buys the toy and, presto, the child is delighted with it—peace and harmony are restored. Imagine, however, that while the mother was indeed more than willing to pay five dollars to soothe and pacify her child, she suddenly ruefully realizes that the toy—nothing more than a clear plastic container containing colored marbles—could easily have been put together in seconds, in her own kitchen, for less than a dollar. She could kick herself for not having done so. (Of course, at the same time that she could now kick herself for the earlier mistake, she may *congratulate* herself for, and feel overjoyed by, her "costly" learning process that has taught her how to save money and soothe bawling babies, in the future. And, of course, *given her earlier errors*, she is, as we have already noted, unquestionably *happy* to pay five dollars for the toy that she needs *now*.) She could kick herself because there was nothing that had prevented her from securing peace and harmony for as little as a dollar—instead of the five dollars which she "stupidly" paid. The extra four dollars which she has paid, has been paid *for nothing*—and has given her nothing that was not within her grasp *without* paying those four dollars. She will explain her mistake by saying that, "stupidly," she did not realize that what she was about to purchase from the vendor was available to her almost instantly in her kitchen for no more than one dollar. She did not, at the moment of purchase, "know" what she now knows. But surely she did *not* lack the *knowledge* needed to have avoided the overpayment. It was simply that that knowledge she indeed *had*, did not inspire her to action. The knowledge she *had was like the set of walking instructions in the pocket of the visiting college professor*—that is, it was not "known" in a manner which shapes action.

In other words, we have here a distinction between knowledge-as-information and action-knowledge—the latter referring to the knowledge which actually spurs and shapes action. Not all one's possessed knowledge, in fact, shapes action. What the mother knew at the moment she purchased the toy for five dollars (instead of creating it herself in her kitchen for less than a dollar) was information-knowledge. But this information-knowledge, just like the instructions possessed by our college professor when he went astray on his way to the station, failed to shape the mother's action. Had she fully realized what was within her grasp, she would under no circumstances have paid five dollars for what was available to her for one dollar. *Action often does unalertly ignore facts, which, in the usual sense of the word, one "knows."* This difference between knowledge-as-information and what we have called action-knowledge is, of course, (a) extremely important, and (b) often, unfortunately, ignored in economic theorizing.

INFORMATION-KNOWLEDGE AND ACTION-KNOWLEDGE: AMBIGUITIES AND SUBTLETIES

Our story of the distraught mother, and the insights we have drawn from that story, abstract, for example, from the "problem-solving costs" facing a busy mother in her kitchen, who has other things on her mind *besides* ensuring the lowest-cost manner of securing toys for her child. We simply assumed that *nothing* prevented her from *realizing* what she *already knew*, viz. how to construct a toy from the materials ready to hand in her kitchen. Our assertion that she "already knew" how to construct the toy, follows everyday language. In this everyday use of language, the itinerant vendor taught her nothing she did not already "know." Such use of language, however, does not, we have wished to emphasize, deny that *in a different sense* she had *not* "known" how to construct the toy; she had not *realized* that her information-knowledge could have been *instantly* applied—without any further costly "learning" process—to practical action. This has given us *two equally* valid possible senses of the term "knowledge": (i) information-knowledge and (ii) action-knowledge.

We do not wish to depart from everyday use of language by reserving the term "knowledge" for action-knowledge only. John Doe is attending a large family wedding. Suddenly he realizes that his checkbook is no longer in his pocket. He is not particularly worried; his name is printed on the checks. He does not think anyone would bother to steal the checkbook, but he would very much want to have it back. He says to himself: "perhaps someone will find the checkbook, and it will be announced on the microphone." About an hour later, when John Doe is deeply engaged in stimulating conversation with fellow-guests at his table, someone at the microphone indeed calls out John Doe's name, asking him to come to the microphone. John Doe's first reaction is one of alarm; he fears that perhaps there has been an emergency that has befallen a member of his family (one of his children has been seriously ill). It is only after several seconds have passed that he realizes, of course, that his name has been called only because someone has found his checkbook. *During* those several seconds it would be surely incorrect to say, in everyday language, that John Doe "did not know" that his name was on his checks, or that it was likely that his name would be called when his checkbook was found. He *did* "know" all this; but the full *realization* of what all this meant was prevented by an initial misinterpretation in terms of a possible family emergency. That is, although he certainly did "know" that his name was likely to be called if the checkbook was found—*that* knowledge was *not foremost* on his mind at the moment of the microphone announcement.

It must be emphasized that while it is an act of deliberate production (the act of "learning") which ordinarily converts information into knowledge, what determines whether knowledge-as-information becomes action-knowledge is not, in general, the result of any deliberate decision. While the relation between information and knowledge can, in general, be analyzed using the economist's standard calculus of benefits and costs, the relation between knowledge-as-information and action-knowledge *cannot* be so analyzed. The college professor who failed to consult his walking instructions may, as we have noted, "justify" his failure to convert the information in his instructions into actual knowledge of that information, by referring to the costs of consulting his instructions. It may have been *inefficient* for him to have sought to confirm his belief (that he knew the way to the train station) by stopping, opening his coat in bitter cold weather, extracting his instructions, and reading them on a busy street. But the distraught mother, given our assumptions, has no such "justification" for not having realized that the five dollars she pays for the toy is more than what is necessary to acquire such a toy. She could kick herself for her "stupidity"; that is, she could kick herself for not having been alert to the information-knowledge which she in fact possessed.

Two individuals may "know" the same facts; one of them grasps the opportunity which these facts represent, the second fails to do so. We may say that the first individual was more entrepreneurial, more alert to opportunities. The second individual has simply been unalert. Our discussion suggests that another way of expressing the difference between these individuals is to say that, although they both "know" the same facts, their knowledge is not the same. The one who failed to grasp the opportunity expressed in these known facts had "information-knowledge" of them, but not "action-knowledge." The one who grasped the opportunity was, presumably through his alertness, somehow able to turn his information-knowledge into "action-knowledge." Here we find a difference between (a) the distinction between information and knowledge, and (b) the distinction between information-knowledge and action-knowledge.

Turning information into knowledge calls for the *learning* of that information, and for such learning "alertness," while perhaps necessary, is certainly not sufficient. But in turning information-knowledge into action-knowledge, alertness is necessary and sufficient. Alertness is the crucial bridge between the two kinds of knowledge.

Despite this important difference between the two distinctions, we have in our discussion emphasized the *parallelism* between (a) the relation of knowledge to information, and (b) the relation of action-knowledge to information-knowledge. This emphasis is justified because standard economic theorizing tends to take *no notice whatever* of the difference between information-knowledge and action-knowledge. The economics of information, for example, in the economics of advertising, almost invariably assumes that once information has been deployed in a process of learning to create "knowledge," utilization of that knowledge follows inexorably. So that much of the significance of advertising activity, which goes so far beyond the mere provision of information, is completely lost sight of. The truth surely is that to inspire the consumer to *act* in a manner which correctly mirrors his preferences and resources calls for more than the provision of information. It calls for him to be *alert* to that information and to its significance. In evoking this alertness, advertising plays an important economic role. But this role is invisible to theorists who treat information-knowledge as *identical* with action-knowledge.

Economic theory surely should explore those aspects of economic processes wherein human beings traverse the gulf that otherwise separates the two kinds of knowledge.

COMMENTS ON R. N. LANGLOIS, "FROM THE KNOWLEDGE OF ECONOMICS TO THE ECONOMICS OF KNOWLEDGE: FRITZ MACHLUP ON METHODOLOGY AND ON THE 'KNOWLEDGE SOCIETY'"

Professor Langlois was, he reveals, invited to discuss the connection between Mises's doctrine of praxeology, and the late Professor Machlup's monumental (and regrettably unfinished) "Knowledge Project." In response to this invitation Langlois has given us an elegant, subtle paper which, when boiled down to its essentials, tells us, elegantly and subtly, that there is in fact *no* connection (or virtually no connection) between the two. Machlup's knowledge project owes virtually nothing, we are given to understand, to his Vienna training at the feet of the most consistent modern exponent of the Austrian tradition, Ludwig von Mises.

In what follows I shall not disagree with Langlois' conclusion; in fact I am strongly inclined to agree with him. Nonetheless, it may at the same time be argued with some cogency, I believe, that Machlup's work indeed offers a consistent development of the position occupied by the Vienna economists of the interwar period. The following pages will argue this case, not so much for its own sake, as for the light it will throw upon the somewhat paradoxical modern development of the Austrian tradition, and upon what that tradition meant for Machlup.

I. THE PATH NOT TAKEN

Let us begin by noticing Langlois' brief but highly perceptive section on the path that Machlup did *not* take. Langlois points out that Hayek, another of Mises's brilliant Vienna followers, went on to focus attention upon *the role of knowledge, and of learning, in the social economic process.* "But this was not Machlup's path" (p. 8). For Machlup, "the connection between knowledge and economics extended only to the role of knowledge as a commodity that can be bought, sold, and invested in" (p. 15).

In other words, for all of Machlup's massive concern with knowledge, he failed utterly to emphasize the role which knowledge, search, and

From *Research in the History of Economic Thought and Methodology*, vol. 3 (1985), 237–41, copyright © 1985 by JAI Press Inc. Reprinted by permission.

discovery play in the achievement (by the competitive market process) of those very results that constitute the core of standard marginalist economics (of which Machlup was so staunch a protagonist). Certainly there is something of a mystery here: for Machlup *markets* were of very great significance indeed; so also was the communication of *knowledge*; yet Machlup never did seem to sense the extent to which the former depend upon, and reflect, the latter.

Indeed, in Machlup's comprehensive and detailed review of Hayek's contributions to economics (1974), the role that market processes play (within the Hayekian system) in the communication of knowledge (and vice versa) is noticed hardly at all. Even where, in that review, Hayek's ideas concerning the "division of knowledge" are described as "most original and most important," there is little evidence that Hayek's understanding of market processes of equilibration as being processes of learning, or Hayek's perception of competition "as a discovery procedure," were appreciated by Machlup. Still less is there any suggestion that Machlup would have understood why Hayek has recently held these ideas to have been his most pathbreaking contributions (Hayek, 1982).

II. THE ROLE OF PROCESS IN AUSTRIAN ECONOMICS

But this difference between Hayek and Machlup on the role of discovery in market processes is consistent with yet another peculiarity in Machlup's economics. We know that Machlup was proud of his training in the Austrian tradition of economics, and that he considered himself a consistent continuator of that tradition (being firmly convinced that this tradition had been successfully absorbed into the mainstream of modern economics). On several occasions Machlup set forth a list of the major tenets of the Austrian school (see e.g. 1981, pp. 21f.). There is one respect in which this list might well appear surprising to anyone familiar with modern Austrian economics: although Machlup lists six tenets of Austrianism, he fails to include any reference to what is today generally recognized as being fundamental to the Austrian view, viz. its emphasis upon *processes* (rather than upon equilibrium states of affairs).

It seems reasonable to suggest that this omission by Machlup is consistent, in turn, with the circumstance that up until the thirties (when the group of Vienna economists, including Machlup, dispersed), this Austrian emphasis upon process (and upon the role of learning in this process) remained virtually unarticulated. (Perhaps the statement that came closest to such articulation was Hans Mayer's 1932 espousal of the "causal-genetic," rather than "functional," approach.) By the end of the thirties, both Mises and Hayek were beginning to spell out this process emphasis (although Mises never did explicitly link this process to the communication of knowledge). Machlup, busy with countless other important researches (and more concerned, perhaps, with what the Austrian tradition shared with other schools of thought than with what set it apart), never learned to appreciate this emphasis upon process as being integral to the Austrian tradition.

III. GROPING FOR SELF-AWARENESS

What appears to have occurred is something like the following. In the earlier development of the various post-1870 schools of modern economic thought, there was little need to emphasize, or even articulate at all, some of the more subtle differences between the schools; in fact, some of these differences may not have been noticed altogether. It was not until a good deal of further development occurred within each of the separate traditions, that some of these more subtle differences became apparent (see Jaffe, 1976). So that it should come as no surprise that an Austrian such as Machlup, trained in the twenties, should not have appreciated the role of process in the Austrian view. Indeed it can be persuasively argued that much of the communication-failure that characterized the famous inter-war debate on economic calculation under socialism is to be attributed to the earlier lack of self-awareness on the part of the Austrians, concerning their own "process"-orientation. Had this emphasis been as clearly seen by the Austrians in the twenties as it was in the forties and later, there can be little doubt that their response to the solutions suggested by Lange and Lerner would have been much more powerfully stated and much more clearly understood. It would then have been apparent that the role of market prices in the Austrian process sense—and in fact even the very meaning of the term "prices"—is totally different from the understanding of prices which Lange and Lerner brought to their proposed solutions to the calculation problem.

IV. MACHLUP AND THE ROLE OF KNOWLEDGE

Against this background in *dogmengeschichte*, it may therefore be suggested, Machlup's work on the economics of knowledge may legitimately be held to offer a consistent development of the position widely held in

Vienna in the interwar period. The market was understood as achieving coordination through a rather vaguely specified interplay of decisions—but there was little recognition that any such process of coordination can be postulated only insofar as market experience spontaneously communicates relevant mutual information to potential buyers and sellers. At the same time, however, the subjectivism that suffused Austrian economics from its inception helped focus attention upon the importance of knowledge and information, and helped Austrians, such as Machlup, appreciate the economic significance of markets in which this elusive commodity of knowledge is produced and exchanged.

So that the answer to the question (noticed at the start of this *Comment*) posed to Langlois appears susceptible to two quite different answers. In terms of the *direction* in which Misesian economics was moving during the interwar period, Machlup's work on knowledge indeed failed to reflect the emerging insights into market processes of discovery that were being glimpsed at the time. But in terms of the body of received Austrian doctrine that was in fact settled and articulated teaching at the time, Machlup's work on the ways in which knowledge, as a commodity, manifests its presence in markets, can be held to represent faithfully and consistently those Austrian tenets that Machlup not incorrectly saw as characterizing the economics of interwar Vienna.

REFERENCES

Hayek, Friedrich A., "Dankadresse," in *F. A. Hayek*, edited by E. Hoppman, Baden-Baden, Nomos, 1982 (2nd ed.); cited in S. Boehm, "The Private Seminar of Ludwig von Mises," unpublished paper presented to meetings of the History of Economics Society, Pittsburgh, May 1984, 9.

Jaffe, William, "Menger, Jevons, and Walras De-Homogenized," *Economic Inquiry*, December 1976, 14.

Machlup, Fritz, "Hayek's Contributions to Economics," *The Swedish Journal of Economics*, December 1974, 76, 498–531. Reprinted in F. Machlup, ed., *Essays on Hayek*, New York: New York University Press, 1976.

———, "Ludwig von Mises: A Scholar Who Would Not Compromise," in John K. Andrews, ed., *Homage To Mises, The First Hundred Years*, Hillsdale College Press, 1981.

Mayer, Hans, "Der Erkenntniswert der funktionellen Preistheorien," in *Die Wirtschaftstheorie der Gegenwart*, Vol. II, edited by H. Mayer, F. A. Fetter and R. Reisch. Vienna: Springer, 1932.

Advertising has been badly treated by many scholars who should know better. Not only Marxists and liberals, but even conservatives have given advertising a bad press. Let us examine some of the criticisms.

First, many advertising message are said to be offensive—by esthetic or ethical and moral standards. Unfettered, unhampered, laissez-faire capitalism, it is contended, would propagate such messages in a way that could very well demoralize and offend the tastes and morals of members of society.

Second, advertising, it is argued, is deceitful, fraudulent, full of lies. Misinformation is spread by advertising, in print, on the airwaves, and this does harm to the members of society; for that reason advertising should be controlled, limited, taxed away.

Third, it is argued that where advertising is not deceitful, it is at best persuasive. That is, it attempts to change people's tastes. It attempts not to fulfill the desires of man but to change his desires to fit that which has been produced. The claim of the market economist has always been that the free market generates the flow of production along the lines that satisfy consumer tastes; their tastes determine what shall be produced—briefly, consumer sovereignty. On the contrary, the critics of advertising argue, capitalism has developed into a system where producers produce and then mold men's minds to buy that which has been produced. Rather than production being governed by consumer sovereignty, quite the reverse: the consumer is governed by producer sovereignty.

A fourth criticism has been that advertising propagates monopoly and is antithetical to competition. In a competitive economy, it is pointed out, there would be no advertising; each seller would sell as much as he would like to sell without having to convince consumers to buy that which they would not otherwise have bought. So, advertising is made possible by imperfections in the market. More seriously, it is contended,

From *The Libertarian Alternative: Essays in Social and Political Philosophy*, ed. Tibor R. Machan (Chicago: Nelson Hall, 1974), 478–91. Reprinted by permission; the original source is *The Freeman* 22, 9 (1972): 3–16 (515–28 bound volume).

advertising leads toward monopoly by building up a wall of good will, a protective wall of loyalty among consumers which renders a particular product immune to outside competition. Competing products, which do not share in the fruits of the advertising campaign, find themselves on the outside. This barrier to entry may gradually lead a particular producer to control a share of the market which is rendered invulnerable to the winds of outside competition.

Finally—and this in a way sums up all of these criticisms—advertising is condemned as wasteful. The consumer pays a price for a product which covers a very large sum of money spent on advertising. Advertising does not change the commodity that has been purchased; it could have been produced and sold at a much lower price without the advertising. In other words, resources are being used and paid for by the consumer without his receiving anything that he could not have received in their absence.

These are serious criticisms. We have learned to expect them to be emphasized by contemporary liberal economists. To Marxist thinkers, again, advertising is essential for capitalism; it is seen as a socially useless device necessary in order to get excess production sold. They see no positive elements in advertising at all. But even conservative thinkers and economists have pointed out some apparent limitations, weaknesses, criticisms of advertising.

THE FREE ECONOMY AND HOW IT FUNCTIONS

It is not my purpose here to defend each and every advertising message. I would rather discuss a free economy, a laissez-faire economy, pure capitalism. I would like to show that in such a world, advertising would emerge with a positive role to play; that it would add to the efficiency with which consumer wants are satisfied; and that, while the real world is far from perfect, a large volume of the criticism would fade away were it understood what role advertising, in fact, has to play in a pure market economy.

Let me imagine a world, a free market, in which there are no deceitful men at all. All the messages beamed to consumers and prospective consumers would be, as far as the advertisers themselves believe, the strict truth. We will consider later the implications of the fact that men are imperfect and that men succumb to the temptation in selling something to say a little bit less, a little bit more, than the exact truth. In the meantime, let us talk about a world of honest men, men who do not try to deceive.

Further, let us imagine a pure market economy with government intervention kept to the absolute minimum—the night watchman role. The government stands to the sidelines and ensures the protection of private property rights, the enforcement of contracts freely entered into. Everyone then proceeds to play the game of the free market economy with producers producing that which they believe can be sold to the consumers at the highest possible money price. Entrepreneur producers, who detect where resources are currently being used in less than optimum fashion, take these resources and transfer them to other uses in the economy where they will serve consumer wants which the entrepreneurs believe are more urgently desired, as measured by the amounts of money consumers are willing to pay for various products.

We will assume that there is freedom of entry into all industries. No entrepreneur has sole control over any resource that is uniquely necessary for the production of a given product. No government licenses are required in order to enter into the practice of a given profession or to introduce a particular product. All entrepreneurs are free to produce what they believe to be profitable. All resource owners are free to sell their resources, whether labor, natural resources, capital goods. They are free to sell or rent these resources to the highest bidder. In this way the agitation of the market gradually shuffles resources around until they begin to be used to produce those products which consumers value most highly. Consumers arrange their spending to buy the commodities they believe to be most urgently needed by themselves. And the market flows on in the way that we understand it.

OPEN COMPETITION

We say this is a free market, a laissez-faire, competitive system. But we do not mean a *perfectly* competitive market, as this notion has been developed by the neo-classical economists. In a perfectly competitive market, each seller faces a demand curve which is perfectly horizontal. That is to say, each seller believes that he can sell as much as he would like to sell without having to lower the price. Each buyer faces a perfectly horizontal supply curve and each buyer believes that he can buy as much as he would like to buy of anything without having to offer a higher price. In such a world of "perfect competition," we have what we call an "equilibrium" situation, that is, a situation where all things have already been fully adjusted to one another. All activities, all decisions have been fully coordinated by the market so that there are no disappointments. No participant in the economy discovers that he could have done something better. No participant in the economy discovers that he has made plans to do something which it turns out he cannot do.

In this model of the perfectly competitive economy, there would in fact be *no* competition in the sense in which the layman, or the businessman, understands the term. The term "competition" to the businessman, the layman, means an activity designed to outstrip one's competitors, a rivalrous activity designed to get ahead of one's colleagues, or those with whom one is competing. In a world of equilibrium, a world of "perfect competition," there would be no room for further rivalry. There would be no reason to attempt to do something better than is currently being done. There would, in fact, be no competition in the everyday sense of the term.

When we describe the laissez-faire economy as competitive, we mean something quite different. We mean an economy in which there is complete freedom of entry: if anyone believes that he can produce something that can serve consumers' wants more faithfully, he can try to do it. If anyone believes that the current producers are producing at a price which is too high, then he is free to try to produce and sell at a lower price. This is what competition means. It does not mean that the market has already attained the "equilibrium" situation, which goes under the very embarrassing technical name of "perfectly competitive economy."

NON-PRICE COMPETITION

Now, economists and others understand generally that competition means price competition: offering to sell at a lower price than your competitors are asking, or offering to buy at a higher price than your competitors are bidding. Entrepreneurs will offer higher prices than others are offering for scarce labor. They will offer to sell a product at lower prices than the competing store is asking. This is what price competition means. This is the most obvious form in which competition manifests itself.

However, we must remember that there is another kind of competition, sometimes called "nonprice competition," sometimes called "quality competition." Competition takes the form not only of producing the identical product which your competitors are producing and selling it at a lower price, not only in buying the identical resource which your competitors are buying and offering a higher price. Competition means sometimes offering a better product, or perhaps an inferior product, a product which is more in line with what the entrepreneur believes consumers are in fact desirous of purchasing. It means producing a different model of a product, a different quality, putting it in a different package, selling it in a store with a different kind of lighting, selling it along with an offer of free parking, selling through salesmen who smile more genuinely, more sincerely. It means competing in many, many ways besides the pure price which is asked of the consumer in monetary terms.

With freedom of entry, every entrepreneur is free to choose the exact package, the exact opportunity which he will lay before the public. Each opportunity, each package has many dimensions. He can choose the specifications for his package by changing many, many of these variables. The precise opportunity that he will lay before the public will be that which, in his opinion, is more urgently desired by the consumer as compared with that which happens to be produced by others. So long as there's freedom of entry, the fact that my product is different from his does not mean that I am a monopolist.

A DISSERVICE TO ECONOMICS

The late Professor Edward H. Chamberlin of Harvard did economics a great disservice in arguing that because a producer is producing a unique product, slightly different from what the fellow across the street is producing, in some sense he is a monopolist. So long as there's freedom of entry, so long as the man across the road *can* do exactly what I'm doing, the fact that he is *not* doing exactly what I'm doing is simply the result of his different entrepreneurial judgment. He believes that he can do better with *his* model. I believe I can do better with *mine*. I believe that free parking is more important to consumers than fancy lighting in the store. He gives a different package than I do. Not because he couldn't do what I'm doing, not because I couldn't do what he's doing, but because each believes that he knows better what the consumer is most anxious to acquire. This is what we mean by competition in the broadest sense, not merely price competition, but quality competition in its manifold possible manifestations.

Professor Chamberlin popularized a distinction which was not original with him but which owes its present widely circulated popularity primarily to his work. That is a distinction between "production costs" and "selling costs." In his book of almost forty years ago, *The Theory of Monopolistic Competition*, Chamberlin argued that there are two kinds of costs which manufacturers, producers, sellers, suppliers incur. First, they incur the fabrication costs, the costs of producing what it is they want to sell. Second, they incur additional expenditures that do not produce the product or change it or improve it, but merely get it sold. Advertising, of course, is the most obvious example which Chamberlin cited. But "selling costs" of all kinds were considered by him to be sharply different from "production costs." In his original formulation, Chamberlin argued that "production costs" are costs incurred to produce the product for a given Demand Curve while "selling costs" simply shift the Demand Curve over to the right. That is to say, the same product is now purchased in greater quantities at a given price but the product is the same.

A FALSE DISTINCTION

The fallacy in the distinction between production costs and selling costs is fairly easy to notice. In fact, it is impossible for the outside observer— except as he resorts to arbitrary judgments of value—to distinguish between expenditures which do, and expenditures which do not, alter the product. We know as economists that a product is not an objective quantity of steel or paper. A product is that which is perceived, understood, desired by a consumer. If there are two products otherwise similar to the outside eye which happen to be considered to be different products by the consumer, then to the economist these *are* different products.

Ludwig von Mises gives the example, which cannot be improved upon, of eating in a restaurant. A man has a choice of two restaurants, serving identical meals, identical food. But in one restaurant they haven't swept the floor for six weeks. The meals are the same. The food is the same. How shall we describe the money spent by the other restaurant in sweeping the floor? "Production costs" or "selling costs?" Does sweeping change the food? No. Surely, then, it could be argued that this is strictly a "selling cost." It is like advertising. The food remains the same; but, because you have a man sweeping out the floor, more people come to this restaurant than to that. But this is nonsense. What you buy when you enter a restaurant is not the food alone. What you buy is a meal, served in certain surroundings. If the surroundings are more desirable, it's a different meal, it's a different package. That which has been spent to change the package is as much production cost as the salary paid to the cook; no difference.

Another example that I recall was the case of the coal being run out of Newcastle and traveling along the railroad toward London. Every mile that coal travels nearer the London drawing room, the Demand Curve shifts over to the right. How shall we describe that transportation cost? "Production cost" or "selling cost?" Of course, it's "production cost." In fact, it's "selling cost" too. All "production costs" are "selling costs." All costs of production are incurred in order to produce something which will be more desirable than the raw materials.

You take raw meat and turn it into cooked steak. The act of changing the raw meat into cooked steak is to make the consumer desire it more eagerly. Does this simply shift the Demand Curve over to the right? Of course, it does that. It does it by changing the product.

Another example supposes there are two identical pieces of steel, except that one piece has been blessed, while the other piece is subject to a spiritual taint, which to the scientist is not there but which is very vivid and vital to the consumer. How shall we describe the expenditure on the commodities? Shall we describe the difference between them as nonexistent? Or should we not recognize that, if something is spiritually tainted to the consumer—in his view, not necessarily in mine or yours or the economist's or other than in the mind of the consumer— then he will not buy the tainted item, even though to the objective laboratory scientist there's no difference between the items? The economist has recognized these as two different commodities. There'll be two Demand Curves. The fact that the scientist doesn't see any difference— they look the same, they smell the same, if you touch them they feel the same—is irrelevant. We know, as economists, that what we find in a commodity is not the objective matter that is inside it, but how it is received by the consumer.

Clearly then, the distinction between a so-called "selling cost" and "production cost" is quite arbitrary. It depends entirely on the value judgments of the outside observer. The outside observer can say that this particular selling effort does not change the product, but in that situation he is arrogating to himself the prerogative of pronouncing what is and what is not a product. That is something which violates our fundamental notions of individual consumer freedom: that a consumer's needs are defined by no one else other than himself. This may seem quite a detour from advertising and yet it is all relevant to the question of what role advertising has to play.

THE PROVISION OF INFORMATION

Let us consider how some of these notions apply to the matter of information. One of the standard defenses for advertising is that it provides a service which consumers value: the provision of knowledge, the provision of information. People buy books. People go to college. People enroll in all kinds of courses. Advertising is simply another way of providing information. To be sure, it would seem that the information provided by suppliers comes from a tainted source, but don't forget that we are imagining for the meantime a world without deceitful people.

We can even relax that assumption for a moment. It may be cheaper for the consumer to get his information from the supplier or the producer than from an outside source. In other words, if you, a consumer, have the choice of acquiring information about a particular product—either more cheaply from the producer or more expensively from an outside, "objective" source—you may decide that, on balance, you're likely to get a better deal, penny-for-penny, information-wise, by reading the information of the producer, scanning it perhaps with some skepticism, but nonetheless relying on that rather than buying it from an outside source. Technically, this involves what is known as the problem of transactions costs. It may be more economical for the information to be packaged together with the product, or at least to be produced jointly with the product, than to have the information produced and communicated by an outside source. This is a possibility not to be ignored.

Advertising provides information, and this goes a long way to explain the role which advertising and other kinds of selling efforts must play. Does this not seem to contradict the point just made, that there is no distinction between "production costs" and "selling costs"? Surely, information about a product is distinct from the product. Surely the costs incurred to provide information are a different kind of costs than the costs incurred to produce the product. The answer is clearly no. Information is produced; it is desired; it is a product; it is purchased jointly with the product itself; it is a part of the package; and it is something which consumers value. Its provision is not something performed on the outside that makes people consume something which they would not have consumed before. It is something for which people are willing to pay; it is a service.

You can distinguish different parts of a service. You can distinguish between four wheels and a car. But the four wheels are complementary commodities. That is to say, the usefulness of the one is virtually nil without the availability of the other. The car and gasoline are two separate products, to be sure, and yet they are purchased jointly, perhaps from different producers, different suppliers, but they are nonetheless parts of a total package, a total product. If it happens that the information is produced and sold jointly with the product itself, then we have no reason to question the characteristics of the costs of providing information as true "production costs," not producing necessarily the physical commodity about which information is produced, but producing information which is independently desired by consumers, independently but jointly demanded, complementarily used together with the "product" itself. In other words, the service of providing information is the service of providing something which is needed just as importantly as the "product" itself.

WHY THE SHOUTING?

There is another aspect of advertising which is often overlooked. Information is exceedingly important. But, surely, it is argued, information can be provided without the characteristics of advertising that we know, without the color, without the emotion, without the offensive aspects of advertising. Surely information can be provided in simple straightforward terms. The address of this and this store is this and this place. These and these qualities of commodities are available at these and these prices. Why do illustrated advertising messages have to be projected? Why do all kinds of obviously uninformative matter have to be introduced into advertising messages? This is what renders the information aspects of advertising so suspect. The Marxists simply laugh it away. They say it is ridiculous to contend that advertising provides any kind of genuine information. If one rests the defense of advertising on its informative role, then one has a lot of explaining to do. One has to explain why information that could be provided in clear-cut straightforward terms is provided in such garish and loud forms, in the way that we know it.

The answer, I think, is that advertising does much more than provide information which the consumer wishes to have. This is something which is often overlooked, even by economists. Supposing I set up a gas station. I buy gasoline and I have it poured into my cellar, my tanks. I have a pump carefully hidden behind some bushes, and cars that come down the road can buy gas if they know that I'm here. But I don't go to the effort to let them know I'm here. I don't put out a sign. Well, gas without information is like a car without gas. Information is a service required complementarily with the gas.

CUSTOMERS WANT TO KNOW WHERE TO FIND THE PRODUCT

Supposing, then, I take a piece of paper, type very neatly in capital letters, "GAS," and stick it on my door. Cars speed down the road in need of gas, but they don't stop to read my sign. What is missing here? Information is missing. Don't people want information? Yes. They would like to know where the gas station is, but it's a well-kept secret. Now, people *are* looking for that information. It's my task as an entrepreneur not only to have gas available but to have it in a form which is known to consumers. It is my task to supply gas-which-is-known-about, not to provide gas *and* information.

I have not only to produce opportunities which are available to consumers; I have to make consumers aware of these opportunities. This is a point which is often overlooked. An opportunity which is not known, an opportunity to which a consumer is not fully awakened, is simply not an opportunity. I am not fulfilling my entrepreneurial task unless I project to the consumer the awareness of the opportunity. How do I do that? I do that, not with a little sign on my door, but with a big neon sign, saying GAS; and better than that I chalk up the price; and better than that I make sure that the price is lower than the price at nearby stations; and I do all the other things that are necessary to *make* the consumer *fully* aware of the opportunity that I am in fact prepared to put before him. In other words, the final package consists not only of abstract academic information but in having the final product placed in front of the consumer in such a form that he cannot miss it.

FREE $10 BILLS!

The strange thing about the world in which we live is that it is a world in which $10 bills are floating around, free $10 bills! The problem is that very few of us notice these $10 bills. It is the role of the entrepreneur to notice the existence of $10 bills. An entrepreneur buys resources for $10 and he sells the product for $20. He is aware that resources available for

$10 are currently being used in less than optimum fashion, that commodities for which consumers are willing to pay $20 are not being produced, and he puts these things together. He sees the $10 bill and makes the combination which other people do not see. Anybody might do it—freedom of entry. The entrepreneur notices the $10 bill, gets it for himself by placing in front of the consumer something which he had not noticed. If the consumer knew where he could buy resources for $10 and get the product that is worth $20, he wouldn't buy from the entrepreneur. He would do it himself. Since he doesn't know, I, as entrepreneur, have to create this opportunity and make the consumer aware.

It is not enough to buy gas and put it in the ground. The entrepreneur puts it in the ground in a form that the consumer recognizes. To do this requires much more than fabrication. It requires communication. It requires more than simple information. It requires more than writing a book, publishing it, and having it on a library shelf. It requires more than putting something in a newspaper in a classified ad and expecting the consumer to see it. You have to put it in front of the consumer in a form that he *will* see. Otherwise, you're not performing your entrepreneurial task.

THE GROWTH OF ADVERTISING

Advertising has grown. Compare the volume of advertising today with the volume of 100 years ago and it has grown tremendously. More! Consider the price of a commodity that you buy in a drug store or in a supermarket. Find out what portion of that price can be attributed to advertising costs, and it turns out that a much larger percentage of the final cost to the consumer can be attributed to advertising today than could have been attributed 50 years ago, 70 years ago, 100 years ago. Why is this? Why has advertising expenditure grown in proportion to total value of output? Why has advertising expenditure grown in proportion to the price of a finished commodity? Why has advertising apparently grown more offensive, more loud, more shrill? It's fairly easy to understand.

I give, as example, the lobby walls of a college building that I know very well. At one time this was a handsome lobby with walls of thick marble; you could walk from one end of the building to the other and the walls would be clear. Some years ago an enterprising entrepreneur decided to use some free advertising space. He pasted up a sign. It was the only sign on the wall; everybody looked at it, saw the message. I don't remember what the message was or whether it was torn down, but I do remember that soon afterward those walls were full of signs. As you walked down the passage, you could read all kinds of messages, all kinds of student activities, non-student activities. It was fairly easy to learn about what was going on simply by reading the signs.

At first, the signs did not have to be big. But as advertisers saw the opportunity, the free space gradually filled up. The Ricardian rent theory came into play; all the free land was in use. And as the free land or space was taken, of course, it became more and more important to get up early to paste up your sign. That was the "rent," the high price, getting up early. But more than that, it became necessary now to arouse all kinds of interest in me in order to get me to read these signs. In other words, the variety and multiplicity of messages make it harder and harder to get a hearing.

THE PRICE OF AFFLUENCE

We live in a world which is often described as an "affluent society." An affluent society is one in which there are many, many opportunities placed before consumers. The consumer enters a supermarket, and if he is to make a sensible, intelligent decision he is going to have to spend several hours calculating very carefully, reading, rereading everything that's on the packages and doing a complete research job before feeding all the information into the computer and waiting for the optimum package to be read off. It's a tough job to be a consumer. And the multiplicity of opportunities makes it necessary for advertisers, for producers, to project more and more provocative messages if they want to be heard. This is a cost of affluence. It is a cost, certainly; something that we'd much rather do without, if we could; but we can't.

The number of commodities that have been produced is so great that in order for any one particular product to be brought to the attention of the consumer a large volume of advertising is necessary. And we can expect to get more and more. Is it part of production costs? Very definitely, yes. It is completely arbitrary for anyone to argue that, whether or not the consumer knows it, the commodity is there anyway, so that when he pays the price which includes the advertising communication he is paying *more* than is necessary for the opportunity made available. For an opportunity to be made available, it must be in a form which it is impossible to miss. And this is what advertising is all about.

One more word about the offensiveness of advertising. Ultimately in a free market, consumers tend to get what they want. The kinds of products produced will reflect the desires of the consumer. A society which wants moral objects will get moral objects. A society which wants immoral objects will tend to get immoral objects. Advertised communication is part of the total package produced and made available to consumers. The kind of advertising we get, sad to say, is what we deserve. The kind of advertising we get reflects the kind of people that we are. No doubt, a different kind of advertising would be better, more moral, more ethical in many respects; but I'm afraid we have no one to blame but ourselves, as in all cases where one deplores that which is produced by a market society.

A final word about deceit. Of course, deceitful advertising is to be condemned on both moral and economic grounds. But we have to put it in perspective. Let me read from one very eminent economist who writes as follows:

> The formation of wants is a complex process. No doubt wants are modified by Madison Avenue. They are modified by Washington, by the university faculties and by churches. And it is not at all clear that Madison Avenue has the advantage when it comes to false claims and exaggerations.[1]

TAKE WITH A GRAIN OF SALT

In other words, we live in a world where you have to be careful what you read, to whom you listen, whom you believe. And it's true of everything, every aspect of life. If one were to believe everything projected at him, he would be in a sorry state.

It is very easy to pick out the wrong messages to believe. Now, this doesn't in any way condone or justify deceitful messages of any kind. We have to recognize, however, while particular producers may have a short-run interest in projecting a message to consumers of doubtful veracity, that so long as there's freedom of competition the consumer has his choice not only of which product to buy but whom to believe. And notice what is the alternative in this world of imperfect human beings. The alternative, of course, is government control—still by imperfect human beings. So there is no way to render oneself invulnerable to the possibility of false, fraudulent, deceitful messages.

It would be nice to live in a world where no deceitful men were present. It would be cheaper. You could believe any message received. You wouldn't have to check out the credentials of every advertiser. But that is not the world in which we live. You check out the credit standing of individuals, the character of people with whom you deal; and this is an unavoidable, necessary cost. To blame advertising for the imperfections and weaknesses of mankind is unfair. Advertising would exist under any type of free market system. Advertising would be less deceitful if men were less deceitful. It would be more ethical, less offensive, if men were less offensive and more ethical. But advertising itself is an integral, inescapable aspect of the market economy.

NOTE

1. H. Demsetz, "The Technostructure, Forty-Six Years Later," *Yale Law Journal,* 1968, p. 810.

This book explores the phenomenon of advertising in considerable detail. It presents and critically examines the "traditional" view in economics that saw advertising as a fundamentally baneful phenomenon, thwarting the tendency of competitive markets to allocate resources efficiently. This book presents, by way of refreshing contrast, an "emerging" view of advertising that recognizes the essential and constructive role it plays in the functioning of markets.

This emerging view is presented here with clarity, and with cogency; it draws upon an impressive literature and reports a wide range of research findings. I believe that the thoughtful reader of this book is likely, after carefully and candidly comparing these two views, to concur with the authors in their conclusions rejecting the traditional sweeping condemnations of advertising on both economic and ethical grounds. While advertising, like every other human activity, is certainly both prone to error and subject to abuse, the insights developed in this book reveal that the phenomenon of advertising as such, is neither the expression of any ethical failure of the market nor the evidence of resources being inefficiently deployed in defiance of consumer preferences.

Yet the very cogency with which Professors Ekelund and Saurman develop their case raises an obvious problem. If advertising is indeed so usefully important for the functioning of markets, why has traditional economics so consistently failed to recognize this? The authors have, quite correctly, cited the excessive preoccupation of economists with equilibrium analysis as being primarily responsible for their failure to grasp the real, beneficial character of advertising. In the following pages I shall try to identify a key element in the economics of advertising which has placed it, so to speak, in the "blind spot" of traditional economics. Once this key element is brought into unmistakable focus, the irrelevance of traditional equilibrium analysis for an understanding of advertising

Foreword to Robert B. Ekelund and David S. Saurman, *Advertising and the Market Process: A Modern Economic View* (San Francisco: Pacific Research for Public Policy, 1988), xv–xxii. Reprinted by permission.

becomes abundantly apparent. So that, I shall argue, an appreciation of the true economic role of advertising, as it emerges from this volume, can lead, in turn, to a more profound and sensitive appreciation for the nature of economic understanding, no longer confined narrowly to the contemplation of states of hypothetical equilibrium. The key element in the economics of advertising to which I wish to draw attention is the *open-endedness* of the universe to which it relates. The concept of open-endedness deserves some elaboration.

THE OPEN-ENDED UNIVERSE AND THE CLOSED

Fundamental to all economic understanding is the analysis of *choice*. Whether probing the nature of individual economic activity or canvassing the options confronting the framers of societal economic policy, economics is deeply involved in the theory of choice. For the greater part economics has dealt with choice, we shall contend, within a framework appropriate to a *closed* world. A closed universe is, for present purposes, one in which relevant alternatives present themselves to the decision-makers in definitely perceived form. The decision maker sees himself confronted by a limited number of clearly marked out possible courses of action, each leading to a definitely perceived outcome. The calculations, on the basis of which the choice among alternatives must be made, are not clouded by any sense of possible surprises (that might reveal the environment to have been different from that envisaged at the moment of choice). What characterizes choice in a closed universe is the circumstance that there is, within its framework, no scope for the decision maker to exercise any foresight, or creative imagination. Once the parameters of this closed universe have been identified, once the decision maker's preferences among the given set of alternative possible outcomes have been recognized, the decision-making process becomes strictly mechanical. Given these parameters and preferences, choice is completely predictable and determined.

The open-ended universe differs decisively in these respects from the closed. Decision-making in the open-ended universe occurs within a context in which key elements required for deliberate, calculative decision-making are totally absent. While some possible courses of action may be more or less clearly perceived, others are not seen at all. While some possible outcomes (of given courses of action) may be glimpsed, others are not recognized. The possibility of utter surprise is central to the open-ended universe. Such a universe provides ample scope for—in fact, it imperiously demands—the imagination, creativity, and prescience of the decision maker. Successful decision-making in such a universe is not at all a matter of scanning and comparing a series of given and known alternative outcomes. Successful decision-making, in the open-ended universe, consists rather in creatively anticipating the as yet unknown, in imaginatively filling in the missing contours of the apparently open-ended environment.

KNOWLEDGE, IGNORANCE, AND OPEN-ENDEDNESS

It is not sufficient, for the description of the open-ended universe, to identify it with imperfect knowledge, on the part of the decision maker, concerning aspects of his environment. As we shall emphasize, a closed universe need not imply omniscience with respect to one's environment; a closed universe merely requires that relevant courses of action be immune to surprise. Thus someone who requires a piece of information (let us say, concerning the climate in a foreign country to which he is considering a visit) knows that a time-consuming trip to the library is needed to acquire the needed information. His decision on whether or not to go to the library is fully consistent with the conditions for a closed universe. Moreover, even should he decide *not* to go to the library, his subsequent decisions (concerning the prospective visit to the foreign country) may nonetheless yet be made in a closed context. It is true that he lacks pertinent information (concerning the climate of the country) but he *knows* that he lacks this information. Within a wide range, he is subject to no surprises.

For the open-ended universe it is not enough that knowledge is incomplete; it is required that the decision maker *be ignorant of the extent of his own ignorance.* He is subject to genuine surprise. One so subject to surprise is not choosing between perceived alternatives about whose outcomes he has specifically incomplete information; he is, in important respects, making a choice without knowing what he is selecting, or what he is giving up.

LIFE IN THE OPEN-ENDED UNIVERSE

As has been pointed out by a number of writers, particularly by Ludwig von Mises, George Shackle, and Ludwig Lachmann, life in the open-ended universe is radically different from life in the closed universe described in textbooks of economic theory. To choose in the open-ended universe is to strike out boldly into a largely unseen world. To act as a producer, in an open-ended world, is not to fabricate a commodity for a perceived market; it is to create a commodity for a market the extent of which must be imagined; it is to create a commodity for a market into which any number of competing producers may be introducing novel products at prices that can only be guessed at. To act as a producer, in an open-ended world, is not to produce a commodity for waiting consumers; it is to try to sell one's product to potential customers who are unaware of what has been made available to them. In other words, potential consumers in the open-ended universe may be ignorant, not merely of the availability of commodities for which they may have urgent need, but also of that ignorance itself. Moreover potential consumers may be ignorant concerning the potential usefulness to them of known available commodities—and may, to boot, be ignorant of their ignorance in this respect as well.

Confronted with markets made up of such "utterly" ignorant potential consumers, producers cannot content themselves with producing goods; nor can they even be content with making relevant information (concerning the availability of these products) available to potential customers. After all, customers who are unaware that they lack vitally important information are in no obvious way motivated to acquire that information—even if it is made costlessly available to them. It is necessary for the producer *to grab the attention of his prospective customers* and somehow to get them to see the product he has prepared for them (or at least to see the information available concerning such products). And it is in regard to the task of attention-grabbing that the economics of an open-ended world must differ most radically from that of a closed universe.

THE GRABBING OF ATTENTION IN A CLOSED UNIVERSE

Economists have learned well Adam Smith's lesson concerning the invisible hand. Economists understand that the butcher's eagerness to help produce my dinner is rooted in and motivated by his knowledge of my own eagerness to have dinner. When economists observe an act of production, no matter how bizarre it may appear, they are thereby alerted to the existence of some anticipated consumer eagerness (outlandish though this preference may seem to the rest of us) to which the producer proposes to cater. This training preserves economists, to a considerable extent, from the error of concluding that producers are somehow ungoverned by the imperatives of consumer sovereignty. But this very training renders it understandable why traditional economists have failed properly to grasp the nature of advertising. It is this very training that has rendered the *activity of grabbing attention* virtually incomprehensible to traditional economists in any but a socially baneful light. The matter is quite easy to see.

For the activity of seeking to grab attention seems, at first glance, to be simply impossible to be subsumed under Smith's invisible hand. It seems impossible to argue that my frantic efforts to grab your attention is in response to your eagerness that your attention be grabbed away from whatever you are now concentrating your attention upon. In fact it seems quite clear that you have definitely chosen to bestow your attention on something else; that you do *not* wish to read the advertising message that I wish you to read. It is, in fact, precisely because you have demonstrated your preference to concentrate on reading something else (say, a book) that motivates me to mobilize all the wiles of Madison Avenue somehow to turn your attention away from what *you* had decided you wished to read, toward what *I* would like you to read.

But of course this conclusion that my efforts to grab your attention violate the invisible hand insights obtains its validity only because it assumes a closed environment. For such a world, indeed, advertising represents a kind of *aggression* in which a powerful advertiser wrenches the consumer away from the purchases which *he* deems the most efficient use of his budget and somehow manipulates him into buying what the advertiser wishes him to purchase.

Moreover, in this same closed universe, it becomes easy to see how disinterested "objective" observers of such a scene might be "scientifically" convinced that the products which the advertiser wishes to ram down the throats of consumers are in fact wasteful or even harmful—and that the consumer himself will soon regret having succumbed to the advertiser's blandishments.

Grabbing Attention in the World of Open-Endedness
Once we escape the confines of the closed world of textbook economics, however, the activity of grabbing attention can be understood much more sympathetically. To grab a consumer's attention may just possibly be to do something for which that consumer will be eternally grateful *even*

though, at the moment, it appears to violate his own expressed preferences. The advertiser has, without violating the consumer's property rights, stimulated the latter's imagination to the point that he recognizes now an opportunity of which he had previously been totally unaware. *The advertiser has, as it were, injected a pleasant surprise into the world of the consumer.* The consumer finds that his world, his range of options, is a little richer than he had dared anticipate.

The advertiser, it should be emphasized, has not *responded* to pre-existing consumer demand, but neither has he, necessarily, violated that preexisting pattern of demand by invasively altering it through psychological manipulation. He has merely opened the consumer's eyes to see what he had earlier failed to notice. In a closed environment, eyes cannot be opened (since they were never closed). The only way consumer behavior could be modified, under closed-world conditions, would be by *engineering* a change of preferences. Advertising, from the closed-world perspective, is naturally seen as constituting such engineering, and hence as unethically and inefficiently unfaithful to the original preferences. But open-endedness means that consumers' eyes *are* likely to be closed, offering scope for entrepreneurial action to bring to consumer notice that which has hitherto escaped them. To widen horizons is not to be unfaithful to what was seen earlier, it is to *add* to what was seen earlier.

Nor can the outside observer, in the open-ended universe, arrogate to himself the authority to pronounce "scientifically" a particular advertising message or a particular advertised product as perverse or inconsistent with the consumer's true preferences. If the consumer himself does not yet know how much he might like a particular product (once a full display of its qualities might be imaginatively laid out by the entrepreneurial producer), it is all the more certain that no outside observer, no matter how knowledgeable, can know what the consumer's "true" preferences may be, once that consumer's world will have been enriched by the surprises injected by the advertiser.

A World of Competing Attention-Grabbers
Once we transcend the confines of the closed analytical universe, in fact, we can begin to appreciate more generally the benign character of social processes that are rooted in the open-endedness of the real world in which we live. The benign character of advertising emerges, then, as merely an

example of a more general phenomenon. Once open-endedness has been recognized, we can understand the need for social processes that might stimulate the *discovery* of unknown opportunities and might reveal pleasantly surprising features of the environment that can be taken advantage of (as well as unpleasant surprises to be wary of). Hayek has taught us to see the *competitive process*, always central to markets, as just such a procedure for discovery. In the competitive process actions are taken that lead to the discovery of interpersonal (and technological) possibilities that no one had suspected. So that the outcome of the competitive process could never have been deliberately achieved without it.

Advertising, the activity of capturing consumer attention, is easily seen to be just one particular dimension of competitive activity. Competing advertisers, vying with each other for the consumer's attention, are inspired to devise attention-grabbing strategies that no one could have foreseen, disseminating information that no one could have known to have been needed (or perhaps even to be available), and stimulating the provision of goods and services the importance to consumers of which no one had suspected.

To be sure, these strategies display features difficult to reconcile with the economics of a closed world. The phenomenon of advertising simply cannot fit a world in which consumers already know what they want. Nor can this phenomenon even fit a world in which consumers know what information they need to obtain, in order to know what they want. Advertising exists in a world in which people do not know what information they need to know.

Ethics, Economics, and the Open-Ended Universe

The world of economic activity is a seemingly chaotic one. The casual, untutored observer finds little that appears systematic in this world of vigorous competition and energetic entrepreneurial innovation. For much of its history the science of economics made important progress by abstracting from such apparently chaotic elements, and by therefore concentrating on only those features of the world that could fit into the model of a closed universe. Undoubtedly these contributions of economics were of enormous value and importance. Much that is central to the working of the market can indeed most easily be grasped by reference to the closed-world model. But this approach to economic understanding has not been without its costs.

Principal among these costs has been the widespread tendency for economists to ignore and even to deny features of the world that do not fit into the closed-world model. This has meant that economists have been inclined to interpret such features of the real world in terms of an ethics and an economics which is significantly inappropriate for them. Advertising, we have seen, is just such a feature. Its ethical and economic treatment at the hands of economists has suffered correspondingly. If the phenomenon of advertising (and other similar phenomena intrinsic to the open-ended universe) are to be adequately understood and evaluated, traditional economics must be regenerated, enriched and deepened to encompass concepts of discovery, surprise, and entrepreneurial competition. It is the outstanding merit of this volume that, in regard to the economics of advertising, it addresses this regenerative task with impressive comprehensiveness and scholarly excellence.

TWO

ESSAYS

ON

MARKETS

HOW MARKETS WORK: DISEQUILIBRIUM, ENTREPRENEURSHIP, AND DISCOVERY

FOREWORD

In the last hundred years or so, the neo-classical school has come to dominate micro-economic thinking. Economists concerned with competition have taken refuge in increasingly complex models which emphasise the end-state of competitive equilibrium; for a time the classical economists' interest in the disequilibrium adjustments which lead up to such a state all but disappeared.

The economic policy consequences of this dominance have been momentous. Concentration on the equilibrium state of "perfect competition" leads to a search for "imperfections" and "failures" in markets. It is a short step to proposals for government action to correct such failures. Indeed, since all real-world markets must appear imperfect when set next to the perfectly competitive ideal, the scope for government intervention seems virtually unlimited.

Criticisms of the market failure approach to policy-making have, however, mounted. Some have arisen from within the economics mainstream—for instance, the "second-best" critique of piecemeal tinkering with markets[1] and the doubts expressed about the practical value of the optimality criterion implicit in the perfectly competitive paradigm.[2] More devastating are the criticisms made by the public choice school which points out that people in the state sector are neither omniscient nor altruistic but just like other people. Consequently, government fails too, and it cannot reasonably be assumed that action to remedy market failures will necessarily be beneficial.[3]

First published by the Institute of Economic Affairs, London, in June 1997. Reprinted by permission.

1. R. G. Lipsey and K. Lancaster, "The General Theory of Second Best," *Review of Economic Studies*, 24(1), October 1956, pp. 11–32.

2. The Pareto optimality criterion, which defines an improvement as a move which makes at least one person better off without making anyone else worse off.

3. For example, Gordon Tullock, *The Vote Motive*, Hobart Paperback 9, London: Institute of Economic Affairs, 1976 (2nd Impn. 1978).

But even more damaging to the neo-classical mainstream is the criticism that competition should properly be seen not as a state but (as in the earlier classical tradition) as a continuous process taking place over time. This view is often labelled "Austrian" and associated particularly with two great 20th-century exponents of the Austrian School—Ludwig von Mises and Friedrich Hayek. According to the Austrians, the long-run equilibrium of perfect competition is not an appropriate policy target because it does not represent competition at all but an end-state in which competition has been exhausted. The market is at rest whereas the essence of competition is disequilibrium characterised by continuous change.

Professor Israel Kirzner, who is one of the leading exponents of Austrian economics, following in the tradition of Mises and Hayek, demonstrates in Hobart Paper 133 the insights the Austrians can provide. His emphasis is on a form of competition far more closely aligned with the real-world markets in which business people operate than are the arid models of neo-classical theorists.

Kirzner uses his unrivalled knowledge of the history and present state of Austrian economics to show how it relates to the older classical tradition and how it diverges from the mainstream. He opens the "black box" of the competitive process, explaining how entrepreneurs drive markets by searching for, discovering and exploiting profit opportunities which had not previously been seized. Entrepreneurial discovery is at the centre of the real-world market process. Knowledge is neither perfect nor is it available from some central pool which can be tapped: it is naturally dispersed and is uncovered by entrepreneurs competing one with another to find better ways of satisfying consumers.

Not only does Professor Kirzner explain the principal features of Austrian economics, he also discusses the insights it offers into practical policy issues (Section V). *Advertising,* for example, is a means in a complex society of alerting consumers to "what they do not know that they do not know": it is a ". . . tool *with which to compete.*" *Anti-trust laws,* intended as well-meaning defences against the emergence of monopoly, may well become obstacles to market processes: freedom of entry is the only requirement for a competitive market to exist and, in general, it is only governments which can erect genuine barriers to entry.

Mainstream welfare economics, with its emphasis on social optimality, is fatally flawed since the dispersion of information means that no "social agent" could conceivably gather the information required to attain optimal outcomes: markets, however, can gather such information and achieve the necessary co-ordination even if their outcomes are not "optimal" in the strict sense. *Socialist economics*, though now discredited in practice, could never even in theory simulate competitive markets because it aimed at mimicking the perfectly competitive outcome rather than instituting a competitive discovery process. As for *justice*, Professor Kirzner maintains that there is nothing unjust about pure profits accruing to entrepreneurs: such profits are "created gain," not a portion of some already existing 'pie' which is available for distribution.

Interest in the Austrian view of economics is growing, especially in industrial economics where researchers place much more emphasis on entry conditions to markets than on the old structure-conduct-performance paradigm. References to Austrian economics now appear even in introductory economics texts. Micro-economic policies, however, with their emphasis on supposed market failures, still seem biased towards the views of "defunct economists" (to use the words of Keynes).

As with all Institute publications, the views expressed in Hobart Paper 133 are those of the author, not of the Institute (which has no corporate view), its Trustees, Advisers or Directors. Professor Kirzner's illuminating paper is published by the Institute to expose the insights of Austrian economics to a wide audience—including policy-makers, for whom it contains many lessons.

April 1997

Colin Robinson
Editorial Director, Institute of Economic Affairs;
Professor of Economics, University of Surrey

I. INTRODUCTION

This paper presents, in non-technical terms, an "Austrian" view of how a market economy works. The theory is "Austrian" in its being derived from insights which matured during the course of the century-and-a-quarter history of the Austrian tradition. These insights came to be articulated with especial clarity and with originality of emphasis in the mid-20th-century contributions, respectively, of two great exponents of the Austrian tradition, Ludwig von Mises and Friedrich Hayek. During the past quarter of a century a number of younger economists working in the Austrian tradition, including the present writer, have contributed to the further crystallisation of the theory of entrepreneurial discovery and of its implications for economic understanding and policy.

Most economists agree that markets "work"—that, through voluntary exchange transactions agents in a market economy are, without central direction or control, able to participate in an enormously productive system, taking advantage of specialisation and division of labour. Moreover, economists generally agree that the overall social pattern of resource allocation spontaneously so achieved is highly and benignly sensitive to changes in consumer preferences, resource endowment availabilities and known technological possibilities.

These shared doctrines enable economists to understand both the dramatic increase in the standard of living achieved in market societies during the past century and the relative failures (and the recent numerous examples of complete breakdown) of socialist economies, whether in Eastern Europe or elsewhere. Yet there remains a fundamental mystery at the heart of these shared doctrines. Surprisingly, standard economics does not provide a satisfying explanation of exactly *why* and *how* markets work. Adam Smith's "invisible hand" turns out to be an apt metaphor for what remains an analytical black box in economic theory. Economic theory, at least in its mainstream version, explains with great sophistication the operation of a smoothly working market economy in which each agent has somehow already found his place. But it turns out to be virtually silent in explaining the course of events which enables agents, starting from initial absence of co-ordination, *to find* their places in the social jig-saw puzzle. So the relatively smooth working of real-world markets remains, after all, a mystery.

It is not the primary purpose of this *Hobart Paper* to demolish mainstream economics. Mainstream theory has limited usefulness for a number of workaday purposes of economics. The paper's objective is to set forth an alternative "Austrian" theoretical approach, grounded in the economics of entrepreneurial discovery, to explain a mystery left unresolved by mainstream theory—how and why markets work. Criticisms of mainstream theory are developed briefly in Section III of the paper, with the aim of highlighting the crucial features of the Austrian approach.

When economists, Austrian or not, talk of markets "working," they have in mind processes of social adjustment in which market participants are spontaneously attracted to offer their fellows exchange opportunities which tend in aggregate to exhaust all potential gains from trade throughout the economy. At first glance such a tendency appears counter-intuitive. For individual activities to become dovetailed in such a benign fashion one would expect a virtually omniscient, omnipotent and benevolent economic czar to survey all individual preferences, endowments and potentialities; he would then compute and enforce a pattern of decision-making that not only co-ordinates all decisions, but also ensures that no opportunities for mutual gain remain unexploited.

Yet the theory of the market claims not only that it is *possible* for a set of decentralised individual decisions to exist on the pattern of the fully co-ordinated state of affairs. It claims also that there is a powerful tendency for market events spontaneously to unfold towards such a fully co-ordinated pattern without any central direction and control. The absence, in mainstream economics, of a satisfying explanation for the validity of such claims, is a troubling hiatus. The Austrian theory of entrepreneurial discovery outlined in this paper aims to fill this gap. But the implications of the theory go much further.

The set of assumptions required by mainstream theory to demonstrate how a smoothly operating market might work are far too demanding in terms of the economic systems we know. The empirical unrealism of that theory's assumptions suggests that it conclusively demonstrates that real-world markets should *not* be able spontaneously to co-ordinate. Thus the obvious co-ordinating properties of real-world markets turn out to be counter-intuitive phenomena crying out even more desperately for an explanation.

Austrian theory, as presented here, places great weight on "entrepreneurial discovery" which enables decentralised decision-makers to recognise when present decisions can be improved upon, and to antici-pate future changes in the decisions being made by others. Movements in prices, production methods, choices of outputs, and resource owner incomes generated by entrepreneurial discovery tend to reveal where cur-rent allocation patterns are faulty, and to stimulate changes in the cor-rective direction. The paper contrasts the element of entrepreneurial discovery which is central to the Austrian theory, with the character of the individual economic decision as it enters into mainstream theory.

It turns out that not only does entrepreneurial discovery theory pro-vide the key to explaining how markets work, on lines foreign to the approach taken by mainstream theory. In addition, its implications for economic policy are at sharp variance with those conventionally held. Even if one's scientific curiosity as to how the market works were some-how to be suspended, attention to Austrian theory would be required in order to choose intelligently among alternative policy options with differ-ent consequences for social well-being. In such areas as anti-trust policy, in particular, Austrian theory suggests policies differing drastically from those conventionally derived from mainstream theory.

Section II of this paper sketches the background, in 20th-century eco-nomics, of the theory of entrepreneurial discovery. Section III briefly examines the mainstream understanding of markets, emphasising those features to which the Austrian theory takes sharp exception. Section IV develops the Austrian theory in positive fashion. Section V discusses the implications of the Austrian theory which differ from those traditionally drawn from mainstream economics. Section VI concludes the paper.

II. THE BACKGROUND IN THE HISTORY
OF ECONOMIC IDEAS

THE EMERGENCE OF NEO-CLASSICAL THEORY

Beginning with the 1870s, there emerged a body of economic doctrines broadly shared by the various schools of economic theory in Europe. Whether under the aegis of the Marshallian school in England, the Mengerian school in Austria, or the then emerging Walrasian tradition on the Continent, up to the 1930s economics came to emphasise the theory of price, held to co-ordinate the decisions of suppliers and demanders. These different schools of thought are often described as making up a single, broadly understood "neo-classical" approach to economic theory.[1]

A central tenet of this neo-classical theory was that price tended towards the market-clearing level in each market. In terms of the simple supply and demand diagram (still taught today to all students beginning economics) this came to mean that prices too high to clear the market tend to fall (due to the competition of sellers trying to sell their unsold surplus); prices too low to clear the market tend to rise (due to the competition of eager, disappointed buyers). These regularities governing price movements provided economists with an insight into markets which appeared perfectly general, applying to all kinds of goods and services and showing how market phenomena systematically express the preferences of market participants. All these neo-classical schools shared the view that it was scientifically fruitful, in examining different kinds of markets, to abstract from the institutional detail, and to focus upon their pure economic structure—an analytical structure from which everything but supply, demand, and price had been stripped away. This aspect of neo-classical economics was successful in pushing the once dominant German Historical School of Economics—with its anti-theoretical bent—from its turn-of-the-century pre-eminence on the Continent.

This awareness by the various theoretical schools of their shared opposition to the German Historical School seems to have misled them into overlooking subtle developing analytical and methodological differences

---

1. In regard to late-20th-century economics, the term "neo-classical" has come to be specifically attached to a much narrower set of theories reflecting a rigorous extension of Walrasian general equilibrium theory, in which the market is seen as made up of perfectly co-ordinated decisions of strictly maximising individuals.

that would subsequently lead into sharply divergent theoretical paths. Indeed, the shared neo-classical theory of price formation came to be developed along sharply different lines. The mainstream (narrowly "neo-classical") approach emerged out of the confluence of the Marshallian and Walrasian traditions. In this approach the focus was placed upon the conditions of market equilibrium seen, in Walrasian fashion, as the expression of the solution to the simultaneous equation system consti-tuted by the relevant supply and demand functions. This diverted ana-lytical attention from the step-by-step process through which one might imagine initially dis-co-ordinated sets of decisions gradually becoming modified towards greater mutual co-ordination. Hence the "mystery" to which we have drawn attention: mainstream theory fails to explain how markets do in fact *come* to work. It explains in great detail the relation-ships that would prevail in markets that already do work; it is silent on the nature of the processes that might generate those relationships.

MENGERIAN AND WALRASIAN TRADITIONS

But the third doctrinal component of the earlier neo-classical alliance of schools came to develop a different understanding of the theory of price. The Mengerian tradition gradually evolved until, at about the middle of this century, it was set firmly in a direction explicitly diver-gent from the Walrasian. It recognised that the mathematical refine-ments occurring in mainstream theory had been won at the cost of obscuring key features of the earlier neo-classical understanding. As explained below, both Ludwig von Mises and Friedrich Hayek articu-lated such views in the 1940s.

These contributions by Mises and by Hayek emerged out of an earlier Austrian tradition that had taken the shared neo-classical theory of price for granted. A prescient paper by Austrian economist Hans Mayer had pointed to key problems in the emerging Marshallian-Walrasian synthe-sis.[2] But as late as 1932 Mises himself (celebrating the definitive burial of the German Historical School) asserted that what separated the "modern"

2. Hans Mayer, "Der Erkenntniswert der Funktionellen Preistheorien," in Mayer (ed.), *Die Wirtschafttheorie der Gegenwart*, Vienna, 1932, Vol. 2, pp. 147–239b. Trans-lated under the title "The Cognitive Value of Functional Theories of Price," in I. Kirzner (ed.), *Classics in Austrian Economics, Vol. II: The Interwar Period*, London: Wil-liam Pickering, 1994, pp. 55–168.

schools of economic theory from one another was largely nothing more than a matter of language and style.[3]

THE RÔLE OF ROBBINS

That the Austrians of the 1920s indeed saw their economics as entirely compatible with the British (Marshallian) mainstream, is well illustrated by the rôle played by Lionel Robbins. Robbins, who emerged as an intellectual leader in the teaching of economics at the London School of Economics at a young age, came to be profoundly influenced by the vibrant Austrian tradition pulsating in the Vienna seminars at the end of the 1920s. His celebrated 1932 book, *The Nature and Significance of Economic Science*,[4] was written, at least in part, to introduce British economists to a number of the fundamental Austrian insights which Robbins (who read German) had absorbed during his visits to Vienna and from the Austrian literature (which he cites freely throughout his book). In his Preface, Robbins acknowledges, in particular, his intellectual indebtedness to Mises.

Yet Robbins did not see himself as calling for any important modification of the substance of British economics; as explained in his Preface, he saw his book as simply introducing British economists to a fresh way of understanding the foundations of *their own* economics. The price theory that Robbins found in Vienna was not seen as antithetical to the theory which developed into the orthodox theory of price to be taught in countless college classes in Britain and in the USA over the rest of the century.

THE SOCIALIST CALCULATION DEBATE

It was the celebrated interwar debate on the possibility of socialist economic calculation which appears to have jolted Mises and Hayek into recognising that the differences between an Austrian theory of price and a Marshallian-Walrasian theory went far beyond matters of language and style. In 1920 Mises had pointed out that central planners under socialism, lacking the guidance provided by market prices for resources, would be unable to plan socialist production projects so as to take into account

---

3. See Ludwig von Mises, *Epistemological Problems of Economics*, translated by George Reisman, Princeton: Van Nostrand, 1960, p. 214. The passage is part of the translation of a paper delivered by Mises on 30 September 1932.

4. Lionel Robbins, *An Essay on the Nature and Significance of Economic Science*, 2nd edition, London: Macmillan, 1935.

the comparative importance of competing projects. This challenge set off a wave of contributions by defenders of the possibility of efficient socialist planning. Hayek contributed a number of papers during the 1930s assessing these contributions, and demonstrating that the Misesian critique of socialist efficiency had not, after all, been adequately addressed.

Best known among the socialist contributions were papers by Oskar Lange and by Abba P. Lerner[5] which suggested that central planners could arbitrarily announce "prices" for resources, and instruct socialist production managers to use these resource prices in making their own respective production plans. Resulting resource surpluses (or shortages) would then indicate to the central planners the need to adjust resource prices downwards (or upwards). In developing such schemes, Lange and Lerner professed simply to be transferring to the socialist model the insights concerning the nature and function of resource prices they had learnt from the theory of price in the market economy.

This use of standard price theory made Mises and Hayek realise *their* understanding of the nature of market prices makes these prices utterly incapable of serving as a model for the purposes envisaged by Lange and by Lerner. In reaction to these developments in the socialist economic calculation debate, Mises wrote his magnum opus, *Human Action*.[6] Hayek responded to the calculation debate by writing a remarkable series of papers, which he collected together and republished in his 1948 *Individualism and Economic Order*. There were significant differences in the ways in which Mises and Hayek respectively identified the essence of their understanding of the theory of price, as distinct from that of mainstream theory.

MISES AND ENTREPRENEURIAL ACTION

Mises emphasised the dynamic character of the market process, driven by a profit-seeking entrepreneurial vision of future conditions in a radically uncertain world. "The driving force of the market process is

5. Oskar Lange, "On the Economic Theory of Socialism, Parts I and II," in Benjamin M. Lippincott (ed.), *On the Economic Theory of Socialism*, Minneapolis: University of Minnesota Press, 1938; Abba P. Lerner, "A Note on Socialist Economics," *Review of Economic Studies*, 4 October 1936, and "Statics and Dynamics in Socialist Economies," *Economic Journal*, June 1937.

6. Ludwig von Mises, *Human Action*, New Haven: Yale University Press, 1949. Its German-language forerunner, *Nationalökonomie*, was published in 1940. A revised edition of *Human Action* has been published by Laissez Faire Books: New York 1996.

provided . . . by the promoting and speculating entrepreneurs . . . Profit-seeking speculation is the driving force of production."[7] The equilibration process, which mainstream theory somehow believed to be instantaneously achieved, consisted of such entrepreneurial speculative activity. "The activities of the entrepreneur are the element that would bring about the unrealisable state of the evenly rotating economy if no further changes were to occur."[8]

For Mises, the important point to be observed concerning the equilibrium state is that in "the imaginary construction of the evenly rotating economy there is no room left for entrepreneurial activity . . ."[9] His title, *Human Action*, reflects his emphasis not on the colourless constrained-maximising decision of mainstream equilibrium theory, but on the actions of purposeful human beings in an uncertain world, who are called upon to exercise their entrepreneurial judgement in making their way in such a world. "Action is always speculation . . . In any real and living economy every actor is always an entrepreneur and speculator."[10] A science of "human action" must be a science of the equilibrative properties of entrepreneur-driven market processes. An economics seen as such a science of human action is distinguished sharply from the mainstream theory of price confined to an analysis of the conditions under which a market, or a market economy, can be pronounced to be in equilibrium.

HAYEK AND THE MARKET PROCESS

Hayek, on the other hand, did not explicitly draw attention to the rôle of entrepreneurial dynamism and speculative drive in the operation of the market process. Instead, in his papers collected in *Individualism and Economic Order*, Hayek explored the ways in which the market process made market participants aware of each other's attitudes and prospective plans. A state of equilibrium, Hayek pointed out, is one in which market participants have somehow come to expect, on the part of other participants, precisely those plans to be made which do in fact turn out to be made. All plans are made in the correct expectation of the corresponding plans being made by others. No one's plan is frustrated on account of others

7. *Ibid.*, pp. 325–26.
8. *Ibid.*, p. 335.
9. *Ibid.*, p. 253.
10. *Ibid.*, p. 253.

failing to act as that plan had anticipated they would act. No realised plan is regretted as having failed to make use of opportunities, made possible by the actions of others, which hindsight reveals but which foresight failed to anticipate. In Hayek's own words of 1937,

> the concept of equilibrium merely means that the foresight of the different members of the society is . . . correct in the sense that every person's plan is based on the expectation of just those actions of other people which those people intend to perform and that all these plans are based on the expectation of the same set of external facts, so that under certain conditions nobody will have any reason to change his plans.[11]

With this profoundly important insight into the state of market equilibrium as consisting in a pattern of mutually sustaining expectations, Hayek identified the crucial ingredients necessary for an equilibrating process to be set in motion. Such a process, Hayek pointed out, must consist in mutual learning, during which market participants come to acquire more and more accurate mutual knowledge concerning what one's fellow participants are able (and in fact plan) to do.

> In the light of our analysis of the meaning of a state of equilibrium . . . the real content of the assertion that a tendency toward equilibrium exists . . . can hardly mean anything but that, under certain conditions, . . . the expectations of the people and particularly of the entrepreneurs will become more and more correct.[12]

In standard price theory, Hayek claimed,

> it is generally made to appear as if these questions of how the equilibrium comes about were solved. But, if we look closer, it soon becomes evident that these apparent demonstrations amount to no more than the apparent proof of what is already assumed. The device generally adopted for this purpose is the assumption of a perfect market where every event becomes known instantaneously to every member.[13]

---

11. Friedrich A. Hayek, *Individualism and Economic Order*, London: Routledge and Kegan Paul, 1949, p. 42.

12. Hayek, *ibid.*, p. 45.

13. *Ibid.*

In subsequent papers expanding on his insights into the rôle of ignorance and knowledge in explaining the market process, Hayek rejects,
explicitly or implicitly, much of the core of mainstream theorising about
the process of equilibration, the meaning of competition, and the criteria
relevant in making judgements about the well-being of society.

MISES AND HAYEK: DIFFERENCES AND SIMILARITIES

In terms of the positive theory of entrepreneurial discovery, the differences between Mises's understanding of the dynamic market process and
Hayek's understanding of that same process, are less important than the
congruence of these two ways of understanding markets. It is true that
Mises did not draw special attention to the mutual learning that must
occur during the entrepreneurially-driven process of equilibration. Nor
did Hayek emphasise the speculative, entrepreneurial character of the
market process. But as Section IV explains, these two ways of articulat-
ing a theory of market process turn out to be two sides of the same coin.
Moreover, in drawing attention to these complementary sets of insights,
Mises and Hayek were explicitly detaching Austrian economics from the
mainstream consensus in price theory. They were, indeed, breaking away
from the mainstream paradigm, as it was coming to be understood by
the middle of the 20th century, and moving towards the creation of a
new, "Austrian," paradigm.

THE NEW AUSTRIAN PARADIGM

Why had this new "Austrian" paradigm not been articulated earlier? A
plausible explanation is that the mainstream paradigm had itself been
gradually undergoing modification (particularly under the impact of the
Walrasian approach) in the decades immediately following 1930. Earlier neo-classical thinking had *not*, in fact, confined price theory to the
analysis of perfectly competitive equilibrium under conditions of perfect
knowledge.[14] The great 20th-century Austrians, Mises and Hayek, gradually realised the direction in which mainstream price theory was moving. The crystallisation of mainstream theory into an approach confined

---

14. See Frank M. Machovec, *Perfect Competition and the Transformation of Economics*, London and New York: Routledge, 1995, where this thesis is convincingly developed in great detail.

to analysis of equilibrium conditions under the assumption of perfect knowledge made it both possible and necessary for the Austrians to articulate, for themselves and others, their own approach.

By mid-century the Austrian tradition—at a time when conventional histories of economic thought were pronouncing that tradition to be in permanent eclipse—had produced at least the elements of a new analytical framework within which to understand price-formation, market processes, and the rôle of equilibrium analysis.

Subsequent developments in the history of Austrian economics during the second half of the 20th century continued this gradual liberation from the mainstream approach. The theory of entrepreneurial discovery (Section IV below) offers a synthesis of Misesian and Hayekian insights which places Austrian understanding of the market process in an entirely different framework from that of contemporary mainstream microeconomic theory. This Austrian framework, unlike the mainstream theory, offers a satisfying explanation of how and why markets work.

Before presenting the theory of entrepreneurial discovery, however, it is necessary to draw attention in more detail to weaknesses in the mainstream approach which have moved contemporary Austrians to embrace the Mises-Hayek paradigm.

The core of the standard theory of competitive price as taught in text-books for the last half century can be presented in the following simplified form:[1]

- the competitive market system ensures instantaneous or rapid attainment, for a given good or service, of the market-clearing price (that marked out by the intersection of the relevant Marshallian supply and demand curves);
- the competitive market system instantaneously or rapidly achieves those adjustments between markets needed to ensure that the market-clearing price is simultaneously attained in *each* market throughout the system; and
- to satisfy the conditions needed to sustain this theory an economy must, at all times, be imagined to display the characteristics of perfect competition. For purposes of our discussion the most significant of these characteristics is perfect mutual knowledge. Each market participant must, at each instant, be fully aware (i) of the decisions that all fellow market participants would make under all conceivable price situations; (ii) of the decisions that are, in fact, being made by all fellow market participants; (iii) that all fellow participants have similar awareness, *ad infinitum*. The notion of an individual decision implies that a decision-maker, having a clearly

1. The version of mainstream theory presented and criticised in this section is a simplified one, but far from a caricature. The main simplification made in the text is to make it appear as if the perfect knowledge assumption in the mainstream theory is such as entirely to rule out the possibility of undesired outcomes due to incomplete information. Mainstream theory has sought to grapple with incomplete information. But it has done so by treating information as a costly resource, concerning which agents have full relevant information. This means that while agents may not know everything, they do know precisely the degree of mathematical risk associated with every risky option taken. They can never be surprised. An undesired outcome can certainly emerge from a choice made under risky circumstances, but, since the risk was deliberately assumed (in the light of the known risks) the "undesired" outcome is no surprise, and was, indeed, in a sense, "desired" (since the statistical possibility of its occurrence was known and the gamble was knowingly accepted in advance).

ranked series of desired objectives and confronted with a perceived outcome, makes decisions with perfect rationality, that is, in strictly maximising fashion and without error.

The picture portrayed by this theory is, of course, that of the perfectly competitive equilibrium model. In reviewing the well-known criticisms of this model, it is not our purpose to deny that this model can serve useful analytical objectives. It is to point out the inadequacies of the model as a self-contained and complete explanation for the price and quantity phenomena observed in the real world. It is then easier to appreciate the Austrian theoretical innovations to be discussed at greater length in Section IV. The perfectly competitive equilibrium model suffers from two difficulties—those arising from the *unrealistic* character of the assumptions of the model, and those arising from the *internal contradictions* from which the model suffers as an explanatory framework for understanding the real world. First we take up the second difficulty.

THE PROBLEMS OF THE ASSUMED SOLUTION

We have already cited Hayek's observation that, while it is generally made to appear, in textbook expositions of mainstream theory, that the question of how equilibrium comes about has been solved, "these apparent demonstrations amount to no more than the apparent proof of what is already assumed."[2] Hayek pointed out this is because mainstream models in effect assume perfect knowledge to have been achieved at the outset, throughout the system.

Once one appreciates the Hayekian insight that an attained state of equilibrium *means* universal perfect knowledge, it becomes obvious that no model in which perfect knowledge is *assumed* can be of direct assistance in explaining how an equilibrating tendency might occur. A model in which perfect knowledge is assumed is necessarily a model of already-attained equilibrium; it cannot grapple with the process in which imperfect mutual knowledge may tend (or fail to tend) to generate improved mutual knowledge. Consequently, quite apart from the unrealistic character of the perfect knowledge assumption in mainstream theory, that assumption renders such theory, when used to explain the equilibrative properties of markets, internally contradictory and incoherent.

2. Friedrich A. Hayek, *Individualism and Economic Order, op. cit.,* p. 45.

Constructing a model in which all decisions are made without error not only paints a picture which does not correspond to reality. It paints a picture in which that configuration of decisions that is mutually sustainable without disappointment and without regret has, somehow, already come to be made. This extraordinarily demanding requirement is implied by the misleadingly simple assumption of perfect knowledge. We cannot imagine a situation in which we simultaneously postulate perfect knowledge (as defined above) and a set of decisions that are *not* mutually sustainable without disappointment and without regret. We cannot imagine decision-makers deliberately undertaking courses of action which they *know* are bound to be disappointed or to be regretted.

So the mainstream theory locks us, at the very outset of analysis, into a pattern of decisions that are all mutually sustainable without disappointment and without regret. No matter how illuminating such a picture may be as providing *in*direct clues as to how such a configuration of decisions might come to be attained, it cannot of itself portray any such process. Any adjustments needed to achieve this equilibrium configuration must have occurred prior to the moment pictured in the equilibrium model. Thus a view which sees the world as *at all times* in the relevant attained states of equilibrium clearly *rules out all the adjustments which might have made such attainment possible.*

This criticism of mainstream price theory applies only to claims that the theory explains *how* equilibrium prices and quantities emerge in the course of the market process. A mainstream theorist may simply *postulate* a universal tendency towards equilibrium, claiming then that the theory provides a valid understanding of market outcomes. If one believes that the market price for a given commodity does, at least roughly, correspond to the price that would prevail under equilibrium conditions, the theory which explains exactly what is implied by the phrase "under equilibrium conditions" is certainly neither internally contradictory nor uninformative.

But our criticism of the theory would still be valid. Instead of charging incoherence in the use made of mainstream theory, criticism would focus on the arbitrariness of the postulate needed to render the theory of any interest in understanding the real world. A theory which relies, for its relevance, upon the arbitrary postulate of a universal tendency towards equilibrium, must be severely circumscribed. *By itself* it offers *no* explanation for the phenomena we are seeking to explain. And mainstream theorists who have honestly confronted the problem of deploying their theory to account for (or even to argue for) the successful achievement of market equilibrating tendencies, have been compelled to concede its fatal limitations in this regard.[3]

Some mainstream theorists dismiss this criticism. Granted, they would say, that the theory does not offer a picture of the equilibrating process. That does not affect the value of the theory in the slightest because the function of a theory is not to offer a picture of reality, even a schematic picture from which irrelevant details have been abstracted. It should provide a "black-box" formula capable of generating predictions; the validity of a theory is not to be judged by the facsimilitude of the picture it presents, with reality, but only by the empirical accuracy of the predictions it generates.[4] This methodological position is considered below, in examining the unrealism of the assumptions of mainstream theory. Here we merely point out that, whatever the epistemological validity of this position, it simply does not satisfy the "scientific curiosity" which inspires such questions as "what is the secret of capitalist success?"; "why and how do markets work so well?" Mainstream theory fails to provide that satisfying explanation which legitimate curiosity is seeking.

THE UNREALISM OF MAINSTREAM THEORY

As mentioned earlier, one line of criticism directed at mainstream theory concerns the unrealism of the assumptions upon which that theory relies. The offending assumptions are, in particular: (i) those relating narrowly to the way in which individual decision-making is modelled in the mainstream theory; (ii) those implied by the perfectly competitive conditions which loom so prominently in mainstream theory.

THE INDIVIDUAL DECISION IN MAINSTREAM THEORY

For mainstream theory, the analytical unit is the decision of the individual. But this decision, and the manner in which it is imagined to be made, turn out to be wholly artificial and stylised. Real-world men and women do not reach their decisions in the mechanical fashion

---

3. See Franklin M. Fisher, *Disequilibrium Foundations of Equilibrium Economics,* Cambridge and New York: Cambridge University Press, 1983, as a prime example of such recognition.

4. This methodological approach is particularly associated with Milton Friedman; see Milton Friedman, "The Methodology of Positive Economics," in his *Essays in Positive Economics,* Chicago: University of Chicago Press, 1953, pp. 3–43. Professor Friedman's paper generated a considerable subsequent methodological literature.

and under the stylised circumstances portrayed in mainstream theory. The theoretical model of decision-making adopted in mainstream
macro-economics abstracts from key features of the real-world context
in which human beings make decisions. Such abstraction denatures
human choice to the extent that the resulting theory of the individual
decision must be pronounced false, as a representation of actual human
choices. A theory of market phenomena, built upon choice-theoretic
foundations which do violence to reality, cannot enable us to trace those
phenomena to the human actions out of which they have been created.

For mainstream decision theory, the context of the decision is "closed."
Analysis of individual market-participating decision-making proceeds by
first imagining each agent to be confronted by a clearly specified problem
in constrained maximisation. The agent has a clearly defined and ranked
set of objectives; he confronts price possibilities governing each prospective trade in which he might participate; and he begins with a known set
of initial human and/or other resources at his disposal. His decision is
made in strict maximising fashion, subject to the constraints of his situation. He is programmed, as it were, to select that combination of transactions which will faultlessly and inevitably convert his initial endowment
into the most preferred combination of attainable objectives. He can
never have any opportunity to exercise imagination or boldness; he can
never be surprised. But this way of imagining decision-making diverges
in crucial respects from the real context of human choice.[5]

It is impossible to imagine any real-world situation in which a
decision-maker does not recognise that he must make his choices
within an *open-ended* context. The decision-maker is *not* presented, as
it were, with given resources. On the contrary, it is *in the course of the
decision itself* that the human decision-maker *determines* what objectives are most important, and what resources are in fact available to
him. The decision-maker must include these determinations under
the rubric of the decision because the situation he confronts is, at each
instant, open-ended. The agent does *not* necessarily know in advance
what courses of action he must choose among; he does not necessarily
know in advance what the consequences of any prospective course of
action will be; he may not even have considered which objectives are

---

5. George Shackle was perhaps the most emphatic critic of the mainstream version
of decision-making. See his *Epistemics and Economics: A Critique of Economic Doctrines*,
Cambridge: Cambridge University Press, 1972.

worth thinking about realistically and in what ranking of urgency he would place them.

The inescapable and radical uncertainty[6] faced by each human agent ensures the open-endedness of human choice. When a human being takes an action, he is, *in that action*, grasping at a specific picture of the future as the relevant framework for his action. Action *consists* in grappling with an essentially unknown future. To imagine human choice as being made within a "closed" framework, with given ranked goals and given available resources, may constitute for some purposes a useful simplification, throwing light on certain aspects of human choice. But such simplification comes at a distressingly high price. It diverts analytical attention from features of actual decision-making which are crucial in understanding the market process.

The mainstream portrayal of the individual decision permits derivation of determinate theoretical conclusions, undisturbed by the vagaries introduced by unsystematic human efforts to cope with open-ended uncertainties of the great unknown. But it *obscures* our understanding of market processes. The drastic modifications with which mainstream micro-economic theory incorporates the individual decision, the filtering out of all potential for surprise, prevent us from seeing the determining forces operating in the market.

MAINSTREAM MARKET THEORY

The core of mainstream theory refers to the perfectly competitive model of markets. To examine the consequences of the unrealism of its assumptions, it is helpful to consider the perfectly competitive model of the Marshallian market for a single commodity. The model explains price, in such a market, as being pushed instantaneously or rapidly towards the market-clearing level, at which all potential sellers are able to sell all that buyers wish to buy (at that price). The assumptions adopted for this model—which ensure the inevitability of this outcome—are well-known, at least ever since Frank Knight's classic articulation of the perfectly competitive market economy.[7] For our purposes, these assumptions include

---

6. The term "radical uncertainty" has been used to emphasise the Knightian character of the uncertainty facing real-world agents (as distinct from insurable risk). See also Gerald P. O'Driscoll, Jr., and Mario J. Rizzo, *The Economics of Time and Ignorance*, Oxford: Basil Blackwell, 1985, chapter 5.

7. Frank H. Knight, *Risk, Uncertainty and Profit*, Boston and New York: Houghton Mifflin, 1921, chapters 3–6.

especially perfect knowledge, and the infinity of buyers and sellers in the perfectly competitive market. Both these key assumptions—which imply that, at the going market price for the relevant good, each buyer expects (correctly) to be able to buy as much as he wishes, and each seller expects (correctly) to be able to sell as much as he wishes—are wildly unrealistic in regard to the commercial world with which we are familiar.

This gaping chasm between the real world and the perfectly competitive theoretical portrayal of it moved Edward Chamberlin to construct more complicated models (of monopolistic competition) which would be less offensive in this regard.[8] Instead of a picture of a world in which each seller believes it possible to sell an unlimited quantity of his product at the market price (that is, he faces a perfectly elastic, horizontal demand curve), Chamberlin built a theory based on the assumption that a seller is typically aware of being able to sell more goods if he is prepared to lower the price. Earlier theory had confined the possibility of a seller facing a downward-sloping demand curve to special cases of pure monopoly. Chamberlin, however, argued for a general theory which recognised the empirical reality of competition between similar, but not identical, products, and the associated empirical reality of sellers' awareness that the price they charge is significantly under their own control.

Despite this valiant attempt to restore a modicum of realism to the theory of markets, and despite an enormous literature that sprang up around this attempt, it failed to make a permanent impact upon mainstream theory. The late-20th-century mainstream theory of price places more, not less, emphasis upon the perfectly competitive model than had been the case when Chamberlin completed his doctoral dissertation in 1927.

Production is of course carried on in markets in which the number of producers (and even of retailers) is far from infinite. The typical producer or retailer agonises over whether or not to raise or lower the price he will ask. The contrast between the picture offered in the model of the perfectly competitive market for a given product, and the real-world business scene, is so striking as to strain credulity. As noted earlier, the perfectly competitive model is inherently, by its very assumptions, incapable of explaining how a market works. But it is not just that it cannot explain how present market phenomena came to be what they are; the model

8. See Edward H. Chamberlin, *The Theory of Monopolistic Competition*, 7th edition, Cambridge: Harvard University Press, 1956. Chamberlin's book was first published in 1933, being based on his 1927 doctoral dissertation.

requires us to see current market phenomena in an analytical framework that cannot fit the empirical pattern we are seeking to understand.

THE PERFECTLY COMPETITIVE MODEL
AND CRITICS OF THE MARKET ECONOMY

The implications of these unrealistic features of the perfectly competitive model have not been lost on critics of the market economy. They do not, in the context of late-20th-century mainstream micro-economics, have to base their attacks on the efficiency of the market, upon any critique of the *logic* of price theory. They merely have to embrace the perfectly competitive model and point out the obvious respects in which real-world capitalism falls short of the ideal conditions required in order for the social welfare optimalities of the perfectly competitive model to apply.

Mainstream micro-economic theory therefore not merely fails to provide the theoretical explanation we seek for the market successes we observe: that theory provides critics of the market economy with the intellectual ammunition they need to press their attacks on the efficiency of capitalism. They merely need to tick off the respects in which real-world capitalism departs from the requirements for perfectly competitive optimality.[9]

Pointing out these implications of the unrealism of the perfectly competitive model used in mainstream theory does not establish the invalidity of that theory. But it does demonstrate the price being paid in order to take advantage of the elegance and orderliness of that theory. Searching for an explanation of how and why markets do work using a patently unrealistic model, such as that of perfect competition, is likely to result in the conclusion (counter to our direct observation) that markets do not, in fact, achieve efficiency at all.

As explained in Section IV, the theory of entrepreneurial discovery finds the explanation for market efficiency precisely in those real-world

---

9. Indeed, mainstream theory has at various times been seen as supporting the economic desirability of the market economy, only on the condition that it be buttressed by decidedly aggressive types of government intervention. For example, the market economy has been endorsed only if it is subject to powerfully intrusive anti-trust regulation; or provided the market's distribution of incomes can be "corrected" by taxation. The strong reservations, discussed in later sections of this paper, concerning such proposals for intervening in market operation and market outcomes, will be seen to derive directly from a rejection of the reservations which circumscribe the mainstream model's arguments in favour of the market economy.

features of commercial markets which have been deliberately excised from the pictures portrayed by the perfectly competitive models. A particular aspect of the real world is its disequilibrium character. At any given moment, the market is *not* characterised by attained equilibrium. In this respect, our positive theory of how markets work differs sharply from the attempts of Edward Chamberlin to introduce realism into price theory by postulating "imperfections" in market competition. The point is worth some emphasis, because it permits us to sum up and make more explicit criticisms of the lack of realism in mainstream theory.

All the points in mainstream theory upon which we have focused on the grounds of absence of realism, turn out to be attributable to the exclusively *equilibrium* character of that theory. Both at the level of individual choice and at the level of market outcomes, mainstream theory deliberately confines itself to situations of attained equilibrium. The first part of this section focused on the incoherency of attempting to explain possible processes of equilibration strictly in terms of models characterised by already-attained equilibrium. The latter part of this section pointed out the numerous aspects of real-world commercial life which are incompatible with the assumption of already attained equilibrium. Now the mere failure of a theoretical picture to replicate with precision all features of the reality it seeks to explain, is not necessarily fatal for the usefulness of that theoretical picture. But mainstream theory filters out of the picture those aspects of reality which are the core of an adequate explanation for market phenomena. Those features of reality which cannot find a place in an equilibrium model turn out to be the keys to the explanation.

Chamberlin's attempt to restore realism by constructing models of monopolistic competition missed the mark. He did not recognise that the source of the offending unrealism lay in the assumption of already-attained equilibrium in the perfect competition model. What he proposed instead was a more complicated equilibrium model. The model of attained monopolistically competitive equilibrium is in a number of respects less insulting to our sense of realism than the model it sought to replace; nonetheless, the new model suffers from the same cardinal fault. By postulating already-attained equilibrium it cannot explain how equilibrium might come to be approached. The theory misses the opportunity to provide a satisfactory explanation by considering the disequilibrium features of the market.

IV. THE THEORY OF ENTREPRENEURIAL DISCOVERY

The theory of entrepreneurial discovery sees the explanation of market phenomena in the way entrepreneurial decisions, taken under disequilibrium conditions, bring about changes in prices and quantities. The market process so initiated consists of continual entrepreneurial discoveries; it is a process of discovery driven by dynamic competition, made possible by an institutional framework which permits unimpeded entrepreneurial entry into both new and old markets. The success which capitalist market economies display is the result of a powerful tendency for less efficient, less imaginative courses of productive action, to be replaced by newly discovered superior ways of serving consumers—by producing better goods and/or by taking advantage of hitherto unknown, but available, sources of resource supply. The theory focuses on the concept of discovery in contrast to the notion of the individual decision in mainstream theory.

BREAKING OUT OF THE NEO-CLASSICAL BOX:
THE CONCEPT OF DISCOVERY

The discovery concept points to a way of escaping from the closed-ended analytical box in which modern neo-classical economics confines the theorist. The stylised decision-maker is unable to exercise genuine choice. Given arrays of objectives and available resources automatically mark out the option-to-be-chosen; any other option is ruled out in advance. It is unthinkable that the decision-maker might deliberately select a less preferred option instead of a preferred option (and what is more preferred and less preferred is known to the agents as defined by and in the given arrays of objectives and available resources).

So the act of choice consists in nothing more than computing the solution *already implicit* in the data. There is nothing creative in such an act. And since it is assumed that decisions are inevitably and inescapably made without error, this mainstream notion of the decision in effect squeezes the decision-maker out of the picture; the decision is "made" by the sets of data which are "given" prior to the decision. Mainstream theorising adopts this stylised concept to render the outcome of decisions determinate, unaffected by unsystematic factors such as impulse, surprise, or fear. But, in order to escape the limitations of such theory, we have to escape this narrow notion of the decision. The notion of discovery points the way.

When a surprising discovery is made, it cannot be ascribed to any deliberate act that can be fitted in to the neo-classical concept of the decision. There has been no deliberate search for a piece of information (the value of which was known in advance, and the cost of finding of which was known in advance). Rather the act of discovery consisted in having "undeliberately" *noticed* what was *already* costlessly knowable. Where the neo-classical concept of the decision makes it unthinkable that an available gainful opportunity has not been grasped, a more realistic perspective permits us to recognise that such opportunities *may simply not have been noticed*. An opportunity may not be grasped not because the information needed to grasp it was too costly to make it worthwhile, but because the costlessly obtainable opportunity (or the costlessly available information that would have brought the opportunity within immediate reach) was simply, "inexcusably," overlooked. An act of discovery occurs when someone notices what has up to now been overlooked.

Recognising the possibility that a gainful opportunity may fail to be grasped because it has not been noticed permits the appreciation of dimensions of individual choice and of social interaction which standard economic theory obscures. It also liberates theorising from the closed-ended neo-classical box in which everything occurs inevitably. We are no longer imprisoned in a world where the course of events unfolds inexorably under the mechanical, clockwork-like programming of the maximising postulate under given initial circumstances. Awareness that opportunities may go unnoticed, and therefore ungrasped, allows us to explore the pure discovery of hitherto unnoticed opportunities. The theory of entrepreneurial discovery offers the key to understanding the market process.

DISCOVERY AND ENTREPRENEURSHIP

Mises's observation that, "in any real and living economy every actor is always an entrepreneur and speculator"[1] draws attention to the link between the "open-ended" conception of individual decision-making, and the entrepreneurial function in the market process. For Mises the analytical unit is the human act, and the essential feature of the human act is its speculative and entrepreneurial dimension. This leads us directly to

1. Ludwig von Mises, *Human Action, op. cit.*, p. 253.

appreciate the parallelism between the individual act and the entrepreneurial function in markets.

Every individual act constitutes, necessarily, an act of discovery. In acting, the individual is not simply (as in neo-classical theory) spelling out the implications of the preference rankings given at the outset; he is, at the moment of action, alertly *establishing* those preference rankings (with all their implications), in the face of the radical uncertainty he confronts. When he acts to seize an opportunity, he is not seizing a "given" opportunity; he is, at that moment, declaring that opportunity to exist. He is, as it were, *discovering* that opportunity's existence. The human act *simultaneously* establishes the framework within which one can imagine deliberate maximisation to occur, and pursues the maximising implications of that framework. The establishment of the framework constitutes an act of discovery; that framework was itself neither "given" to the decision-maker nor inexorably implied in some prior "given" meta-framework.

The most careful prior deliberation could not define the framework established at the moment of action. Establishing the existence of an opportunity framework calls for *alertness* to a set of circumstances hitherto not yet noticed. A "framework" involves not only assumed given arrays of goals and of resources; it involves *expectations* of relevant goals and of relevantly available resources *in the future*. The uncertainty enveloping the future means that the establishment of such an expectational framework of ends and means constitutes, necessarily, a creative act of discovery. To act means to grasp an opportunity; to grasp an opportunity means to discover it, to identify it out of the ambiguities and clouds of an infinite array of alternative prospective futures.

Such an act of discovery involves more, however, than finding something that happens to attract attention. The discovery of an *opportunity* means the discovery of anomaly. Discovering an attractive opportunity always represents something of a pleasant *surprise*. If the gain embodied in the opportunity had been fully anticipated, grasping it would hardly represent a creative act of discovery. The gain would be nothing but the realisation of something fully expected. Because, for Mises, human action is essentially geared to the radical uncertainty of an unknowable future, it is inescapably speculative. Human action *is* discovery.

An act of discovery in which resources are deployed to achieve an objective represents the realisation that, before the discovery, the relevant resources had been *undervalued*. The full potential of these resources had not been up to now understood. Thus the act of discovery, and thus indeed every human action, represents the discovery of hitherto *unsuspected value* in hitherto undervalued resources. Here we have the key to the profoundly significant Misesian parallelism between the individual act and the pure entrepreneurial function. The pure entrepreneurial function consists in buying cheap and selling dear—that is, in the discovery that the *market* has undervalued something so that its true market value has up to now not been generally realised. This permits the pure entrepreneur to buy something for less than he will be able to sell it for. His act of entrepreneurship consists in realising the existence of market value that has hitherto been overlooked.

Pure entrepreneurship in the market bears, then, the very same relationship to the decision-making that occurs in the neo-classical theory of the firm as does Misesian human action to the neo-classical model of the individual maximising decision. In the neo-classical theory of the firm the owner of the firm maximises the difference between revenues and costs. Both the revenues and costs associated with alternative levels of output are given. The "profits" the firm so maximises are thus fully expected and known to be available *before* the firm's output decision is made. There is no surprise whatsoever in the "profits" grasped through the firm's decision. Winning them constitutes, in effect, nothing more than mechanically carrying through a plan firmly settled on in advance.

But the entrepreneurial decision in the context of a market is quite different. The entrepreneur who "sees" (discovers) a profit opportunity, is discovering the existence of a gain which had (before his discovery) not been seen by himself or by anyone else. Had it been seen previously, it would have been grasped or, at any rate, it would have been fully expected and would no longer then be a fresh discovery made *now*. When the entrepreneur discovers a profit opportunity, he is discovering the presence of something hitherto unsuspected.

Exactly the same kind of liberation for the individual decision inside or outside a market setting provided by the human action concept (as opposed to the closed-ended-context version of neo-classical decision-making) is to be found (for the theory of markets) in the notion of pure entrepreneurship.

EITHER ENTREPRENEURSHIP OR EQUILIBRIUM

Recognition of the parallelism between the Misesian concept of human action in the face of open-ended uncertainty, and the purely entrepreneurial rôle in markets, highlights the limitations surrounding the use of exclusively equilibrium models.

An equilibrium world is one without scope for entrepreneurial discovery and creativity: *the course of market events* is foreordained by the data of the market situation. No entrepreneur can, within the straitjacket assumptions of the equilibrium model, alter the foreordained sequence of market events. The only circumstance which can induce a genuine change[2] in the sequence of market events is an exogenous shock to the system.

The only changes that can occur in a neo-classical market are those traditionally analysed with comparative statics, in which history is seen as a sequence of equilibrium situations. Consequences of exogenous changes in the data are "explained," not by tracing through the step-by-step changes that might ensue from such exogenous changes, but by jumping from a picture of one inexorably foreordained world to a picture of a different inexorably foreordained world. While this approach fulfils its presumed objective of filtering out unsystematic sources of change, it does so at the price of providing any genuine explanation of how the world could in fact possibly make the (non-foreordained!) transition from the first picture to the second.

THE DRIVING FORCE OF ENTREPRENEURIAL ALERTNESS

In contrast, the world of disequilibrium offers scope for entrepreneurial discovery and consequently for genuine change. Consider a situation in which a commodity is being sold at two different prices in two separated parts of the market (between which transportation costs are zero). Such a situation of disequilibrium is, within the scope of mainstream theory, strictly impossible. In mainstream theory, with all parties being aware of the two prices being accepted, those paying the higher prices are clearly failing to pursue their preferences consistently (since they presumably prefer paying less to paying more). Similarly, those accepting the lower prices are acting at variance with their own preferences.

But in the framework of the Austrian theory of entrepreneurial discovery such a situation is not merely possible, it is unavoidable. Complete

---

2. The term "genuine change" distinguishes such changes from those mechanically generated, fully anticipated "changes" that are programmed to emerge from the clockwork-like operation of multi-period, intertemporal equilibrium conditions.

relevant information is no longer assumed. Those paying the higher price do so simply because they are unaware of the lower price that is available. Those accepting the lower price do so simply because they are unaware of the higher price being paid. The divergence between the two prices constitutes an opportunity for pure profit. A buyer buying at the lower price may sell it at the higher price and thus win the difference as pure profit. It is important to notice that, until we introduce the element of entrepreneurial alertness, we have no basis upon which to postulate any change in the situation—ever. Those unaware of prices lower than the price which they are paying, may remain so unaware indefinitely; those unaware of prices higher than the price they are accepting may remain so unaware indefinitely.

As soon as entrepreneurial alertness is introduced, however, matters are drastically altered. There is now room for the possibility, if not near certainty, that the profit opportunity constituted by the price difference will be noticed by an alert entrepreneur. Once noticed, the pure profit opportunity will be promptly seized (since it is now perceived pure gain, costlessly available). This will involve additional buying in the low-price market (tending to push price up) and additional selling in the high-price market (tending to push price down).

Entrepreneurial discovery of the profit opportunity constituted by the initial price differential is thus a powerful force pushing the two prices towards each other, eliminating both the price differential and the profit opportunity it offered. The most fundamental law of price theory, Jevons's Law of Indifference, asserting a tendency for a single price to emerge throughout the market for a given commodity, thus finds its place and its explanation within the theory of entrepreneurial discovery. The constant changes occurring in the world continually occasion new situations concerning which market participants will typically be unaware. New causes of disequilibrium and of price differences are continually arising. But, at the same time, these disequilibria continually generate forces tending to discover the opportunities so created. The tendency towards a single price is continually interrupted—but continually resumed.

The entrepreneur's discovery is not a deliberate act of learning nor of search. He had previously been unaware of the existence of the price differential. Transition from unawareness to awareness was not a deliberately taken step. Nor is it a step that can be explained by invoking any action that has a place within mainstream theory. In order to understand the most powerful (and characteristic) moving force within the market economy, it is necessary to step outside the paradigm of mainstream theory, and invoke pure entrepreneurial discovery.

For mainstream theory, the very possibility of two different prices existing disequilibrium-fashion simultaneously in the market is one that is, strictly speaking, unthinkable. Jevons's Law of Indifference has, in mainstream theory, come to mean nothing more than that anything except a single price for a commodity through the market is ruled out by assumption.

It might, however, be argued that mainstream neo-classical theory *can* handle both the possibility of the two-price situation, and the tendency for both prices to move towards each other, within its equilibrium framework. We rule out, of course, a neo-classical explanation referring to differences in commodity quality, or in differences between the convenience of shopping for the commodity in different locations. Such explanations are illegitimate and irrelevant because they do not represent two prices for the *same* commodity (defined to include not only the quality dimension but also the utility of activities which come packaged with the physical commodity whose price is under discussion). But at first glance it would seem possible, in a neo-classical world, to postulate the existence of two prices for the same commodity, as soon as we admit the possibility of imperfect information.

Neo-classical economics proceeds as if full awareness exists of all relevant aspects of the situation. But this need not imply omniscience. The neo-classical theorist understands that the buyer paying the higher price knows that the commodity is available at a lower price, but also knows that in order to find out exactly how to take advantage of the lower price he would have to expend learning or search resources on such a scale as to make it worthwhile to continue paying the higher price. Such a situation is an equilibrium, and therefore acceptable from the point of view of neo-classical economics because there *is* an explanation for the price divergence. If it *is* worthwhile to undertake deliberate learning or search, and if the learning or search process is itself a time-consuming one, then we can expect, within the neo-classical framework, that the initial price differential will gradually disappear, as the additional information gradually spreads throughout the market. At each point in time each market participant, and the entire market, is in complete neo-classical equilibrium. The dynamic version of Jevons's Law of Indifference has, it might thus be argued, been retrieved within the neo-classical framework.

However, while imperfect information certainly can account in the neo-classical framework for two prices for the same commodity, this does *not* generate the dynamic version of the law of the single price. While the time-consuming character of learning may explain why it takes time for two prices to converge, the possibility of such deliberate learning does not ensure any converging tendency. On the contrary, it is eminently possible that the very costs of learning which prevented *earlier* learning from having occurred will *continue* to deter market participants from learning how to take advantage of better prices available in the market. The initial equilibrium multi-price situation may, therefore, prevail indefinitely precisely because it *is* an equilibrium.

What renders the two-price-for-the-same-commodity case a possibly genuine disequilibrium situation is the possibility that there may be *no* "rational" explanation (that is, an explanation in terms of deliberate knowledgeable decision-making) for the price differential. It may be that, after the costs of learning have been tallied (or, in the extreme case when these costs are zero because the existence of the two prices is plain to see) we have *no* explanation for the buyer who pays the higher price, and the seller who accepts the lower price other than that market participants have simply failed to notice what was staring them in the face. This glaring absence of a "rational" explanation for the price differential renders it a disequilibrium situation—a situation which cannot be expected to last for long because the pure profit opportunity constituted by the price differential will attract entrepreneurial discovery.

The driving force of entrepreneurial discovery refers to the prevalence of pure profit opportunities, that is, of situations which seem to *defy* rational explanation. Moreover, such situations can be expected to be systematically whittled away by spontaneous entrepreneurial discovery of the pure profit opportunities they represent. Entrepreneurial discovery exercises a systematic force upon markets, tending to drive them at each moment *away* from the disequilibrium situations which cried out for discovery.

SYSTEM OUT OF CHAOS: THE PARADOX OF ENTREPRENEURSHIP

The paradox of entrepreneurship in a market economy is as follows. Mainstream theory left entrepreneurship out of its picture because entrepreneurship seems chaotic and unpredictable. Boldness, impulse, hunch are the raw materials of entrepreneurial success (and failure);

they seem to render the possibility of systematic, determinate chains of events unlikely. In order to perceive regularities amidst the apparently chaotic vagaries of real-world market volatility, it may seem methodologically sound to imagine a world with *no* scope for entrepreneurship. Yet, paradoxically, exactly the opposite is the case. It is *only* when entrepreneurship is introduced that we begin to appreciate how and why markets work. Without the possibility of entrepreneurship, no genuine explanation for market co-ordination is possible (aside from arbitrarily *postulating* that co-ordination always fully and instantaneously prevails). The "chaos" introduced by entrepreneurship is required to account for the systematic character of real-world market processes.

Introducing scope for entrepreneurship permits a degree of freedom which makes it possible for errors to be made—that is, for decisions to be made that fail to take full account of relevant circumstances. It may indeed not be possible to explain how errors come to be made or which specific errors occur. There is no economic theory which describes which features of reality are likely to be "unexplainedly" and irrationally overlooked. But understanding how the market phenomena of any moment reflect errors made as a result of unawareness opens up possible understanding of the way such phenomena change over time.

It might at first glance seem that, just as one cannot understand which specific features of reality come to be unaccountably overlooked in the first place, it might also be impossible to predict whether any of these overlooked features will be noticed later. After all, what was overlooked yesterday, may be overlooked today and tomorrow. But such a conclusion would be too hasty. Economists *are* able to identify one feature of a market economy which acts powerfully to direct (or to attract) entrepreneurial alertness towards the correction of earlier errors—such errors of the kind we have discussed made in a market economy manifest themselves *as opportunities for pure profit.*

These earlier errors may come systematically to be discovered because of the tendency for entrepreneurial alertness to "smell" or sense where pure entrepreneurial profits can be won. The systematic character of the market process stems from the human propensity to sense (*without* deliberate search) where to find pure gain. Our economic analysis teaches where and how errors come to be translated into opportunities for pure profit, and so provides understanding of the tendencies these errors create for their systematic correction.

JEVONS'S LAW OF INDIFFERENCE EXTENDED

The fundamental law tending to ensure convergence among the market prices for a given commodity also operates with powerful consequences in less obvious circumstances. Consider a production process in which a given combination of different resources is deployed to fabricate a product. The producer buys each of the necessary resources in order to produce the product, which he sells to consumers. To say that an entrepreneur-producer is making pure profits in the production and sale of this commodity means that, after calculating the prices he pays for *all* resources needed to produce the product and deliver it to the door of the consumer, their sum is less than the amount paid by the consumer. This situation, too, is an example of the "same commodity" being sold at different prices in different parts of the "same" market.

The sum of the prices paid for the resource bundle needed to produce and deliver the product, is lower than the price paid by the consumer for that delivered product. But the bundle of *all* the required resources *is*, in effect, the commodity that bundle is able to produce. Nothing more is needed than, so to speak, to say "Go!" To possess that bundle is, in effect, *already* to possess the commodity. So that the possibility of earning pure profit through selling the commodity at a price higher than that at which the resource bundle is being sold is because the "same" commodity is being sold in some parts of the market at a lower price (in the form of resources) than it is being sold at in other parts of the market (that is, as a finished consumer good).

If the resource bundle did indeed include all necessary resources, we have no "rational" explanation for this multi-price situation. There is no reason why consumers should be willing to pay more for a finished product than the sum needed to obtain command of *all* the resources (including all the time and trouble needed to buy and assemble the resources used in fabrication itself) required to deliver the finished product to the consumer. The only explanation for this price discrepancy lies in awareness of pure error on the part of market participants.

Such error means that some market participants have undervalued these resources relative to the future eagerness of consumers to acquire the product in question when it can be produced. This undervaluation can be "explained" only as an "unexplainable" error, a failure to see a future that is in fact staring one in the face. Such error manifests itself, exactly as in the simple case of the commodity selling for more than one price, in a pure profit opportunity.

Whenever an entrepreneur senses the possibility of pure profit by moving into a new line of production, or by innovating a new method of production, he is taking advantage of what he believes to be a case where the market is erroneously assigning two different values to what is, in economic reality, the same item. The powerful driving force of entrepreneurial alertness is always and everywhere at work, noticing such errors through the attraction provided by the pure profit which such errors create. Entrepreneurial profit-making is occurring, not only through bringing the prices of a given physical good towards equality throughout the market. The same entrepreneurial profit-making operates towards bringing resource prices into relevant equality with future product prices.

Ludwig von Mises expressed this with great clarity:

> What makes profit emerge is the fact that the entrepreneur who judges the future prices of the products more correctly than other people do buys some or all of the factors of production at prices which, seen from the point of view of the future state of the market, are too low.[3]

What is important is that, in operating along this dimension, entrepreneurial alertness is not only pushing prices towards relevant "equality," it is also *moving resources from one line of production to another*. The tendency, in a market economy, for resources to become reallocated from less productive uses (as judged by consumers) towards more productive uses, operates through the same entrepreneurial discovery procedure which creates a tendency for the prices of a given commodity to move towards equality. The extension of Jevons's Law of Indifference turns out to explain the market forces responsible for capitalist allocative efficiency.

For this allocative tendency to be set into motion, it is not necessary that the entrepreneur is aware of the present misallocation of resources. He does not need detailed knowledge of the industries in which the resources are currently employed; he does not need to be familiar with technical production conditions of, and consumer interest in, the

---

3. Ludwig von Mises, "Profit and Loss," in his *Planning for Freedom and Other Essays and Addresses*, 2nd edition, South Holland, Ill.: Libertarian Press, 1962, p. 109.

products in those industries. He merely has to sense that pure profits may be won by buying the necessary resources.

Of course, in order to sense the possibility of pure profits in a particular line of production, through having a "nose" for price differences, it is most helpful for the entrepreneur to have a keen sense (or, at least, a keen sense of where to hire employees with this keen sense) both for technical production possibilities and for future consumer preferences in *this* line of production. But ultimately it is his sense for the possibility of pure profit (because of differences between resource prices and product prices) which drives his activity and motivates his alertness to technical production possibilities and to future consumer preferences. It is the law of the single price which, working through the process of entrepreneurial discovery, powerfully redirects the pattern of capitalist production into more, rather than less, allocatively efficient channels.

ERRORS OF OVER-PESSIMISM AND ERRORS OF OVER-OPTIMISM

The errors which express themselves as pure profit opportunities are not the only ones which can be made in a disequilibrium world of open-ended uncertainty. Errors which result in pure profit opportunities are errors stemming from over-pessimism. There are, in addition, errors of over-optimism which also play important rôles in the entrepreneurial discovery process of the market economy.

Errors of over-pessimism are those in which superior opportunities have been overlooked. They manifest themselves in the emergence of more than one price for a product which these resources can create. They generate pure profit opportunities which attract entrepreneurs who, by grasping them, correct these over-pessimistic errors. The other kind of error, error due to over-optimism, has a different source and plays a different rôle in the entrepreneurial discovery process.

Over-optimistic error occurs when a market participant expects to be able to complete a plan which cannot, in fact, be completed. A buyer mistakenly plans to buy a commodity or a resource at a price so low that the item is not obtainable at the price. A seller plans to sell an item at a price so high that in fact no buyer is willing to buy at that price. This kind of error does not generate pure profit opportunities which are corrected through entrepreneurial alertness. Over-optimistic errors tend to be corrected by more direct market forces, calling for less creative entrepreneurial alertness.

An over-optimistic error tends to manifest itself in a price either too high or too low to clear the market for that good. Thus if sellers have been, in general, over-optimistic, they will be expecting higher prices than buyers are, in general, prepared to pay. If buyers have been over-optimistic, they will be expecting prices that are lower than sellers are, in general, prepared to accept. Such mistaken expectations do not necessarily mean that the market price will be at variance with those expectations. After all, if sellers are unwilling to sell at a price below $300 (because they mistakenly believe that at this price they can sell all that they wish to sell), then any units sold will indeed have been sold at that price or higher (since no one who expects to be able to sell at $300 will accept less). The over-optimism will be revealed not necessarily by an initial failure of the market price to be at $300, but by the unexpected failure of some or all sellers to sell what they had expected to be able to sell at that price.

Market price, in this kind of disequilibrium situation, will be too high to clear the market. It is a case of disequilibrium because we feel fairly confident that, if the market price for a good is indeed higher than the market-clearing level, sellers will soon realise this (as a result of the pile-up of unsold goods), and will lower their expectations and reduce their asking prices. Similarly, if over-optimism on the part of buyers has resulted in prices being below the market-clearing level, this situation will reveal itself in the form of shortage, and buyers, realising their error, will bid higher prices to obtain the commodity or resource they wish to buy.

Where over-pessimism arises from failure to realise that more eager buyers or sellers for a commodity indeed exist than had been expected, over-optimism arises from believing that buyers and sellers are *more* eager than they actually are. Errors arising from over-optimism are more likely rapidly to be discovered than are errors arising from over-pessimism. An opportunity which has not been seen *may* (even though it offers its discoverers pure profit) continue to remain unnoticed in the future. But an error arising from over-optimism *must* surely be discovered simply because it involves making a plan which cannot and will not be completed. Prices which are too high will be revealed to have been too high by piles of unsold goods; prices which have been too low will be revealed to have been too low by the shortages they create. Certainly, entrepreneurial judgement may be required to interpret these shortages (or surpluses) correctly. But, sooner or later, prices that are too high must come down, and so on.

The major insights of the theory of entrepreneurial discovery can now be summarised:

- At any given moment market participants are (virtually inevitably) likely to be suffering from unawareness of the true (present and future) plans of other market participants.
- Such unawareness may take the form of undue optimism (as when sellers of a good expect buyers to be more eager to buy that good than they really are), leading to a disequilibrium price for a good that is too high or too low to clear the market. Disequilibrium prices generate direct *disappointment* of plans (as when sellers who have refused to sell for lower prices, discover their customers are simply not buying at the high prices). Such disappointment can be expected to alert entrepreneurs to the true temper of the market. Prices that were too high will tend to be lowered; those that were too low will tend to be bid upwards.
- Unawareness may also (and generally more importantly) take the form of undue pessimism. Sellers may underestimate the eagerness of buyers to buy. Buyers may underestimate the eagerness of sellers to sell. Such unawareness leads to more than one price for the same good (or a lower price for the resources bundle, and a higher price for the product the resources can deliver). Such price differences constitute opportunities for pure profit and therefore tend to attract entrepreneurial attention. The price differences will tend to be eroded by entrepreneurial action to grasp these profit opportunities.
- If one could, for purely analytical purposes, imagine consumer preferences, resource availabilities, and technical possibilities as frozen in time, then the entrepreneurial discovery processes will tend to ensure that the price of any given good or service will tend towards equality throughout the market; that resource-bundle prices will tend to equality with the prices of the respective commodities they can deliver through production; that, at the uniform prices so achieved, the market for each consumer good or service, and for each resource service will tend to clear; and that all prospective buyers will find what they wish to buy at the price they expect and all prospective sellers will find buyers prepared to pay the prices which the sellers are expecting and are prepared to accept.

- In the course of the market movements achieved through these tendencies, not only will resource and product prices be modified as described but, more importantly, resources will be shifted continually from less important uses (as measured by the prices consumers are prepared to pay) to more important uses; less productive technological uses for resources will come to be replaced by more productive technologies; and undiscovered sources of new resources will tend to be discovered.

- In the real world of incessant change in underlying consumer preferences, resource availabilities and technical possibilities, these corrective tendencies may be partly or wholly frustrated or interrupted. In addition, these tendencies, operating in different parts of the ever-changing market, may interrupt and confuse *each other*. But the direction of the powerful forces of entrepreneurial discovery will be shaped and moulded by the above-described systematic and corrective processes of error, disappointment, discovery, and surprise.

A number of important features of the theory of entrepreneurial discovery remain to be briefly discussed.

COMPETITION AND ENTREPRENEURSHIP

The critical discussion of mainstream neo-classical theory in Section III focused particularly on features of the model of perfect competition central to that theory. The concept of competition used in mainstream theory is quite different from the corresponding concept in the Austrian theory of entrepreneurial discovery. For mainstream theory competition is the closer to perfection as market conditions approach the ideals of complete information throughout the market, and infinite numbers of buyers and sellers of each commodity or service. For the theory of entrepreneurial discovery, on the other hand, the relevant concept of competition involves only one condition, that of *freedom of entry* into each conceivable market.

Both for mainstream neo-classical theory and for the Austrian theory of entrepreneurial discovery, competition is required in order to account for the phenomena which are to be explained. But here the common ground ends. For mainstream theory, competition is a required assumption in order to ensure that the situation described is indeed an equilibrium and to distinguish it from other possible equilibrium con-figurations (for example, that under pure monopoly). But, for the theory of entrepreneurial discovery, competition is required to account for the dynamic entrepreneurial process described above. Consider the case in which freedom of entry has been sharply abridged.

Where (for example as a result of a government grant of monopoly privilege to a favoured manufacturer) potential entrepreneurs are blocked from entering a particular industry, this must paralyse the market discov-ery process. Suppose, as is plausible, the protected monopolist is enjoy-ing monopoly rents and so is able to charge a price which substantially exceeds relevant costs of production. Then this situation will not be eroded by competitive forces, since entry is blocked.

The monopolised product may be urgently needed by potential con-sumers, and resources now employed in other, less urgently needed industries, might more productively and profitably be used in this (monopolised) industry. But discovery of the profit possibilities is ren-dered less likely because entry restrictions prohibit the grasping of such profits by new entrepreneurs even if the existence of these profits is dis-covered. Perhaps the technology now in use in the monopolised industry could be dramatically improved, resulting in a substantial reduction in costs of production. Such new production techniques might have been discovered, under conditions of free entry, by potential entrepreneurs on the prowl for pure profit opportunities. But such discovery is rendered less likely because entry restrictions prevent the winning of such profits by innovative entrepreneurs. Where the grasping of profit is prohibited, the process of technical discovery is sharply inhibited or totally paralysed. The entrepreneurial discovery process depends upon the awareness by potential entrepreneurs that any pure profit opportunities they may dis-cover will redound to the discoverer's benefit.

The dynamic character of the competition central to the process of entrepreneurial discovery exercises powerful forces operating not only on prices, but on the quality characteristics of products and on the tech-niques of production. The driving force of entrepreneurial, competitive entry redirects resources from industries in which their productivity is low, as measured by consumer eagerness, and willingness to pay, towards industries or techniques in which their productivity is higher. Competitive entry and the threat of competitive entry bring about the lowering of product prices towards their lowest possible costs of production and alert incumbent producers to the possibility of lowering the costs of production and to the competitive necessity to lower product prices accordingly.

The contrast between the notion of competition in mainstream neo-classical theory and that in the theory of entrepreneurial discovery can most effectively be presented in terms of knowledge. Mainstream competition theory calls for knowledge as a *prerequisite:* without complete knowledge throughout the market, competition is imperfect. But, for the theory of entrepreneurial discovery, competition is the process *through which* knowledge is discovered and communicated. It was Hayek who put his finger on this cardinal difference separating these two notions of competition.[4] Whereas the mainstream concept sees competition as referring to one particular *state* of equilibrium, the dynamic concept of competition refers to a *process* through which disequilibrium states are gradually modified in the equilibrative direction. It is the difference between an imagined state of completely attained information throughout the system, and a process of discovery through which both activities and mutual information become more closely co-ordinated.

The close relationship between the dynamic concept of competition and entrepreneurial alertness has been explored in the literature of the theory of entrepreneurial discovery.[5] It turns out that the two notions, dynamic competition and entrepreneurship, are two sides of the same coin. Every act of competitive entry is an entrepreneurial act; every entrepreneurial action is necessarily competitive (in the dynamic sense of the word). To compete is to act (or to be in a position to act) to offer buyers a more attractive deal, or to offer sellers a more attractive deal, than others are offering. To do so it is necessary to discover situations where incumbent market participants are offering less than the best possible deals, and to move to grasp the profits made possible by filling the gap so created by the incumbents. Such activity is strictly entrepreneurial. To act

---

4. See especially: (a) Friedrich A. Hayek, "The Meaning of Competition," in his *Individualism and Economic Order, op. cit.,* Chapter 5, pp. 92–106; (b) Friedrich A. Hayek, "Competition as a Discovery Procedure," in his *New Studies in Philosophy, Politics, Economics and the History of Ideas,* Chicago: University of Chicago Press, 1978, Chapter 12. (This paper was first presented as a lecture on 29 March 1968.)

5. See especially Israel M. Kirzner, *Competition and Entrepreneurship,* Chicago: University of Chicago Press, 1973.

entrepreneurially is to enter a market with a new idea, with a better product, with a more attractive price, or with a new technique of production. Any such act necessarily competes with others.

In the theory of entrepreneurial discovery, competition can (apart from governmental restrictions on entry) be limited only as a result of monopoly ownership of unique and scarce resources.[6] If an individual enjoys sole ownership over such a resource, he may be invulnerable to competitive entry, because potential competitors are precluded from access to the unique resource. Entrepreneurial discovery, in such cases, must necessarily be channelled into other productive activities for which the required resources are available to all willing to pay the market price.[7] Entrepreneurial activity is possible only to the extent that no resource monopoly obstacles exist to block entry. Dynamically competitive activity which involves not duplication of *existing* offers made by others but the innovative offering of *superior* opportunities to others is possible only because entrepreneurs are alert to the possibilities available through innovation.

MISES, HAYEK AND THE THEORY OF ENTREPRENEURIAL DISCOVERY

Thus the theory of entrepreneurial discovery emerges as a synthesis of complementary ideas developed separately by Mises and by Hayek. In Section II we saw that Mises emphasised the entrepreneurial character of the market process, while Hayek drew attention to the character of that process as being one of mutual learning. We observed there that these two elements of emphasis turn out to be two sides of the same coin, a coin which represents an Austrian paradigm, sharply at variance with the mainstream neo-classical paradigm. This observation can now be reviewed.

The key to appreciating the complementarity between the Misesian and the Hayekian insights is the distinction to be drawn between the

6. On this see Ludwig von Mises, *Human Action, op. cit.,* pp. 354–74.

7. In any monopolised industry, in fact, the market process proceeds through entrepreneurial competition being re-channelled to other markets. The process through which the monopolist arrives at the monopoly price for his product is one in which activity in the production of possible substitute products, and activity in markets for alternative uses of other, non-monopolised resources, impinge on the prices on the basis of which the monopolist calculates his own pricing policy.

discovery so central to the Austrian approach, and the deliberate search which finds its place in the mainstream neo-classical approach. Mainstream theory has developed the important theory of search, significantly enriching the realism of the theory. Recognising the ubiquity of imperfect information, search theory ingeniously incorporates into the mainstream paradigm the possibility of imperfect information. It assumes that those whose information is incomplete know how much information they lack, that they know the value to them of the missing information, and that they know precisely how (and at what cost) it is possible to obtain the missing information. Mainstream theory is then able to "explain" exactly how much additional information will be obtained, through deliberate, cost-benefit-calculative search. Obtaining information in this mainstream approach is a special kind of production activity, an activity which can and is, therefore, incorporated into the enriched equilibrium picture which search theory makes possible. The discovery central to the Austrian approach is entirely different.

The difference is between the unawareness which is corrected in the course of entrepreneurial discovery, and the imperfect information which is completed in the course of deliberate search. The latter kind of ignorance is an ignorance deliberately chosen, as it were; the agent knows exactly how much information it is worth acquiring. The information which he deliberately refrains from acquiring is simply not worth the cost of acquisition. The ignorance with which he remains is, from this neo-classical perspective, *optimal* ignorance. But the unawareness corrected in the course of the entrepreneurial discovery process is an unawareness of which the agent is himself utterly ignorant. This ignorance is not "justified" by the high cost of deliberate learning; it is not justified at all. It is simply the expression of one having unaccountably failed to notice what is, in effect, staring one in the face.

Entrepreneurial discovery represents the alert becoming aware of what has been overlooked. The essence of entrepreneurship consists in seeing through the fog created by the uncertainty of the future. When the Misesian human agent acts, he is determining what indeed he "sees" in this murky future. He is inspired by the prospective pure-profitability of seeing that future more correctly than others do. These superior visions of the future inform entrepreneurial productive and exchange activity. The dynamic market process is made up of such profit-motivated creative acts in regard to the future.

In so acting, the Misesian entrepreneur drives the market process which reflects the flow of new discoveries these entrepreneurial visions have uncovered. If all exogenous change (in consumer preferences, resource availability, and technological possibilities) could be suspended, this dynamic, entrepreneur-driven market process would proceed until all uncertainties, arising out of unawareness of what others are able and willing to do, would gradually become resolved. In emphasising the entrepreneurial character of the Misesian market process, we are at the same time drawing indirect attention to the Hayekian mutual-discovery aspect of that very same process. While certain elements in Hayek's expositions of the 1940s do seem to differ from elements emphasised in Mises's expositions of that same decade, an entrepreneurial discovery theory of the market process can be developed which draws on the complementarity between the Misesian and the Hayekian insights.

THE THEORY OF ENTREPRENEURIAL DISCOVERY
AND THE MAINSTREAM NEO-CLASSICAL PARADIGM

It might be argued that the theory of entrepreneurial discovery provides crucial, badly needed *support* for neo-classical equilibrium theory which does a superb job in explaining the conditions fulfilled once all the co-ordinative steps taken in the course of the market process have been completed. But, because it does not of itself account for the process through which such co-ordinative steps come to be taken, it needs the contribution of the theory of entrepreneurial discovery. In this way, it might be argued, Austrian theory supports the mainstream neo-classical approach.

For many workaday purposes in applied economics, mainstream equilibrium theory offers a useful short-cut to understanding what happens in markets. In considering what the consequences are of specific governmental interferences in markets (for example, in seeing how price ceilings generate shortages or minimum prices generate surpluses), the Austrian economist is likely to find himself using the same simple Marshallian supply-and-demand diagrams as his neo-classical colleagues. The technique of comparative statics analysis has for many decades been a simple but powerful tool for the applied economist. Nothing in this paper is intended to denigrate the possible usefulness of mainstream equilibrium theory to serve as the algorithm for roughly identifying the consequences of specific kinds of exogenous change. It may indeed seem that the theory of entrepreneurial discovery provides not much more than a helpful explanatory footnote, as it were, to mainstream theory.[8] But in fact the relationship between the theory of entrepreneurial discovery and mainstream neo-classical theory can and should be seen in a different light.

If the purpose of economic theory is seen as no more than offering short-cuts to statements linking causes to effects, then "black-box" theorising may appear adequate. But if the purpose of theory is to help us understand *how* the market economy works, things are quite different. For purposes of achieving understanding, a black-box "theory" is no theory at all. It explains nothing, in the sense in which people usually understand "explanation." Thus the theory of entrepreneurial discovery provides far more than a moderately interesting supplement to mainstream equilibrium theory; it provides the explanation which is lacking in mainstream theory.

As will be shown in the remaining sections of this paper, the theory of entrepreneurial discovery has implications which go beyond the simple satisfaction of scientific curiosity. The explanation which it provides drastically alters the way in which significant features of the market economy and of contemporary economic reality are understood or appreciated. The differences in understanding should, in turn, entail important modifications both in the "moral" evaluation of key features of capitalism, and in the formulation of practical economic policies to permit the economy to reap its greatest potential in efficiency and in prosperity.

8. Cf. Karen I. Vaughn, *Austrian Economics in America: The Migration of a Tradition,* Cambridge: Cambridge University Press, 1994, pp. 139ff.

Understanding the market process as a systematic, error-corrective sequence of profit-inspired entrepreneurial discoveries, continually reshuffled and redirected as a result of the ceaseless impact of exogenous changes, should drastically alter our appreciation of key features of capitalism. In this section a number of examples of such alterations are examined.

A good deal of the argument stems from refusal to accept perfectly competitive equilibrium as an ideal. Many features of real-world markets which appear, from a perfectly competitive-ideal perspective, to be direct evidence of inefficiency turn out to be wholesome features of a vigorously and dynamically competitive world. So-called "imperfections" of competition emerge as crucial elements in the market process of discovery and correction of earlier entrepreneurial errors. Each example in this section demonstrates how the Austrian view of the competitive process contrasts with the norm of perfect competition.

THE ECONOMICS OF ADVERTISING

Advertising cannot easily be fitted into the perfectly competitive equilibrium model. Hence it has been seen as a generally harmful and wasteful phenomenon, responsible for serious divergence of capitalist performance from the efficiency conditions in the perfect competition model. It appears to be expenditure of resources designed to manipulate consumer preferences, shifting the demand curves for given advertised products to the right. Such manipulation can only benefit firms in monopolistic or quasi-monopolistic situations. Further, advertising adds insult to injury by requiring consumers to pay more for the privilege of buying commodities which they would not want in the absence of manipulation.

Neo-classical theory recognises that advertising may perform a productive rôle in providing consumers with useful information (for which they may be entirely willing to pay). There may be sound economic reasons why this information is provided by those with an interest in promoting sales of the advertised product (rather than by impartial, disinterested market purveyors of information). But it hardly explains the enormous volume of advertising, and especially its provocative, attention-grabbing, shrilly persuasive character. However, it is the analytical framework of the neo-classical paradigm which prevents critics of advertising from recognising its important rôle in the entrepreneurial discovery process. This paradigm has led critics to see advertising as decisively refuting the notion that under capitalist market constraints and incentives, producers are governed by consumer sovereignty.[1]

The theory of entrepreneurial discovery opens up a new perspective into which advertising can be fitted far more easily and in which it fills a different rôle. In order to serve the preferences of consumers, producers have to do far more than merely fabricate and make available the goods they believe consumers desire most urgently. They must do more, even, than to make available the information they believe consumers need to acquire and appreciate the goods on offer. After all, the entrepreneurial discovery perspective shows that mere availability does not guarantee that those needing information will have it. Even if information is staring them in the face they may simply not notice it, and remain unaware that there is anything further to be known.

It is therefore necessary for producers, intent on winning the profits from innovatively serving consumer preferences, also to *alert consumers* to the availability and the qualities of goods. Clearly there is a rôle for advertising beyond "providing information in response to consumer demand." There is, in addition, a rôle for advertising to grab the attention of potential consumers and direct them both to the information and to the goods that are available. This information may be such that, once aware of the goods, consumers may wish to buy them. But their demand may not yet be active as long as they remain unaware of their existence.

Such arguments may be presented in different terms. Mainstream theory sees consumers entering the market-place with given demand curves for each product. The success of the market in serving consumers is then judged by its success in responding to these demands. Advertising by producers is therefore immediately suspect, because its function

---

1. This has been repeatedly argued, for example, by Professor Galbraith: see John K. Galbraith, *The Affluent Society*, Boston: Houghton Mifflin, 1958, Chapter 11; John K. Galbraith, *The New Industrial State*, Boston: Houghton Mifflin, 1967, Chapter 18; John K. Galbraith, *Economics and the Public Purpose*, Boston: Houghton Mifflin, 1973, Chapter 14.

appears not to satisfy the given demand, but rather to manipulate those demand curves better to suit the profit-seeking motives of the producers.

But from the Austrian perspective, the notion of demand cannot be given coherence unless the consumer is aware of the buying opportunities he faces. If a consumer has, say, never seen a pair of gloves and has no inkling of their existence or purpose, it is meaningless to speak of his demand curve for gloves. Yet we would not deny that an innovative, imaginative and creative entrepreneur who invents gloves, produces them, and offers them to satisfied customers, has correctly anticipated their demand for gloves. Surely we would agree that this entrepreneur has served consumer sovereignty, broadly understood.

The notion of "serving the consumer" must be broadened to mean fulfilling consumer preferences, not as they were before the entrepreneur began his activities, but as they will be once the entrepreneur has made consumers aware of his product. The idea of "manipulation of consumer demand by producers" then becomes unclear. It is part of the producer's function to acquaint consumers with what has been made available to them. So it becomes virtually impossible to distinguish in practice between selling activity designed to persuade consumers to buy something which they would not wish to buy and "selling activity"[2] designed to make consumers fully aware of the qualities of the product which satisfies a demand of which they were previously unaware.

The provocative, attention-grabbing character of modern advertising is easily understandable as part of the efforts of producers, not only to make goods available to consumers, but also to ensure that consumers are aware of what is before them. The entrepreneur-producer must, in addition, be entrepreneurial enough to recognise that effort must be expended to awaken potential customers to new preferences. To dismiss such an argument as cynical sophistry would be to ignore two factors.

First, in a world of complexity, change and uncertainty, it is inevitable that consumers *are* imperfectly aware of the qualities and promise of the multitudes of goods. The need to alert consumers to *what they do not know that they do not know,* is very real. *Second,* to interpret advertising effort as primarily designed to persuade consumers to buy what they

2. Elsewhere the writer has pointed out that this kind of "selling activity" is not conceptually distinguishable from a broadly understood notion of "production activity." See Israel M. Kirzner, *Competition and Entrepreneurship, op. cit.,* Chapter 4.

really do not want, raises an obvious difficulty. It assumes that producers find it more profitable to produce what consumers do *not* want, and then to persuade them to buy it, with expensive selling campaigns, rather than to produce what consumers do already in fact want (without need for selling effort). While producers may make errors of judgement, and may then see advertising as a way of minimising losses from having produced the wrong products, it seems highly implausible that the volume of advertising we observe can be explained in this way.

The entrepreneurial discovery perspective illuminates the obviously *competitive* character of modern advertising, which is difficult to appreciate within the neo-classical framework. From the mainstream perspective, advertising makes sense only as a weapon in the arsenal of the monopolist. From the perspective on advertising described here, however, advertising is plainly a tool *with which to compete*.

Once we see advertising as an activity through which entrepreneurs alert consumers to new goods and to qualities which the consumers may value highly, advertising appears as simply one more avenue for competitive entrepreneurship. Where two entrepreneurs have correctly anticipated the urgency of consumer eagerness to buy gloves, a new avenue opens for them to compete in serving the consumer. The producer who judges more correctly what kind of dramatic advertising message will best awaken consumer interest has the more successfully served those consumers. In exactly the same way as glove manufacturers compete in selecting those features (such as colour choice, style, durability and so on) most likely to appeal to glove consumers, they compete also on the most effective (and most cost-effective) way of attracting consumer attention. Advertising is thus an activity in which entrepreneurship is required. Apart from special cases (in which, perhaps, government regulation has given one producer unique access to advertising media), such entrepreneurial activity is essentially competitive because no one advertiser can prevent competing producers from advertising *their* products.

None of this can guarantee that each and every advertising message is necessarily truthful and in the consumers' interest. But it does point to the superficiality of sweeping attacks on the economic rôle of advertising. It demonstrates also that the entrepreneurial discovery perspective presented in this paper has important consequences for the way in which we "see" significant features of the market economy.

THE ECONOMICS OF ANTI-TRUST

An important alteration in approach to anti-trust policy is entailed by the insights of the theory of entrepreneurial discovery.

Laws attempting to prevent the emergence of (or to curb the use of) monopoly power antedate mainstream neo-classical theory. Consumer fear of monopoly power does not depend on the dominance of the model of perfectly competitive equilibrium. But modern anti-trust policy draws upon that model for much of its intellectual ammunition. If one begins from the premise that complete allocative efficiency depends upon the attainment of the conditions necessary for perfect competition, any departure from those conditions appears as a threat, not merely to consumers who might be subjected to "higher" monopoly prices but also to the allocative efficiency properties of the entire market system. The extraordinarily demanding conditions required for perfectly competitive equilibrium render mainstream neo-classical economics not so much a body of market theory demonstrating the efficiency of real-world capitalism, as one demonstrating its departures from allocative efficiency. Vigorous anti-trust legislation and enforcement came, therefore, to be seen by defenders of the market economy steeped in the mainstream paradigm, as steps urgently needed in order to *defend* the capitalist system against criticism of its otherwise non-competitive character.[3] But the theory of entrepreneurial discovery throws a different light on such issues.

Section IV explained that in the theory of entrepreneurial discovery the relevant notion of competition depends on the fulfilment of only one condition—unhampered freedom of entrepreneurial entry into any and all sectors of the market. So long as no potential entrepreneur finds himself blocked from carrying out and profiting from any entrepreneurial venture he initiates, every activity undertaken in the economy is taken under the threat of the competition of others, and itself offers competitive challenge to others.

The social advantage provided by dynamic competition is the incentive it offers for the discovery and correction of earlier entrepreneurial errors. This social advantage does not consist in an assurance of "optimal"

3. See in this regard Henry C. Simons, *Economic Policy for a Free Society*, Chicago: University of Chicago Press, 1948, pp. 81ff.

allocation of resources. It consists of a systematic process of discovering and correcting entrepreneurial errors, especially errors which have left open opportunities for as yet unexploited mutual gain through trade among market participants. Consequently, departures from the optimality conditions of perfectly competitive equilibrium are not a threat to any relevant notion of economic efficiency. Equilibrium is not an attainable ideal, nor are perfect or "near perfect" competition attainable. What is important is to ensure that opportunities for mutual gain are rapidly noticed and exploited; that market participants are not misled by over-optimism or by over-pessimism to undertake activities which they will subsequently regret. Dynamic competition offers the incentive and the pressure which alert entrepreneurs to the opportunities created by such errors of over-optimism and over-pessimism.

A single producer who enjoys privileged protection against the entry of other potential entrepreneurs enjoys a monopoly position. A single producer not protected against entry of potential competitors does not constitute a monopoly in the relevant sense. It is true that a single producer is confronted by a downward sloping demand curve because the demand he faces *today* is the demand of the entire market, which is downward sloping. So it is certainly likely that such a single producer will be able to exercise control over price. But such "power" over price does not threaten the competitive process, because it can be exercised only with full awareness that raising the price may in fact simply invite new producers to compete in "his" market.[4] The shape of the demand curve facing a producer at a given point in time has virtually nothing to do with the competitive character of the market for his product.

Only a barrier against entrepreneurial entry into a favoured sector can confer a relevant monopoly position upon the agent engaged in that activity, deflecting potential entrepreneurial discoveries into other areas. Such a barrier can be created by governmental grants of monopoly to favoured individuals or groups; it may also arise through sole ownership of a uniquely essential ingredient for a production process.

---

4. This of course means that the demand curve that confronts this single producer is subject to drastic modification through competitive entry. It is no longer true, simply and without qualification, that he faces the entire market demand curve for the product he sells.

In the absence of such a barrier, even if only a few producers (or even only one) are active in a particular industry, there is no monopoly power in the relevant sense. No producer is sole owner of the capacity of entrepreneurial alertness. The fact that only one producer has chosen to enter this line of production simply means that other entrepreneurs have either failed to see the profit opportunities that the producer has correctly seen, or that *they* have correctly understood that no such profit opportunity exists. In the process of discovery entrepreneurs pursue opportunities which they see. This process is not in the slightest impeded by the downward slope of the demand curve which momentarily faces a single producer who enjoys no protection against competitive entry.

Even more compelling, entrepreneurial competition takes the form, not of producing a product identical to that produced by a single producer, but of producing other products competitive with it. Ultimately, of course, all products compete with each other. In a world of scarce resources, resources allocated to the satisfaction of one set of consumer desires have been diverted from the satisfaction of other consumer desires. In buying the resources needed to produce any one good, an entrepreneur has succeeded in competing away these resources from other possible uses. When a producer, not enjoying protection against competitive entry, finds himself as sole producer he still has to worry about the activities of competing entrepreneurs. They are channelling their energies and their alertness into producing *other* products, which are competing for consumers' attention also. Inter-product competition will not guarantee horizontal demand curves facing each producer. But it offers assurance that errors made in the identification of the most urgently needed consumer products (and/or of the most easily accessible resources) will tend rapidly to be noticed and exploited by alert, competing entrepreneurs.

This view of competition casts doubt on the idea of government policy designed to create or maintain competition. That idea developed out of a conviction that, without such a policy, market competition might degenerate into monopoly or near-monopoly. Economies of scale might, for instance, promote mergers among firms in an industry, pushing the structure of that industry further and further away from the perfectly competitive pattern. Without steps to prevent such mergers, the structure of an industry might easily become non-competitive. Similarly, even without mergers, collusion (tacit or explicit) among large firms in an industry might result in near-monopolistic pricing policies. Active anti-trust legislation and enforcement therefore seem to be required to create and to maintain competitive structures, and to avoid collusion. The enormous literature on anti-trust economics that grew up over the best part of this century was based, for the most part, on these general presumptions. The entrepreneurial discovery perspective seriously challenges these presumptions, or at least, their relevance for industrial policy.

From that perspective it is quite clear that (except in the extraordinary circumstances of single ownership of a uniquely essential scarce resource needed in the production of an important consumer good, for which there are no reasonably close substitutes) no special governmental legislation or enforcement activity are necessary to ensure the dynamically competitive character of the market process. Freedom of entry (that is, absence of privilege) is the only requirement. In most instances of blocked entry, the source is grants of governmental privilege or governmental obstacles to entry (such as licensing requirements). The *only* government action needed to ensure the dynamically competitive character of market activity is to remove all such government-created obstacles.

The market itself is unable to erect such obstacles against entrepreneurial entry. Collusion among "dominant" firms in an industry (unless it takes the form of effectively monopolising the control of essential scarce resources), while it may appear to be effective in keeping up prices, is incapable of preventing entry. Any attempt to keep prices collusively high will be undertaken with awareness of such competitive threat.

Certainly, collusively-engineered high prices are inconsistent with perfectly competitive equilibrium. But they do fit the pattern of dynamic entrepreneurial competition; they emerge out of free competition among unconstrained entrepreneurs. Outright merger between "dominant" firms in an industry may indeed create a single-large-firm-industry, but entry by others is not blocked by that circumstance alone. If the size of such a large firm permits economies of large-scale production which potential entrants may not be able to match, that does not constitute an entry barrier. Quite the contrary; it is desirable that such economies should be reaped through alert entrepreneurial action. Merger activity motivated by the prospect of lowering costs is precisely the kind of competitive entrepreneurship of which the market discovery process consists.

This view of the rôle of competition in markets casts anti-trust activity not as helpful public policy designed to improve the efficiency of the market by limiting its divergence from the competitive ideal. On the contrary, anti-trust activity emerges as a well-meaning but clumsy interference in the market process, which has the effect of *hampering* competition. This paradoxical conclusion follows because blocking a merger, for instance, means blocking a possibly more efficient entrepreneurial venture. Previous processes of production had failed to take advantage of available economies of scale. Entrepreneurial alertness to the profits to be grasped by innovating a large-scale process of production inspires a merger. Governmental obstacles to such a merger are clearly blockages of entrepreneurial entry. What is designed to enhance competition turns out, in fact, to slow down or prevent competitive entry.

Scepticism about conventional anti-trust policy is not the exclusive prerogative of the entrepreneurial discovery approach. Much good sense has entered professional understanding of the nature of real-world competition and the potential threat to its healthy operation which conventional anti-trust policy represents.[5] But, within the mainstream neo-classical framework, it is difficult consistently to defend what appears as non-competitive industrial concentration. The entrepreneurial discovery approach offers a consistent theoretical framework within which to place the dynamic character of the competitive process. To encourage the spontaneous dynamism of the competitive process what is required is not large numbers of small producers producing exactly the same product in exactly the same way; the requirements are freedom of entrepreneurial entry and the elimination of privileges to incumbent producers that might switch off alertness of potential competitors to superior innovative possibilities.

THE ECONOMICS OF WELFARE

Along with the development of 20th-century neo-classical price theory, there developed modern welfare economics. There has never been a time when economic theorists have not sought to evaluate the impact upon society's economic well-being of specific pieces of legislation or policies, or of major historical events. The objective has been to use economic theory to understand how economic phenomena affect some index of social economic well-being.

---

5. For examples see Yale Brozen, *Concentration, Mergers, and Public Policy*, New York and London: Macmillan, 1982; Yale Brozen (ed.), *The Competitive Economy, Selected Readings*, Morristown, N.J.: General Learning Press, 1975.

Changes have, of course, occurred in what economists have understood as the relevant interpretation of "economic well-being." Classical economics, beginning with Adam Smith, saw the "wealth of nations" as an aggregate of objectively measurable items: the economic "goodness" of a policy could be measured by its impact upon the nation's wealth.

With the infusion of subjectivist insights into early neo-classical (late 19th-century) economics (and especially its recognition of diminishing marginal utility), aggregate wealth could no longer be accepted as a simple index of a society's economic well-being. Mainstream economic theory sought to replace aggregate wealth with the more abstract aggregate economic "welfare." Extensive and subtle discussions on how to define aggregate economic welfare (especially how to deal with interpersonal utility comparability) created a significant literature during the middle third of this century. The notion of "Pareto optimality"—a pattern of resource allocation and consumption such that no opportunities exist for a reshuffling of resource uses and consumption patterns that might benefit one or more members of the economic system without harming anyone else—came to be widely used in discussions of economic efficiency.

Modern welfare economics defined with considerable sophistication the conditions under which a market economy in perfectly competitive equilibrium satisfies the requirements for Pareto optimality. Mainstream neo-classical economists who have ascribed social-efficiency properties to the capitalist system have generally treated that system as a reasonably acceptable approximation to the perfectly competitive state of affairs. Mainstream economists who have found fault with the capitalist system on social-efficiency grounds have done so through pointing out the features of the system which violate the conditions required for perfectly competitive equilibrium.

Recognising one salient feature of mainstream economics allows us to appreciate how entrepreneurial discovery opens up a new way of evaluating the economic effectiveness of alternative institutional arrangements. Mainstream welfare economics assesses the economic well-being of a society by adopting the perspective of an omniscient observer. Looking down on an economy, seeing exactly where every unit of resource is being allocated, knowing exactly what the resource supply functions and the consumer demand functions are, welfare economics sets out to pin down the conditions under which an omniscient, omnipotent, and benevolent leader of society, intent upon improving the economic well-being of society, would have nothing left to do. This reduces the economic problem facing society to exactly the same as that defined by Lionel Robbins as the economic problem facing the individual agent—to allocate given resources among given alternative ends.[6]

It was Hayek who pointed out most emphatically, however, that this is *not* the economic problem facing real-world economies[7] where information is widely scattered. The real economic problem is bringing to bear upon decision-making all this available, scattered information—mobilising all the bits of knowledge which exist in decentralised form throughout the economy. *This* problem is one which would have to be solved *before* one could even consider the allocation-of-social-resources problem which mainstream textbooks assure us is *the* economic problem facing society. As Hayek pointed out, the perspective from which mainstream economics proceeds rules out by assumption any consideration of the prime economic problem which societies face.

Hayek's critique of the mainstream notion of the economic problem was not intended by him as a direct attack on the foundations of modern welfare economics. He was pointing out that, if we are in any way concerned to improve the economic well-being of society, it will not do to proceed as if the prime obstacle to achieving that goal simply does not exist. He was inspired to point this out as a result of his debates with socialist economists who failed to recognise the contribution the market makes to mobilising scattered information. Hayek was drawing attention to the blame attached to mainstream theory in simply assuming that this problem did not exist. But he was indirectly also offering a powerful and profound critique of the mainstream theory of economic welfare.

Once it is realised that the relevant information is scattered among many minds, it becomes apparent that the notion of social efficiency central to modern welfare economics is no longer coherent. A social efficiency objective implies a single mind to which all resource supply conditions and all consumer attitudes are simultaneously given. Otherwise, there can be no coherent notion of a relevant optimum. The entire notion of a "social choice" presumes, in principle, the relevance of imagined

6. Lionel Robbins, *An Essay on the Nature and Significance of Economic Science, op. cit.*, Chapter I.

7. Friedrich A. Hayek, *Individualism and Economic Order, op. cit.*, p. 77.

omniscience. In drawing attention to the dispersed information problem Hayek was pointing out that the fundamental ideas at the basis of modern welfare economics lack coherence and relevance for the world in which we must live.

The entrepreneurial discovery approach exposes this fatal flaw in modern welfare economics. Indeed, Hayek's own indictment of mainstream theory for falsely characterising the economic problem facing society (because it fails to consider the problems raised by dispersed information) is effective only within the entrepreneurial discovery perspective. That is so because a hard-boiled modern neo-classical economist might be inclined to shrug off Hayek's problem of dispersed information.

Such an economist might argue that Hayek's observation is not fatal to a neo-classical view which sees the economy as facing a social choice problem, in exactly the same way as the Robbinsian individual agent faces an allocation problem in his quest for individual efficiency. What must be known, to the social agencies charged with achieving social efficiency, need not be specific details of supply conditions and consumer preferences. All that would need to be known, in a world of dispersed information, would be: (i) the costs required in order to acquire, through search, central command over that information, and (ii) the value to society of the information now dispersed (but potentially available to the central social economic agency at the known costs of search). Such information (concerning search costs and information values) *must* be assumed available within the mainstream neo-classical framework, as explained in earlier sections of this paper. So, the neo-classical economist might maintain, the social-efficiency paradigm *can*, after all, still be applied to the Hayekian world of dispersed information.

But the entrepreneurial discovery approach, with its emphasis on the kind of ignorance which cannot be reduced by deliberate search (because the agent is unaware of his ignorance, or at least unaware of how his ignorance could be reduced), demonstrates the insurmountable difficulties for mainstream theory raised by Hayek's insights. Those difficulties defy any effort to fit the situation into a Procrustean bed of neo-classical constrained maximisation. An imagined social agent lacking omniscience would simply not be aware of how much dispersed information he lacks, of where to look for it (even if he realises his ignorance), or what questions to ask in pursuing a hypothetical search.

At the same time, the entrepreneurial discovery approach offers the germ of a potential reconstruction of welfare economics. Once we understand the difficulties constituted by unknown ignorance, we realise the possibility of evaluating economic policies and/or historical events, not in terms of the flawed notion of social efficiency, but in terms of a different criterion—ability to encourage entrepreneurial alertness to valuable knowledge the very existence of which has not previously been suspected.

The entrepreneurial discovery approach focuses on the social advantages conferred by the competitive market process during which earlier errors become translated into pure profit opportunities which, in turn, attract entrepreneurial alertness and are thus corrected. The social advantages thus achieved do not constitute "social optimality" as defined from the perspective of imagined omniscience. They constitute instead a co-ordinative process during which market participants become aware of mutually beneficial opportunities for trade and, in grasping these opportunities, move to correct the earlier errors.

Focusing in this way on *co-ordination* as the criterion for evaluating the successful functioning of economic institutions, should not be misunderstood. The term "co-ordination" suffers from some ambiguity. It *can* refer to a state of affairs in which all conceivable plans of all potential market participants *are already* in full co-ordination with one another. Such a state of affairs would be achieved, for example, in perfectly competitive equilibrium, thus returning us to the Pareto Optimality criterion.

The term "co-ordination" is used here to refer to the *co-ordinating process*. An important dimension of proper economic functioning is the sensitivity with which a society's institutions reveal when avoidable, wholly unnecessary errors have been made. We can hope, therefore, to develop ways of assessing the comparative success of alternative institutional arrangements in this regard and of identifying the impact of specific pieces of legislation. We may not have any coherent notion of global well-being that can withstand a methodologically individualistic critique. We may not have any coherent notion of global efficiency that can withstand a Hayekian critique based on the dispersed nature of information. But we can, nonetheless, recognise a supra-individual "social" benefit bestowed by benign economic institutions and policies in stimulating the co-ordinative process of entrepreneurial discovery. This possible reconstruction of welfare economics can help us understand the inter-war debate about the possibility of rational socialist economic calculation.

THE ECONOMICS OF SOCIALISM

One unfortunate consequence of the mainstream neo-classical approach to understanding markets has been to support socialist contentions that the efficiency advantages of markets can be relatively easily simulated under socialist central planning. This may seem paradoxical, since both admirers of the market and admirers of central planning have recognised neo-classical economic theory as the intellectual bulwark of the capitalist system. Yet it was neo-classical price theory that was skilfully applied by defenders of socialism to deflect Mises's famous 1920 critique of the possibility of rational socialist economic calculation. One is reminded of the aphorism attributed to Abba P. Lerner: "Marxism is the economics of the capitalist system; neo-classical price theory is the economics of the socialist economy." The entrepreneurial discovery approach to understanding markets enables us properly to appreciate Mises's critique, and to recognise that the most celebrated of the socialist attempts to refute this critique in fact failed to understand it.[8]

In 1920, Mises pointed out[9] that socialist planners, lacking the guidance provided by market prices for resources, would be unable to plan rationally. In choosing a method of production for a given project, for example, they would be unable rationally to choose that method of production which would be the most economical (that is, which would interfere least with the fulfilment of other desirable social objectives). Socialist production could certainly be undertaken, but socialist planners could not ensure that the array of outputs produced represented the most desirable possible array. The devastating implications of this critique were not lost upon socialist writers, and a vigorous inter-war debate ensued. We can focus on the work of Oskar Lange and of Abba P. Lerner, who (as mentioned in Section II above) recognised the force of Mises's critique, but believed that it was possible to fashion a socialism

8. For a book-length treatment of this issue see Donald C. Lavoie, *Rivalry and Central Planning, The Socialist Calculation Debate Reconsidered*, Cambridge: Cambridge University Press, 1985.

9. This paper was translated as Ludwig von Mises, "Economic Calculation in the Socialist Commonwealth," in Friedrich A. Hayek (ed.), *Collectivist Economic Planning, Critical Studies of the Possibilities of Socialism*, London: Routledge and Kegan Paul, 1935, pp. 87–130. See also Ludwig von Mises, *Socialism: An Economic and Sociological Analysis* (1922), translated by J. Kahane, London: Jonathan Cape, 1936, Chapter 6.

that would be able to avoid the harsh implications of that critique for socialist efficiency.

Lange[10] was explicit in linking his suggested solution to the Misesian economic calculation problem to mainstream theory. He proposed a form of socialism in which non-market "prices" for resources would be announced by the central economic authorities and used by socialist managers of state enterprises in exactly the same way as neo-classical theory sees owners of capitalist firms using market prices for resources. The socialist managers would be instructed to use these resource "prices" in conjunction with the prices of their products to select output levels and methods of production that would maximise "profit." They would do so by aiming at precisely those same marginal equalities which neo-classical theory sees as being achieved by capitalist firms in competitive markets. The central economic authorities would periodically adjust the announced resource "prices" upwards (or downwards) in response to resource shortages (surpluses) generated by the socialist managers' demands for resources under earlier resource "price" announcements. In this innovative way, Lange believed, the socialist economy, by simulating the operation of the perfectly competitive capitalist market economy, would achieve the same allocation of resources as that resulting from the competitive market—while being able to fulfil the distributive and other goals of traditional socialism.

Mises (and Hayek, who had in 1935 published two important essays[11] supporting Mises in the economic calculation debate) did not concede that Lange and Lerner had responded at all usefully to their criticisms of the possibility of rational socialist planning. Nevertheless, the post-war literature somehow concluded that these criticisms of the possibility of socialist efficiency had been decisively refuted. The reason is the same as that which was responsible for Lange's solution, viz. that other writers, like Lange, were thinking in terms of the neo-classical equilibrium paradigm. Consequently, Lange was unable to grasp the full meaning of Mises's and

10. Oskar Lange, "On the Economic Theory of Socialism," *op. cit.*, reprinted in Oskar Lange and Fred M. Taylor, *On The Economic Theory of Socialism*, edited by B. E. Lippincott, University of Minnesota Press, 1938, pp. 55–129.

11. Friedrich A. Hayek, "The Nature and History of the Problem," published as the Introduction to F. A. Hayek (ed.), *Collectivist Economic Planning: Critical Studies on the Possibilities of Socialism*, London: George Routledge and Son, 1935; *ibid.*, Chapter 5, "The Present State of the Debate."

Hayek's critique—which proceeded, at least implicitly, from an Austrian understanding of price theory in the entrepreneurial discovery approach.

Lange's solution for Mises's problem is to simulate the operation of the competitive market imagined to be in equilibrium. Mises had argued that socialist planners, unlike capitalist entrepreneurs, are unable to use the prices of resources in order to calculate the most economical ways in which to achieve given goals. Lange's response was that announced prices could serve exactly the same "parametric" function as served by market prices for resources in competitive equilibrium.

But Mises had not understood the rôle of market prices as serving such a parametric rôle at all. He had not seen the ability of capitalist entrepreneurs to use resource prices as in any way depending on the properties of prices under competitive equilibrium conditions. Quite the contrary, he understood the resource prices which emerge in markets as expressing the entrepreneurial bids and offers of market participants competing with each other under disequilibrium conditions. In bidding for a resource an entrepreneur is both guided by the judgement of the entrepreneurs with whom he is competing, and expressing his own judgement concerning the future value of his projected product to tomorrow's consumers (to whom he hopes to offer his product). There is nothing in Lange's scheme of simulating perfectly competitive equilibrium markets under socialism remotely corresponding to the alert, profit-stimulated entrepreneurial judgement which is both guided by market prices and itself drives the course of such prices. To imagine that Lange's scheme could simulate capitalist efficiency is grossly to misunderstand the way in which capitalist markets work. The virtue of the entrepreneurial discovery approach is that it clearly identifies the flaw in Lange and Lerner's response to the Misesian critique of the possibility of socialist efficiency.

The demise of socialist economic systems in Eastern Europe during the past decade has focused renewed attention on the Misesian critique. It is true that the Lange-Lerner proposed solution was never implemented in socialist practice. Nonetheless, the widespread conclusion in the post-war literature on comparative economic systems that the Misesian critique can, at least in principle, be met by appropriate simulation of neo-classical markets in equilibrium, makes it doubly important to appreciate the true content of this critique. Such an appreciation simply cannot be achieved within the mainstream neo-classical paradigm. The entrepreneurial discovery approach from which Mises's work proceeded illuminates Mises's real meaning.

ECONOMICS, MARKETS, AND JUSTICE

The entrepreneurial discovery approach offers insights into philosophical discussions of the possibility of *justice* in a capitalist society. An understanding of the market economy which is based on seeing it, in mainstream neo-classical terms, as being in the competitive equilibrium state, is likely to arrive at sharply distorted philosophical conclusions in regard to capitalist justice. Philosophical conclusions are likely to be decisively shaped by the way the operation of capitalism is understood. Moving from a mainstream paradigm to an entrepreneurial discovery paradigm entails profound differences in philosophical judgements concerning the justice of the system. In order to rebut widespread philosophical condemnation of the market society on justice grounds, it may not be necessary to engage in philosophical disputation at all. It is simply necessary to correct mistaken ideas (taken unquestioningly from mainstream economics) concerning the positive economic operation of the system. Once these strictly economic-theoretic misunderstandings have been cleared up, the philosophical conclusions typically drawn from them are likely to collapse without further argumentation. In other words, moral judgements have been reached on the basis of a flawed understanding of the system being evaluated.

Criticisms of the market society on grounds of its alleged injustice traditionally proceed from a variety of concerns. The institution of private property is criticised; the inequality of incomes is criticised; effects of the price system are criticised. Our focus here is on criticisms of the justice of capitalism which arise from its permitting—indeed its resting upon—the possibility of pure entrepreneurial profit. The market system relies for its driving force on the profit motive. The justice of the system is often criticised on the grounds that profits have not been *earned* or deserved, that they are pure surplus captured at the expense of labourers and/or of consumers. Justice, critics maintain, requires that all gains received be *deserved*. A system in which the distribution of incomes includes a significant share of pure entrepreneurial profit cannot be just.

Critics of the justice of profits make a sharp (and proper) distinction between incomes received in return for services rendered (whether by one's own labour or by material resources justly owned) and pure profit. Incomes received for services rendered are considered to have been justly earned; they represent a *quid pro quo*. Even the return on invested capital (although often loosely called "profit") may, at least for the non-Marxist critic of capitalism, be recognised as having been earned and deserved. But pure entrepreneurial profit—an amount received over and above the full value of all resource services rendered—is seen as defying the traditional justifications offered for factor incomes.

Quite correctly, it is recognised that pure profit cannot be treated or justified *as a factor income*. The entrepreneur who pays out the sums needed to acquire *all* necessary inputs for a production process, and who is able to sell his output for greater sums, has captured thereby a pure gain, which does not correspond to a service rendered by any identifiable input. Such profit can appear to be derived either from "exploitation" and/or deceit, or as being the result of sheer, undeserved luck. Regardless of the relative size of the pure profit share in market-determined incomes, because this "undeserved" share offers the primary incentives for the operation of the entire system, that is sufficient in the eyes of critics of capitalism to render that system unjust. But the entrepreneurial discovery approach suggests otherwise.

That approach reveals a category of gain which is neither the deliberately aimed-at result achieved by the expenditure of productive resources, nor the wholly fortuitous result of pure luck: the gain is revealed and grasped through alert *discovery*. Within the neo-classical paradigm there can be no such category. Mainstream economics proceeds by fitting the economic phenomena of the market economy into a framework from which all but deliberately aimed-at results on the one hand, and the fruits of pure luck on the other hand, have been carefully excluded. This neo-classical world excludes all possibility of *surprise*. Explanation, in this analytical world, is achieved by attributing all phenomena to deliberately and correctly made choices between known alternatives.[12] Within such a framework there is no room for pure entrepreneurial profit. There is no opportunity, in such a world, to discover what one had hitherto not sought.

If the possibility of discovered gain is ruled out by the analytical framework employed, it follows that all questions of distributive justice boil down to questions of how justly to share *a given pie* (or, what amounts to

---

12. Luck has a place, in a modified neo-classical world, only to the extent that the relevant probability functions are fully known. One may be the fortunate beneficiary of good luck. But since one knew exactly the chances one had of being lucky, good fortune is not anything that can be considered a genuine *surprise*.

the same thing, of how to share the given pie-ingredients). Either the pie we see (which is to be justly distributed) has already always existed (with just claims for shares of it somehow established by history). Or the pie we see has been produced, and just distribution requires that it be justly shared out among the owners of the ingredients (assumed always to have existed, with historically established title claims to them) combined in the pie-baking process. There is, in this world without discovery, no scope for considering how just principles can be applied to a pie (or its ingredients) which did not, for all relevant purposes, exist at all prior to its having been discovered.

It is the concept of discovery which permits and requires us to recognise that "pies" (or their ingredients) may have *come into existence* as a result of acts of discovery. An act of discovery is not an act of deliberate production (out of known ingredients); nor is it simply the passive reaction to a stroke of pure luck. An act of discovery is one during which *one becomes aware* of a costlessly available gain. Clearly, pure entrepreneurial profit fits into the pigeon-hole reserved for such discovered, costlessly available gain. The entrepreneurial discovery approach, in recognising discovery as the driving force in the disequilibrium world, also recognises pure profit as a category that may be defensible, on justice grounds, along lines that would not be relevant in a world in which there was nothing left to be discovered.

For discovery relates to alert action which brings new things into the world *without expenditure of resources*. It differs from deliberate production in that production requires resources (whose value therefore tends to rise to the level of the value of what they produce, leaving no surplus for pure profit). It differs from what becomes available as a result of pure luck, in that the latter calls for no human action whatever. Discovered gain is gain that, despite its possible prior *physical* existence was, as far as human cognisance is concerned, simply "not there." What brings it into existence, *ex nihilo*, is human (entrepreneurial) alertness. That act of alertly grasping what one sees is a creative act, since it instantaneously brings into existence what was previously, to all human intents and purposes, non-existent.

Claim to what one has "created" in this fashion cannot be based on ownership of the resources which produced it: there were no such resources. This gain is not in any sense the fruit of a tree justly possessed. The gain may be claimed by its discoverer on the grounds that he has "created" it by bringing it into existence, as it were, out of nothingness. Unlike the fortunate beneficiary of a stroke of good luck, the discoverer of a hitherto unnoticed desirable object *acted* to "create" that object. *He* noticed it; no one else did so before he grasped the object he noticed. Discovery may take the form of alertly noticing how to produce, out of available resources, something desired. While the subsequent deliberate act of production is not an act of discovery, the *discovery of the opportunity* to gain through subsequent deliberate production, *is* creative.

The entrepreneurial discovery approach permits us to see pure entrepreneurial profit as *created* gain, the surplus value created by the alert entrepreneur who discovers the opportunity of converting resources valued by society at a low value, into products which society values more highly. The slice of pie grasped by successful entrepreneurs has not been sliced from a pre-existing pie at all; it is a portion which has been created in the very act of grasping it.

There certainly is room within the theory of entrepreneurial discovery for understanding incomes received in return for providing the productive process with the services of resources which one owns. And neoclassical marginal productivity theory, ever since John Bates Clark, has clarified the nature and the justice of such earned income.

But we live in an open-ended world, in which as yet unseen opportunities always exist for improving human well-being through the discovery of new resources or of new ways of deploying resources productively. So the creative character of the actions taken alertly to notice and to grasp these opportunities should be recognised. An enormous volume of pure entrepreneurial activity takes place in capitalist society; a theory of economic justice must be grounded in an analytical framework which can accommodate such activity, not in a framework built upon the premise that no scope whatever exists for such activity. The theory of entrepreneurial discovery drastically alters conventional conclusions regarding capitalist distributive justice.

VI. CONCLUSION

The purpose of a theoretical framework is to foster understanding of phenomena encountered in the real world. Any such framework necessarily abstracts from details of the real world in order to develop an explanatory model able to provide insight into the complexities of that world. Different explanatory models are designed to help us understand different facets of the world.

There is no doubt that important aspects of the market economy can be helpfully illuminated by mainstream neo-classical economics. But there are even more important aspects of the economy which remain obscure when the mainstream framework is applied. Among the important questions which that framework is, by its very construction, unable to answer, are: How do markets work? How are the individual decisions of millions of market participants able to become as co-ordinated as they are in the market economies we know? These questions are surely the most fundamental which arise when we consider the extraordinary prosperity achieved in market economies during the past two hundred years.

The theory of entrepreneurial discovery, derived from the Austrian tradition, offers a framework within which satisfying, coherent answers to these fundamental questions can be found. This theory enables us, at the same time, to "see" important features of market economies in a different light from that provided by the mainstream approach. Deploying the Austrian insights provided by this approach can help avoid policy pitfalls, as well as satisfying our purely scientific curiosity about the way in which the world works.

Hayek, F. (1948): "The Use of Knowledge in Society," *American Economic Review,* September 1945; reprinted in Hayek, *Individualism and Economic Order,* London: Routledge and Kegan Paul.

Hayek, F. (1978): "Competition as a Discovery Procedure," in Hayek, *New Studies in Philosophy, Politics, Economics and the History of Ideas,* Chicago: University of Chicago Press.

Ikeda, S. (1990): "Market-Process Theory and 'Dynamic' Theories of the Market," *Southern Economic Journal,* July.

Kirzner, I. M. (1973): *Competition and Entrepreneurship,* Chicago: University of Chicago Press.

Kirzner, I. M. (1985): "The Perils of Regulation: A Market Process Approach," in Kirzner, *Discovery and the Capitalist Process,* Chicago: University of Chicago Press.

Kirzner, I. M. (1997): "Entrepreneurial Discovery and the Competitive Market Process: An Austrian Approach," *Journal of Economic Literature,* March.

Lavoie, D. (1985): *Rivalry and Central Planning: The Socialist Calculation Debate Reconsidered,* Cambridge: Cambridge University Press.

Littlechild, S. C. (1978/1986): *The Fallacy of the Mixed Economy: An "Austrian" Critique of Recent Economic Thinking and Policy,* Hobart Paper 80, Second Edition, London: The Institute of Economic Affairs.

Machovec, F. M. (1995): *Perfect Competition and the Transformation of Economics,* London and New York: Routledge.

Mises, L. von (1949): *Human Action,* New Haven: Yale University Press.

Rizzo, M. J. (1979): "Uncertainty, Subjectivity, and the Economic Analysis of Law," in Rizzo (ed.), *Time, Uncertainty, and Disequilibrium,* Lexington, Mass.: Lexington Books.

ENTREPRENEURIAL DISCOVERY AND THE COMPETITIVE MARKET PROCESS: AN AUSTRIAN APPROACH

I

The Austrian tradition is represented in modern economics by a "very vocal, feisty and dedicated subset of the economics profession" (Karen Vaughn 1994, p. xi). Much of the work of this group of scholars is devoted to the most fundamental problems of microeconomics.[1] This Austrian work, therefore, differs in character and content from a good deal of neo-classical theory which, despite widespread and growing awareness of its limitations, continues to serve as the analytical core of mainstream economics. This paper sets forth the outlines of one important approach within modern Austrian economics, an approach offering a perspective on microeconomic theory which (while it has generated a considerable literature of its own) is not ordinarily well-represented either at the (mainstream) textbook level, or in the (mainstream) journal literature. Although the author subscribes to and has contributed to this approach, the purpose of this paper is exposition, not advocacy. References in the paper to criticisms of mainstream microeconomics which have been discussed in the Austrian literature should be understood here not as arguments in favor of the Austrian approach, but as clues that may be helpful in understanding what the Austrians are saying, and how what they are

The author is deeply grateful to Mario Rizzo, Peter Boettke, and Yaw Nyarko, for extensive and helpful comments on an earlier draft. Further helpful comments were provided by Joseph T. Salerno, and by other members of the Austrian Economics Colloquium at New York University. Several anonymous referees provided many additional valuable suggestions. The author is grateful to the Sarah Scaife Foundation for research support.

From *Journal of Economic Literature* 35, 1 (March 1997): 60–85. Reprinted by permission.

1. The emphasis here on microeconomics expresses the focus of the present paper, not the scope of modern Austrian economics. For important modern Austrian contributions to macroeconomic and to monetary theory, see Roger Garrison (1978, 1984), Lawrence White (1984), George Selgin (1988), Selgin and White (1994), Steven Horwitz (1992). See also Brian Snowdon, Howard Vane, and Peter Wynarczyk (1994, ch. 8). For a link between Friedrich Hayek's macroeconomics and the Austrian microeconomics set forth in this paper, see Dieter Schmidtchen and Siegfried Utzig (1989).

saying is to be distinguished from the approach taken by other modern economists.

This paper does not offer anything like a survey of modern Austrian economics. It does not deal at all with such major areas within it, such as cycle theory, monetary theory, capital theory. Within its chosen scope of microeconomics, it does not claim to represent a universally accepted Austrian position (or even to cover its entire range of topics). Nonetheless, the approach described here is arguably central to the reviving contemporary interest in Austrian ideas, and has been treated as such in a number of recent general surveys of modern Austrian economics (Stephen Littlechild 1986; Bruce Caldwell and Stephan Boehm 1992; Vaughn 1994).[2]

During the past two decades modern Austrian economics has emerged out of the classic earlier "subjectivist" tradition[3] (which began in the late nineteenth century with Carl Menger, Eugen von Boehm-Bawerk, and Friedrich von Wieser),[4] particularly as that tradition came to be represented in the midcentury contributions of Ludwig von Mises and Friedrich Hayek.[5] The early work of the Austrian School until the 1930s was correctly perceived as simply one variant of the dominant early twentieth century mainstream approach to economic understanding (often loosely referred to as "neoclassical"). But the work of Mises and Hayek from the thirties on, steered the Austrian tradition in a direction sharply different from that being taken at that time by mainstream neoclassical microeconomics.[6] By 1950 both Mises and Hayek had crystallized separate, definitive, statements of their disagreements with mainstream

2. For an authoritative, encyclopedia-style set of surveys of modern Austrian economics, see Boettke (1994).

3. For discussions of Austrian subjectivism (and also on its influence on other schools of economic thought) see Alfred Coats (1983), Jack Wiseman (1983, 1985), Gerald O'Driscoll and Rizzo (1985, ch. 2), James Buchanan (1982), Ludwig Lachmann (1982).

4. For general surveys of the history of the Austrian tradition, see Hayek (1968), Vaughn (1994), Kirzner (1992). For collections of papers representing the work of the Austrian School from 1870 to the present see Littlechild (1990), Kirzner (1994).

5. Among the principal relevant works are Mises (1949), Hayek (1941, 1948, 1978).

6. For the thesis that these developments in the work of Mises and Hayek stemmed from their participation in the interwar debate on the possibility of socialist economic calculation, see Kirzner (1992, ch. 6).

microeconomics, and of their own substantive approaches. These were indeed separate statements, differing from one another certainly in style and, no doubt, to some degree also in substance. But it can be argued that they are best understood as both overlapping and complementary, rather than as contrasting alternatives. It was these contributions of Mises and Hayek which, while almost entirely ignored by the midcentury mainstream of the profession, have nourished the Austrian revival of the past two decades, and which have generated the modern Austrian approach to understanding the competitive market process set forth in this paper.

At the basis of this approach is the conviction that standard neoclassical microeconomics, for which the Walrasian general equilibrium model (in its modern Arrow-Debreu incarnation) is the analytical core, fails to offer a satisfying theoretical framework for understanding what happens in market economies. This conviction is rooted (a) in criticisms of the lack of relevance in models which seek to explain market phenomena as if they were, at each and every instant, strictly equilibrium phenomena, and (b) in the belief that it is a methodologically legitimate demand to be made of a theory of the market, that it not merely begin with the instrumentalist assumption of already-attained equilibrium, but also realistically offer a plausible explanation of how, from any given initial set of nonequilibrium conditions, equilibrating tendencies might be expected to be set into motion in the first place. As will be noted below, such criticisms are not (or, at any rate, no longer) *exclusively* "Austrian" criticisms. In fact, a good deal of recent non-Austrian work in microeconomics has in some fashion attempted to grapple with these difficulties. What stamps the entrepreneurial discovery approach as Austrian is not these criticisms themselves, but rather the specific positive elements of the approach.

These positive elements focus on the role of knowledge and discovery in the process of market equilibration. In particular this approach (a) sees equilibration as a systematic process in which market participants acquire more and more accurate and complete *mutual knowledge* of potential demand and supply attitudes, and (b) sees the driving force behind this systematic process in what will be described below as *entrepreneurial discovery*. Although, of course, much contemporary mainstream work in microeconomics takes its point of departure from the imperfection of knowledge (relaxing the older standard neoclassical assumption of complete, universal information), the Austrian approach set forth in this paper has little in common with this work.

For the mainstream, imperfect information is primarily a circumstance constraining the pattern of attained equilibrium (and introducing a new "production" cost, that of producing or searching for missing information). For the Austrian approach imperfect information is seen as involving an element which cannot be fitted at all into neoclassical models, that of "sheer" (i.e., unknown) ignorance. As will be developed below, sheer ignorance differs from imperfect information in that the discovery which reduces sheer ignorance is necessarily accompanied by the element of *surprise*—one had not hitherto realized one's ignorance. Entrepreneurial discovery is seen as gradually but systematically pushing back the boundaries of sheer ignorance, in this way increasing mutual awareness among market participants and thus, in turn, driving prices, output and input quantities and qualities, toward the values consistent with equilibrium (seen as the complete absence of sheer ignorance).

What will emerge from this paper is thus the exposition of an Austrian way of understanding the systematic character of markets which, while sharply differing from the mainstream competitive equilibrium model, does not necessarily see that model as totally irrelevant. (Many practical questions, such as those regarding the effects of price controls, minimum wage laws, and the like, can be answered quite adequately without going beyond simple competitive supply-and-demand equilibrium models.) The dynamic competitive process of entrepreneurial discovery (which is the driving element in this Austrian approach) is one which is seen as *tending systematically toward,* rather than away from, the path to equilibrium. Therefore, the standard, competitive equilibrium model may be seen as *more* plausible as an approximate *outcome,* in the Austrian theory here presented.[7] This aspect of the entrepreneurial discovery approach troubles a number of the Austrian economists who have not accepted it. In order to clearly locate the entrepreneurial discovery perspective within the range of modern Austrian theoretical points of view, it will be necessary briefly to identify more precisely the various disagreements which other Austrians have had with this approach.

Section II of this paper will review the Austrian criticisms of the equilibrium emphasis of the neoclassical models. Section III will develop the

7. For a critique of the use by Austrian economists (such as Mises and Murray Rothbard) of a concept (the "evenly rotating economy") which parallels that of the equilibrium state, see Tyler Cowen and Richard Fink (1985).

Austrian understanding of the market process, based upon the twin concepts of sheer (i.e., unknown) ignorance and entrepreneurial discovery. Section IV will survey several areas of applied microeconomics (anti-trust economics, welfare economics, the theory of justice, and the possibility of socialist economic calculation), taking special note of the significant differences which the Austrian approach entails in regard to policy recommendations in these areas. Section V will note the various criticisms to the entrepreneurial discovery theory developed in this paper, offered by several contemporary Austrian economists. Section VI concludes the paper by clearing up certain misunderstandings concerning the Austrian approach.

II

Mainstream microeconomics interprets the real world of markets as if observed phenomena represent the fulfillment of equilibrium conditions.[8] Markets consist of successfully maximizing agents whose decisions are held to fit in together perfectly, in the sense that each maximizing decision being made correctly anticipates, in effect, at least, all the other maximizing decisions being made simultaneously. It is this latter condition which mathematically constrains the attained values of the key decision variables. For this condition to be fulfilled, only that set of input and output prices and quantities can prevail which simultaneously satisfies the relevant equations of supply and demand (themselves constructed by aggregating the selling and buying decisions consistent with maximizing under a range of hypothesized states of affairs). It is this aspect of modern neoclassical economics which accounts for its characteristic emphasis upon: (a) the constrained maximization pattern imposed by the theory upon individual decision making, and (b) the mathematics of simultaneous equation systems. Valiant attempts have been made to enrich the realism of these equilibrium microeconomic models by building into them assumptions acknowledging imperfections in competition. Nonetheless, the dominant trend has been to concentrate upon models of *competitive* equilibrium, that is, upon models in which both prices and product/resource qualities are taken as given to each decision maker, and as being independent of the decisions made. Not

8. It has been strongly argued by Frank Machovec (1995) that the great neoclassical economists of the period before 1930 did *not* proceed in this manner.

only do these competitive models (like all equilibrium models) assume complete mutual knowledge (in the relevant sense), they also assume, in effect, that the crucial market variables of price and quality are somehow presented to each decision maker as an external fact of nature. Neoclassical economics operates on the assumption that the world reflects the relationships that would prevail in such equilibrium models—with the model of competitive equilibrium being the favorite one. While Austrians have not been alone in criticizing this approach to understanding markets, their criticisms have been both pioneering and trenchant.

Austrian dissatisfaction with this standard approach to understanding real world market phenomena emerged most clearly in the forties. Both Mises and Hayek expressed dismay at models labeled as competitive, in which market participants are forbidden, as it were, from competing (in the sense in which, in everyday discourse and experience, market participants compete by bidding higher prices or by offering to undersell competitors, by offering consumers better quality merchandise, better service, and the like; see Mises 1949, p. 278ftn; Hayek 1948, pp. 92–118). Their unhappiness with models of so-called perfect competition ultimately stemmed from their unwillingness to surrender the economists' insights into the dynamic character of active markets to equilibrium models, in which all decisions have somehow been pre-reconciled, held as at all times governing market phenomena. It seems accurate to understand their impatience with the neoclassical preoccupation with equilibrium models as arising from (a) the blatantly false nature of the assumption that market conditions are at all times in equilibrium, and (b) methodological unease with an instrumentalist mode of theorizing and empirical analysis that finds it useful to presume that equilibrium always prevails, while recognizing no obligation to account theoretically for any equilibrative process (from which equilibrium might be explained as emerging).

Modern presentations of the entrepreneurial discovery approach have echoed these criticisms of equilibrium economics, and have deployed these criticisms in seeking to demote the concept of perfect competition from its position of dominance in modern neoclassical theory, in order to replace it by notions of dynamic competition (in which market participants are, instead of exclusively price takers, competitive price—and quality—makers). Within the two broad bases for Austrian (as well as for non-Austrian) criticism, several strands of difficulty with the neoclassical

competitive equilibrium paradigm may be distinguished. The clear identification of these strands will help us understand the Austrian character
of the positive approach, based on entrepreneurial discovery, to be developed in Section III.

(a) Criticisms of the unrealistic character of neoclassical theory relate
to both the way in which individual decisions are modeled in that theory,
and the way in which that theory sees real world market outcomes as satisfying the conditions for equilibrium.

(i) At the individual level Austrians have taken sharp exception to the
manner in which neoclassical theory has portrayed the individual decision as a mechanical exercise in constrained maximization. Such a portrayal robs human choice of its essentially open-ended character, in which
imagination and boldness must inevitably play central roles. For neoclassical theory the only way human choice can be rendered analytically trac-
table, is for it to be modeled as if it were *not* made in open-ended fashion,
as if there was *no* scope for qualities such as imagination and boldness.
Even though standard neoclassical theory certainly deals extensively with
decision making under (Knightian) risk,[9] this is entirely consistent with
absence of scope for the qualities of imagination and boldness, because
such decision making is seen as being made in the context of known
probability functions. In the neoclassical world, decision makers know
what they are ignorant about. One is never surprised. For Austrians, however, to abstract from these qualities of imagination, boldness, and surprise is to denature human choice entirely.[10]

Now we should emphasize that a good deal of critical attention has been
directed in recent years by non-Austrians at the neoclassical assumption
of perfect information. A significant literature has shown how imperfect
information may, as a consequence of entailed externalities, render the
equilibrium outcomes of market economies inefficient in terms of Paretian criteria. It is however necessary to dispel a certain confusion which
has arisen in this regard. Joseph Stiglitz (1994, pp. 24f.) who has been
a central contributor to this critical literature, has taken note of what he
believes to be the parallel Austrian concern with imperfect information.

9. Frank Knight developed his classic distinction between risk and uncertainty in
Knight (1921).

10. (See for example, Ernest Pasour 1982 and Naomi Moldofsky 1982; see also
George Shackle 1972; Buchanan 1979.)

He has also (1994, p. 43) drawn attention to what he understands as the contrary Austrian view, namely, that it claims informational efficiency for the price system. We should emphasize that, on both these points, he has missed the crucial element that sharply distinguishes the unknown ignorance (with which Austrians have been concerned) from the imperfect information (central to the critical literature in which Stiglitz himself has been a pioneer). For Stiglitz "imperfect information" refers to known-to-be-available information which it is costly to produce. But for Austrians the focus is upon what has been termed "previously unthought-of knowledge" (Esteban Thomsen 1992, p. 61). In Section III we shall return to see how, as a consequence of this distinction, Austrian appreciation for the discovery potential of market processes does not at all imply that "informational efficiency" for market outcomes which Stiglitz has denied.

(ii) At the market level, Austrians have rebelled against a microeconomics which can find coherence in markets and can explain market phenomena only by asserting that markets are, at all times, to be treated as if already in the attained relevant state of equilibrium.

Such a picture of the world Austrians find simply false, not merely in the sense that an explanatory theoretical model may, obviously, not offer a photographic representation of the richly complex reality it is being used to explain, but in the sense that this picture falsely labels important features of reality. For Austrians it is unacceptable to claim that, at each and every instant, the configuration of production and consumption decisions currently made, is one which could, in the light of the relevant costs, not possibly have been improved upon. To claim that, at any given instant, all conceivably relevant available opportunities have been instantaneously grasped, is to fly in the face of what we *know* about real world economic systems. It is one thing to postulate rapid equilibrating processes as imposing systematic order upon markets; it is quite another thing (in the *absence* of any theory of equilibrative processes!) to treat the world as at all times already in the attained state of equilibrium.[11]

(b) The basic methodological foundation for Austrian unhappiness with mainstream neoclassical preoccupation with equilibrium models, has not so much to do with the false and misleading picture of real

---

11. For examples of Austrian literature critical of the standard equilibrium approach see Rizzo (1979), Sanford Ikeda (1990). For a mainstream reaction to this literature see Christopher Phelan (1987). See also Brian Loasby (1994), David Harper (1994a).

markets, which standard deployment of these models entails, as with the instrumentalist view of theory which the neoclassical equilibrium-preoccupation came to express. Austrians, in this version of their criticism, need have no quarrel with equilibrium models as such. No doubt significant features of real world market economies can indeed be illuminated by use of such models. But, the Austrian criticism runs, we are surely entitled to demand a theoretical basis for the claim that equilibrating processes systematically mold market variables in a direction consistent with the conditions postulated in the equilibrium models. If competitive markets are to be explained in terms of Marshallian supply-and-demand diagrams, surely we are entitled to a theoretical process— "story" which might account for the economists' confidence in the special relevance of the intersection point in that supply-and-demand diagram. In our undergraduate freshman classes we do offer such stories: if above equilibrium prices prevail, this generates surplus of supply over demand; these surpluses force prices downwards, etc., etc. But strictly speaking, these plausible stories are, within the neoclassical framework, quite illegitimate. That framework requires us simply to accept equilibrium models as the only explanatory tool necessary for understanding prices and outputs. This, for Austrians, is methodologically unacceptable. What, we must ask, accounts for the powerful equilibrating tendencies which economists believe to be operating in markets? If, at any time, real world limitations upon the perfection of information possessed have prevented instantaneous attainment of equilibrium, why should we have confidence in any possible equilibrative process?[12] And how, if we do observe such equilibrating processes, can we understand what has generated them?[13]

Kenneth Arrow's well known paper of 1959 offers an excellent illustration of (a) how a foremost exponent of the neoclassical approach perceptively recognized one aspect of the problem upon which this latter Austrian criticism has focused, and (b) how this led him to develop an analytical dynamics from which the standard competitive equilibrium model emerges only as the outcome of a process. Arrow focused his

12. This confidence has, in recent literature, been challenged also on the grounds of possible path-dependency. See for example Brian Arthur (1989), Robin Cowan (1990).

13. For literature on the role of process theory in economics, see particularly Jack High (1990), Lachmann (1986), Ikeda (1990, 1994), Wolfgang Kerber (1994). For a pioneering contribution, see George B. Richardson (1960).

attention upon the Marshallian perfectly competitive supply-and-demand model in the single commodity market, and especially, upon the requirement of this model that supply equal demand. He draws attention to the logical gap in the perfectly competitive model:

> Each individual participant in the economy is supposed to take prices as given and determine his choices as to purchases and sales accordingly; there is no one left over whose job it is to make a decision on price. (Arrow 1959, p. 43)

He overcomes this difficulty by proposing that it be recognized "that perfect competition can really prevail only at equilibrium" (Arrow 1959, p. 41). In disequilibrium each supplier faces a downward sloping demand curve and, acting "monopolistically," seeks an optimal price-quantity combination. The equilibrating process operates through each supplier discovering that (as a result of the comparable activities of his fellow "monopolists") his demand curve is shifting "at the same time as he is exploring it" (Arrow 1959, p. 46).

Arrow recognized that the very notion of a perfectly competitive market in disequilibrium is incoherent. And he recognized an obligation to offer a model that might account for the emergence, out of initial disequilibrium, of an equilibrating process. His critique of the core of neoclassicism illustrates well the vulnerability of mainstream theory to the Austrian criticisms discussed in this section. A number of non-Austrian writers have followed Arrow's critique, and Franklin Fisher's (1983) important contribution attracted a modest amount of professional attention. Nonetheless, the mainstream has proceeded by virtually ignoring these criticisms, and operating as if its core paradigm was, by and large, as relevant as ever.

Austrians maintain that a theoretical framework for understanding the equilibrative process is available. This framework offers its explanation not by denying the operation of competition in disequilibrium but per contra (and in sharpest contrast to Arrow's labeling system), by reformulating the notion of competition to make it utterly *inconsistent* with the equilibrium state.

III

The entrepreneurial discovery approach which has emerged in modern Austrian economics during the past quarter of a century was developed out of elements derived from Mises and from Hayek. From Mises the modern

Austrians learned to see the market as an *entrepreneurially* driven *process*. From Hayek they learned to appreciate the role of *knowledge* and its enhancement through market interaction, for the equilibrative process. These two distinct elements have been welded into an integrated theoretical framework which, on the one hand, is consistent with and, on the other hand, is articulated in a manner more explicit than the earlier Austrian expositions.[14]

Mises' conception of the market as an entrepreneurially driven process pervades his mature theoretical work.

> The driving force of the market process is provided neither by the consumers nor by the owners of the means of productions—land, capital goods, and labor—but by the promoting and speculating entrepreneurs ... Profit-seeking speculation is the driving force of the market as it is the driving force of production. (Mises 1949, pp. 325–26)

"The activities of the entrepreneur are the element that would bring about the unrealizable state of the evenly rotating economy if no further changes were to occur" (Mises 1949, p. 335). "In the imaginary construction of the evenly rotating economy there is no room left for entrepreneurial activity ..." (Mises 1949, p. 253). The focus here is on the market *process*, as opposed to the "imaginary construct" of the "evenly rotating economy" (corresponding roughly to the state of general market equilibrium).

Entrepreneurial activity has no place at all in neoclassical equilibrium microeconomics (because it is inconsistent with the conditions satisfied in the equilibrium state; William Baumol 1993, ch. 1). But for Austrians the entrepreneurial role provides the theoretical key with which to account for the market as a process. For Mises, the economist

> shows how the activities of enterprising men, the promoters and speculators, eager to profit from discrepancies in the price structure, tend toward eradicating such discrepancies ... He shows how this process would finally result in the establishment of the evenly rotating economy. This is the task of economic theory. The mathematical description of various states of equilibrium is mere play. The problem is the analysis of the market process. (Mises 1949, pp. 352–53)

14. For excellent modern Austrian expositions of the approach developed in this section see Martti Vihanto (1989, 1994). For discussions which are at least partly critical of the Austrian approach see Loasby (1989, ch. 10) and Claudia Loy (1988).

Hayek's emphasis on the role of knowledge and its enhancement in the course of the market process goes back to his work in the thirties. It was Hayek who insisted that

> the concept of equilibrium merely means that the foresight of the different members of the society is . . . correct . . . in the sense that every person's plan is based on the expectation of just those actions of other people which those other people intend to perform and that all these plans are based on the expectation of the same set of external facts . . . Correct foresight is then . . . the defining characteristic of a state of equilibrium. (Hayek 1948, p. 42)

In his pioneering discussion of the equilibrating process Hayek pointed out that, "if we want to make the assertion that, under certain conditions, people will approach (the equilibrium state), we must explain by what process they will acquire the necessary knowledge" (Hayek 1948, p. 46).

For Hayek the equilibrating process is thus one during which market participants acquire better mutual information concerning the plans being made by fellow market participants. For Mises this process is driven by the daring, imaginative, speculative actions of entrepreneurs who see opportunities for pure profit in the conditions of disequilibrium. What permits us to recognize that these two perspectives on the character of the market process are mutually reinforcing, is the place which each of these two writers assigns to *competition* in the market process. The Austrian approach includes a concept of competition which differs drastically from the encapsulated in the label "competitive" as used in modern neoclassical theory.

For neoclassical economics the maximum possible degree of competition is represented by the equilibrium notion of perfect competition, in which all traces of rivalry are absent. Anything less than perfect elasticity in the supply/demand curves faced by potential buyers/sellers corresponds, in neoclassical terminology, to some degree of monopolistic power.[15] Mises rejected this nomenclature, in that it implies that monopoly prices are somehow determined without that competitive process which constitutes for Mises the essence of the market. "Catallactic competition is no less a factor in the determination of monopoly prices than it is in the determination

---

15. See George Stigler (1957) for the emergence of the view that explicitly rejects rivalrousness as an ingredient in competitive analysis.

of competitive prices . . . On the market every commodity competes with all other commodities" (Mises 1949, p. 278). He cites Hayek's critique of the doctrines of imperfect or monopolistic competition (Mises 1949, p. 278 fn.), and emphasizes that competition (far from being defined, as in the perfectly competitive model, as the state in which all participants face identical prices) "manifests itself in the facts that the sellers must outdo one another by offering better or cheaper goods and services and that the buyers must outdo one another by offering higher prices" (Mises 1949, p. 274). In other words, the essence of competition is precisely that dynamic rivalry which the neoclassical equilibrium notion of competition is at great pains to exclude. Hayek's pathbreaking critique of the dominance of the perfectly competitive model (and hence also of the corollary doctrines of imperfect and monopolistic competition) takes as its point of departure precisely this feature of the model. That model, he points out, deals

> with a state of what is called "competitive equilibrium" in which it is assumed that the data for the different individuals are fully adjusted to each other, while the problem which requires explanation is the nature of the process by which the data are thus adjusted. (Hayek 1948, p. 94)

For Hayek, on the other hand, "competition is by its nature a dynamic process whose essential characteristics are assumed away by the assumptions underlying static analysis" (Hayek 1948, p. 94). "Competition," he insists,

> is essentially a process of the formation of opinion . . . a process which involves a continuous change in the data and whose significance must therefore be completely missed by any theory which treats these data as constant. (Hayek 1948, p. 106)

In other words the role of competition in economic theory must, for both Mises and Hayek, focus not on the state of affairs at the end of the market process, but upon the character of that process itself. More recently Hayek has emphasized the nature of competition as a "discovery procedure"— i.e., as generating "such facts as, without resort to it, would not be known to anyone . . ." (Hayek 1978, p. 179).

For the modern Austrian approach, this perception of competition as the dynamic, driving force for discovery in the market process has become central. The key to an explanation of the equilibrative process is to recognize the pivotal role of dynamic competition in that process. This equilibrative process of competition is at work even in markets in which one firm may enjoy monopolistic privilege. This is because even a monopolistic equilibrium can be approached, in a world of uncertainty, only through a process whereby market participants can become better aware of one another's attitudes and plans. Only the process of competition can achieve this.[16]

We have thus placed our finger on the key interrelated analytical concepts with which the modern Austrian entrepreneurial discovery theory of the market process operates. These concepts are: (a) the entrepreneurial role; (b) the role of discovery; (c) rivalrous competition. Each of these requires some brief discussion.

A. The Entrepreneurial Role

In standard neoclassical equilibrium theory there is, by its very character, no role for the entrepreneur. In equilibrium there is no scope for pure profit: there is simply nothing for the entrepreneur to do. (If textbooks do speak of the entrepreneur in the theory of the firm this turns out to refer simply and imprecisely to the owner of the firm who, operating in equilibrium markets, is indeed able to "maximize," but who has no opportunity to sell output at a price exceeding costs.)[17] If the entrepreneur grasps the opportunities for pure entrepreneurial profit created by temporary absence of full adjustment between input and output markets, the neoclassical market in full equilibrium can, of course, find no room for him. In Austrian theory the entrepreneur is an agent whose character has been carefully explored.

---

16. It follows that monopolistic (or monopolistically competitive) equilibrium *states* are entirely compatible with the notion of dynamic competition (which might in fact bring about such states).

17. The statement in the text presumes that rents earned by firms who own scarce, non-reproducible resources used in their production operations are (although included in accounting "profit") properly to be included in the firms' economic costs. These firms certainly enjoy an advantage over other firms who, not owning these resources, must produce with resources of lower productivity. But this advantage consists, for the economist (as distinct from the accountant), not in entrepreneurial profit won by the fortunate firms, but rather in rental income earned through asset *ownership*. The entrepreneur is considered as hiring these resources from himself as owner, and should then include this rental income as part of his (implicit) economic costs. For a full and classic discussion of the sense in which differential rent on assets owned are properly included in the firm's economic costs, see Fritz Machlup (1952, pp. 237f., 288ff.).

For Mises the term "entrepreneur" refers to "acting man in regard to the changes occurring in the data of the market" (Mises 1949, p. 255). Entrepreneurship is human action "seen from the aspect of the uncertainty inherent in every action" (Mises 1949, p. 254). The Misesian concept of human action thus implies the open-ended framework within which all decisions made must necessarily partake of the speculative character essential to the notion of entrepreneurship. "In any real and living economy every actor is always an entrepreneur" (Mises 1949, p. 253). By freeing microeconomic analysis from the constrictions of the equilibrium state, Austrian theory is able to recognize the speculative element in all individual decision making, and to incorporate the activity of the real world businessman into a theoretical framework that provides understanding of the market process. In focusing upon the entrepreneurial decision in a Knight-uncertain world, Austrian theory thus diverges sharply from the notion of the individual decision that constitutes the analytical building block of neoclassical microtheory. For neoclassical microtheory each decision, whether made by consumer, firm, or resource owner, is made within a definitely known framework made up of a given objective function, a given set of resource constraints, and a given set of technologically or economically feasible ways of transforming resources into desired objectives. (Uncertainty, while of course recognized as surrounding each decision, expresses itself in the form of known probability distributions relating to the given elements of this known framework.) In this neoclassical context, there is no room for entrepreneurship, not only in the sense (mentioned earlier) that no opportunities for pure profit can possibly exist, but also in the sense that the model precludes all Knightian uncertainty that might affect the character of the individual decision. Boldness, imagination, drive are characteristics which are simply irrelevant to individual decision making in neoclassical microtheory.

This Austrian emphasis on the entrepreneur is fundamental.[18] Whereas each neoclassical decision maker operates in a world of *given*

18. For an example of Austrian work in an applied field in which this emphasis on entrepreneurship is central, see Charles Baird (1987). For general discussion of this Austrian emphasis, see also Jochen Runde (1988). A work which, while on the whole sharply critical of the Austrian approach, provides a very insightful exposition of it, is Stavros Ioannides (1992, especially chs. 3, 4, 5). Other valuable recent critical discussions of Austrian entrepreneurial theory include Martin Ricketts (1992), Vaughn (1994, pp. 141ff.), Harper (1994b).

price and output data, the Austrian entrepreneur operates to *change* price/output data. In this way, as we shall see, the entrepreneurial role drives the ever-changing process of the market. Where shortages have existed, we understand the resulting price increases as driven by entrepreneurs recognizing, in the face of the uncertainty of the real world, the profit opportunities available through the expansion of supply through production, or through arbitrage. Except in the never-attained state of complete equilibrium, each market is characterized by opportunities for pure entrepreneurial profit. These opportunities are created by earlier entrepreneurial errors which have resulted in shortages, surplus, misallocated resources. The daring, alert entrepreneur discovers these earlier errors, buys where prices are "too low" and sells where prices are "too high." In this way low prices are nudged higher, high prices are nudged lower; price discrepancies are narrowed in the equilibrative direction. Shortages are filled, surpluses are whittled away; quantity gaps tend to be eliminated in the equilibrative direction. In a world of ceaselessly changing tastes, resource availabilities, and known technological possibilities, this entrepreneurial process cannot guarantee rapid (or slow) convergence to a state of equilibrium. But it does at each moment guarantee profit-incentives tending to nudge the market in what, from the perspective of that moment, must be recognized as the equilibrative direction.

The critical question for an entrepreneurial theory of market process is how to understand, in the existence of such profit-incentives, the existence also of a systematic tendency for entrepreneurial errors to be replaced by profit-making entrepreneurial corrections. For this aspect of the entrepreneurial discovery theory we must postulate a tendency for the profit opportunities generated by earlier entrepreneurial error, *to be noticed and grasped.* The Austrian approach indeed includes such a postulate. To appreciate this we turn to the second of the above listed three key analytical elements in this approach.

B. The Role of Discovery

We have already seen that Hayek pioneered in interpreting the equilibrative market process as a process of mutual discovery. In the course of this process market participants become better informed of the plans being made by other participants. Whereas some initial plans must, as a result of initial entrepreneurial error, turn out to have been mistaken, these errors tend systematically to become eliminated as market experience reveals the infeasibility of some (hitherto sought after) courses of action and the (hitherto unnoticed) profitability of other courses of action. In the world of static equilibrium, a chosen course of action, because it was pronounced mathematically to have been the optimal course of action within the given decision framework, cannot fail to be chosen again and again, so long as that given framework prevails. In the market-process world of entrepreneurial discovery, on the other hand, flawed plans (i.e., those made on the basis of an erroneously imagined decision framework) can be expected to tend to be corrected through the responsiveness of alert, imaginative entrepreneurs to the opportunities revealed as a result of the initially flawed plans. In other words, this approach postulates a tendency for profit opportunities to be *discovered* and *grasped* by routine-resisting entrepreneurial market participants.

In the neoclassical context a decision can never be *corrected*—because no decision can ever be *truly* mistaken. The reason for a *change* in a decision, thus can be found only in an exogenously generated change in the relevant decision-framework. But in the Austrian context a decision can be *corrected* as a result of the decision maker's discovery of an earlier *error* in his view of the world. Whereas earlier plans had overlooked available profit opportunities (as, for example, where some buyers buy goods at high prices, that were being sold elsewhere in the same market for lower prices), subsequent plans can be expected to reflect discovery of the profit opportunities implicit in (and constituted by) the earlier plans. We should acknowledge that, from the neoclassical perspective, it is not at all obvious why we should expect such discoveries to be made.

After all, it may be objected from the mainstream economist's point of view, if an available opportunity for profit was universally overlooked yesterday, why should we expect that opportunity to be noticed today? It is not as if that profit opportunity was the object of systematic search (in which case it might be expected that a time consuming search process would identify it sooner or later). An opportunity for pure profit cannot, by its nature, be the object of systematic search. Systematic search can be undertaken for a piece of missing information, but only because the searcher is aware of the nature of what he does not know, and is aware with greater or lesser certainty of the way to find out the missing information. In the economics of search literature, therefore, search is correctly treated as any other deliberate process of production. But it is in the nature of an overlooked profit opportunity that it has been *utterly* overlooked, i.e., that one is not aware at all that one has missed the grasping of any profit. From the neoclassical perspective, therefore, a missed opportunity might seem (except as a result of sheer, fortuitous good luck) to be destined for permanent obscurity.

It is here that the Austrian perspective offers a new insight, into the nature of *surprise* and *discovery*. When one becomes aware of what one had previously overlooked, one has not produced knowledge in any deliberate sense. What has occurred is that one has discovered one's previous (utterly unknown) ignorance. What distinguishes *discovery* (relevant to hitherto unknown profit opportunities) from *successful search* (relevant to the deliberate production of information which one knew one had lacked) is that the former (unlike the latter) involves that *surprise* which accompanies the realization that one had overlooked something in fact readily available. ("It was under my very nose!") This feature of *discovery* characterizes the entrepreneurial process of the equilibrating market. What accounts for a systematic tendency toward that succession of wholesome surprises which must constitute the equilibrative process, is not any implausible series of happy accidents, but rather the natural *alertness* (Kirzner 1973, pp. 35f., 65f.) to possible opportunities (or the danger of possible disaster) which is characteristic of human beings. In the world of uncertainty such natural alertness expresses itself in the boldness and imagination which Austrian theory ascribes to entrepreneurs in the context of the market. Entrepreneurial alertness refers to an attitude of receptiveness to available (but hitherto overlooked) opportunities. The entrepreneurial character of human action refers not simply to the circumstance that action is taken in an open-ended, uncertain world, but also to the circumstance that the human agent is at all times spontaneously on the lookout for hitherto unnoticed features of the environment (present or future), which might inspire new activity on his part. Without knowing what to look for, without deploying any deliberate search technique, the entrepreneur is at all times scanning the horizon, as it were, ready to make discoveries. Each such discovery will be accompanied by a sense of surprise (at one's earlier unaccountable ignorance). An entrepreneurial attitude is one which is always ready to be surprised, always ready to take the steps needed to profit by such surprises. *The notion of discovery, midway between that of the deliberately produced information in standard search theory, and that of sheer windfall gain generated by pure chance, is central to the Austrian approach.*[19] The profit opportunities created by earlier entrepreneurial error do tend systematically to stimulate subsequent entrepreneurial discovery. The entrepreneurial process so set into motion is a process tending toward better mutual awareness among market participants. The lure of pure profit in this way sets up the process through which pure profit tends to be competed away. Enhanced mutual awareness, via the entrepreneurial discovery process, is the source of the market's equilibrative properties.

Austrians are careful to insist (i) that continual change in tastes, resource availabilities, and known technological possibilities always prevent this equilibrative process from proceeding anywhere near to completion; and (ii) that entrepreneurial boldness and imagination can lead to pure entrepreneurial losses as well as to pure profit. Mistaken actions by entrepreneurs mean that they have misread the market, possibly pushing price and output constellations in directions not equilibrative. The entrepreneurial market process may indeed reflect a systematically equilibrative *tendency,* but this by no means constitutes a *guaranteed* unidirectional, flawlessly converging trajectory. What the Austrian entrepreneurial discovery process seeks to explain is not any imaginary mechanical sure-fire convergence to equilibrium, but rather the existence and nature of those important tendencies which markets display toward continual discovery and exploitation of pure profit opportunities thus tending to nudge the market in the equilibrative direction. In this process the capacity of market participants to discover earlier error, is central.[20]

C. Rivalrous Competition

What drives the market process is entrepreneurial boldness and imagination; what constitutes that process is the series of discoveries generated by that entrepreneurial boldness and alertness. Austrians are at pains to emphasize the dynamically competitive character of such a process. The process is made possible by the freedom of entrepreneurs to

19. For further discussion of the Austrian concept of discovery, see Kirzner (1989, ch, 2). See also Littlechild (1982a), Michael Beesley and Littlechild (1989), Manfred Streit (1992).

20. For clarification of possible misunderstandings concerning this claim for equilibrative tendencies in markets, see Section VI below.

enter markets in which they see opportunities for profit. In being alert to such opportunities and in grasping them, entrepreneurs are competing with other entrepreneurs. This competition is not the competitive state achieved in neoclassical equilibrium models, in which all market participants are buying or selling identical commodities, at uniform prices. It is, instead, the rivalrous process we encounter in the everyday business world, in which each entrepreneur seeks to outdo his rivals in offering goods to consumers (recognizing that, because those rivals have not been offering the best possible deals to consumers, profits can be made by offering consumers better deals).[21]

It is from this perspective that Austrians stress (i) the discovery potential in rivalrous competition, and (ii) the entrepreneurial character of rivalrous competition. The competition that characterizes the market process reveals information which no one was aware of its having been lacking. (This, as we shall see in Section IV, will be of importance in assessing the possibility of the deliberate engineering, in a socialist economy, by central planners, of the kinds of outcomes yielded in a capitalist economy by the competitive market process.) This is what Hayek had in mind when he referred to competition "as a discovery procedure" (Hayek 1978, p. 179). The competitive process is an entrepreneurial one in that it depends crucially on the incentives provided by the possibility of pure entrepreneurial profit. From this perspective profit emerges most importantly not as evidence of entrepreneurial error (which it certainly is), but as the powerful incentive to keep down the incidence of entrepreneurial error.

As noted in Section II, Stiglitz saw Austrians as claiming "informational efficiency" (in the Paretian sense) for this "discovery procedure" of the market. This is not the case. The knowledge gained through the discovery process of the market refers to the "unthought-of knowledge" with which Austrians have been concerned. Ignorance of this unthought-of knowledge is responsible for failure to attain equilibrium. Attainment of equilibrium, imagined as the eventual outcome of an uninterrupted process of market discovery, does not attribute informational efficiency

21. For the existence of a long tradition in economics in which rivalrous competition was recognized, see Paul McNulty (1967), Robert Ekelund and Robert Hebert (1981). For modern Austrian (or Austrian-influenced) discussions of dynamic competition, see Donald Boudreaux (1994), Dominick Armentano (1978), Mark Addleson (1994), Thomas Arthur (1994), Harald Kunz (1989).

to that state of equilibrium. The informational inefficiency which Stiglitz and his colleagues have attributed to equilibrium states, relate, on the other hand, to "known ignorance," that is, to "known-to-be-available" information which it is costly to produce.[22]

IV

The entrepreneurial discovery approach offers a theoretical framework for understanding how markets work. This framework has important practical implications for applied economics and for economic policy. We briefly take note of four areas of application where the Austrian approach implies sharply different practical conclusions from those usually derived from neoclassical economics. A number of additional areas of application might also have been explored here. Examples of such areas, omitted here because of space constraints are: law and economics (see for example Rizzo 1979), and the economics of transition (see for example Boettke 1993). The four areas examined are: (a) antitrust policy; (b) the applicability of accepted theories of economic justice; (c) welfare economics; (d) the workability of central planning under socialism.

A. Antitrust Policy

Standard economics, built upon neoclassical insights into the Pareto-efficiency qualities of perfectly competitive equilibrium, has for most of this century been deployed to support antitrust policy limiting firm size (both absolutely and relative to the industry). Despite the healthy dose of realism introduced into antitrust economics in recent decades, and despite the substantive theoretical improvements introduced into our understanding of competition by the theory of contestable markets, it remains the case that standard microeconomics sees the ideal degree of competition as represented by the perfectly competitive model. The Austrian view sees matters quite differently.

For the Austrian approach competition is socially beneficial primarily in a dynamic sense. Coordination tends to be induced among the

---

22. The paragraph in the text has the objective of making clear the distinction between the quite separate aspects of imperfect information treated respectively by Stiglitz and by the Austrians. It does not have the objective of providing an Austrian critique of Stiglitz's position. For such a critique see Thomsen (1992, ch. 3). See also Boehm (1989, pp. 208f.), and Thomsen (1994).

decisions made in the market place under the pressure of rivalrous entrepreneurs alert to the profit-opportunities created by initial discoordination. To harness the entrepreneurial initiative intrinsic to this kind of dynamic competition, we do not require fulfillment of the classic Knightian conditions for perfect competition—in fact those conditions *preclude* scope for (and, in fact, any need for) entrepreneurial initiative. The perfect knowledge requirement central to the perfectly competitive model can in fact be satisfied only by assuming away the need for any coordinative process. To induce dynamic entrepreneurial competition we require the fulfillment of only one condition: guaranteeing free entrepreneurial entry into any market where profit opportunities may be perceived to exist. Most of the insights of contestable market theory turn out not only to be consistent with the entrepreneurial discovery approach, but in fact to be implied by that approach. To limit the size of firms (for example by obstructing mergers) is, in the entrepreneurial discovery approach, to block entrepreneurial entry, and is thus *anti*-competitive in the relevant sense. Conversely, many aspects of real world business activity, involving such practices as advertising, or any of innumerable forms of product differentiation, set down as imperfectly competitive or even as "monopolistic" in the standard framework (because they imply less than perfectly elastic demand curves facing firms), are precisely the kinds of entrepreneurial initiative which make up the dynamic competitive process.[23]

B. Economic Justice

There are many policy issues which hinge upon public perceptions of economic justice or injustice. In recent decades economists have explored the economic justice of alternative economic policies. In this they have been following a venerable tradition in economics. When John Bates Clark wrote his *Distribution of Wealth* almost a century ago, his motivation, in developing the tools of marginal productivity theory, was to demonstrate the consistency of capitalism with economic justice. One significant implication of the entrepreneurial discovery approach has

23. For an excellent example of non-Austrian appreciation for these considerations, see Fisher, John McGowan, and Joen Greenwood (1983), Yale Brozen (1982). Among Austrian (or Austrian-inspired) writers on this issue, see Armentano (1986), Beesley and Littlechild (1989), Thomas DiLorenzo and High (1988), Michael DeBow (1991).

been that it appears to cast crucial aspects of the capitalist system in a drastically different ethical light than has traditionally emerged from the neoclassical perspective.

Neoclassical economics asks us to rule on the justice of the method through which or the pattern in which a *given* (known-to-be-knowable) *pie* is distributed among the potential claimants to it. This may be seen as a pie of given output; or, in more sophisticated versions, it may be seen as the yet-to-be-determined pie to be baked out of given inputs. This "given-pie" framework for discussion of economic justice restricts us to considering the justice of capitalist earnings or receipts in regard only to already existing goods (including already existing inputs with the capability of generating alternative outputs). From the Austrian perspective, such restriction places artificial blinders upon our ethical assessment of capitalist incomes.

In the Austrian perspective there must be afforded the possibility, at least, of considering the justice also of *discovered* income. A discovered income is one gained not by earning or otherwise receiving a share of any given pie, but one gained by discovering the existence of something valuable, the very existence of which was hitherto wholly unknown. Discovery would include not only one of hitherto unknown natural resources (as in an oil discovery) but also of new kinds of output (as through entrepreneurial product-innovation), or of new additional productivity (of known outputs) available from known inputs (as when an entrepreneur innovates a new productive technique). The earmark of a genuine discovery is that it reveals the existence of something concerning which one had not been merely ignorant, but in fact *utterly* ignorant (in the sense that one was not even aware of one's ignorance). All kinds of discovery essentially create something genuinely new, something simply not present (as far as human knowledge up until now could fathom) in the pie of available inputs and outputs given just prior to the moment of discovery.

The making of a genuine discovery is not an act of deliberate production (in this it differs also from a successful deliberate search). Neither is it simply the fortuitous outcome of a stroke of wholly undeserved luck. Discovery is attributable, at least in significant degree, to the entrepreneurial alertness of the discoverer. A theory of justice built upon a perspective which compels us to refrain from considering and therefore recognizing the moral character of discovered gain must, from the Austrian perspective, appear seriously incomplete if not wholly misconceived.

All this has, of course, particular relevance to judging the justice of *pure entrepreneurial profits*. Such profits simply do not fit into the neo-classical distributional scheme, and, therefore, defy any justification within standard theories of justice otherwise sympathetic to capitalist distribution patterns.[24] For the Austrian viewpoint, however, pure entre-preneurial profits emerge clearly as the wholly discovered gains, which accompany entrepreneurial creation and discovery in the sphere of pro-duction. An understanding of pure profits in this manner permits the economist to explain more accurately (to the philosopher, citizen, or statesman engaged in moral judgments concerning capitalist justice) the true economic character of what they are evaluating.[25]

C. Welfare Economics

Neoclassical economics includes an analytical framework designed to assess the social efficiency of alternative arrangements, policies, and events. The Austrian approach to understanding markets outlined in this paper, implies a certain dissatisfaction also with the neoclassical approach to welfare economics. The cause for this dissatisfaction can be identified in straightforward fashion.

Standard welfare theory considers the allocation pattern governing the uses made of society's resources at a given instant (or, by strict extension, to a given intertemporal allocation pattern being irrevocably adopted at that instant). The theory then analyzes that pattern from a perspective of imag-ined omniscience, against the socially optimal allocative pattern implied by the data. Austrian economists along with many other economists are of course deeply concerned by the well-understood analytical difficulties (especially for methodological individualists) of defining what "socially optimal allocation" is to mean, within the neoclassical framework.[26] But

24. See for example Clark (1899, p. 201). For a discussion of Robert Nozick's (1974) theory of justice in regard to profit, see Kirzner (1989, p. 69f.).

25. These observations on an Austrian view of economic justice have been advanced by the present writer (Kirzner 1989). They do not substantially overlap with the observations concerning justice expressed either by Mises or by Hayek.

26. For Austrian critiques of standard notions of social efficiency, see Rizzo (1979), Rothbard (1979).

the Austrian dissatisfaction of interest to us in the present context has a different root. The entrepreneurial discovery approach reminds us that the degree of achieved social efficiency (or even the degree of efficiency that will be achieved in the equilibrium state toward which a market may be converging) is not the only dimension along which to judge the economic success of a social system. Just as important, surely, is the speed and accuracy with which the system is able to identify and overcome the waste and discoordination of disequilibrium situations. Standard welfare theory provides no scope for considering this dimension, because this discoordination involves that sheer ignorance which cannot be incorporated into neoclassical analysis (so that intertemporal welfare analysis cannot grapple with, or even consider, the question of how rapidly—or whether— the volume of sheer ignorance is being reduced).

Up to now, it must be acknowledged, Austrian economics has—with one important exception to be noted below—not done much more than to identify this serious shortcoming of standard welfare economics. But this identification (and its being related to the social function of the entrepreneurial discovery process) must be considered already a significant step forward.[27] As a result of this step, Austrian economists are not satisfied to ask, in regard to issues such as tax policy and the like, merely what impact will a given program have upon the allocative efficiency of the system (as an exercise, say, in applied comparative statics). They also ask what impact it will have in regard to the stimulation of those acts of entrepreneurial discovery upon which the equilibrative process must depend. The one area in which Austrian economics has not merely raised new questions but has in fact fruitfully pursued the entrepreneurial discovery approach to its full welfare-economic implications, is in the modern version of its long-standing Misesian critique of central planning. To this we now turn.

D. Central Planning under Socialism

In a famous 1920 article Mises asserted on theoretical grounds, the "impossibility" of rational economic calculation under socialism and hence the impossibility of central planning. In a series of essays during

---

27. Roy Cordato (1992) has done valuable work exploring this avenue for Austrian normative economics. For a critique of Cordato's work, see David Prychitko (1993). See also Vihanto (1989, pp. 86f.), Alan Hamlin (1992), Robert Sugden (1992) and White (1992, pp. 263f.).

the thirties, Hayek supported Mises' contention and responded to several attempted solutions by socialist economists to refute that contention. Out of all these attempted solutions, the "decentralized" solution of Oskar Lange and Abba P. Lerner became the most famous. For decades the mainstream literature on comparative systems routinely cited these solutions by Lange and Lerner as having definitively laid to rest the critiques of the possibility of socialist calculation argued by Mises and Hayek.

During the past 15 years, largely as a result of the resurgence of interest in the Austrian tradition, a different assessment of the interwar calculation debate has emerged.[28] Especially as an implication (or application) of the entrepreneurial discovery approach to understanding the market process, it has come to be recognized that Lange and Lerner had not, in fact, refuted the theoretical challenge leveled by Mises and Hayek. The history of the economic calculation debate is not our concern here. What is important is that a modern Austrian understanding of the market process is able to show the limitations of the Lange-Lerner solution. In seeking to simulate, through decentralized socialist production, the conditions satisfied in a perfectly competitive equilibrium market system, that solution in fact misses the difficulties which Mises had seen for the possibility of socialist planning.

The Lange-Lerner solution requires the central planning authority to announce non-market prices for resources and commodities. Working with these prices as "parameters" (see Lange 1938, p. 70)—as if they corresponded to the prices under perfectly competitive equilibrium—decentralized socialist managers would then plan their resource "purchases" (from state suppliers), their output production and input mix, in a manner designed to equalize marginal cost and marginal revenue (*as if* maximizing firm "profit" under perfectly competitive conditions). The extent to which the announced prices in fact diverged from the "correct" values would be revealed in the surpluses and shortages generated for the various resources, thus permitting the central authority to adjust prices accordingly in the directions necessary to achieve resource market

28. Major contributions to this literature have been Don Lavoie (1985), Vaughn (1980), Boettke (1993, ch. 3); see also Willem Keizer (1989) and J. Huerta de Soto (1992).

clearing. The entire scheme is based, explicitly, on the view that the capitalist market economy operates in this way; that resource and output prices are given to entrepreneurs, and that firms then use these prices parametrically to maximize the excess of revenue over cost. The Austrian entrepreneurial discovery approach sees the market economy quite differently, and therefore sees the problem facing the socialist central planning authority quite differently.

The economic problem facing any society, in this view, is primarily that of how, in a world of incessant changes in tastes, resource availabilities, and technological possibilities, to generate mutually sustaining expectations on the part of agents in the economy, such that (a) the series of actions taken are in fact able to be completed as planned, and (b) that that series of actions tends to reveal and exhaust all the available opportunities for social economic gain. Under the imagined conditions of perfectly competitive equilibrium this problem does not exist, not because it has already been successfully solved, but because the equilibrium state has been constructed to avoid the problem in the first place. Whether under socialism or under capitalism, reference to the equilibrium state offers no clues as to how to solve the problem; it offers only a picture of a world in which the problem has never existed.

From this perspective the Austrians understand that whatever social efficiency may be achieved in the market economy is not achieved at all by its participants behaving as if they were agents in a perfectly competitive equilibrium state—but precisely by their behaving entrepreneurially and (dynamically) competitively, under conditions of disequilibrium. The Lange-Lerner solution, in which the socialist managers are instructed to act as perfectly competitive agents, and in which resulting resource surpluses and shortages lead the central authority to adjust resource prices, is simply *not* a simulation of how markets actually operate under capitalism. This solution has *not* successfully incorporated the techniques to which any capitalist successes may be attributed. Central adjustment of non-market prices in response to resource surpluses and shortages (generated by socialist managers having mistakenly behaved as if the originally announced prices were in fact "correct") corresponds to nothing that occurs in capitalist markets (despite its similarity to certain highly dubious textbook stories of how perfectly competitive market clearing prices are arrived at). The Lange-Lerner solution offers no scope whatsoever

for anything in socialism that might correspond to the pure profit motivated entrepreneurial acts of discovery which drive the capitalist market
process.[29]

V

It remains to relate the entrepreneurial discovery approach outlined in
this paper to alternative viewpoints within the universe of modern Austrian economists. The entrepreneurial discovery approach embraces
elements, especially elements in its criticisms of neo-classical microeconomics, with which all Austrian economists broadly agree. But the
specific framework of the entrepreneurial discovery approach—seeing
the market process as consisting of systematic equilibrating tendencies, made up of episodes of mutual discovery and learning (by market
participants)—has been rejected by a number of modern Austrian economists. These economists emphasize, more than does the entrepreneurial discovery approach, the radical uncertainty of the future, with which
market participants must contend. We may distinguish two groups
of Austrians who have, as result of such emphasis, dissented from the
entrepreneurial discovery approach: (a) those who object radically to the
asserted equilibrative character of the market process, and (b) those who
object to the emphasis of the entrepreneurial discovery approach upon
systematic mutual learning as the key feature in the market process (as
well as to what they believe to be the implication of the entrepreneurial
discovery approach, that the market in fact successfully attains *approximate* equilibrium).

(a) Those who object to the asserted equilibrative character of the market process (as explained in the entrepreneurial discovery approach), have
been led by one of the leading figures in the modern Austrian revival,
Ludwig Lachmann. A significant number of younger "Austrian" economists have followed Lachmann in this regard, and their debates with
exponents of the entrepreneurial discovery approach have enlivened and
enriched Austrian economics during the past decade. A careful exposition and analysis of these critics of the entrepreneurial discovery theory
is beyond the scope of this paper. The following thumbnail sketch of the
Lachmann position undoubtedly fails to do justice to the subtleties of that

29. For a valuable non-Austrian paper independently recognizing much of what is
here argued in the text, see Louis Makowski and Joseph Ostroy (1993).

position, and is offered here only to identify, at least, a stream of Austrian dissatisfaction with the entrepreneurial discovery approach. Lachmann (1986, 1991) saw the market process as one not only in ceaseless motion (on which the entrepreneurial discovery theorists would be in thorough agreement) but in a ceaseless motion in which *at no time* is there any assurance that the equilibrative forces are stronger than the disequilibrative forces (set in motion by changes in the independent variables of the system)—so that one may not presume to say that the market process even *tends* to promote mutual discovery among market participants. Following on the later work of George Shackle (Lachmann 1976) this group of Austrians has questioned the very meaningfulness of any equilibrium concept at all. They have deplored an approach (the entrepreneurial discovery approach) which appears to them simply as an attempt to rescue what they believe to be an unsalvageable way of understanding markets, viz. within the neoclassical paradigm. In a world of incessant change, they argue, it is precisely those acts of entrepreneurial boldness which must frustrate any discovery efforts made by fellow entrepreneurs. The entrepreneurial character of the market process (which is not disputed) must virtually guarantee, indeed, that that process must *fail* to be characterized as a systematic procedure of mutual discovery.[30]

Some followers of Lachmann, as well as others, have questioned, not so much the meaningfulness of the equilibrium concept itself (or of the notion of an equilibrating tendency), as the idea that we can, even in principle, identify an equilibrium position. In an open-ended world there is, these critics argue, no equilibrium position "out there" that can serve as a reference point for discussion of the presence or absence of "equilibrating tendencies" (see for example, Buchanan and Viktor Vanberg 1991).

(b) Those who object to the systematic learning character of the market process (as claimed by the entrepreneurial discovery approach) have been led by Murray Rothbard (1994; a foremost late twentieth century exponent of Austrian economics) and by Joseph Salerno (1993, 1994). Although their position is a relatively new one and has not yet generated sustained debate within the Austrian camp, it has already elicited a good

---

30. Among those who have been deeply influenced by Lachmann's position, see Christopher Torr (1981), O'Driscoll and Rizzo (1985), Lavoie (1994), Wiseman (1989), Loasby (1992). See also Peter Lewin (1994). For critical reaction to Lachmann's position, see O'Driscoll (1978), Garrison (1987).

deal of attention, and seems likely to stir up vigorous discussion in the immediate future. Rothbard and Salerno's understanding of the market process sees it not as a continual process of knowledge acquisition, but as a continual process of entrepreneurial decision making which, at each moment, encourages the most perceptive entrepreneurs to make their best judgments in a world of incessant change, through the use of monetary calculation of estimated profits and losses. The degree to which the market achieves coordination is attributed, in the Rothbard-Salerno view, not to any systematic process of knowledge enhancement (through entrepreneurial alertness or anything else), but to the ability of shrewd entrepreneurs, using money prices as tools for calculation, to deploy resources at each moment, in what they believe to be their most urgently demanded uses—as judged ultimately by the consumers. At each moment, it is then claimed, the market has generated that "constellation of resource prices" which *always* reflects the circumstance that existing resources are devoted to their most valuable uses (Salerno 1993, p. 124). Rothbard and Salerno do not deny that the entrepreneurial approach accurately captures the insights pioneered by Hayek in his papers on knowledge (Hayek 1937, 1945, 1948). Their position is simply that this approach differs sharply from a distinctly Misesian paradigm, a paradigm which they endorse.

One important implication of this position is the assertion that, because of the incessant changes in the external data of the market, it leads to the denial of any actual progression in historical time toward long-run equilibrium (Salerno 1993, p. 122). This assertion claims, it appears, not merely that exogenous changes prevent the equilibrating process in any given period of time, from going very far (a claim which, it is recognized, the entrepreneurial discovery approach would certainly endorse), but also that unless one "invokes the ideas of quiescent calendar periods which separate successive exogenous shocks" (an invocation attributed by Salerno to the entrepreneurial discovery approach; Salerno 1993, p. 129), exogenous changes are *continually* frustrating any tendencies toward eventual equilibration.

The brief remarks in this section concerning debates within the "Austrian camp" should help dispel any illusion (possibly created by this paper) that the entrepreneurial discovery approach is seen as a cut-and-dried, completed body of Austrian doctrine. Most "Austrians" see this approach as an important but still debated development in work still in progress. They see it as inviting further exploration and application to such areas as: law and economics (see, for example, Rizzo 1979), the interface between Austrian and mainstream neoclassical paradigms, and the evaluation of mainstream neoclassical attempts to confront the kinds of concerns which have motivated Austrian economics. The theory of entrepreneurial discovery is thus seen as embodying a set of ideas able to inspire several new research programs, rather than as constituting any kind of definitive orthodoxy.

VI

These concluding observations take up briefly the question of whether there exists any necessary relationship between an Austrian approach (such as the entrepreneurial discovery perspective discussed here) and support for a policy of uncompromising laissez faire. A complete and careful discussion of this relationship is beyond the scope of this paper (and, if it were to be successful in expounding the relevant nuances, would require far more space than is here available). Nonetheless it seems useful to offer the following outline for such a discussion. This will (a) respond to frequently expressed (and fully justified) curiosity concerning this relationship, and (b) perhaps provide necessary further clarification of the Austrian position presented in this paper.

It is true that, in their policy judgments, economists in the Austrian tradition have tended overwhelmingly to favor market solutions for solving society's economic problems. Certainly, this tendency is largely rooted in a shared and appreciative understanding of the coordinative properties of the entrepreneurial market process. There are, indeed, Austrian grounds for arguing that government regulation of market activity is likely to obstruct and frustrate the spontaneous, corrective forces of entrepreneurial adjustments. Yet to conclude that Austrian economics by itself rigorously entails adoption of unbridled laissez faire as the scientifically endorsed economic policy for nations, is a far too oversimplified—and inaccurate—conclusion.

Let us not forget that traditionally the economic case for laissez faire depended, for whatever its worth, on the claim that spontaneously achieved outcomes *are*, in a relevant sense, *efficient* (and can therefore only be worsened, not improved, by regulatory interference). Austrian economics cannot, strictly speaking, possibly offer a case for laissez faire based on this claim. After all, Austrian economics makes *no* claim that the market outcomes at any given date are efficient and socially optimal (in any sense in which traditional neoclassical welfare theory would use these terms). It is therefore certainly a misreading of the Austrian theory to construe it as claiming that the entrepreneurial discovery process ensures an unerring trajectory toward the attainment of that complete mutual awareness which is necessary for any notion of social optimization. What the Austrian theory argues is the far more nuanced thesis that the unbridled market tends to offer the incentives likely to stimulate movement in the direction of complete mutual awareness. To the extent that a case for laissez faire must rest on the claim that the market *attains* complete mutual awareness, Austrian economics provides no basis for such a case.

In addition it should be emphasized that, although the entrepreneurial discovery approach throws significant light on the incentives which stimulate movements in the direction of full mutual awareness, this does not amount to the assertion that *all* movements *must* be in that direction. Still less is it the case that entrepreneurial discovery is claimed successfully to *attain* full mutual awareness. As was noted in Section III entrepreneurial decisions may be entirely mistaken; they may in fact be *more* mistaken than those other entrepreneurial judgments they are replacing. So that, instead of correcting the earlier misallocations of resources, the entering entrepreneurs may be making matters even worse. And such errors may generate still more errors. Moreover, even if one imagined that, in a world of stable resource availabilities and consumer preferences, entrepreneurial judgments tend to avoid new errors, the possibility of volatile changes in resource supply and consumer demand conditions must inevitably prevent the entrepreneurial discovery process from proceeding very far toward complete mutual awareness by market participants.

If the Austrian theory claims that entrepreneurial discovery can account for a tendency toward equilibrium, that vague-sounding term "tendency toward" is used deliberately, advisedly, and quite precisely. Such a tendency does exist at each and every moment, in the sense that earlier entrepreneurial errors have created profit opportunities which provide the incentives for entrepreneurial corrective decisions to be made. These incentives offer rewards to those who can better anticipate precisely those changes in supply and demand conditions which we have seen to be so disconcertingly possible. What our understanding of the entrepreneurial discovery process provides, is not conviction that an unerringly equilibrative process is at all times in progress, but rather appreciation for the economic forces which continually encourage such equilibrative movement.

Such Austrian appreciation for the market forces encouraging the equilibrative tendency certainly does offer support for laissez faire. It is no accident that Austrian economists have tended to see economics as showing the unwisdom of government regulation. For, although entrepreneurs can, as noted above, make errors, *there is no* tendency *for entrepreneurial errors to be made.* The tendency which the market generates toward greater mutual awareness, is not offset by any equal but opposite tendency in the direction of diminishing awareness. Understanding how government regulation of entrepreneurial activity is likely to frustrate the coordinative tendency toward error-correction, is often believed sufficient to permit the Austrian economist roundly to condemn such intervention.[31]

REFERENCES

Addleson, Mark. "Competition," in Peter J. Boettke, ed. 1994, pp. 96–102.

Arrow, Kenneth J. "Toward a Theory of Price Adjustment," in *The allocation of economic resources.* Eds.: Moses Abramowitz et al. Stanford, Calif.: Stanford U. Press, 1959, pp. 41–51.

Armentano, Dominick T. "A Critique of Neoclassical and Austrian Monopoly Theory," in Louis M. Spadaro, ed. 1978, pp. 94–110.

———. *Antitrust policy: The case for repeal.* Washington, D.C.: Cato Institute, 1986.

Arthur, Thomas C. "The Costly Quest for Perfect Competition: Kodak and Nonstructural Market Power," *New York U. Law Rev.,* Apr. 1994, 69(1), pp. 1–76.

Arthur, W. Brian. "Competing Technologies, Increasing Returns, and Lock-In by Historical Events," *Econ. J.,* Mar. 1989, 99(394), pp. 116–31.

Baird, Charles W. "Labor Law and Labor-Management Cooperation: Two Incompatible Views," *Cato J.,* Winter 1987, 6(3), pp. 933–50.

Baumol, William J. *Entrepreneurship, management, and the structure of payoffs.* Cambridge, Mass., and London, England: MIT Press, 1993.

Beesley, Michael E., and Littlechild, Stephen C. "The Regulation of Privatized Monopolies in the United Kingdom," *Rand J. Econ.,* Autumn 1989, 20(3), pp. 454–72.

Boehm, Stephan. "Hayek on Knowledge, Equilibrium and Prices," *Wirtschaftspolitische Blatter,* 1989, 36(2), pp. 201–13.

Boettke, Peter J. *Why perestroika failed.* London and New York: Routledge, 1993.

———, ed. *The Elgar companion to Austrian economics.* Aldershot: Edward Elgar, 1994.

Boettke, Peter J., and Rizzo, Mario, J., eds. *Advances in Austrian economics.* Vol. I. Greenwich, Conn., and London, England: JAI Press, 1994.

Boudreaux, Don. "Schumpeter and Kirzner on Competition and Equilibrium," in *The market process: Essays in contemporary Austrian economics.* Eds.: Peter J. Boettke and David L. Prychitko. Aldershot: Edward Elgar, 1994, pp. 52–56.

31. For an example of such a belief see Kirzner (1985).

Brozen, Yale. *Concentration, mergers, and public policy.* New York and London: Macmillan, 1982.

Buchanan, James M. "Natural and Artifactual Man," in *What should economists do?* Indianapolis: Liberty Fund, 1979, pp. 93–112.

———. "The Domain of Subjective Economics: Between Predictive Science and Moral Philosophy," in *Method, process, and Austrian economics: Essays in honor of Ludwig Von Mises.* Ed.: Israel M. Kirzner. Lexington, Mass., and Toronto: Heath, Lexington Books, 1982, pp. 7–20.

Buchanan, James M., and Vanberg, Viktor J. "The Market as a Creative Process," *Econ. Philos.,* Oct. 1991, 7(2), pp. 167–86.

Caldwell, Bruce J., and Boehm, Stephan. *Austrian economics: Tensions and new directions.* Boston: Kluwer Academic Pub., 1992.

Clark, John Bates. *The distribution of wealth.* New York and London: Macmillan, 1899.

Coats, Alfred W. "The Revival of Subjectivism in Economics," in *Beyond positive economics.* Ed.: Jack Wiseman. London: Macmillan, 1983, pp. 87–103.

Cordato, Roy E. *Welfare economics and externalities in an open-ended universe: A modern Austrian perspective.* Boston/Dordrecht/London: Kluwer, 1992.

Cowan, Robin. "Nuclear Power Reactors: A Study in Technological Lock In," *J. Econ. Hist.,* Sept. 1990, 50(3), pp. 541–67.

Cowen, Tyler, and Fink, Richard. "Inconsistent Equilibrium Constructs: The Evenly Rotating Economy of Mises and Rothbard," *Amer. Econ. Rev.,* Sept. 1985, 75(4), pp. 866–69.

DeBow, Michael E. "Markets, Government Intervention, and the Role of Information: An 'Austrian School' Perspective, with an Application to Merger Regulation," *George Mason U. Law Rev.,* Fall 1991, 14(1), pp. 31–98.

DiLorenzo, Thomas J., and High, Jack C. "Antitrust and Competition, Historically Considered," *Econ. Inquiry,* July 1988, 26(3), pp. 423–35.

Ekelund, Robert B., Jr., and Hebert, Robert F. "The Proto-History of Franchise Bidding," *Southern Econ. J.,* Oct. 1981, 48(2), pp. 464–74.

Fisher, Franklin. *Disequilibrium foundations of equilibrium economics.* Cambridge: Cambridge U. Press, 1983.

Fisher, Franklin M.; McGowan, John J., and Greenwood, Joen E. *Folded, spindled and mutilated: Economic analysis and U.S. v. IBM.* Cambridge, Mass.: MIT Press, 1983.

Garrison, Roger W. "Austrian Macroeconomics: A Diagrammatical Exposition," in Louis M. Spadaro, ed. 1978, pp. 167–204.

———. "Time and Money: The Universals of Macroeconomic Theorizing," *J. Macroecon.,* Spring 1984, 6(2), pp. 197–213.

———. "The Kaleidic World of Ludwig Lachmann," *Critical Review,* Summer 1987, 1(3), pp. 77–89.

Hamlin, Alan P. "On the Possibility of Austrian Welfare Economics," in Bruce J. Caldwell and Stephan Boehm, eds. 1992, pp. 193–206.

Harper, David. "A New Approach to Modeling Endogenous Learning Processes in Economic Theory," 1994a in Peter J. Boettke and Mario J. Rizzo, eds. 1994, pp. 49–79.

———. *Wellsprings of enterprise: An analysis of entrepreneurship and public policy in New Zealand.* Wellington: NZ Institute of Economic Research, 1994b.

Hayek, Friedrich A. von. "Economics and Knowledge," *Economica, N.S.,* Feb. 1937, 4, pp. 33–54.

———. *The pure theory of capital.* Chicago: U. of Chicago Press, 1941.

———. "The Use of Knowledge in Society," *Amer. Econ. Rev.,* Sept. 1945, 35(4), pp. 519–30; reprinted in *Individualism and economic order* by Friedrich A. Hayek. London: Routledge and Kegan Paul, 1948.

———. *Individualism and economic order.* London: Routledge and Kegan Paul, 1948.

———. "Economic Thought VI: The Austrian School," in *International encyclopedia of the social sciences.* Vol. 4. Ed.: David L. Sills. New York: Macmillan, 1968, pp. 458–62.

———. "Competition as a Discovery Procedure," in *New studies in philosophy, politics, economics and the history of ideas.* By Friedrich A. Hayek. Chicago: U. of Chicago Press, 1978, pp. 179–90.

High, Jack. *Maximizing, action, and market adjustment: An inquiry into the theory of economic disequilibrium.* Munich: Philosophia, 1990.

Horwitz, Steven. *Monetary evolution, free banking, and economic order.* Boulder, CO: Westview Press, 1992.

Huerta de Soto, Jesús. *Socialismo, calculo economico y funcion empresarial.* Madrid: Union Editorial, 1992.

Ikeda, Sanford. "Market-Process Theory and 'Dynamic' Theories of the Market," *Southern Econ. J.,* July 1990, 57(1), pp. 75–92.

———. "Market-Process," in Peter J. Boettke, ed. 1994, pp. 23–29.

Ioannides, Stavros. *The market, competition, and democracy: A critique of neo-Austrian economics.* Aldershot: Edward Elgar, 1992.

Keizer, Willem. "Recent Reinterpretations of the Socialist Calculation Debate," in *Austrian economics: Roots and ramifications reconsidered.* Part 2. Eds.: J. J. Krabbe, A. Nentjes, and H. Visser. Bradford: MCB U. Press, 1989, pp. 63–83.

Kerber, Wolfgang. "German Market Process Theory," in Peter J. Boettke, ed. 1994, pp. 500–507.

Kirzner, Israel M. *Competition and entrepreneurship.* Chicago: U. of Chicago Press, 1973.

———. "The Perils of Regulation: A Market-Process Approach," in *Discovery and the capitalist process.* By Israel M. Kirzner. Chicago: U. of Chicago Press, 1985, pp. 119–49.

———. *Discovery, capitalism, and distributive justice.* Oxford: Basil Blackwell, 1989.

———. *The meaning of market process: Essays in the development of modern Austrian economics.* London and New York: Routledge, 1992.

———, ed. *Classics in Austrian economics: A sampling in the history of a tradition.* London: William Pickering, 1994.

Knight, Frank H. *Risk, uncertainty and profit.* Boston: Houghton Mifflin Co., 1921.

Kunz, Harald. "Der Wettbewerb Als Entdeckungsverfahren," *Wirtschaftspolitische Blatter,* 1989, 36(2), pp. 214–19.

Lachmann, Ludwig M. "From Mises to Shackle: An Essay on Austrian Economics and the Kaleidic Society," *J. Econ. Lit.*, Mar. 1976, 14(1), pp. 54–62.

———. "Ludwig von Mises and the Extension of Subjectivism," in *Method, process, and Austrian economics: Essays in honor of Ludwig von Mises*. Ed.: Israel M. Kirzner. Lexington, Mass., and Toronto: DC Heath, 1982, pp. 31–40.

———. *The market as an economic process*. Oxford: Basil Blackwell, 1986.

———. "Austrian Economics as a Hermeneutic Approach," in *Economics and hermeneutics*. Ed.: Don Lavoie. London: Routledge, 1991, pp. 134–46.

Lange, Oskar. "On the Theory of Socialism," in *On the economic theory of socialism*. Ed.: Benjamin E. Lippincott. Minneapolis: U. of Minnesota Press, 1938, pp. 55–143.

Lavoie, Don. *Rivalry and central planning: The socialist calculation debate reconsidered*. Cambridge: Cambridge U. Press, 1985.

———. "Introduction: Expectations and the Meaning of Institutions," in *Expectations and the meaning of institutions: Essays in economics by Ludwig Lachman*. Ed.: Don Lavoie. London and New York: Routledge, 1994, pp. 1–19.

Lewin, Peter. "Knowledge, Expectations, and Capital: The Economics of Ludwig M. Lachmann," in Peter J. Boettke and Mario J. Rizzo, eds. 1994, pp. 233–56.

Littlechild, Stephen C. *The fallacy of the mixed economy: An Austrian critique of conventional mainstream economics and of British economic policy*. London: Institute of Economic Affairs, 1978; 2nd ed., 1986.

———. "Controls on Advertising: An Examination of Some Economic Arguments," *J. Advertising*, 1982, 1, pp. 25–37.

———. *Austrian economics*. Vol. I. *History and methodology*; Vol. II. *Money and capital*; Vol. III. *Market process*. Aldershot: Edward Elgar, 1990.

Loasby, Brian J. *The mind and method of the economist: A critical appraisal of major economists in the 20th century*. Aldershot: Edward Elgar, 1989.

———. "Market Co-ordination," in Bruce J. Caldwell and Stephan Boehm, eds. 1992, pp. 137–56.

———. "Evolution Within Equilibrium," in Peter J. Boettke and Mario J. Rizzo, eds. 1994, pp. 31–47.

Loy, Claudia. *Marktsystem und Gleichgewichtstendenz*. Tubingen: J. C. B. Mohr (Paul Siebeck), 1988.

Machlup, Fritz. *The economics of sellers' competition: Model analysis of sellers' conduct*. Baltimore: Johns Hopkins Press, 1952.

Machovec, Frank M. *Perfect competition and the transformation of economics*. London and New York: Routledge, 1995.

Makowski, Louis, and Ostroy, Joseph M. "General Equilibrium and Market Socialism: Clarifying the Logic of Competitive Markets," in *Market socialism: The current debate*. Eds.: Pranab K. Bardhan and John E. Roemer. New York and Oxford: Oxford U. Press, 1993, pp. 69–88.

McNulty, Paul J. "A Note on the History of Perfect Competition," *J. Polit. Econ.*, Aug. 1967, 75(4), pp. 395–99.

Mises, Ludwig von. *Human action*. New Haven: Yale U. Press, 1949.

Moldofsky, Naomi. "Market Theoretical Frameworks—Which One?" *Econ. Rec.*, June 1982, 58(161), pp. 152–68.

Nozick, Robert. *Anarchy, state and utopia.* New York: Basic Books, 1974.

O'Driscoll, Gerald P., Jr. *Economics as a coordination problem: The contributions of Friedrich A. Hayek.* Kansas City: Sheed Andrews and McMeel, 1977.

———. "Spontaneous Order and the Coordination of Economic Activities," in Louis M. Spadaro, ed. 1978, pp. 111–42.

O'Driscoll, Gerald P., Jr., and Rizzo, Mario J. *The economics of time and ignorance.* Oxford: Basil Blackwell, 1985.

Pasour, Ernest C., Jr. "Economic Efficiency and Inefficient Economics: Another View," *J. Post Keynesian Econ.*, Spring 1982, 4(3), pp. 454–59.

Phelan, Christopher. "A Defense of Rational Expectations General Equilibrium Analysis Against Austrian Objections," *Critical Review*, Fall 1987, 1(4), pp. 1001–08.

Prychitko, David L. "Formalism in Austrian-School Welfare Economics: Another Pretense of Knowledge?" *Critical Review*, Fall 1993, 7(4), pp. 567–92.

Richardson, George B. *Information and investment.* London: Oxford U. Press, 1960.

Ricketts, Martin. "Kirzner's Theory of Entrepreneurship—A Critique," in Bruce J. Caldwell and Stephan Boehm, eds. 1992, pp. 67–84.

Rizzo, Mario J. "Uncertainty, Subjectivity, and the Economic Analysis of Law," in *Time, uncertainty, and disequilibrium.* Ed.: Mario J. Rizzo. Lexington, Mass.: Lexington Books, 1979, pp. 71–89.

Rothbard, Murray N. "Comment: The Myth of Efficiency," in *Time, uncertainty, and disequilibrium.* Ed.: Mario J. Rizzo. Lexington, Mass.: Lexington Books, 1979, pp. 90–95.

———. Book Review (of *Austrian Economics: Tensions and New Directions*), *Southern Econ. J.*, Oct. 1994, pp. 559–60.

Runde, Jochen H. "Subjectivism, Psychology, and the Modern Austrians," in *Psychological economics: Development, tensions, prospects.* Ed.: Peter E. Earl. Boston/Dordrecht/London: Kluwer, 1988, pp. 101–20.

Salerno, Joseph T. "Mises and Hayek Dehomogenized," *Rev. Austrian Econ.*, 1993, 6(2), pp. 113–46.

———. "Mises and Hayek on Calculation and Knowledge: Reply," *Rev. Austrian Econ.*, 1994, 7(2), pp. 111–25.

Schmidtchen, Dieter, and Utzig, Siegfried. "Die Konjunkturtheorie Hayeks: Episode in Einem Forscherleben Oder Ausdruck Eines Lebenslangen Forschungsprogramms?" *Wirtschaftspolitische Blatter*, 1989, 36(2), pp. 231–43.

Selgin, George A. *The theory of free banking: Money supply under competitive note issue.* Totowa, N.J.: Rowman and Littlefield, 1988.

Selgin, George A., and White, Lawrence H. "How Would the Invisible Hand Handle Money?" *J. Econ. Lit.*, Dec. 1994, 32(4), pp. 1718–49.

Shackle, George L. S. *Epistemics and economics: A critique of economic doctrines.* Cambridge: Cambridge U. Press, 1972.

Snowdon, Brian; Vane, Howard, and Wynarczyk, Peter. *A modern guide to macro-economics: An introduction to competing schools of thought.* Aldershot. Edward Elgar, 1994.

Sowell, Thomas. *Knowledge and decisions*. New York: Basic Books, 1980.

Spadaro, Louis M. *New directions in Austrian economics*. Kansas City: Sheed, Andrews, and McMeel, 1978.

Stigler, George J. "Perfect Competition, Historically Contemplated," *J. Polit. Econ.*, Feb. 1957, 65(1), pp. 1–17.

Stiglitz, Joseph E. *Whither socialism?* Cambridge, Mass., and London, England: MIT Press, 1994.

Streit, Manfred E., and Wegner, Gerhard. "Information, Transactions, and Catallaxy: Reflections on Some Key Concepts of Evolutionary Market Theory," in *Explaining process and change: Approaches to evolutionary economics*. Ed.: Ulrich Witt. Ann Arbor: U. of Michigan Press, 1992, pp. 125–49.

Sugden, Robert. "Commentary: Austrian Prescriptive Economics," in Bruce J. Caldwell and Stephan Boehm, eds. 1992, pp. 207–14.

Thomsen, Esteban F. *Prices and knowledge; A market process perspective*. London and New York: Routledge, 1992.

———. "Prices and Knowledge," in Peter J. Boettke, ed. 1994, pp. 167–72.

Torr, C. S. W. "The Role of the Entrepreneur (Review Note)," *S. African J. Econ.*, Sept. 1981, 49(3), pp. 283–88.

Vaughn, Karen I. "Economic Calculation under Socialism: The Austrian Contribution," *Econ. Inquiry*, Oct. 1980, 18(4), pp. 535–54.

———. *Austrian economics in America: The migration of a tradition*. Cambridge: Cambridge U. Press, 1994.

Vihanto, Martti. "The Austrian Theory of Price: An Example," *Finnish Econ. Pap.*, Spring 1989, 2(1), pp. 82–94.

———. "Introductory Essay: The Nature and Main Content of Austrian Economics," in *Discovering a good society through evolution and design, studies in Austrian economics*. By Martti Vihanto, Turku: Turku School of Economics, 1994, pp. 18–99.

White, Lawrence H. *Free banking in Britain: Theory, experience and debate, 1800–1845*. Cambridge: Cambridge U. Press 1984.

———. "Afterword: Appraising Austrian Economics: Contentions and Misdirections," in Bruce J. Caldwell and Stephan Boehm, eds. 1992, pp. 257–68.

Wiseman, Jack. "Beyond Positive Economics—Dream and Reality," in *Beyond positive economics*. Ed.: Jack Wiseman. London: Macmillan, 1983, pp. 13–27.

———. "Lionel Robbins, The Austrian School, and the LSE Tradition," *Research in the History of Economic Thought and Methodology*, 1985, 3, pp. 147–59.

———. *Cost, choice and political economy*. Aldershot: Edward Elgar, 1989.

INDEX

Abbott, Lawrence, 47*n*16
action-oriented knowledge,
    information differentiated, 222–27
advertising: for alerting consumers, 217,
    240–42, 302–4; and competition
    arguments, 234–36, 304; and costs
    distinctions, 236–40; criticisms
    summarized, 232–33, 301–2;
    efficiency arguments, 233–34,
    240; growth factors, 242–43; harm
    arguments, 232, 244–45, 301–2;
    information arguments, 211, 239–41;
    in open-ended universe, 247–52;
    scholarly neglect, 246–47, 253
"Antitrust and the Classic Model"
    (Peterson), 41–42
antitrust policy, 69–71, 305–9,
    343–44
Arrow, Kenneth, 331–32
Austrian economics, overview, 323–26,
    353–55. *See also specific topics, e.g.,*
    competition models, comparisons;
    entrepreneurial discovery;
    knowledge dispersal problem
automobile manufacturing example,
    coordination arguments, 156, 159

barter economy, 99–102
Berle-Galbraith doctrine, 5–6, 14
Boulding, K. E., 207–8
bridge arguments, economic thinking,
    154–55, 157–58
Brozen, Yale, 45
Buchanan, J. M., 89, 150–51, 154–55,
    162–63, 217
business cycle, Austrian economics
    perspective, 176–78. *See also*
    competition models, comparisons
Butos, William W., 129, 145

capital access, monopoly arguments,
    4–5, 10–13
capital availability, as trade cycle
    explanation, 175–77
capitalist role *vs.* entrepreneur's role,
    overview, 7–9, 14–15
central planning: and bridge
    arguments, 154–55, 157–58;
    and economic calculation
    debate, 113–15, 265–66, 314–16;
    impossibility arguments, 159–60,
    347–50; knowledge problem,
    80–82, 84–85; Leontif-Stein
    debate, 169–73; motivation
    arguments, 150–51; society as
    entity error, 152–54, 155, 162–64.
    See also socialist calculation debate,
    scholarship impact
Chamberlin, Edward, 34, 36, 236–37,
    277, 279
chaos requirement, entrepreneurial
    process, 287–88
checkbook example, in knowledge
    discussion, 225
civilization and knowledge, 88–90,
    95–102
Clark, John Bates, 344
Clark, John Maurice, 40, 41, 42
closed universe: advertising's role,
    247–52; of equilibrium models,
    283–84; and individual decision-
    making, 280–81; in perfect
    knowledge assumption, 275–76
coal transportation example, in costs
    argument, 238
competition models, comparisons:
    overviews, 50–51, 63–64, 257–59,
    271–72, 294–95; advertising's
    role, 301–4; assumed knowledge

measurement system examples, social
system evolution, 95–96, 98–99
medical patient analogies, market
conditions, 169–73
medical school example, coordination
arguments, 156, 159
Menger, Carl, 99, 101–2, 324
merger restrictions. *See* antitrust policy
metacoordination idea, 147*n*7
metric system examples, social
institution evolution, 98–99
microfoundations theme, 141
Mises, Ludwig von. *See specific topics,*
e.g., entrepreneurial process;
socialist calculation debate,
scholarship impact
money, emergence of, 99–102
monopoly arguments: advertising
criticisms, 232–33, 301; capital
ownership, 4–5, 10–14; competition
models, 40–43, 55–57, 277, 279;
government interventions, 57–58;
resource ownership, 9, 58–63;
terminology difficulties, 61–62. *See*
also antitrust policy; entry barriers
motivation arguments, in central
planning debate, 150–51, 161–63

The Nature and Significance of
Economic Science (Robbins), 265
Nelson, Richard R., 124

O'Driscoll, Gerald P., 59–62, 62*n*21,
64*n*6, 128, 130, 141, 158, 179
offensive advertising, 239, 244
oil production example, coordination
arguments, 156, 159
oligopoly, 43, 45
open-ended universe: advertising's
role, 247–52; of knowledge,
198–202; uncertainty factor,
275–76, 337–38

optimality *vs.* feasibility, in Leontif-
Stein debate, 172
optimism-oriented errors, 91–93,
94–95, 291–92
orange juice example, capital access, 9
order, Hayek's word usage, 133–36
over-optimism errors, from knowledge
problem, 91–93, 94–95
ownership arguments, 3–7, 10–16,
58–63

Pareto optimality criterion, defined,
257*n*2
perfect competition model. *See*
competition models, comparisons
perfect knowledge assumption,
209–11, 271–76, 329–30
pessimism-oriented errors, 92–95,
291–93
Peterson, Shorey, 14, 41–42
prices: in central planning model,
348–49; and entrepreneurial
process, 121–24; knowledge
assumption problem, 271–74,
296; and knowledge dispersal
problem, 22–28; and misdirected
production, 130–31; restriction
effects, 70–71; as signaling system,
140; subjectivism's premise,
206–7; unrealism critique,
274–80. *See also* cost arguments;
profit opportunities
Prices and Production (Hayek), 129–30,
174–78, 180–84, 186–89
pride and knowledge, 202
private ownership arguments, 3–6,
14–16
production costs, 237–39, 289
production errors, 176, 177–78,
289–91
profit opportunities: economic justice
arguments, 317–20, 344–46; from

This book is set in Scala and Scala Sans, created
by the Dutch designer Martin Majoor in the 1990s.

This book is printed on paper that is acid-free and
meets the requirements of the American National
Standard for Permanence of Paper for Printed Library
Materials, z39.48-1992. ∞

Book design by Richard Hendel, Chapel Hill, North Carolina
Typography by Apex CoVantage, Madison, Wisconsin
Printed and bound by Edwards Brothers Malloy, Ann Arbor, Michigan